The Golden Phoenix

A Three Continents Book

The Golden Phoenix

Seven Contemporary Korean Short Stories

translated by

Suh Ji-moon

with the editorial assistance of Daisy Lee Yang

LYNNE
RIENNER
PUBLISHERS

BOULDER
LONDON

Published in the United States of America in 1998 by
Lynne Rienner Publishers, Inc.
1800 30th Street, Boulder, Colorado 80301

and in the United Kingdom by
Lynne Rienner Publishers, Inc.
3 Henrietta Street, Covent Garden, London WC2E 8LU

Library of Congress Cataloging-in-Publication Data
The golden phoenix: seven contemporary Korean short stories /
    translated by Suh Ji-moon.
    A three continents book.
    ISBN 0-89410-862-X (alk. paper)
    ISBN 0-89410-882-4 (pbk. : alk. paper)
    1. Short stories. Korean—Translations into English.   2. Korean
fiction—20th century—Translations into English.   I. Sŏ, Chi-mun.
PL984.E8G65   1999
895.7'3010804—DC21   98-39396

British Cataloguing in Publication Data
A Cataloguing in Publication record for this book
is available from the British Library.

Printed and bound in the United States of America

⊗   The paper used in this publication meets the requirements
     of the American National Standard for Permanence of
     Paper for Printed Library Materials Z39.48-1984.

5   4   3   2   1

*This volume was published
with the support of the
Daesan Foundation,
Seoul, Republic of Korea*

Contents

Preface

$\curlywedge$

As a translator for whom translation is an avocation rather than a vocation, I am sometimes troubled to find the process addictive. Every time I work on a project of translation, I vow to myself that I will return to my vocation proper as soon as that project is completed and remain faithful to it, but when I find a seductive story, my vow of fidelity to my primary occupation breaks down. So, each of the stories in this collection represents my capitulation to the temptation of Korean literature. The temptation, however, was a temptation of nine parts agony and only one part pleasure. So, there can be no denying that I am a fool. But I take comfort in the thought that the world might be a pretty dreary place if not for people who are willing to be fools.

I am a most lucky fool, for I have been able to seduce some extremely smart people into giving their time and effort to aiding and abetting my foolishness. My friend Daisy Lee Yang has rendered me priceless editorial assistance, going over the stories many times with scrupulous attention. She has also given me her unfailing moral support, which I needed often in the course of the agonizing and frustrating work of translation. Our mutual friend Esther Arinaga, a retired attorney residing in Hawaii, also lent her superb literary sensibility to further refining the stories. The seven original authors represented in this collection deserve my thanks for their kind permission to use their stories and their helpful explanations of dialectical expressions, regional customs, and other matters. The Daesan Foundation kindly put its faith in me and aided the project with a generous grant. Finally, it was a pleasure to work with Dan Eades, Leanne Anderson, and Steve Barr of Lynne Rienner Publishers, who were friendly, efficient, and punctual throughout the process.

—Suh Ji-moon

Introduction:
A Context for Korean Fiction

Suh Ji-moon

Koreans credit themselves with having five thousand years of history, dating the founding of their first state in 2333 BC. Their long past is often hailed as "five thousand years of shining history." As a small country neighboring a colossal power (China) and several belligerent tribal nations whose fortunes have fluctuated violently, however, Korea's long history has been frequently one of tribulation. It is quite amazing that a nation that has undergone so many hardships and insecurities could attain such an advanced level of culture—in law, government, philosophy, education, literature, architecture, music, and in customs and ritual.

Korean literature has traditionally been written in both Korean and Chinese characters. In native Korean, writers have produced the Sijo—sparkling little gems of short poems, which express exquisite romantic yearning, unflinching loyalty, the joys of carefree pastoral life, worldly wisdom, or any number of emotions. Then there are the Kasa—long, rambling, loose poems, also in Korean, which often run very long and can be the vehicle for a wide variety of narratives or philosophies. Poems composed in Chinese characters, written by the cultured literati, tend to be delicately romantic, elegantly philosophical, and subtly ironic, sometimes flashing devilish humor and cutting sarcasm.

Prose literature can also be divided into tales written in Korean and those written in Chinese characters. Most of the tales written in Korean are of unattributed authorship. They may have been written by discontented noblemen who did not want their authorship revealed, both because prose compositions were considered beneath their dignity and because such works frequently contained strong criticism of the establishment. An author of common origin would also have wanted to avoid the complications and hazards

1

that could arise from irreverent passages in the book. Even though the tales are incredibly erudite and clever, they also abound in earthy humor, zest for life, and satire—both broad and subtle. There are also many improbable but exciting adventure stories—a number of which feature female generals who save the country from ruin and teach a lesson to their spouses who neglected or underestimated them.

Prose literature written in Chinese characters show elaborate plot complications and serious and learned didacticism. There are also eerie, supernatural tales in the Chinese tradition of ghost and fox tales.

An interesting feature of Korean folk and orally transmitted literatures is the appearance of funny goblins and comical tigers. Koreans believed (or hoped) that one could take advantage of goblins because they were easily offended and prone to the all-too-human weakness of wanting to get even. So, in a typical goblin story, humans first ingratiate themselves with a goblin, and tell him in confidence that they dread or loathe money above all else. And then they provoke him. The goblin is sure to try to persecute the humans by heaping tons of money on them. Tigers, on the other hand, befriended men through their generous good nature, although some tigers, like goblins, were greedy and gullible. A clever man or woman could take advantage of both types. A typical tiger story has humans convincing a tiger that it not only must not eat them, but owes them a favor. All of which indicate that Koreans tamed goblins and tigers—their most dreaded persecutors—in their imagination and turned them into their friends and benefactors. There is ample evidence to indicate that Koreans, in spite of their recurring and almost constant troubles and hardships, had abundant zest for life, fertility of invention, and buoyant optimism.

This rich literary tradition was unfortunately neglected when "modern" literature was inaugurated by a few Western-influenced writers early in the twentieth century. It was at a time of violent reaction against almost any legacy of the Chosŏn Dynasty as being benighted, inefficient, and responsible for the backward and helpless state of the country. The pioneers of modern literature were bent on making literature an instrument of enlightenment, and the dark and gloomy years that lasted almost the entire century didn't provide a favorable soil for liveliness, humor, and playfulness. It is only through an assertion of irrepressible artistic instinct and determined dedication that Korean writers could reach the kind of artistic achievement shown by the writers represented in this collection. Since the long-yearned-for and fought-for termination of military dictatorship in the late 1980s, however, Korean literature is experiencing a dynamic resurgence, experimenting exuberantly and delighting in uninhibited self-expression. Ch'oe Yun is one of the contemporary authors who is delving into the fertile inventiveness of premodern Korean literature for inspiration. In "The Flower with Thirteen Fragrances" Ch'oe, who is serious and playful by turns, uses the fairytale format to register her acute criticism of the contemporary academic climate and the fickleness of the populace.

Other forms of Korean art—calligraphy, painting, and music—also embody the lofty idealism and stately elegance on the one hand and love of fun and enthusiasm for life on the other, as well as the spectrum of moods and perspectives in between. The Korean scholar-artist's aspiration to ennoble his character to attain pure, untainted sublimity in his art is finely portrayed in the title story of this collection, written by a descendant of a scholar-literati clan. But Korean art did not always dwell in such lofty realms and was often friendly to simple folk even while satisfying the fastidious tastes of the connoisseurs.

Koreans often define themselves as a people of "*Mŏt*" and "*Hŭng*," two words that have no counterparts in English but which may roughly be rendered as "elan" and "exhilaration." Koreans still like to think of themselves as being a people "who know" Mŏt and Hŭng, but in recent years, they are much more likely to use the concept of *Han* to identify their national character.

Han is a concept quite antithetical to Mŏt and Hŭng. Mŏt and Hŭng are what Koreans have retained in spite of their sufferings; Han is a residue from the manifold and severe tribulations they bore in the course of their long history. Han covers a wide range of emotions originating from a sense of unjust injury and suffering. It is an emotion that transcends resentment toward the specific oppressor or wrongdoer, however, and which does not seek to resolve itself through wreaking vengeance on a specific person. It is rather a sorrowful brooding over one's own misfortunes and the pitiful helplessness of most human beings in the hands of evil malefactors and unfeeling fate. Thus, it contains both self-pity and bitterness, and seeks a sublimated outlet rather than an active redress. Although the energy and enthusiasm of modern Koreans would never suggest that Koreans harbor such a residue of bitterness from their past, it is true that most Koreans of middle age and older embrace this definition of themselves. Even many among the younger generations seem to feel a congenital affinity for this concept of their collective identity.

It is a misunderstanding that Koreans harbor Han from having been poor. Poverty, simply as poverty, does not generate Han. Poverty was not a dishonor in Korea; in the Confucian ideology it had an honorable place, implying absence of greed in those who bear it uncomplainingly. However, extreme poverty, if it was so extreme that it left lasting bodily impediments (due to malnutrition or inability to procure medical attention) or brought one excruciating mortification or injury at the hands of the wealthy and powerful, could well leave one with Han. In principle, it was injustice suffered at the hands of man that generated Han. But injuries inflicted by blind chance could also be a cause of Han if it wrecked a long-cherished hope or carefully built-up plans.

Poverty and suffering, of course, were hardly unique to Korea, especially in medieval and premodern times. But Koreans lacked cosmopolitan awareness; and their suffering was enough to implant infinite sorrow and undying regret in their hearts.

From time immemorial the great mass of Koreans were poor and oppressed. On top of that, there were internal warfares and foreign invasions that caused the loss of many lives and wrecked the basis of innumerable livelihoods. The Japanese invasion of the sixteenth century laid much of the country to waste and took countless lives, civilian as well as military, before the Japanese were driven out.

Korea was defeated and subjugated by the Mongols and Manchus when they invaded Korea after conquering China. Korean kings formally surrendered to the Yuan in the thirteenth century and to Q'ing in the seventeenth century, securing a very costly peace. Being a vassal state hurt the national pride of Koreans and caused many inconveniences. Throughout, however, Korea was able to maintain her sovereignty and was able to create a unique and highly developed culture.

Moreover, Koreans formulated and developed elaborate rituals and ceremonies and observed them in minutest detail. When one considers what precarious lives they led and how deprived most of them were, Korean respect for tradition, customs, and rituals is truly remarkable, and bears witness to the stability of the Korean character and the firmness of the Korean spirit.

But the Korean spirit, which had remained resilient through so much, received a deadly blow early in the twentieth century, when Korea was "annexed" by Japan, to remain its colony for thirty-five years. Several Western powers as well as China, Russia, and Japan competed to lay their hands on Korea, but Japan won the prize by defeating China and Russia in the Sino-Japanese and Russo-

Japanese wars and bribing off the Western powers. Such a historical experience inevitably aggravated the Han in the Korean psyche.

The unfair means Japan had adopted for annexation of Korea, and its ruthless oppression and unscrupulous exploitation of the Korean land and people, triggered protest movements and armed resistance, but the ingrained tradition of patient suffering formed by their settled agricultural way of life and the influence of Shamanism, Buddhism, and Confucianism made many Koreans endure their humiliation and extortion rather than desperately struggle against their oppressors. Shamanism, the first religion of Koreans, taught that man could attain his end by propitiating and winning over various gods and deities, rather than by fighting and subduing nature and man. Buddhism, which came next and partly superseded and partly merged with Shamanism, preached acceptance of this world's hardships and tribulations as a consequence of one's karma in past lives. Buddhism commended respect for others' rights but did not encourage fighting for one's own rights.

Confucianism, which replaced Buddhism as the state religion and ideology at the beginning of Chosŏn Dynasty, did not foster a fighting spirit, either. The main focus of Confucianism was self-discipline of the elites in preparation for looking after the spiritual, moral, and material welfare of the masses. But the masses were regarded as the herd, who were to be the beneficiaries of enlightened governance by the nobility, but who could not be trusted to govern themselves. The Confucian ideology thus called for the noblesse oblige of the literati, but provided no defense for the lower classes when the literati became collectively corrupt and became oppressors and exploiters of the powerless instead of their guardians. In this philosophy based strictly on the hierarchical concept of social organization, any improvement had to come through the good will and wisdom of the ruling class, and self-determination of the masses was regarded as an impossibility, or at least very dangerous. So, when kings and ministers were wise and benevolent, the people fared relatively well; but when kings were perverse or stupid and their ministers corrupt, the people suffered. When the governed are utterly powerless, there is always a temptation for the governing elites to abuse their power. The bureaucratic corruption and despotism reached a nadir in the first half of the nineteenth century when kings were mere boys and royal in-laws wielded powers greater than any king ever did—while the commoners and outcasts were crushed under continuing and grinding extortion.

The Confucian ideology strengthened the strong family ties fostered through several millennia of an agrarian lifestyle. Confucianism, with its reverence for elders and ancestors, elevated the family and the clan as the focus of one's loyalty and primary sources of one's identity. There was little room for individualism to develop, and even today, after half a century of often desperate and fierce struggles for democracy, individualism is still synonymous with self-aggrandizement for many Koreans. The valorization of and reliance on family ties inevitably gave rise to nepotism, dependency, and a host of other evils, although at the same time family ties and clan solidarity gave one a great sense of security and safe haven from the storms and tempests of the world. We see the homage Koreans paid to the Confucian values vividly portrayed in the figure of the narrator's grandfather in "The Sunset over My Hometown." The narrator's affection for the kind of figure his ancient grandfather represented is shared by many Koreans, though mixed with a bigger dose of negative feelings for the past and its legacies.

With modernization of the country, breakdown of the class structure, and opening up of economic opportunities, the situation has changed. Now, Koreans are individualistic and self-reliant as never before; still, familial, regional, academic and other ties are fostered and exploited for collective self-promotion. Modern Koreans often find themselves in the self-contradictory position of priding themselves on the strength of their kinship and other social ties while at the same time denouncing the evils generated by those very ties.

The forced opening of the country at the end of the last century after being a "hermit kingdom" for many centuries was painfully disorienting to most Koreans. There had been only a few opportunities for importation of Western thought and science through China in the seventeenth and eighteenth centuries. Crown Prince Sohyŏn (1642–1645), King Chŏngjo (1752–1800), and a number of scholars became aware of the advanced science and technology of the West and the need to reform and modernize the country. But the crown prince was eliminated by his own father; the king did not live to completely root out the conservative elite clique and accomplish the reforms and innovations he had envisioned; and the scholars were kept out of the power structure. Then, in the first half of the nineteenth century, the seed of reform was ruthlessly eradicated by the royal in-laws who monopolized power. Prince Regent Taewongun, who expelled the in-laws from power in 1863 by successfully installing his twelve-year-old son on the throne as heir to the childless Chŏljong, was an energetic reformist but a xenophobic. His son Kojong (1852–1919) did his very best to strengthen the country through importing Western technology while soothing and stemming the big powers, but he could not reverse the current of history. It was most unfortunate that Korea's awakening came a few decades later than Japan's. Japan, under the leadership of Emperor Meiji, opened its doors and channelled all its energies into modernizing itself. A few decades of head start by Japan in opening that country led to a powerless and helpless Korea and a mighty and aggressive Japan at the end of the nineteenth century.

Thirty-five years of colonial subjugation (1910–1945) remains an open wound to Koreans, even a half a century later. Not content to simply appropriate Korea's resources, Japan sought to crush the Korean spirit by debasing and vilifying Korean history. Independence movements were ruthlessly quelled, and any "subversive" moves were extinguished with imprisonment, torture, and execution. Citizens were humiliated and taunted. Toward the end of the colonial rule, use of the Korean language was forbidden, and Koreans were required to adopt Japanese names and give up their own. The colonial exploitation culminated in massive conscription of the labor force into mines and war factories and some 200,000 young women for sex services in Japanese army camps during World War II.

Such an experience would have been enough to severely hamper Korea's forward progress for many decades, but there were more ordeals in store for Korea. Almost as soon as the country was liberated, it became a stage of conflict again. Upon the defeat of the Japanese army, the Soviet Union occupied the northern half of Korea, and the United States the southern half. The United States and the U.S.S.R. quickly turned into rival superpowers, and a struggle between Soviet-backed communists and U.S.-backed liberal democrats raged across the whole country. "The Monument Intersection" shows innocent common people caught in this struggle, many of whom left behind all their possessions and ties and made a desperate flight to the South to escape the sinister fate that apparently awaited them in the Soviet-occupied and communizing North Korea.

The conflict divided the country in two, struck terror into the mass of simple folk, and culminated in the outbreak of the Korean War in 1950. The material damage and loss wrought by the war was nothing compared to the psychic wound it left. The ideological split resulted in brother killing brother and friend killing friend. Having cherished and relied so heavily on human ties from time immemorial, Koreans were traumatized. "The Rainy Spell" demonstrates the human cost of the Korean War most poignantly, through the confrontation of two old women who are in-law counterparts, with sons in the Republic's (South Korea's) army and in the Communist guerrilla troupe. The confrontation is tragic, but the story ends with the two old women's reconciliation through their common loss, thereby holding out a possibility of national healing. Syngman Rhee, the first president of the Republic, was, however, bent on eradicating all communist sympathizers and retarded rather than promoted the healing of the wound. The hostile acts and rhetoric of North Korea also kept the threat of another communist invasion alive and reinforced the concept of communists as criminals, or ogres, in the popular consciousness. The Syngman Rhee government was also corrupt, and economic recovery from the devastation of the war was very slow. The 1960 Student Revolution seemed to promise a new beginning, at least politically, but an explosion of suppressed desires and demands drove the country to the brink of chaos, providing a pretext for General Park Chung Hee to seize power in a coup d'état the next year.

The military government of Park Chung Hee vigorously implemented economic development plans, and the long-repressed energy of Koreans seized the new opportunities opened thereby, resulting in an economy that grew by leaps and bounds. The reverse side of economic growth, however, was political oppression and curtailment of citizens' rights. Park Chung Hee ruthlessly squelched all opposition. Many dissidents who criticized and resisted his rule were imprisoned, tortured, or died of "accidents." Park seemed to have firmly installed himself as the country's head for good. But in 1979, after eighteen years of dictatorship, he was assassinated. There followed a brief "Spring of Seoul," but the illusion of a big swing toward democracy was shattered with the brutal suppression of the Kwangju Uprising in May 1980 and the emergence to the foreground of military strongman Chun Doo Hwan.

Chun's reign of terror lasted for seven years, and those were the darkest years of modern Korean history. Park Chung Hee, even though he was a dictator, led the country out of poverty into prosperity, and all Koreans, even those who hated him, acknowledged that fact. But Chun Doo Hwan came to power through a massacre and stood for nothing virtuous. Koreans hated him and despised themselves for living under his dictatorship, even though any active resistance to his rule meant danger to their lives and limbs. So, in the 1980s, Koreans lived under the oppressive sense of their own helplessness, powerlessness, and cowardice. The lassitude and lack of self-determination of the narrator of "The Girl from the Wind-Whipped House" reflect the mood so many Koreans were in during those dark years, even though the original wound dates all the way back to the Korean War. "The Mural" portrays a painter who tries to be a painter rather than a professional dissident during the 1980s but who finds himself without an aim in life when the object of resistance was gone.

Fortunately, Chun Doo Hwan stepped down at the end of his seven-year term as he had promised, though not all Koreans had believed he would. When he tried to install a crony of his as his replacement, nationwide protests and demands for the restoration of the system of direct presidential election won out. Chun's capitulation to that demand, in June 1987, marked the end of military dictatorship in Korea.

The problems Koreans have to cope with are complicated and manifold. The legacy of the Confucian past; injuries and humiliations suffered as a vassal state to the courts in China and as a colony of Japan; postliberation ideological conflict; national division; the Korean War; and finally the three-decades-long military dictatorship—all of these left painful memories and practical problems needing to be addressed. Resolving these problems is especially difficult because the Koreans have been shaped by historical experience into sufferers rather than doers, endurers rather than redressers. Moreover, the government and the ruling powers were traditionally not objects of resistance but rather of loyalty and obedience. Ingrained mental habits had to be overcome and physical courage mustered. But the spread of the ideas of democracy, equality, and the duty of fighting for justice and the rights of citizenship gradually penetrated the Koreans' consciousness and convinced them that they owed a duty to themselves and their posterity to fight for those ideals.

The influx of Western civilization was another source of mental and psychological conflict. Western material civilization as well as some Western ideologies and institutions such as democracy and constitutional government inspired profound reverence. But Western customs and mores, as well as much of Western pop culture, were perceived to have a corrupting influence on Korean morality and manners. Koreans are still torn between nostalgia and shame for their legacies. Many Koreans still praise and defend their heritage in one breath and blame and denounce them in the next. And many do the same to Western culture as well. The economic opportunities that mobilized national energies and the resultant prosperity resolved many of the conflicts but, at the same time, aggravated some of the old problems while ushering in new problems.

These are the factors and conditions that modern Koreans have to deal with and struggle against, to arrive at a viable self-image and way of life. Political development and the advancement of democratic institutions will relieve some of these problems, but there are other issues that every Korean has to work out and find a solution for on his or her own. This is the background against which the characters in these stories have to live and make something of their lives.

The Golden Phoenix

Yi Mun-yol

*Yi Mun-yol (b. 1948) has been a reigning figure in Korean literature
since the late 1970s. He has won both high critical acclaim and huge
popular following. But he has not always been so lucky. In fact, he was
extremely unhappy throughout his childhood and youth, his family
having been on the police surveillance list as the family of a communist defector to North Korea. So, he had to struggle against poverty and
social prejudice, and he repeatedly dropped out of school for financial
and psychological reasons. However, throughout his boyhood and
youth he read omnivorously, and his vast store of reading as well as his
early sufferings became his great assets as a writer. And his vigor
matched his creative fervor as well, so he has produced a dozen novels,
several collections of short stories, and two collections of essays, besides
two ten-volume translations of classical Chinese romances and other
writings. Like most serious Korean writers, Yi criticized the economic
inequality and political oppression that existed in the Korean society
under military dictatorship. But he is more concerned with the national heritage and what it means and does to modern Koreans, and how
modern Koreans could deal with it. So, he is a "must" read for those
who want to understand the Korean culture and the burdens contemporary Koreans carry.*

*"The Golden Phoenix" (1981) reflects his serious interest in the
Oriental heritage and its modern applicability. In this story, Yi
explores the love-hate relationship between an old calligraphy master
and his rebellious disciple, who stand for the traditional Oriental and
the modern aesthetics, respectively. The gifted disciple rebels against the
teacher's overly ethicized and ascetic principles, in preference for a more
formal concept of beauty. The conflict results in a painful rift between
the two, and their reconciliation is achieved through the teacher's last
wish to have his disciple write the banner on his coffin. However,*

11

though not an ascetic himself, the disciple turns out to be as rigorous about his art as his old teacher in the end. Yi's thoughtful approach to tradition, his in-depth knowledge of the Oriental heritage, and his serious and measured prose style are all finely showcased in this story.

K ojuk woke up, as if hit by a strong and swift stroke of light. He thought he had heard the morning bells of the nearby church only a moment ago, but already it was broad daylight. The lattice of the sliding door facing east looked dark against the lit-up panel of the rice paper. He tried to look around. Perhaps stirred by that tiny movement of his head, a faint fragrance of India ink spread into his nostrils. It must be the ink rubbed with the Taiwanese ink stick presented to him by Professor Pak, a self-declared "disciple" of his, upon the latter's return last spring from a tour of Southeast Asia. As Kojuk was already bedridden at the time and unable to use the brush and ink, the gift had made him rather more sad than happy. So, when the professor told him he bought it for him "so he could at least enjoy the fragrance," Kojuk had snubbed him with, "Do you take me for a ghost already?" But he did enjoy the fragrance. His daughter Ch'usu rubbed ink on the ink slab every morning to preserve the atmosphere of a calligrapher's room. Kojuk appreciated her thoughtfulness as much as the rare fragrance of the ink.

The fragrance of the ink told Kojuk that Ch'usu had already been in the room. The stroke of light was probably the sunlight that stole in when Ch'usu opened the paper door to go out. Kojuk tried to raise himself. It wasn't easy, because half of his body was nearly paralyzed. He thought of calling for someone but changed his mind and turned over. He did not want the peace and quiet and the solitude to be disturbed by cumbersome inquiries after his health and fuss over his comfort.

How often—Kojuk mused, gazing at the pattern of plywood on the ceiling—yes, how often have I awakened to this kind of quiet, solitary morning, with no one beside me? Yes, with no one beside me. It began in his childhood numerous years ago. One morning when he was five or six, he woke up to see a paper-covered window brightly lit. From outside came the sound of muffled sobbing. He was about to cry, feeling deserted, when his mother came in and fainted on him. She was clad all in white and her hair was dishevelled. Then there was another morning when he was seven or eight. He had gone to bed the night before with his mother beside him but woke up alone. After a while he felt a sudden dread at the stillness of the room and was about to go out into the yard, but his grandmother came in and hugged him and groaned: "My poor, poor child! What will become of you. To run away, leaving you behind, even before the mourning period's over!"

After he had moved to his uncle's, he was usually alone when he awoke in the morning in his uncle's study, which smelt of books. His aunt always stayed in her own room because of her illness, and his uncle spent more nights out of the house than in it.

When Kojuk thought of his childhood, he could not help recalling the day he was thrown into the life that became his. How many decades ago was it? Anyway, he was about ten when he was led by his uncle to Sŏkdam's old house.

Maybe it is a characteristic of old age that certain moments in your long-forgotten past come back vividly to you. In recent years Kojuk could recall his old teacher more clearly than at any time in the past couple of decades. The teacher was only just forty when they first met, but he already looked old and worn out by poverty.

"What can I do? I have only you to thrust this burden on. If I weren't leaving this country, I'd take the boy with me wherever I drift to and feed him when I can, but . . ." His uncle, who had decided to go to Shanghai, began. "I couldn't ask my wife's family to take another burden on top of my sick wife. Please let me leave him with you. He is my older brother's only child."

Sŏkdam, who was listening with an expressionless face, asked, "So you're planning to go to Shanghai. Do you know how things really stand there? I heard that all they do in the provisional government there is squabbling, even though they don't have enough money to pay rent for the office. Moreover, how can you be sure our teacher Ch'un'gang is still there?"

"But what hope is there here? Anyway, will you take him in or not?"

Sŏkdam gazed at young Kojuk for a long time in silence, and then said with a sigh: "Feeding and clothing him I can do. But raising a child involves more than that . . ."

"Thank you, Sŏkdam. That's all that's needed. Don't worry about his education. God only knows how long this country's going to last, so what would be the use of education? I've already taught him to read, so that ought to be enough for these times." Then his uncle turned to him and said, "Pay your respects to this gentleman. He is your teacher Sŏkdam. You must look upon him as your own father until I come to take you back."

But his uncle never came back. After many years—more than

twenty years later—Kojuk heard that his uncle was among the members of the provisional government that came home upon liberation, but when Kojuk went to Seoul to look for him the next year he could not find him.

Sŏkdam, who was an old friend of Kojuk's uncle from childhood and studied under the same teacher, was a descendant of a great Confucian scholar of the Yŏngnam (the present Kyŏngsang Province) area. He was often listed as one of the three great calligrapher-painters of the late Yi Dynasty for his bold and soul-stirring calligraphy and sublime painting. But, like the great Ch'usa, whom Sŏkdam's teacher Ch'un'gang revered all his life, he was more a scholar than an artist.

"What books did you study?" were the first words of the teacher after his uncle left.

"I've read the *Children's Primer.*"

"Then read *The Minor Learning.* If you don't read it, you won't know how to hold yourself up."

That was all. Buried among the half a dozen students of the teacher, he read *The Minor Learning* over and over in the schoolroom, but the teacher paid no attention to him. Then, when he turned thirteen, the teacher unexpectedly took him to a nearby primary school. "The times have changed. It isn't too late for you to learn something new," was his only explanation. So Kojuk acquired a primary school education. Judging from that, it was obvious that the teacher did not intend to make him a disciple of his.

When he recalled his late teacher, Kojuk's eyes automatically turned to the teacher's own calligraphy on the wall. Written in penurious times and left unframed for too long, the paper had yellowed and the red ink of the seal had faded into reddish yellow, but the master's strokes were vigorous and alive.

The golden phoenix splits open the sea and the elephant parts the river.

As Sŏkdam's only son died of cholera and Sŏkdam had not picked a disciple to cast his mantle upon, after his teacher's death Kojuk looked after the dilapidated old house and inherited a good number of his teacher's calligraphy works and paintings. But because of his long vagabondage and the civil war, now he only had a handful of the teacher's own works. Kojuk had once lamented, after he became ill, how could he dare face his old teacher when he went to the other world? Included in the lament was his guilt for neglecting the teacher's works. But the calligraphy hanging on the wall was one work of his teacher's that he did not, could not, neglect. It contained the teacher's principle that he resented and dreaded, but wanted to attain and transcend. Even in these days when he could no longer write or paint, he felt the stern eyes of his teacher staring down at him out of the bold letters.

An incident occurred when he was twenty-seven. Feeling elated from a sense of attainment, he escaped from the teacher's house without saying a word to his teacher. Charitably speaking, he did it to get material proof of his own artistic attainment. But more accurately, he wanted opportunities to show off his talent. The three-month period that followed was a highly gratifying one for him. He won the top prize in the calligraphy competition in Chŏkpa; he was a valued guest in the Confucian academies in Naeryŏng, Ch'ŏngha, Tusan and other towns of the Yŏngnam area. Sometimes he stayed in the guest quarters of a millionaire's house and was feasted day after day with all the delicacies from the sky, earth and water. It was on a triumphal road he thought he was marching when, after three months, he returned to his teacher's house with a great big bag of rice that he had a coolie carry on an A-frame. But it was an icy welcome he received from his teacher.

"Put that down." Sŏkdam blocked the gate and commanded the coolie. Then he turned to Kojuk. "Take off your brush bag and put it on the rice bag." It was a voice that admitted no protest, no demur. Kojuk unslung the brush bag from his shoulder and placed it on the rice bag. Then the master took out of his sleeve a matchbox and set the A-frame on fire.

"What are you doing, teacher?"

Sŏkdam's reply was as cold as ice: "I took charge of you from your uncle, so I'll let you eat and sleep in my house. But don't you dare call me 'teacher' ever again. I never gave teaching to a dauber who learned to draw in the morning and show off his skill in the evening."

Kojuk had to do two years of harsh penance before his teacher forgave him. It was an incomparably harsher penance than that he did to be admitted as a disciple initially. And the calligraphy hanging on the wall is what the teacher wrote for him on the unforgettable day of pardon.

It meant: In writing with brush, you must have the spirit of the golden phoenix as it splits open the sea and snatches up a dragon; and in its thoroughness it should have the force of the mythical elephant parting the river in two to cross it.

The teacher's first acceptance of Kojuk into discipleship was also clothed with bitter regret in his memory. Perhaps from some premonition, Sŏkdam always treated Kojuk coldly and guardedly. It couldn't have been because Kojuk was an added financial burden to him, even though being a house of a true scholar his land estate was small and the household was run mostly by the rice offered by his students' parents. There must have been some deep-seated problem other than the financial one, for the teacher's attitude did not change in the least after Kojuk grew up and was as good as supporting the teacher's family by working on the teacher's farm. It must have been for a very special reason that Sŏkdam made Kojuk read *The Minor Learning* over and over for many years, and made him go to a primary school when he was thirteen and study "new" subjects instead of calligraphy and painting.

What was just as hard to understand as the teacher's attitude was his own feelings towards such a teacher. Till the end of the teacher's days, Kojuk was tormented by an ineffable yearning towards his teacher and at the same time a violent hatred of him. It was not a very logical state of mind, which continued in its most intense form from the time he finished primary school at age sixteen to when he was formally admitted as the teacher's student at eighteen. In those two years he had turned down a distant cousin's offer to send him on to higher schools and, stifling his interest in the changing world and the new learning that flooded into the country, he worked like a common field hand and managed the teacher's household. He farmed the teacher's small remaining land himself, and he trudged many miles to gather wood for fuel.

The neighbors praised him for his loyalty. But in his heart there was already a burning flame of mixed love and hate for his teacher. The teacher's style of living, which seemed as calm, clean and pure as a rivulet in the autumn valley or the winter sky over snow-covered fields, filled him with a nameless longing and also an uneasy premonition. The teacher, when sitting before a calligraphy table with a mysterious smile playing around his lips; or when wielding his huge brush with the force of a storm, with fiery spirit darting out of his eyes; or when sitting under a sweet briar tree in the backyard like a mountain spirit and playing the Kŏmun'go zithers, epitomized a venerable life. But when Kojuk thought of his teacher's penurious household which would become ruinous within half a year but for his service, or of the decaying house visited only by a few old men and fewer than a dozen students, or when encountering the teacher's helpless gaze as he looked at Kojuk coming back from the field, Kojuk felt that the teacher's lot was an accursed one, and he resolved to escape a like fate at all costs.

But what governed Kojuk's life in the end was love and rever-

ence for the teacher. Having resisted the temptation of the new
world and the new learning, he was imitating his teacher in secret.
He picked up his teacher's discarded calligraphy pieces to use as
models for practicing basic styles. Sometimes he stole them from
the teacher's drawers.

Resentment surged in his heart even in his old age when he
recalled his secret apprenticeship of those years. For lack of paper
and brush, he practiced the small letters with a discarded brush on
a sand board or chalkboard of his own making. And he used the
smooth stone offering table before other people's tombs to practice large letters with a dogtail broom. He washed the letters off
afterwards. He bought his own paper and brush for the first time
by selling a sheaf of wood to a stationery shop without the teacher's
knowledge.

He heard that Sŏkdam later blamed such acts of his as springing from stubborn pride. Anyway, even though he lived in the same
house with his teacher and saw him day and night, he never once
asked his teacher to accept him as a disciple nor even breathed a
word about wanting to become a calligrapher-painter like him. It
must have been his artist's pride, an instinctive pride possessed by
geniuses.

Then one day an incident occurred that forced the teacher to
accept or reject him as a disciple once and for all. The teacher and
his wife had both gone out early in the morning, and Kojuk felt a
strange impulse while cleaning his teacher's study. It was a desire
to see plainly on paper how much progress he had made up to that
time. His teacher had set out for a poetry contest in a town many
miles away and was not expected back that day.

He prepared the writing table and began to rub ink in his
teacher's ink slab. He made sure not a drop of ink splashed on the
rim of the ink slab. When the inkwell was filled with rubbed ink, he
took out precious mulberry papers and brushes from the stationery chest.

First, he copied out the *Shuang-ho Inscription* in the square style
of the poet-calligrapher Yen Chen-ch'ing. Just as Ch'usa valued Ou
Yang-hsun's *Li Ch'uan Inscription* most highly for practicing the
orthodox style, Sŏkdam always urged his students to practice copy-
ing the *Shuang-ho Inscription* more than anything else. As he got
used to writing with a good brush on real paper, Kojuk's copy
resembled the original fairly closely. Next he moved on to *Ch'in-li
Epitaph*, also in the Yen Chen-ch'ing style. Though the effort made
him groan and perspire, he fell by degrees into ecstasy.

He had just finished the first line of the Wang Hsi-chih's

Lan-t'ing Shu, when he was brought to his senses by a sudden thunderous yelling.

"Stop it! How dare you?"

Into his frightened eyes came Sŏkdam's figure looking down at him in the already darkened room. Even though the voice was sharp, on his teacher's face there was more anxiety and resignation than anger. Beside the teacher stood Ungok, who had a nickname of "the seven-faced talent" for his mastery in poetry, calligraphy, painting, Go games, fortunetelling, medicine and physic. Ungok was observing him with an interested look.

Kojuk quickly gathered up the papers scattered all over the room. Sŏkdam wasn't scolding him anymore and was just looking at him absently. Ungok spoke instead: "Leave them there."

Kojuk almost automatically put down the sheets of paper and left the room. But he couldn't resist silently stealing up to the study and straining his ears to hear the conversation inside. His heart was pounding.

In the meantime the room was lit up, and for a long time the only sound from within was the rustling of papers. Ungok spoke first: "Do you really mean you never taught him at all?"

"He may have overheard me teaching the others. But I never taught him directly." Sŏkdam's voice was gloomy and weak.

"Then it is truly a wonder. He is a born genius."

There was no response from Sŏkdam.

"Why don't you make him a disciple?"

"'If one has not the right character, one should not be taught.' Have you forgotten the famous principle of Wang Hsi-chih?"

"Do you mean that boy has a mean character?"

"Well, in the first place that boy's talent surpasses his character. He can copy the letters he doesn't know the meaning of and he can imitate the various styles of calligraphy without knowing their principles. He is a born artisan whose road to greatness is blocked by excessive talent."

"It's so unlike your gentle self to be so hard on a mere lad. Why don't you remove that impediment with your teaching?"

"How can that be easy? Moreover, that boy can have neither depth of feeling nor integrity of character yet. But look how this orchid has all the appearance of deep feeling."

"How can the boy fail to acquire depth of feeling and integrity of character once he becomes your disciple? I don't think it's right to deny him your teaching."

"I undertook nothing more than to feed and clothe him. I only wanted him to be able to support himself, with a modicum of new learning."

"Why are you so severe? You don't deny instruction even to a stranger when he asks for it. How can you be so heartless to the boy who's been a member of your household for seven, eight years? I also heard that he's been as good as supporting your family these past couple of years. Don't you think you ought to take pity on him and reward his loyalty?"

Ungok's voice was sharp. Ungok, too, must have heard about the strange relationship between the old master and his non-disciple.

"Don't blame me too much. To tell you the truth, I myself don't understand why I'm so reluctant to teach that boy. For some reason I keep thinking, when I look at him, that it was an evil fate that brought us together." Sŏkdam's voice was a little tremulous.

"In that case, what if I were to teach that boy? You can send him to me about once every three days or so. I don't think he can be made to take up any other calling now."

There was only silence for a long while. Then Sŏkdam's low but resolute voice came.

"There's no need for you to take the trouble. I'll try teaching him."

What did Sŏkdam mean when he said that an evil fate brought them together? And why did Sŏkdam decide to make him his disciple nevertheless?

The next day Kojuk was formally admitted as Sŏkdam's disciple. It was not as if there was a formal initiation ceremony or anything. Kojuk was setting out for the fields with an A-frame carrier on his back as usual, when Sŏkdam called him.

"Don't go out to the fields anymore," Sŏkdam said in a casual tone. Then, as Kojuk stood there trying to figure out the meaning of those words, Sŏkdam said a little more sharply: "Put that A-frame down and come into the study."

That was Kojuk's inauguration to Sŏkdam's discipleship.

Kojuk returned to reality at the sound of the paper door sliding open. When he strained his eyes, he saw Maehyang stepping in. Then he felt a chill running down his spine and his sight brightening up. What great bitterness must have brought her here? Kojuk looked at Maehyang with a feeling akin to penitence. But it was not Maehyang.

"Are you awake, father?"

It was Ch'usu. There was deep anxiety on her face, which had no trace of make-up. He raised himself, straining to the utmost. Ch'usu, sensing his effort, quickly helped him sit up, and placed a cushion behind his back against the wall. Kojuk could feel distinctly that he had more difficulty moving than the day before.

"Would you care for some juice?" Ch'usu inquired.

Instead of answering, he gazed at her face for a minute and asked, "Do you remember your mother?"

Ch'usu looked at him in surprise. Even though she had been living with him and looking after him for seven years since his third and last wife died, it was the first time that he had ever mentioned her mother. In fact, he had not uttered Maehyang's name from long before Ch'usu joined him.

"I've only seen her in a photograph."

Poor thing! How otherwise could she know her mother, who left her with her grandparents as soon as she was born and committed suicide less than two years afterwards?

"But why, father?"

"I thought you were your mother just now."

Ch'usu just sat there silently.

"She wasn't the kind of woman who could live to old age, but why did she have to quit the world in such a hurry?"

Ch'usu's face, which had become rigid at the mention of her mother, became soft again when she saw the sadness on his face.

"Shall I bring some orange juice?" Ch'usu repeated her question, perhaps to change the subject.

"Bring me tea if you have some," he answered, hurriedly shaking off the thoughts of Maehyang.

Ch'usu opened the window for a while to ventilate the room, and quietly left.

What passion drove me to such madness? Sipping the tea Ch'usu had brought, Kojuk recalled the time of his first meeting with Maehyang. After he left his teacher for the second time at age thirty-five, he wandered around for nearly ten years.

Even though it was near the period of the China-Japan War of 1938, Confucian academies and scholarly communities were still in existence, and poetry and calligraphy competitions continued to be held. Whether it was because he was a recognized disciple of Sŏkdam, who was deemed one of the three great masters of the late Yi Dynasty, or whether it was because of the prizes he won in the National Art Contests that he entered despite his teacher's objection, his wanderings turned out to be lucrative although the times were destitute. About once a month he was an honored guest at a party somewhere, and in every town or city there was at least one local rich man who would give him one month's travel fund in return for a painting or a calligraphy.

On one occasion his wanderings took him to Chinju. After about ten days of luxury and ease, he was about to leave the city when a rickshaw arrived at his inn and asked him to get in. It wasn't the first time such a thing had happened to him. The rickshaw carried him off to a plush restaurant. In one of its rooms there were several Japanese and a couple of Koreans seated around a table laden with all kinds of delicacies. They were chiefs of local offices and Korean men of influence in the area.

Maehyang was one of the entertaining women summoned there when the hosts and guests were drunk and merry. When everyone was pleasantly inebriated, an executive of the Korea Development Company, who seemed to be the host for that evening, grinned and said, "Who will give this honored guest here pleasant dreams tonight?"

The entertaining girls giggled for a while. Then one of them trotted up to him and lifted her long red skirt, revealing a full-length chemise as white as the best-quality mulberry paper. She looked about twenty-two, and, though neither a great beauty nor a seductive glamour, she had an undefinable attractiveness. While untying his brush sack, he felt the alcohol coursing through his head.

"What's your name?"

"It's Maehyang, the fragrance of plum." Her voice was natural and clear. It was he who was flustered.

"Then I must draw a plum tree," he tried to say casually, but his hand shook as he tried to draw. What he really couldn't understand was the plum he drew. It was not his own plum tree that was drawn on the girl's chemise but his teacher's. It was a lean, twisted plum, with only a couple of unopened buds on the boughs. And the caption was also his teacher's: "Even though the plum is cold all its life, it does not sell its fragrance."

Ostensibly the plum tree was a tribute to the girl's name. But how could the lean, gnarled plum and the lofty caption suit the chemise of an entertaining woman under the colonial rule? But what made his face tingle with shame every time he recalled it was what followed.

"Why is this plum tree so frozen and lonely?" Maehyang asked when he finished pressing his seal beside the drawing.

"Have you ever seen an orchid by Cheng Szu-hsiao that didn't have exposed roots?" He answered in a low voice to be heard only by the girl. Then he explained to the company that the plum was gnarled and twisted because it was a January plum, but Maehyang seemed to have got his meaning. The orchid of Cheng Szu-hsiao whose exposed roots bespeak the sorrow and bitterness of losing the sovereignty of one's country . . .

That night, Maehyang accepted his embrace without any hesitation.

He spent four months with Maehyang from that night. Those four months remained in his memory like the abstract idea of sweetness, like the memory of a flower-strewn hill he climbed one spring day in his childhood. Then their days together came to an end. Just as he was not a scholar who roamed around trying to soothe his bitter regret over the loss of his country through calligraphy and painting, she was no noble *kisaeng* like the renowned courtesan in the times of the Hideyoshi invasion who jumped into the river gripping an enemy general. He was no more than an artist driven hither and thither by a passion he did not comprehend himself, and she was only an entertaining woman with eight mouths to feed.

They parted, without hatred or bitterness, as if following an agreed-upon course. Maehyang went back to the call-office of entertaining women, and he left for the calligraphy exhibition in Chŏnju. That was the last he saw of Maehyang.

Then the next year he got word that Maehyang had given birth to a baby girl. As he was lodging at the time in a temple in the Sorak Mountains, he wrote her to name the child Ch'usu, Autumn Brook, without giving it a serious thought. Did he have some premonition of the child's lonely future, when he named her after the clear, cold water of the mountain valley?

A few years later he heard that Maehyang had died. She had become the mistress of a rich man, but unable to stand the persecution of the wife, took her own life by drinking a huge amount of opium dissolved in water. Perhaps because he was heartless, he hadn't felt much sorrow when he heard of her death. He had only wondered, for a moment, where their daughter might be.

He met Ch'usu for the first time when she began a girls' high school in the city where he was living then. Maehyang's brother, who had had a good start in life thanks to his unfortunate older sister, took good care of his niece. Ch'usu was not lonely or destitute but Kojuk went to see her at school from time to time. Nearing the threshold of old age, he had begun to long for a family.

Only recently had the father and daughter begun to live in the same house. Seven years ago, the death of the woman with whom he had been living since he settled down in this city and opened a studio left him a widower. Ch'usu had lost her husband in the Vietnam War. The poor thing was only twenty-six at the time.

Drinking the porridge Ch'usu had brought in with as much distaste as if swallowing an herb medicine concoction, Kojuk raised himself. Picking up the empty porridge bowl, Ch'usu helped him up and asked: "Are you going out today, too?"

"I have to."

"But you didn't find anything yesterday. Why don't you just send Ch'ohŏn to go around and look?"

"I have to go myself."

Ever since he came out of the hospital four months ago last summer, he toured all the downtown art galleries daily. He bought up all his works whenever and wherever he found them. At first he didn't have a clear purpose, but these days he was approaching a resolution.

That resolution was connected with the certain premonition of his own death. Even though Dr. Chŏng, his doctor, assured him of a full recovery, he knew his discharge from the hospital amounted to an admission of hopelessness. He knew why so many people came to ask after him. He knew the reason for the dark shadow on his daughter's face, as she tended him day and night. His stomach, too, didn't behave like an organ on its way to complete recovery. Although there were no more sharp and violent pains, he could feel his body being destroyed inexorably, cell by cell.

"Has Ch'ohŏn phoned yet?"

Ch'ohŏn was the sobriquet of a student of Kojuk's, the last disciple to receive a sobriquet from him. Ch'ohŏn lived in Kojuk's studio.

"He called to say he'll come in half an hour. But I think you'd better stay home today . . . "

"No, I must go out. Help me get ready." He cast a stern glance at Ch'usu, who was looking at him pleadingly. He tried to take a few steps around the room but before he could walk a few steps, he felt dizzy and his balance became uncertain. Ch'usu regarded him with anxious eyes and when he sat down again on the bedding, she went out. Kojuk cast his eyes once more upon Sŏkdam's calligraphy.

Was it really an evil fate that brought Sŏkdam and him together? Even after he was admitted to discipleship, their relationship continued to be a strained one. Sŏkdam was chary of giving instruction, so much so that it remained a bitterness in Kojuk's heart well into his middle age. He began with the basic square style. Before he took up the brush, Sǒkdam ordered him to learn by heart Ch'usa's *Principles of Calligraphy*, which began:

> The principle of calligraphy lies in letting the brush move freely on the blank paper. A blank paper is like the Great Void. The Great Void is held together by the invisible axis running from the North Pole to the South Pole. Calligraphy works on the same principle. The letters are written by the brush, the brush is moved by the fingers, the fingers by the elbow, the elbow by the arm, and the arm by the shoulder. And the elbow, arm and shoulder are all moved by the body.

Kojuk had to memorize the four-hundred-word long *Principles* from the beginning to the end. Next, the teacher gave him a copybook of Yen Chen-ch'ing style.

"If you copy this a hundred times, you will be able to write. If you copy this a thousand times, you will earn people's praises. If you copy this ten thousand times, you will be pronounced a master."

That was about all the instruction he had. The only thing that had changed was that he could now practice openly and that he was sent to Ungok every other day to learn Chinese Classics. Then, after three years, the teacher told him simply, "Hold your breath." The instruction was given when, even after practicing the square characters in the copybook three thousand times, he could not write them as he wished and was almost in despair.

It was not much different in practicing drawing. In teaching orchid drawing, the teacher simply gave him a copybook he made of the Prince Regent Taewǒn's orchid drawings and said: "You can't attain awakening without many years of meditation, and you can't kill a dragon with unpracticed hand. You can draw only after years of unremitting practice." That was all. Sometimes the teacher cast a glance in his direction to observe him practicing, but he never gave detailed comments on his work. Then, when his orchid began to look real, the teacher suggested casually: "Do it from the left. To draw rocks you have to use the brush against the texture."

The teacher never showed much pleasure in his progress. When it was approaching ten years since his admission to discipleship, his work elicited praise from even the teacher's friends. But the teacher's invariable response to such admiring comments were, "Oh, he can make reasonably good copies now."

It must be in protest against this coldness that he left the teacher's house at twenty-seven. But, the more he earned the praises of the worldly crowd, the more he yearned for his teacher's praise. That desire made him return to the teacher's house and endure two more years of penance and humiliation until he was forgiven and readmitted to discipleship.

During the two years that he again worked in the field and gathered wood for fuel, the teacher avoided him like the plague. Once, out of irresistible impulse, he secretly practiced writing and drawing. The teacher, finding it out, ordered him sternly: "Wash yourself at once. The smell of ink on you is more repugnant than the smell of perfume on a prostitute."

The teacher's attitude did not change even after Kojuk was forgiven and was allowed to practice with brush and ink in the master's study. It looked as if the teacher's eyes grew even more critical and anxious. Kojuk, in contrast, gained confidence. He had not only grown accustomed and insensitive to the teacher's coldness, but he even began to enjoy provoking the teacher's grief and fury by doing things the teacher disliked and disapproved, such as participating in group exhibitions or entering the National Art Contests given by the Japanese colonial authorities.

But the day of their final unhappy parting was drawing near. As time passed, the thing that made the teacher uneasy, the thing that separated the teacher and disciple, was brought out into the open. What separated them essentially was the difference in their artistic principles and premises. Sŏkdam valued vigor, integrity and nobility in calligraphic writing. But Kojuk valued beauty and tried to express his emotion and will in calligraphy. Their views differed, too, with regard to painting; Sŏkdam focused on expressing the soul of the objects, while Kojuk tried to give a faithful rendering. The debate between the master and disciple on plums and bamboos well illustrates that conflict.

Bamboos and plums were Sŏkdam's specialty as a painter. In his youth his bamboos and plums were healthy and exuberant. But, after the colonization of the country by Japan, his bamboos and plums had begun to grow withered, lean and gnarled. So that in later years there were no more than three leaves to one stalk of bamboo and fewer than five blossoms to a bough of plum. It made Kojuk extremely unhappy.

"Why are your bamboos and plums so withered and poverty-stricken?" Kojuk protested.

"How can a bamboo tree in a fallen country be exuberant, and what scholar of a colonized country would have the heart to make the plums blossom?" Sŏkdam responded.

"Cheng Sou-nan expressed his grief for the fall of Sung by exposing the roots of his orchids, while Chao Meng-fu served in the court of his country's conqueror Yuan. But I never heard anyone argue that only Cheng Sou-nan's orchids are fragrant and Chao Meng-fu's calligraphy is base," Kojuk objected.

"Calligraphy and painting are reflections of the soul. You borrow the shapes of things to give form to your spirit and soul. There's no need to be governed by the outward forms of things," was the teacher's reply.

"If calligraphy and painting are simply means of expressing a scholar's grief and pain, they're futile and worthless as arts! Isn't it a shame, in that case, for a man to rub ink and foul up paper all his life? If one's country is of such great value, wouldn't it behoove a man to join the underground army and die in fighting the enemy? Isn't it deceiving yourself and the world, to sit in your study and draw lean and twisted bamboos and plums in lament for your lost country?" Kojuk pursued obstinately.

"That's not so. In literal representation, you can't top the sidewalk painters. But because their souls are shallow and spirits base, their pictures are cheap and end up as floor papers. You try to deny the spirit of calligraphy and drawings, but, without their lofty spirit, all drawings are simply ink smeared on paper," Sŏkdam countered.

Another instance of their conflict was their debate on artistic principles. It was also provoked by Kojuk in his mid-thirties, when Sŏkdam was growing weak with old age.

"Are calligraphy and painting arts, laws or ways?" Kojuk asked, to open the debate.

"They are ways," Sŏkdam returned.

"Then, why are there words like 'the art of calligraphy' and 'the laws of calligraphy'?" Kojuk challenged.

"Art is the fragrance of the Way, and laws are the garments of the Way. Without the Way, there can be no art, no law," Sŏkdam enunciated.

"Isn't it said that refinement of art will ultimately bring one to the Way? Isn't art the gateway to the Way, not just its fragrance?" Kojuk objected.

"That's what artisans say. Everything must reside in the Way at all times," Sŏkdam insisted.

"Then the first step in learning calligraphy and painting must be purification of the mind and soul?" Kojuk pursued.

"Yes. That's why Wang Hsi-chih said, 'If one has not the right character, one must not be taught.' Can you see the meaning now?" The teacher's withered face brightened up with those words and he studied his disciple's face with hope. But Kojuk refused to understand him to the end.

"If the noble mind and soul are prerequisites, how is it that you teach calligraphy to little children? If the noble mind and soul are prerequisites, how many could there be who are worthy to take up the brush before death?" Kojuk protested.

"It is to teach the technique while waiting for the Way to take root. If one progresses no further than the technique, one is an artisan; if one can advance to the next stage, one is an artist; if the technique and the Way can both be perfected, one becomes a master," Sŏkdam explained.

"Then, it means that artistry is more basic than the Way. So, to suppress the refinement of the technique for the refinement of the soul is like putting the cart before the horse. Can you deny it?"

That was Kojuk's objection to the whole of his teacher's principles and instruction. Seeing his lifelong dread materialize in concrete form, the teacher's response was sharp.

"You low-down! How dare you try to cover up your deficiency in discipline and scholarship with your sophistry? Scholarship is the road to the Way. But you are neither interested in the classical canons nor take delight in poetic composition. You only try to refine your wrist and fingers to imitate the ultimate attainments of past masters. How can this be different from base artisanship? And you aren't ashamed of yourself in the least, but rather presume to pass judgment on the great masters!"

Then there came the day of their fatal separation. This happened when Kojuk was thirty-five years old.

At that time Kojuk was exhausted for many reasons. His training over the eight years since his readmission to discipleship was a period of long penance. Because he sat in the same position all day long, day after day, practicing writing and drawing, boils erupted on his buttocks in the summer, and in the winter his joints became so stiff that he had difficulty standing up. He didn't so much as glance at or bother to listen to anything unrelated to calligraphy and brush painting. Afterwards, Kojuk always thought of those eight years as the most valuable years of his training. If his first ten years under Sŏkdam could be called the years of struggle to reach Sŏkdam's stage, the later eight years embodied his struggle to transcend Sŏkdam's methods and principles.

His artistry grew more sophisticated, and his name began to be

known. Some critics still rate his works of that period as the best of
all his life's works, for their wit and imaginativeness. Still, Kojuk
was oppressed by a sense of loneliness and emptiness.

There were two factors at the base of his loneliness and emptiness. The first was the feeling that his youth had gone by while he
was wrestling with paper and brush. He had a wife and two children from his marriage arranged by Ungok. But, from the first,
they were articles of necessity, like the stationery chest or the writing table, not objects of desire. All his youth, hope, love and yearning were dedicated to calligraphy and painting. But he found that
though his youth was almost gone, he was still not much nearer the
rainbow peak of his desire.

The second factor was the problem of self-esteem. As he came
out of his trancelike immersion in practice, he often asked himself,
derisively: What am I doing? Does what I do have any meaning? In
a different mood from when he protested to his teacher, he asked
himself whether it is worth a man's while to spend his entire life
rubbing ink and wielding the brush. Men were getting killed,
imprisoned, or fleeing abroad fighting for their country's independence. Some men built industries and fed their starving neighbors.
Some became educators and enlightened their ignorant compatri-
ots, introducing the advanced learning of the new world. But what
had he achieved? he asked himself. His whole concern centered on
himself and he had deemed his goal absolute—was it not, in fact,
an escape from the meaninglessness of his life? A life lived only for
oneself! Ah, he had lived his life only for himself!

Then, on an autumn day it happened. At the time Sŏkdam was
often bedridden with illness. One morning, after a spell of illness,
he asked for brush and paper, not just ordinary brush and paper
but a big brush and full-size paper. Kojuk, who was himself staying
away from calligraphy and painting for several months, felt inwardly cross with his teacher and left the teacher's study as soon as he
had rubbed ink for him. He felt as if his teacher's dedication was a
mocking commentary on his lack of self-trust. After circling the
yard a few times, he was impelled by curiosity to look into his
teacher's study.

He found his teacher panting breathlessly, leaning his brush
against the rim of the ink slab. On the floor lay the paper with the
first three letters of the four-letter phrase, "Though writing ten
thousand strokes, the force does not vary in the least."

"It is said that Su Ch'i wrote 'All the world's at peace' on a
sesame seed at age seventy-eight. I am not seventy yet, but I don't
have enough strength to write these four letters in one breath."

There was mournful despair on the teacher's face as he said

this. But Kojuk, instead of being moved to pity, felt perverse anger. To him, the mournful despair on his teacher's face looked like a veil drawn over arrogant self-confidence.

"What could it avail you even if you could write those four letters in one breath and on top of it could see the golden phoenix and the mythical elephant rise from those letters?" Kojuk challenged with a smirk.

"How dare you blaspheme? Such a plateau is what every calligrapher yearns to attain, if only once in a lifetime."

"But what could it avail us even if we reach it?"

"You are like the one who worries that there won't be higher peaks, even before trying to climb Mount Tai. Do you mean to say that the divine achievements of those great masters of old are useless and worthless?"

"They deceived themselves and others. How can there be any sublimity in smearing paper with ink? How profound and subtle can that Way be? Speaking of the 'Way,' wouldn't you say that there's a way in butchery and robbery as well? And, speaking of subtlety and profundity, isn't it true that they are also found in the work of the bricklayer and the plumber? You speak of leaving behind one's name, but what does it mean to have an empty sound circulating after you've ceased to be? And as for leaving behind your calligraphy and paintings—how can fragile paper and ink endure, when even hard stones are eroded by wind and rain? Moreover, calligraphy and painting can't help you live comfortably, nor can it help feed and clothe your hungry neighbors. The so-called great masters set up a certain goal that can neither be reached nor defined, to hide from the emptiness and meaninglessness of their pursuit and to deceive themselves and others."

Kojuk could not go on any more; he fell forward with a sudden pain in his forehead. The teacher had thrown the stone lid of his ink-slab at Kojuk. While trying to stop the blood gushing from his forehead, Kojuk heard the teacher's enraged wail.

"I should have recognized your hopeless baseness long ago. Go away. You should have become a sidewalk painter long before this. Go away. You'll have no difficulty peddling your paintings for rice, as you could hide your base nature this long."

It was their last meeting. Kojuk left his teacher's house that same day. When he returned many years later, the teacher was already in a coffin.

Kojuk fingered the little scar on his left forehead, faintly recalling the pain of more than thirty years ago. But that touch called up the teacher's face, invoking in him neither fear nor hatred but longing.

"Father, Ch'ohŏn's here."

Ch'usu's voice awoke him from his reverie. Soon the door slid open and Ch'ohŏn's round face appeared. Ch'ohŏn was a student of his whom he cherished like his own son. It was partly because the young man was running Kojuk's studio by himself for nearly a year now without any complaint or demand, but more because of his attitude toward calligraphy and painting. Unlike most young men of recent times who want to jump onto the next step before mastering the preliminary steps, Ch'ohŏn stuck to the basic square style for three full years. And, even after devoting seven years wholly to practice, he participated in the joint exhibition of Kojuk's students that spring with only two pieces of calligraphy. His calligraphy, though lacking slightly in fluency, had an indefinable force that moved Kojuk strangely. It reminded him of his own teacher's style, which he had so vehemently rejected at one time but which filled him with yearning in his old age.

"Are you going out today, too? Your daughter told me you had difficulty moving . . . " Ch'ohŏn said slowly. The young man's hesitant manner of speaking would have exasperated Kojuk when young, but he simply said, reassuringly: "All the more reason why I should find even one more piece. So, the city library won't hear of selling or trading it?"

"It won't. The director said he couldn't allow it to be sold or exchanged, because it's clearly listed in their book."

"Not even to trade with Maekye's calligraphy?"

"No. The director said it can't be removed under any condition."

"What fools. I'll have to talk to the director myself."

"Are you really going out?"

"Yes. Don't waste any more words and go fetch a taxi."

Ch'ohŏn went out silently. His face was full of questions but he still didn't ask what his teacher intended by collecting all his works.

It was a fine day. Kojuk got off the taxi with the help of his young disciple at the entrance of the street lined with art galleries and began checking the galleries. It was a daily pilgrimage that had been going on for several months now.

"Oh, come in, come in, sir! But nothing has come in since yesterday. I suppose everyone's holding onto your work, now that it's known your health is poor." All gallery owners greeted him with words to the same effect.

Then, in the sixth gallery he found a familiar piece. It was a calligraphy in the semicursive style. As it bore the signature of "ko" for lonely instead of "ko" for ancient, it must be a piece written in the period of his second vagabondage.

"I'll give you an orchid of Ungok's in exchange. Would that do?"

The gallery owner seemed delighted. He knew that Kojuk's works signed with the "lonely ko" were rated relatively low. Furthermore, all gallery owners knew that such barters with Kojuk were always to their advantage.

"Well, if you really must have it," the gallery owner said, like one bestowing a great favor.

"Thank you. I'll send you the orchid by this young man."

"Oh, I'll send someone over to your house. No. I'll come myself. Will late afternoon be okay with you, sir?"

"Yes."

The gallery owner began wrapping up the scroll.

"There's no need. Just give it to me," Kojuk said, extending his gaunt hand. When the owner put it in his hand, he sat down on the sofa and unrolled it.

Rubbing the ink stick on the slab, I see a dense mist rise.
Writing with a fine brush, I see a thin cloud floating.

It was written in the semicursive style of Huang Shan-ku that had fascinated him for a while. It must have been in repayment for a banquet or something; the strokes were very unsettled. Then the memory of the days of his wandering came back again, bringing neither sorrow nor regret, but a kind of longing.

For a while after leaving his teacher's house for the second time, Kojuk believed that he was thrown out by his teacher. Even though he sold his calligraphy and paintings indiscriminately and lived the life of a prodigal, he told himself he was taking a just revenge upon the cruel teacher. But, when he got accustomed to the money and acclaim offered by the worldly crowd, and the pleasures he could buy with money, it occurred to him from time to time that it was he who had deserted his teacher. It also dawned on him that the praises and pleasures he was enjoying had nothing to do with what he strove to attain in his life, and that they were poor recompenses indeed for the unremitting penance of his entire youth and young manhood. He realized that, though politely offered, the money he got for his calligraphy and paintings was no different in essence from tips given to entertaining women, and that the loud praises showered on him were no different from the applause given to circus clowns. The money and acclaim, far from quenching his thirst, made it the more urgent, like saltwater that makes one more thirsty the more one drinks it.

But it was that very emptiness that held him fast in the rut of waste and dissipation. Base pleasures aggravated his emptiness, which in turn demanded more violent stimulations.

His repressed lust also helped prolong his wanderings. Around that time he found out that his father had debauched away a substantial family fortune and died of exhaustion in his early thirties, and his mother had run away with a neighborhood widower before she was out of mourning, leaving behind her only child. Lust was in his blood. The lust had lain dormant in his boyhood in his stern teacher's house and in his youth by the urgency of his desire to attain mastery in his chosen field. But, once awakened, it completely overwhelmed him and drove him to banquet after banquet and woman after woman.

His dissipation did not abate even when the Pacific War broke out and the whole nation was impoverished and devastated. There are always people who can take advantage of a general calamity. Such renegades were his patrons. The pro-Japanese Koreans, the cultured Japanese aristocrats, the merchants of war supplies . . .

Then there came a turning point. It occurred while he was a guest of a pro-Japanese landowner. Calligraphers and painters loved to be guests of this landowner because he was a connoisseur of fine arts and well-to-do enough to be munificent to his artist guests. Moreover, he himself did not commit any dishonorable acts against the country but simply enjoyed the protection of the Japanese because his son was a high official at the Japanese governor-general's office. Anyway, while Kojuk was a guest at this landowner's, Ungok came by one day. Kojuk was happy to see the guest who had been his teacher of Chinese Classics for about six years. Ungok was also one of the few friends of his teacher, Sŏkdam. Besides, Ungok had arranged Kojuk's marriage, even though the marriage did not end very happily. It was Ungok, too, who had understood him better than anybody else when he left Sŏkdam. But Ungok's response to Kojuk's warm greeting was one of cold accusation.

"Ah, how does the lofty soul who disclaims ancestor, teacher and family still remember this miserable old man?" Ungok said in cold mockery of Kojuk's sobriquet, "Thrice Bereaved," that Kojuk once used in self-derision. Then he turned back in spite of the host's earnest entreaties. "Sŏkdam must be near his end, to be waiting for the return of a wretch like you!" Ungok spat out the words as he passed the gate. As Ungok had always been a warm and friendly soul, his blame was like an ax cleaving Kojuk's heart.

By that time Kojuk was already sick and tired of his vagabond life. His loneliness and emptiness could not be allayed by the senti-mental pleasures of travel or the acclaim and money offered by the worldly crowd. Nor could cheap romances veil the meaninglessness of his existence from his own eyes. Moreover, he was already well past forty, and the fury of the lust in his blood had abated.

After that momentary encounter with Ungok, Kojuk went into the Odae Mountains where an old friend of his was the superior of a temple. He wanted to collect and purify himself there before returning to his old teacher.

He lived like a monk in the mountains for almost half a year. But the accumulated dust of the world and the age-old resentment towards his teacher could not be washed away even by half a year's ascetic life. He did not feel like going back to the old teacher even when spring came.

Then, one day, while sitting down to take a rest on the embankment behind the main hall, after gathering the inner bark of pine trees with one of the monks, his eyes lighted on a faded wall painting. At first he thought it must be a painting of one of the twelve Buddhist demigods. But, on looking more carefully, he found that it was the painting of a huge bird with a head like an eagle, body like a human, and great golden wings.

"What kind of a bird is that?" Kojuk asked the superior who appeared just at that moment. The superior glanced at the wall and said, "Oh, that's a Karura bird. It's a huge mythical bird that has cintamani in the middle of its forehead, spouts fire from its mouth, and eats dragons. It lives in the Sumisan Ocean and is the fifth of the eight guardian angels of Buddha's Ways. It is also called a Kŭmsijo, or a golden phoenix."

At that moment, the phrase "the golden phoenix splits open the sea" flashed through his head like lightning. It was the first phrase in the calligraphy that the teacher wrote for him to warn him against his talent overwhelming his character. But until then the golden phoenix was no more than an abstract metaphor for him. To him it was a kind of symbol of hardy strength that could be seen in the teacher's calligraphic style. But now, the metaphor came alive from out of the faded picture; the bird began to move. For a moment Kojuk seemed to behold a colossal golden phoenix flying across the vast firmament, flapping its huge golden wings, and splitting the ocean and snatching up a great dragon. Kojuk thought he could at last understand what his teacher meant when he said that if one could see a golden phoenix fly up from one's

calligraphy or painting, even if only for once in one's life, then that
life has meaning, regardless of any external recognition or value or
standard.

The next day Kojuk packed his things and came down from
the mountains. It was the year before the end of World War II and
the country's liberation.

The teacher was already dead—Kojuk thought of the day he
reached his teacher's house again with a feeling akin to regret. The
house, which was always quiet and lonely, bustled with the
teacher's friends and disciples. But no one greeted Kojuk warmly.
Only Ungok told him coldly: "You write the banner on the coffin.
That is the teacher's wish. Don't write his titles and honors but simply write, 'Scholar Kim Sŏkdam's hearse.'" Then he added, with
tears streaming down his face: "Do you know what that means, you
wretch? He means to carry your calligraphy to the other world. He
loved your calligraphy that much, you idiot!"

In that instant, Kojuk's hatred and bitterness of many years
towards his teacher melted away without a trace. Kojuk felt an irresistible longing to see his teacher once more, but the coffin had
already been nailed.

"Hadn't we better leave, sir?" Ch'ohŏn asked diffidently of
Kojuk, who sat gazing into space, sunk in revery. Kojuk came back
to himself and stood up slowly. But, after four more visits to the
galleries, Kojuk suddenly felt dizzy and his legs caved in.

"What's the matter, sir?" Ch'ohŏn asked, hurriedly supporting
him.

"I'm all right. Let's go on to the next shop," Kojuk said, but he
couldn't move. An electric current ran down his spine and cold
sweat broke out on his forehead. When they stepped into the next
gallery even his consciousness was dim.

"Why don't you go home and rest? I don't think you'd find any
more of your works even if you went to all the other galleries," the
gallery owner also suggested. But Kojuk, almost toppling down on
the sofa, told Ch'ohŏn: "You go and look in the rest of the galleries. And come here at once if you find anything."

Ch'ohŏn went out, after watching Kojuk anxiously for a while.

"What are you going to do with all the works you buy?" The
gallery owner asked, seeing that Kojuk had caught his breath. It
was a mystery to all the gallery owners for the past several months.
But Kojuk never told anyone his real intention. It was the same
that day.

"Well, there will be some use for them."

"Then, are you really going to build a commemorative hall for yourself? That's what people say."

A commemorative hall . . . Kojuk smiled thinly at the idea. An ineffable loneliness and emptiness welled up in his heart. How could you understand, even if I were to explain it to you? he thought.

"That's not a bad idea," Kojuk said and changed the subject. "Is that a genuine Ch'usa?" he said, pointing to a copy of Ch'usa, knowing only too well that it was a copy. *The soul of brush painting is illimitable as a flowing river. The art of calligraphy is as lonely as a branch of pine.* As it represented one section of a folding screen, it couldn't be floating around as an independent scroll if it had been an original.

"It's a copy made by a young calligrapher who goes by the sobriquet of Unbong. I thought it's a copy worth hanging, as it has a lofty air," the gallery owner said, regarding the scroll with some satisfaction.

"True enough," Kojuk said, gazing at the scroll like one trying to find the face of the ancient master in it. Ch'usa! How that great man once held him in thrall!

After returning to his teacher's house for the second time, Kojuk abided there for nearly ten years. He looked after the teacher's lonely widow and his young adopted son, and began another period of penance-like self-training. He started again from the very beginning, and practiced all the styles all over again.

He collected copies of all the monumental inscriptions, beginning with the hieroglyph of Early Ch'in, and studied all the specimens of every different style, from ancient to recent times, all over again. Judging from the depth of scholarship Kojuk exhibited in later years, it is obvious that this period of intensive study improved his understanding of the classics most markedly. The outside world was in a huge turmoil from the aftermath of the country's liberation and the maelstrom of a civil war, but nothing could draw him out of his old teacher's study.

It was during that period that Kojuk began to have a true appreciation of Ch'usa, whose *Principles* he had learned by heart at his teacher's order. He encountered the great man here and there in the course of his third period of self-flagellation, and ended up being completely enthralled by him. That thralldom grew out of Kojuk's renewed appreciation of, and love for, his teacher Sŏkdam. Although Sŏkdam had never explicitly said so, he was the last true

follower of Ch'usa. And it could well be that the reason Sŏkdam
was so chary of giving instructions was that he thought he had
nothing to add to the great man's teaching.

But even Ch'usa could not hold him in thrall forever. Kojuk's
artistic passion, which made Sŏkdam so reluctant to accept him as
a disciple, and which Sŏkdam had tried so hard to suppress, re-
asserted itself, though in an ennobled form. Despite his admiration, Kojuk could not accept Ch'usa's view of art. Kojuk was convinced that art should be an art from first to last, whereas Ch'usa's
view of art seemed to be based on a confusion of art with scholarship. To Kojuk, true understanding of the text, both emotional and
scholarly, manifested in works of calligraphy, can be an aid to artistic beauty, but is not its essence or basis. Kojuk did not regard
Ch'usa's greatness as a calligrapher and brush painter to be stemming from his greatness as a scholar. Ch'usa was simply an artistic
genius who happened to be a great scholar and thinker at the same
time. Moreover, the "Principle of Textual Criticism" of the Q'ing
scholars that was at the basis of Ch'usa's principles was responsible
for stifling the development of a uniquely Korean philosophy and
artistic tradition. That was another factor that turned Kojuk away
from Ch'usa. Kojuk decided at last that Ch'usa was, like his teacher
Sŏkdam, a great man to be admired and venerated but not one to
follow as an artistic model.

As the gallery owner had predicted, Ch'ohŏn came back
empty-handed in about an hour. He reported that he had been to
the six remaining galleries but found nothing that had come in
since the day before.

Kojuk asked Ch'ohŏn to accompany him to the City Library,
though the young man tried to dissuade him. His purpose was to
persuade the director of the library to yield up his calligraphy
piece there. But his stubbornness was his undoing. He fainted
while arguing heatedly with the inflexible director.

It was early afternoon when Kojuk came to his senses again. He
was lying in his own room and there were a few familiar faces looking at him anxiously. Kojuk gazed at them one by one, slowly.
Besides Ch'ohŏn's expressionless face were two of his old pupils'.
Ch'usu, who was sitting beside them with a tear-stained face, asked
in a tearful voice; "Are you all right, father?"

Kojuk nodded a couple of times and continued looking
around. Next to Ch'usu sat a familiar face. It was Nanjŏng, the first
student of his to whom he had given a sobriquet. Impudent fellow!
Kojuk stared at him with fury. Nanjŏng was his student for ten years

from shortly after his second return to Sŏkdam's house at the time of the teacher's death to shortly after he opened his own studio in the city. It was true that there was only about a dozen years' difference in their ages and Nanjŏng had prior training before coming to receive his teaching, but there was no question that he was Kojuk's student, who was honored with the gift of a sobriquet by Kojuk. Anyway, this impudent fellow suddenly stopped coming to receive instruction one day, and a few years later opened his own studio-institute. Kojuk was hurt that his student ignored him, but he wasn't prepared for what followed. It was reported to him that Nanjŏng went around saying that he was a disciple of Sŏkdam, not of Kojuk, and that Kojuk was just a senior fellow student with whom he studied for more than a decade. Kojuk had rushed to Nanjŏng's studio in fury. Although he had gone to scold him, the visit resulted in Nanjŏng's claims being confirmed publicly.

"Oh, dear brother! Welcome, welcome!" Nanjŏng greeted him with a broad smile in front of his own numerous students. He concluded every sentence with "brother," and often prefaced it with "When we were studying together." Later on, he even sued Kojuk for having maligned him to other people.

"Father, this gentleman has brought two bamboo drawings of yours." Ch'usu hurriedly explained, seeing the fury in her father's eyes.

"I heard you were collecting your own works. They're all I have," Nanjŏng stammered. He did not look cunning anymore. Wasn't he close to sixty already? Kojuk noted the wrinkles on the treacherous disciple's face and closed his eyes. But he did not find it easy to forgive the fellow even now.

"Thank you. You needn't stay any longer," Kojuk said weakly after calming himself with difficulty.

"Goodbye . . . sir."

Nanjŏng left with a heavy countenance. Silence reigned in the room for a while. Ch'usu broke the silence.

"Chaesik phoned today."

"Did he say when he'll come?"

"He'll arrive tonight. Would you like me to contact Yunsik, too?"

"Yes, do."

Kojuk sighed. Chaesik was his son by his first wife. He had a son and a daughter by his first wife, but the daughter had died during the Korean War and only the son survived. Yunsik was his youngest child, a son by his last wife. Chaesik was forty-three, and owned a shop in Pusan. Yunsik was just twenty, and was going to college in Seoul. Kojuk was not a loving parent, but he always felt guilty towards his youngest son, who lost his mother at thirteen and was raised by his stepsister. But today, Kojuk called to mind Chaesik's face and felt a painful tenderness. It wasn't his face as a tired shop owner in his early forties. It was his face as a boy of sixteen, who looked no better than a beggar boy when Kojuk went to get him back. And he recalled the face of his first wife, which he had not done for many decades.

Kojuk got married at twenty-two through Ungok's arrangement. His wife was a distant cousin of Ungok's. She was neither a beauty nor very plain. Anyway, she was of a mild temperament, so that she had never, in his memory, yelled at him or nagged at him viciously. It wasn't a very happy marriage from the start, because Kojuk's passion was all for calligraphy and brush painting. Except for a few days after the wedding, Kojuk spent almost all his daytime at Sŏkdam's house. Even at home, Kojuk's thoughts were far from household matters. Moreover, since his entire contribution to household finances consisted of an occasional gift of rice from Sŏkdam, she worked incessantly at sewing but could hardly make ends meet.

Even so, the first few years were the best years of their marriage. As long as Kojuk studied under Sŏkdam he slept in his own house at night, and they had two children together. But that came to an end with the beginning of Kojuk's vagabondage. For nearly ten years after he left the house without any explanation, Kojuk roamed around, rarely if ever remembering that he had a wife and children. His wife and children meant no more to him than a cumbersome garment he had to keep wearing, for appearance's sake. It was because they meant so little to him that he could leave them so easily and forget them so completely.

His wife sought him out several times during his years of drifting. But Kojuk always turned a cold shoulder on her. Perhaps such a cruelty stemmed from the fact that she reminded him of his own baseness and selfishness more than she aroused pity and guilt in him. Once he gave her a little money and bought her a pair of rubber shoes when she came to him with their daughter strapped to her back. But he did that not out of his sense of responsibility as husband and father but rather out of charity for shivering and starving poor folk: his baby daughter was feverish and his wife's torn rubber shoes kept slipping off her feet. That was their last meeting.

Five years after Kojuk left his teacher and his family, his wife went back to her parents' house with the two children. That was the year Kojuk began living with Maehyang. The next year his wife went to Osaka, Japan, where her brother was living. It was rumored that she remarried there. It must be true, since she never came back to take away her children as she had promised her parents. It was several years after he returned to his teacher's house from that long wandering that he sent for his children. His son Chaesik was sixteen and his daughter was eleven.

Just as Kojuk never blamed himself for neglecting and deserting his wife, he never blamed his wife for leaving him and their children, either. It was the same with all the women who were his temporary lovers. None of the women—whether entertaining women like Maehyang who had been his mistress, or the two "wives" of his later years, or women calligrapher-painters who became his lovers—could captivate him for long. Because of his character Kojuk was fated to be lonely.

Then, what was it that I really loved, passionately and truly? What was it that I strove so hard to attain all my life? Kojuk sank into a revery that was akin to sorrow, as he looked around the room in which only he and Ch'ohŏn were left. It was, of course, the art of calligraphy and brush painting. He was not interested in family or social life. He did not covet possessions or wealth. He had no burning desire for fame and power. Though his life had periods of hectic activity, on the whole it was a very simple life he had led. He was always faithful to the strongest impulse of the moment, regardless of social norms and ethical convictions. Well, his strongest and most persistent impulse was that for beauty, so he cultivated the art of calligraphy and brush painting.

But what did I get from my dedication to that art? Kojuk asked himself, a little mockingly. Can it give me anything even now?

In the first half of his life Kojuk had been continuously torn between two conflicting artistic principles. In the Orient, art was from the first an aid to and a means of statecraft. And it not only never achieved independence from statecraft, but scholarship and religion infringed upon it as well. Its most frequent subjects were such notions as loyalty and integrity. And such concepts as "nobility of character" and "depth of scholarship" were terms of higher praise for the arts than beauty or grace.

Of course things weren't much different with art in the West in ancient times. For a long time art was used to glorify God. But, since the Renaissance, with the formation of citizenry, art became

independent of other values and was recognized as a unique entity
of its own. In other words, such artistic values as sensitivity and
imaginativeness were recognized as values in themselves.

Well, throughout Kojuk's youth the Oriental view of art
reigned supreme. Artists were considered a pariah and their talent
was a kind of stigma. True art was believed always to be based on
depth of scholarship, and its perfection was always compared to
the attainment of religious awakening or of sublimity of character.
Sŏkdam was perhaps the last true adherent of this traditional view
of art.

From the Western viewpoint, Kojuk was a born artist. But, to
Sŏkdam, he was not much better than a base entertainer. The conflict between the teacher and the disciple might not have been so
persistent nor so miserable, had Kojuk's character been weaker or
had he been born a little earlier. But Kojuk could not stand for his
art to be trammeled by anything that was not art in essence, and
the changing times were on his side as well. Fortunately for the
two, Kojuk had a deep reverence for the integrity of his teacher,
and the teacher had an irrepressible love for his disciple's talent,
so that there could be a reconciliation between them, albeit a
posthumous one.

But Kojuk's journey was not over when he returned to his
teacher's house. For ten years he strove to reconcile himself with
his teacher's vision, but he had to give it up in the end. His thralldom to Ch'usa and his eventual estrangement from him were
emblematic of this process. Another twenty years passed after that.
He had striven and searched ceaselessly. But did he really get what
he wanted? Kojuk fell into sleep that was more a swoon.

It was after sunset when Kojuk woke again from a strange commotion in the room.

"There'll be another attack of pain. I can stop that at least,"
someone said and pulled back the quilt cover. It was Dr. Chŏng.
The cold needle of the syringe sent a shiver through his body as it
pierced his skin. There were many more people in the room.
Kojuk knew instinctively what it meant.

"Father, it's me. Chaesik. Can you recognize me all right?"
Chaesik said in a tearful voice, holding his hand, as soon as the
injection was over. He was never happy at home, even after he
began living with his own father at sixteen. Kojuk recalled the day
Chaesik first ran away from home. It was the day after Kojuk first
bought him an inkstone and a brush. He had disappeared from
home before anybody was up, leaving behind him the inkstone
pounded to powder, the brush handle split to shreds, and a handful of scattered hair. Thereafter Chaesik was a source of continuous

trouble for Kojuk. He sometimes disappeared with Kojuk's unfinished calligraphy and paintings, or stole money from the safe. But, after being discharged from the army, he asked for money to buy a delivery truck and disappeared with it. It was only the year before last that Chaesik began coming to see him again.

"Yunsik's here, too." Ch'usu's eyes were badly swollen from crying. Poor things. He had sinned against them all. Could the small property he was leaving them be some recompense? Kojuk had already specified in his will that Chaesik was to have the orchard in the suburbs of the city; Yunsik to have the building housing his studio; and Ch'usu the present house. Then he thought that he did well indeed to cancel the plan to endow an arts prize by selling all his movable property. He did not want to fawn on the world at his death, when he had lived his life in such utter disregard of it.

"Stop crying. This isn't the proper way to bid farewell." A woman's voice said. Then the woman held his hand. "Do you recognize me?" she said to Kojuk. Kojuk looked at her weakly. It was a lady calligrapher–brush painter whose sobriquet was Okkyŏ. She was a woman he had passionately loved at one time, and was rumored far and wide to be his mistress. She ran a studio of her own in a nearby city and lived in semiretirement. Of course I recognize you. Of course. Of course. But he fell into slumber again before he could say it.

The golden phoenix was in flight. Flapping its mile-long wings, it was flying over the blue ocean. But the bird was not an awe-inspiring bird about to dispel an army of devils and snatch up an evil dragon. It was simply flying to reach a brighter, more beautiful world. On its sublime forehead the cintamani shone radiantly, and from its lips scattered crimson petals. Kojuk himself was riding on its back. He was holding onto it by a feather, straining not to slip off. The golden phoenix soared suddenly. A gust of wind rose and Kojuk dangled by a feather. He lost strength and his grip loosened. Ah! Waking, he heard the clock in the living room strike four. The painkiller must have spent its power. He felt a sinister pain that couldn't be pinned down to any specific source invading all parts of his body. But his consciousness was as clear as could be.

The visitors were all gone and only his sons and Ch'ohŏn were dozing, leaning on the wall. Kojuk tried to sit up. It was unexpectedly easy. The pain in the small of his back had markedly subsided. Then he recalled that he still had a big task left.

"Sangchŏl!" He called his disciple quietly by name. When he called three or four times Ch'ohŏn woke up.

"Yes, sir, what is it?" Ch'ohŏn answered and hurriedly went up to him to give him support. But Kojuk stopped him by a motion of his hand and said, "Bring me all the calligraphy and brush paintings we've been collecting."

Ch'ohŏn did as bidden. When brought out from closets and stationery chests they made quite a heap, even without the frames, and amounted to more than two hundred items.

"What are you doing, father?" His sons also woke up at the noise and asked. Kojuk did not at all look like a sick person nearing his death. But he didn't bother to answer his sons' questions and instead asked Ch'ohŏn: "Can you make this room a little brighter?"

"I know there's a lampstand somewhere. I'll go and look for it."

Ch'ohŏn went out, without asking his teacher what he meant to do with the calligraphy works and paintings and more light, and returned with a lampstand. When the room became twice as bright, Kojuk ordered Ch'ohŏn again: "Now straighten them out one by one and hold them up for me."

Ch'ohŏn simply did as bidden. The first one was a calligraphy written in his fifties, in the style of Yu Shih-nan.

"That's Yu Shih-nan's text. It doesn't have the five virtues it ought to have. Put it on my left."

The next one was a brush painting of an orchid.

"It's an orchid still in the shadow of Prince Regent Taewŏn. It's neither a wild orchid nor an orchid of my heart. Put it on my left."

Kojuk criticized each piece, as severely and mercilessly as one criticizing a lifelong enemy's works. In commenting on calligraphy works he criticized the uncertainty of strokes or lack of fidelity or force for those in any of the traditional styles. For those in his own style, he criticized their artificiality or lack of dignity. He ordered every one of them to be put on his left. It was the same with brush paintings. Judged with the double severity of the old laws and his own high standard, nothing was pronounced worthy to be put on his right.

The operation that began at dawn continued till it was broad daylight. It was almost a superhuman strength that he exhibited, as Dr. Chŏng was to marvel again and again afterwards. Kojuk's spacious room was soon densely crowded with visitors. But because the proceeding was so solemn, no one dared to dissuade him from that enervating operation. And Kojuk seemed oblivious of anyone except Ch'ohŏn.

The operation came to an end after ten o'clock. But there was not a single piece that was on Kojuk's right.

"Aren't there any more?" Kojuk asked in a tremulous voice, even though he could see as plainly as anyone that there was no more.

"No," Ch'ohŏn answered simply. Then, grief covered Kojuk's face for a moment, his head dropped, and his body slid down weakly. Several of the visitors screamed and surrounded him. But Kojuk was muttering to himself even at the moment. He muttered over and over, "No, it didn't appear. I longed to see it if only for once, but it didn't rise. Perhaps I knew from the first I'd never see it. Maybe that's why I put it off till this last moment . . ."

What was it that Kojuk wanted to see rise from his works? It was a golden phoenix, such a phoenix as he saw in his dream of that dawn. The phoenix that flew to him from his teacher Sŏkdam was an emblem of such Oriental virtues as integrity and sublimity of character. But the bird was transformed in Kojuk's mind. It had become a bird symbolizing aesthetic fulfillment or artistic perfection.

Kojuk's artistic principle that was embodied in both his calligraphy and paintings and expressed verbally to his students had two main points. One was that whereas in the traditional aesthetics even painting was looked upon as a form of writing, he regarded even writing as a form of drawing. Calligraphy was not worth dedicating one's life to if it meant no more than transmitting meaning through letters. With a brush one can convey one's meaning sufficiently well after a few month's training. With instruments like a pencil or a ball-point pen, a few days' practice is enough. So, calligraphy has meaning not as a medium of message but as formal art. If it wasn't a formal art, then there is no explaining why calligraphy was developed only in the Orient, which used the Chinese ideograms, and not in the West, which used phonetic letters. But because it was regarded as a medium of message, it and its companion brush painting were never accorded independent values.

The second point of Kojuk's artistic principle was to distinguish between realistic painting and expressive painting. Realistic painting strove to paint objects faithfully, while expressive painting used objects to express the painters' emotion; so the objects could be modified or transformed by the emotion of the painters. Thus, the two kinds of painting had correspondence to nonabstract and abstract paintings of the West. Kojuk was of the opinion that in Oriental painting the two kinds of painting were curiously confused, and he was convinced that there should be a clear distinction between the two. Moreover, neither kind was superior to the other, and it was simply a matter of preference for the painter to cultivate either kind. So, ideas like integrity of character and depth of scholarship were simply elements of expressive painting, and not the essential bases of all superior paintings.

So, Kojuk's Kraken was a bird soaring from out of the sea of his artistic convictions to aesthetic perfection. When he reached the age he had to prepare for death, his ardent wish was to see a Kraken rise from the strokes of his brush. He thought that would give meaning to his lifelong struggle and reconcile him to his lonely and painful life. But, he did not see the bird rise. It was not solely from physical exhaustion that his body collapsed weakly.

None of the people in the room thought Kojuk would regain consciousness, but he woke up again within five minutes. Then, disregarding pleas to keep lying still, he sat up again and called Ch'ohŏn in a commanding tone.

"Take all of these out to the flower bed by the storage place."

Ch'ohŏn, who as a rule never asked questions and simply did as he was told, looked at him questioningly without moving.

"With those things I deceived myself and the world all my life. I made myself believe I was doing something worthwhile and accepted the praise and respect of other people as my due."

"They were your due."

"No. Maybe there are people who deserve such praise and respect. But I'm not one of them." He paused. "Until just now I yearned to see a Kraken rise from my works—if only for once. I thought then my life would be fulfilled. But now I doubt if my life would have gained meaning even if I had seen a Kraken rise from my works."

Ch'ohŏn was silent.

"Well, do as I tell you. If I leave them behind, I will be deceiving the world even after death."

Ch'ohŏn silently went out with the sheaf of painted and written papers. There is no telling whether it was because he understood his teacher or whether because he could not disobey him. Anyway, no one there dared to detain Ch'ohŏn. Everyone was overwhelmed by Kojuk's imperious solemnity.

"Leave it open," Kojuk commanded sharply when someone touched the door. Then, in a clear and forceful voice, unlike that of a man at the gate of death, he ordered his disciple who was walking toward the storage platform: "There. Put them all down."

The young man had reached the flower bed by the storage platform. When Ch'ohŏn put down the pile beside some withered flower plants, Kojuk gave his order again: "Set them on fire."

A commotion rose in the room. Some tried to talk to Kojuk, and some rushed out to grab Ch'ohŏn's arms. But all to no avail. Kojuk thundered imperiously: "I said set them on fire!"

Ch'ohŏn's reaction amazed everyone. For a minute he stared at his teacher with furious eyes, but then, shaking off those people grabbing him by the arm, he set fire to the pile. Judging from the fact that Ch'ohŏn later accused his teacher of being a fake, it must be that his scholarly and ascetic temperament rebelled against Kojuk's excessive self-abnegation and self-negation. The pile of paper soon burst into flames. Sighs and groans and sobs broke out from everyone.

To some, Kojuk's entire life was burning. To others, Kojuk's truth was in flames. To still others, it was like sheaves of high-denomination currency burning. The works of a celebrated old master, whose works no less than two presidents had sought and who had refused to serve on the prestigious screening committee of the National Art Exhibition, were being destroyed all at once by the flames.

But Kojuk saw in the flames a golden-winged phoenix soaring. He saw its astonishing beauty and its vigorous flight.

Kojuk breathed his last around eight o'clock that evening. He was aged seventy-two.

The Girl from
the Wind-Whipped House

∽

Yun Hu-myŏng

Yun Hu-myŏng, born in 1946, started out as a poet but became better known for his fiction. He studied philosophy at Yonsei University, and his training in philosophy shows up throughout his poetry and fiction. In his works, past and present merge and fantasy and reality intersect and coalesce. His characters are all alienated from society and carry mysterious wounds. Suffering from a feeling of their own unreality, they are at a loss as to how they can connect with reality, establish contacts with other people, and make sense of life. So, his stories tend to be rather involved. He has stood somewhat aloof from the issues of social injustice and political oppression, choosing instead to explore man's inner consciousness and existential wounds. Yun is not a prolific writer, and his favorite medium of expression is the long short story.

"The Girl from the Wind-Whipped House" (1982) has a somewhat simpler structure than his usual stories. It deals with a childhood trauma that leaves a lasting scar on the protagonist and relationships gone awry without anybody being responsible for them. And the alienation of the father is passed down to his children, as if it is part of the basic condition of being human. The ardent yearning of his characters for connection and their repeated failures to connect strike a chord in modern people who keep experiencing similar frustrations and despair.

1

When I was told at last that I could go out and play even though I wasn't completely well yet, I went over to Sehwa's house. The world had changed greatly while I had been in bed with the measles. It was almost uncannily quiet though it was broad daylight. I was vaguely aware of changes taking place in the outside

world while I was convalescing. But I could never have imagined
the village being weighed down by such an awesome stillness. The
stillness was not peaceful, but threatening, as if something sinister
lurked there. My legs shook from long disuse. The incandescent
daylight made me dizzy. I went to the plank wall dividing my house
from Sehwa's and peeked at her house through the hole in the
wall. Her house, which had been shrouded in silence even before I
became sick, now seemed sunk in even greater silence. It looked as
though a goblin with a dark blue face might spring out from the
rotting gables. It was hard to believe that little Sehwa lived and
breathed in such an eerie, decrepit house.

"Don't go out anywhere. Strangers will snatch you away to a
terrible place if they see you," Mother had said as she carefully
poured the water from the soaking potatoes down the drain. She
was probably going to mash the potatoes and make potato cakes.

I crawled through the hole into Sehwa's yard, hoping her
grandmother would not come out. The hole, made by knocking
planks out from the wall, was big enough for grown-ups to crawl
through and served, for all practical purposes, as a passage.
Sehwa's grandmother was not in the yard. She must be poring over
her sewing in the house, lost in her own world. The old woman,
who had gone deaf, was always sewing something, peering with her
gummy eyes. I had heard that she was strong enough to act as a
midwife as recently as when I was born, but in those few interven-
ing years she had become completely senile and spent her days
sewing up everything in sight. She rarely left her house, only coming over to mine when she had nothing else to sew. Whenever she
came to my house, nodding her head up and down, my mother
would search through our clothes chest and put some pieces of
worn-out clothing into her gnarled hands. There was no need for
Mother to say anything, because the old woman was deaf. The old
woman would then grin and disappear into her house again. At
such times she looked like a witch. Sehwa was an expert at threading needles because her grandmother sewed all the time. Even my
mother would ask Sehwa to thread needles when she was around.
Sehwa's grandmother sewed up all the tears and the holes in clothing, even pocket openings and buttonholes, so that when she was
done with a piece of clothing it didn't look like a garment any
more.

"Sehwa! Sehwa!" I shouted up at the broken window, not having to worry about Sehwa's grandmother hearing me. I heard a
door sliding open and soon I could see Sehwa standing before the
dust-encrusted window.

"Are you well?"

"Yes."

Sehwa smiled, perking up her nose like a baby rabbit. We passed through the hole in the plank wall to my side of the house in order to go out into the street. The gate of Sehwa's house had been nailed shut a long time ago. Luckily, Mother wasn't in the yard. We both winced because the gate squeaked loudly. Perhaps it sounded so loud because it'd been a long time since it was last opened. We closed the gate carefully and took stealthy steps toward the main street.

The main street was completely empty; not even an insect could be seen. It was the time of year when a long procession of women usually came into town from the mountains, carrying baskets filled with big, ripe ears of corn. As it was the crops and fruits that told people the time of the year, it looked as if even the seasons stood still on this forsaken white road.

"Where're all the other kids?"

"They've all gone to hide in the country. They're going to come back when the war is over," I told Sehwa, as if I were a grown-up who knew everything. But the presence or absence of other kids didn't make any difference to us. They didn't play with us and we didn't play with them. Even when the other children went in groups to gather shellfish on the beach, Sehwa and I preferred to play in the mossy backyard of my house.

"It was so boring when you were sick."

While staying in bed covered with a thick cotton-wool quilt, I could hear Sehwa calling me several times a day. Lingering around the veranda of my room, Sehwa tried to catch a glimpse of me through the door. Even though feverish and covered with a rash, I could have exchanged a few words with her without much difficulty if I had wanted to. But for some reason, I kept quiet and pretended to have excruciating pain, even though she could not see me. At such times Mother appeared from somewhere and told Sehwa to go back to her house.

"I'm afraid he'll have to stay in bed for a few more days. We should've fed him shrimp and sped up the eruption, but where can we find shrimp these days? You must be tired of playing all by yourself. Is your grandmother all right?"

I knew Sehwa would nod "yes" to this. Then Mother would say, "Here," and give her a ball of seasoned rice. Sehwa usually ate her meals at my house, so the rice and potatoes were for her grandmother. Sometimes Mother would give Sehwa a moistened piece of cotton cloth. "Here, take this and clean your grandmother's eyes. That's a good girl," Mother would say encouragingly. Sehwa's mother had run away from home, and her father, in his fury, had

also left home for a mining town, so there was no one to look after
the young girl and the old woman.

I once overheard the grown-ups say that Sehwa's father roamed
mining towns and sent some money to us once in a while for the
child's and the old woman's sustenance.

Sehwa always came to our house through the hole and climbed
over the mound that served as the roof for our emergency dug-out.
Sehwa's house stood with its back towards the mountain and ours
stood facing it, so that when she crossed the mound, gusts of wind
sometimes blew her long hair, scattering them over her face. It
always looked as though the wind blew only to pester her. At such
times Sehwa would frown and try to push back her hair.

Without either of us suggesting it, we both began walking
towards the marketplace. When we went to the market, it always
used to be to eat grilled mackerel. The middle-aged women who
sold the fish grilled on the open stove were all our old acquain-
tances. They all wore baggy pants with elastic bands at the ankles,
and had uneven eyebrows, which were singed by the sparks from
the open charcoal stove.

"Don't you wish you could eat some mackerel?" I asked. Sehwa
swallowed. Grilled mackerel was a favorite snack for people in this
mountainous area. Both grown-ups and children loved its taste.
Once we saw a grown-up man eating up even the head and tail of a
mackerel, and we whispered to each other that we were lucky our
fathers didn't eat like that!

We hesitated before the fork in the road leading to the market.
Both paths were terrifying to us. It was said that on the path to the
left a man once electrocuted on top of an electric pole now
screamed at passers-by, "Gosh, it's hot!" On the path to the right
there was a madwoman who marched up and down the road flail-
ing her arms. Ordinarily we hung around at the junction until we
saw someone taking one of the roads, and then rapidly followed
him or her. But now the roads were completely deserted save for
us, so there was no use waiting for someone to come along.

"Which way shall we go?"

"I don't know."

Sehwa looked at the path on the left, as if trying to detect a
voice saying, "Ouch, it's hot!" She then moved toward the path
with the madwoman. Perhaps she was hoping that the madwoman
had either fled entirely or gone into hiding with the rest of the
people.

"Come this way," I whispered. Grasping each other's hand
tightly, we groped along the path on the right. All the gates were

firmly closed, and most of them were nailed up with bars in the figure X. Sehwa looked around even more attentively than I. The empty village was like a page of hieroglyphics. The fading graffiti on a wall looked like some secret code. The drawing of a child's face on another wall looked like the face of a little goblin that seemed to be mocking our fears. I grasped Sehwa's hand more tightly so she wouldn't be afraid. Our hands became clammy with sweat. Suddenly, the little goblin seemed to put on a sorrowful face, saying, "Where are you going? I live here. I live here all alone on this wall. I have to live here until I find someone to take my place. Won't either of you please live here instead of me?" Where did I hear a story like that? It must have been from the pock-marked man who showed us children kaleidoscopes or slides for a penny. I shook my head forcibly towards the little goblin and quickened my steps. When we came out of the path Sehwa whispered, "She's gone."

"Who?" I said, having forgotten the madwoman in my fear of the little goblin.

"The madwoman."

"That's right!" I said.

The madwoman was never seen outside that pathway, so she must have fled like everybody else. I thought that if the madwoman fled from the war while we were braving it, there was no reason to be scared of her, even if she were to come back after the war.

We walked on, clinging to the edge of the road. We moved carefully, ready to run at the least sound, as if we were playing hide-and-seek.

"How come there's nobody here?" Sehwa asked, breaking the silence.

"I told you, everybody's gone to hide in far-off places. My mom said we must hide if we see somebody."

"Why?"

"Because he would grab us and take us to a terrible place. See, that's why even the madwoman's gone and hid herself."

"I see." Sehwa nodded, but I saw her eyes dropping to the ground and her face becoming thoughtful. I glimpsed loneliness alighting on the bridge of her straight high nose. We both knew very well that whereas my family couldn't flee from the war because I had measles, her family couldn't seek refuge because her father hadn't come home to take them away. We were silent for a good while. With each step we took, we heard the noise of sand crushing under our shoes. The crunchy noise felt like another one of the goblin's tricks.

When we passed the watchtower of the fire station, the shopping arcade came in sight. The arcade consisted of a few general stores, one hardware store, one sporting goods store and one stationery store. Sehwa always wanted to have the round-eyed doll that was in the display window of one of the general stores. I wondered if the doll might still be waiting for an owner, lying inside the window behind the heavy wooden shutters. If it were, it must be feeling very hurt that everybody had left, leaving her behind.

"Do you think it's still in there?"

Sehwa was startled when I asked. She must have been thinking the same thing.

"Dolls can't walk, so it must still be there," Sehwa said apprehensively, as if afraid I'd contradict her.

"The owner must have taken everything away with him," I ventured.

"No!"

I was surprised by the vehemence of her response, but I wasn't going to give in so easily.

"How do you know? It's an expensive doll. Didn't you see its eyes close when the owner laid it on its back?"

It was a doll that falls asleep when it is laid on its back and wakes up and looks at you with twinkling eyes when it sits upright. Sehwa seemed discouraged by this allusion to its costliness and just stared at the thick shutters. After several minutes had passed, she turned to me.

"My dad promised to buy me that doll. He'll buy it for me no matter how much it costs, 'cause he'll be coming back with lots and lots of money. My dad digs up gold from the earth. Honest. And my dad always keeps his promises." Sehwa babbled rapidly. I, too, had heard that Sehwa's father was a gold prospector. I had long been afraid that when her father came back with a mountainous heap of gold and bought Sehwa lots of toys, she wouldn't play with me any more. When I first heard about Sehwa's father prospecting for gold, I had a dream. I dreamt of Sehwa's grandmother wearing a golden dress and sewing a golden rag with a gold thread and needle. When someone in Sehwa's family touched anything, it turned into gold like in the story the pockmarked man had told us. Even the matter in the corners of the grandmother's eyes was gold.

"Will you play with me even after your father comes back with lots of gold?" I asked fearfully. I felt Sehwa's eyes fixed on me, but I kept my eyes on the ground and waited for her reply.

"What're you talking about?" was the girl's response.

"I said are you going to play with me even when you have lots of gold!" I repeated huffily.

"What's gold got to do with it? I can't play with gold."

"Why not?"

"How can people play with gold? Stupid!" Sehwa retorted angrily.

"If I'm stupid, you're an idiot!" I shouted, pushing her, enraged at being called stupid.

"Stupid!"

"Idiot!"

"Stupid! Dummy!"

We yelled at each other without knowing what we were angry about. I searched my brain for something to make Sehwa desperately mad. I glared at her, panting.

"Idiot, your mommy's run away!"

For a moment Sehwa looked at me with dazed eyes. I could see that my taunt had hit home. I felt triumphant, but Sehwa seemed to recover pretty quickly.

"No, she hasn't! She's just gone somewhere because she's sick."

"That's a lie. She ran away because she didn't like you."

"That's not true!"

"It is, too. And she ran away so far she'll never come back!"

"How do you know! My mommy's sick."

Something glistened in Sehwa's eyes.

"I know, too. She ran away."

"No, she didn't! She didn't, either."

Her voice was tearful. But it was very soothing to me, and sweet as the faintly acrid but sweet taste of corn on the cob when you chewed it. Then Sehwa must know about her mother, too. She began to sob in earnest when I said nothing.

"She didn't!" Sehwa insisted. I was then satisfied, thinking that Sehwa, who was crying in front of me, wouldn't desert me for lumps of gold. I nodded at her tear-stained face apologetically.

"But isn't this the marketplace?"

We had already reached our destination, but no one was there. Since we didn't have any money anyway, it would have been rather embarrassing if there had been women selling mackerel. But we felt sorry nonetheless. Sehwa rubbed her eyes to brush away her tears and looked around. A few empty stalls were left standing, but there were neither vendors nor buyers.

"There's nobody here," Sehwa said, sitting on a big stone near one of the empty stalls.

"Not one," I agreed, squatting beside her.

"You already said everybody's fled our town."

"But there isn't even a rat."

"Oh, there are rats all right. One stared at me a long time and scurried away a little while ago."

"Honest?"

"Honest. That's why there are cats around. There're cats because there are rats for them to eat."

"But they're stray cats."

"They're cats all the same. They all eat rats."

Sehwa was right. We had seen stray cats jumping from roof to roof after dark. First they arched their backs like balls and sprang; the next moment they were on the opposite roof.

"Where shall we go?" I asked Sehwa thoughtfully.

"I suppose it's all the same everywhere," Sehwa answered weakly. She seemed to have lost her spirit. Her pale face was as white as Snow White's. Her head, sitting on top of her small squatting body, made me think of the girl in the story who was kidnapped by a tiger. While listening to Mother telling that story one nightfall with Sehwa, I had looked often towards the big mountain, even though I couldn't see it through the door. In the story, the girl, a rich man's daughter, was carried off by a tiger while washing her hair in her backyard. Her folks searched everywhere but couldn't find her. They were bitterly aggrieved, especially as she was their only daughter. Then one day, while crossing a mountain with a cart, one of her father's hired hands saw her. He rushed up to her and found that it was only her head, placed on top of a rock. After that, every year on the anniversary of her disappearance, tigers rushed into her house and demanded to be treated as sons-in-law. The tigers ate and sang and danced all night long and only returned to the mountain at daybreak.

"How about going to the cathedral?" I suggested hastily, because I was now afraid she might be snatched away by a tiger.

"The cathedral?"

"Yes. There might be someone there. Maybe there are grown-ups singing."

"That's right. I hope there are."

We headed towards the cathedral. One time, Sehwa and I had stood before the white statue in the cathedral yard with our heads bowed and our eyes closed, because someone had told us that if you prayed to the statue your wishes would come true. At that time I prayed that Sehwa and I would like each other even better and play together every day, and hoped that Sehwa prayed for the same thing. But my wishes had not come true.

"What did you pray for?" I had asked Sehwa secretively. But she didn't answer and just gazed at me. That made me believe she had prayed for the same thing as I. So I said, "I prayed that you and I would like each other even better and play together every day. What did you pray for?"

Sehwa answered, reluctantly, "I prayed for my mommy to get well. And for my dad to come home."

Her answer made me feel as if I had fallen into an icy pond.

Now we walked at a much quicker pace than when we were heading for the market. I don't know what made us walk so fast. We raced past nailed-up houses. We were going to pray before the statue again, and I thought Sehwa would again pray that her mother would get well and her father would come back, because contrary to what my mom and dad had said she insisted her mother hadn't run away. I regretted having agreed with her when she insisted her mother hadn't run away. If she knew her mother had run away, then she might pray that we would like each other better and always play together.

The cathedral stood on a hill. Sehwa climbed the hill breathing hard. The sycamores along the road also looked as if they were weary of the endless silence. I thought I could see a genie dancing behind the drooping leaves. Because I walked faster, Sehwa panted and lagged behind.

"Don't walk so fast. I can hardly breathe."

"This is not fast," I said testily.

"What if there's nobody there, either?" Sehwa said anxiously. She sounded as if she already knew that nobody would be there. I also fully anticipated that. No one was going up or coming down the usually busy road. There wasn't going to be anybody in the cathedral.

"The priest said he'll always be with us," I said, trying to sound hopeful. In fact, I wasn't really concerned about whether or not the priest was going to be there. I was only interested in what Sehwa would ask of the statue in her prayer. If Sehwa prayed for her mother's recovery, then that must mean that her mother was seriously ill somewhere. Otherwise, the statue, who made everybody's prayer come true, wouldn't let her continue to pray so long for her mother's recovery.

But a surprise awaited us at the cathedral. Even before we could go into the building to see if anybody was there, we saw that the statue had fallen to the ground. And it had mud spattered all over its body. With pounding hearts we went nearer and looked down at the face, the same face we had to tilt our heads far back to

look at. The face looked rather like Sehwa's tear-stained face of a
while ago.

"What do you think happened?"

"How awful!" Sehwa fretted.

I was just as sorry. "Did they run away, leaving her behind like
this?"

"Is there anything we can do?"

"I suppose the priest isn't here, either."

"Shall we try and pull her up?" Sehwa suggested. But I hesitated, because it didn't look as if we could manage.

"No, because the priest must have left it like this. Perhaps
that's the way they keep it when there's no one in the cathedral."

"But there's mud even in her ears!"

"Even so."

"What can we do?"

"I don't know."

We were at a loss. It occurred to me that if we dropped the statue while trying to pull it up and it broke, it wouldn't be able to
hear our wishes any more. We sat on the stone steps of the chapel,
trying to think of something to do. The statue lying in the empty
yard looked sad, as if it missed people praying to it.

At last Sehwa said, petulantly, "There really is no one. When do
you think everybody's going to come back?"

"I wish they'd come back soon."

"I do, too."

Even while talking of other things, I kept worrying about the
statue. Sehwa also cast an anxious eye on it. Whenever our voices
ceased, the silence of the empty village swept over us. The silence
seemed to have taken on a note of sorrow from passing over the
statue. I suddenly became frightened. There were goosebumps on
Sehwa's arms, too. The goosebumps seemed ready to taste our terror, rising like so many taste buds.

"Are you scared?" I asked, taking hold of Sehwa's hand.

"Yes, I'm scared. Let's go home."

"All right. Let's go."

"But let's pray first," Sehwa said and looked at my face.

"Pray to whom?" I said and looked at her. Sehwa pulled at my
hand. I followed her, wondering. Sehwa stopped in front of the
fallen statue. Sehwa blinked her eyes at me, as if to say, "Do you get
my meaning?" I blinked back at her. We dropped our heads and
prayed. This time I didn't ask Sehwa what she prayed for. For my
part I remembered Sehwa's sobbing of a while ago, and prayed for
the same thing she did. As we came out of the cathedral gate, I

looked back at the toppled statue and hoped that it would be fixed again and make our prayers come true.

When I got back home I started running a high fever and had to stay in bed again. My sickness got so bad that I became delirious the next day, but even then I could perceive that only total silence enveloped the village. It was as if all the world had stopped still. I thought that this state might go on forever, and if so, Sehwa might have to grow old and die living with her deaf grandmother. But soon all such thought melted in the furnace of my feverish body. Mother kept murmuring about being unable to heat the room for fear of the smoke being seen.

"You were getting well, all right. If only you hadn't traipsed around all day yesterday!" Mother complained, but she seemed to be grateful that I had come back alive. "I told you a thousand times you shouldn't go out of the house. Do you know what could have happened to you?"

I couldn't imagine what could have happened to me in a village where the only live things were rats and cats. However, it was only for a short time that Mother fretted about not being able to heat the room. From the next morning on, the sounds of distant cannon broke the silence of the village. The noise became louder in the afternoon, and we all moved into the emergency dugout. As there was no facility for heating the dugout, I was glad Mother didn't have that to worry about, at any rate. But I was excited that the silence of the village was broken at last. However, there was no one with whom to share my excitement. Sehwa and her grandmother were still living in their eerie house, even though the cannon now sounded quite close. Mother had tried to induce them to come into the dugout, but in vain. Sehwa's grandmother, being impervious to any noise, simply ignored Mother's hand-communicated danger signals and went on with her sewing, saying that she would wait for her son in her own house. And Sehwa also refused to leave her grandmother, at least during the night.

"I wish Sehwa's father would come. He said he'd come back soon, but I guess he can't because the war is going on," Mother murmured to herself, sitting on the dirt floor of the dugout. It was humid in the dugout and the smell of earth made us nauseous. The noise of the cannon was coming frighteningly near. The reverberating noise made me think of the thunderous steps of a giant whose footprint was on the stone in the courthouse yard. It was said that the giant was born just before the Japanese drove iron stakes into certain famous mountains in our country, to cut off the auspicious mountain forces that could foster heroes and sages in

Korea. The step was longer than Sehwa's height. Now this terrible thunder approached nearer and nearer.

After sunset we began to hear gun and cannon firing. The guns were fired so rapidly it sounded like corn popping. It was a dark, moonless night. In the dugout it was pitch dark. Earth shaken loose by the firing cannon fell from the ceiling and walls of the dugout. I saw Mother look up at the ceiling and make the sign of the cross. It occurred to me that as the statue was now lying on the ground, Mother should cross herself towards the floor.

The cannon and gun firing ceased awhile and then it resumed at much closer range. We could hear windows breaking. We could also hear screaming from somewhere, and the loud swish of a bullet flying. The darkness brightened up spasmodically and the report of guns fell like hail. I thought I also heard a groan, but as I was losing consciousness I thought it might be my own. I didn't know how long into the night it would go on like this. Before drifting away, I dimly heard the noise of desperate steps amidst the gunfire. And I saw Mother make the sign of the cross again. Then I passed into a fever-induced oblivion. But there were momentary gaps of lucidness, so that I was conscious from time to time that a fierce battle was going on outside. Perhaps I was dreaming. In any case, I wanted to be awake the whole night, so I was grateful that I had intervals of consciousness.

Finding myself alone in the dugout when I awoke at dawn, I sat up. My whole body ached, and I was still feverish. The world was again deathly silent, so I became frightened. Maybe the world was going back to the empty, silent world of a few days before. I crawled up the dirt steps of the dugout and came out into the yard. I wanted to see if Sehwa was safe. Luckily, her house was standing as solid as ever, like her grandmother's impervious eardrums. The sky was clear, and I was glad to hear the noise of people murmuring. The world wasn't emptied of humanity, after all. I headed towards Sehwa's house. But just as I was turning the corner I saw something strange. Mother emerged from the backyard carrying an empty straw sack and covered a large, dark object with it. At that moment I distinctly saw what it was.

It was Sehwa's father. As he was lying on his back, with his head pillowed on the threshold of our gate, I saw his face upside down. Because I was familiar with his upside-down face from when he used to whirl me in the air for an "airplane ride," I knew instantly it was Sehwa's father. Mother was covering his face with the straw sack so that Sehwa would not accidentally see it. He lay there in our yard for many hours.

"Is that a dead man?"

Sehwa was beside me, asking timorously, before I heard her approach. She was covered all over with dust, and mice dung clung to her worn sweater. It must have dropped from the ceiling when the cannon's reverberations shook the house. Sehwa's lips were bluish from fright and tension. A gust of mountain wind swept past us. Sehwa's hair blew back and the mice dung fell from her sweater.

"Yes, you idiot. That's a dead man." I answered sharply. I felt dizzy and confused.

"Why am I an idiot?" Sehwa retorted, though her eyes were still glued on the object covered with the straw sack.

"There's no reason. If you're an idiot, you're an idiot, that's all."

"Then if I'm an idiot, what are you?" Sehwa yelled at me. I thought of telling her the truth. I thought of saying, "Your father's dead." But my throat tightened and I couldn't say anything. If Mother hadn't appeared then and chased us into the room, there's no telling what might have happened.

"Go into the room and stay there. You, you're still sick, so you must stay in bed and rest. Sehwa, you stay with him. And don't budge until I come back."

We both nodded. We didn't fight any more. It was the first time we were allowed to stay together since I had gotten sick. I took down the bedding from the closet and plopped down on the mattress. My whole body shook with pain, but I couldn't get Sehwa's father's face out of my mind.

"Are you hurting much?" Sehwa asked anxiously. I blinked affirmatively. "I think people have come back," Sehwa went on. I blinked again. I pointed to my left and told Sehwa to lie down. "I think people have come back from hiding," Sehwa said, reclining.

"Yeah," I said.

"But why is that man dead?" Sehwa asked.

"He died last night. He came back too soon," I said knowingly. Or pretending ignorance.

Sehwa also knew there had been fierce fighting the night before.

"A poor man, isn't he?" Sehwa whispered, taking hold of my hand. Her hands felt icy cold in mine, still fiery hot from fever.

"I'll get well quickly and play with you," I whispered into Sehwa's ears.

Sehwa looked up at the ceiling and said, with dreamy eyes, "Yes, and my dad will come back, too. I'll tell him to give you some gold, too."

"No, no. I don't want any gold," I said, feeling my consciousness dimming again.

"Then what do you want? You can buy anything if you sell
gold."

"I just want to play with you," I said, and strained my ears to
hear what was going on outside. I couldn't hear any specific sound.
I closed my eyes. Sehwa also kept silent, perhaps bemused in
thought. Then fever assailed me again and I sank into sleep.

I awoke to the sound of the door opening. Some time must
have elapsed. Sehwa must have fallen asleep; she didn't stir. With
dim eyes I watched Mother stepping in.

"Sehwa's asleep," Mother said, half to herself.

"Yeah," I murmured. My head whirled. Sehwa's father had
returned with the other folks, but not in the way Sehwa had wanted
him to.

"What dreadful times!" Mother sighed. She sat beside my head
and reached out to feel my forehead. At that moment, my dim
eyes, which had been vacantly staring at the ceiling, caught sight of
the object Mother shifted from her right to her left hand.

I almost sprang up. It was the doll. I collected myself and
looked at it carefully. When laid down beside Mother's knee it
closed its eyes, just like Sehwa sleeping at my side.

2

I have a glass doll the size of a child's forearm. I have moved quite
a few times, but in each abode I kept bumping into it in unexpected places at unexpected times. It always evoked a strange feeling in
me. I became aware of its existence at such times as when looking
through my toolbox or an old suitcase in search of some tool or
rags, and found the dusty doll lying there. At such times, I would
wipe it clean with a cloth, but that was all. I didn't caress it lovingly
or put it in some visible place. I always put it back where I wouldn't
see it.

I said a glass doll, but to be more precise it was only a mis-
shapen mass formed by molten glass. Its uneven surface was
stained with pale green streaks and spotted black in a few places.
You could see that it had been a doll only if you looked at it with
that knowledge. A mangled and disfigured doll, its look always
makes me inexplicably sad.

I had moved into this apartment last year, and for the first six
months I was totally oblivious of the doll's existence. Then I discovered it again, unexpectedly, as in former times. This time I found it

among the items I no longer used, such as a dog chain and bird dish. I suppose while packing to move I had put it with things to be discarded. The moment I saw the doll among those things I picked it up, feeling as if a great mishap had been prevented. Even though it had no useful function, for people like us who have lived through the turmoil of war and revolutions, a thing that has been kept for three decades is bound to have some special meaning. It is true that I never took any particular care to preserve it, but whenever I dug it out from somewhere I couldn't help becoming excited that it had stayed with me for so long.

I took the doll to the bathroom and washed it clean. Then I dried it with a new towel. It hadn't changed a bit: the same light green stain; the same dark spots; the same burned and shriveled arm.

This time I put the doll in a file box with my important documents. Sleep well, my doll, I said to it. Darkness was descending, but I kept looking out the window vacantly without turning the lights on. With the onrush of darkness a nameless longing invaded the room and gripped me. I bit my lip from a feeling of indefinable guilt. I tried to smile to myself about the burnt doll, and about how I came to possess it, but I couldn't. The face that belonged to the owner of the doll appeared before me faintly, like the face of a Buddha sculpted on the top of a precipice. Only the touch of her long, thin fingers and her soft, moist lips came back vividly.

I remember the day when I went to see her at the orphanage where she stayed after she gave me the doll and left my house. It was an early spring day when the cold wind petulantly whipped us, as if loathe to give way to spring. I walked to the orphanage, hugging myself tightly, feeling like an aimless vagabond. Even at that age I was wishing there would never be a day like that again in my life. But when I reached the orphanage I realized that I didn't have the courage to go in, and that I had no pretext whatsoever for entering.

All I could do was to stand tiptoe on a stone and look into the orphanage yard. I could only stand there and wait.

It occurred to me that Sehwa might have already left. I became anxious and impatient. But I didn't know what I would say even if she were to appear. I searched my brain for something appropriate to say, but I couldn't think of anything. On the contrary, my head felt hollow inside, I shivered with cold, and I felt like going to the toilet.

For a long time, there was no sign of movement in the orphanage building. I wondered if I had come to the wrong place. The longer I waited, the more pitiful I looked to myself. But I couldn't

leave. I knew this would be my last chance to tell her how I felt
about her.

Then I heard a bell ring. I stretched as far as I could and
stared at the yard. A group of children emerged from the building
and dispersed into the yard. My heart beat wildly. I was terrified
lest Sehwa would look at me doubtfully, as if I were a stranger.

Was Sehwa still here? Or has she already gone to the country
called America? My palms grew wet. I kept wiping my palms on my
pants and kept my eyes fixed on the children. Boys came out after
the girls. One, two, three, four, five . . . But Sehwa was nowhere in
sight. She must have already left for a faraway place . . . I thought I
heard a rumbling sound in my chest.

Sehwa was not there even though it seemed that all the girls
had come out. I surveyed them one by one again, but to no avail.
The girls, all with bobbed hair, were wearing checkered skirts and
colorful sweaters that came as relief goods from overseas; they
looked like wealthy children. Suppressing my sorrow and desolation, I kept gazing into the yard. I wouldn't see her ever again. Why
couldn't I grow up faster? If I had been a grown-up, I'd never have
let her go. I'd surely have done something to make her stay with
me if I'd been a grown-up, like marrying her, for example.

I regretted not coming earlier. But in fact I couldn't have come
any earlier, because I had to wait until the gash on my forehead
closed. It was a deep cut. So today, I had to pull down my bangs
and cover the long scar that looked like an earthworm.

My fall from the tree was the immediate cause of Sehwa having
to leave my house. Of course, she was bound to leave us sooner or
later, but her departure had been put off from one day to another.
But when it became known that I had climbed up the tree to catch
a bird for her, she had to leave immediately.

"What did you want the bird for, you fool? What stupid bird
would be caught by you?" My uncle scolded me harshly.

"Why not? I can catch birds," I protested, but didn't believe it
myself in the least. I was scared of birds, and had nightmares of
birds pecking out my eyes and things like that. I had even confided
my fears to my uncle, who hadn't brushed them off as nonsense.

"I suppose there are such terrible birds in other countries,"
Uncle had said at the time.

"Other countries? Then, where are those birds out there
from?"

"Some are from other countries. Some always live in our country," Uncle had said and grinned. He hadn't said whether the birds
in our yard were the kind that peck out people's eyes or not. Years

later, I saw Hitchcock's movie *The Birds* and thought that my fears were not unique. Anyway, it was a few days after this conversation with Uncle that I had fallen out of the tree.

"So, what were you going to do with the bird?" Uncle queried sarcastically. At first I kept my mouth firmly closed, because I wasn't sure what Sehwa had planned to do with the bird. Did she really mean to ride it?

"I said, what were you going to do with the bird?" Uncle pressed me. It looked as though he wasn't going to give up until he found out. And I couldn't hope that he'd give up, as he cared so much about birds that he had once nabbed and turned over to the police those farmers who caught pheasants with poisoned beans. But I really didn't want to answer him.

"I was going to fly on it," was what came out of my mouth. I studied Uncle's reaction. As expected, he looked astonished.

"What did you say?"

"I was going to fly on it," I repeated sullenly.

"Do you mean it?"

"Yes," I nodded obstinately.

Uncle shook his head as if to say, "This kid really worries me." He looked as if he believed I was capable of trying to fly on a bird. My response evoked a serious reaction. I could see that my whole family watched me carefully, as if to see if I were all right in the head. I regretted having blurted it out. It was stupid of me to think that my folks would give up questioning me after I gave such a preposterous answer! At last I had to confess that it was not me, but Sehwa, who wanted to fly on the bird.

I thought it was a mistake for the grown-ups to have told Sehwa, after her house burned down with her grandmother in it and she came with us to my uncle's house in this remote hamlet, that her father and mother were in a faraway country where the birds come from. Sehwa knew lots more things than I did, but not where it concerned birds. She insisted that one could ride birds.

"How can people ride a bird?" I asked irritably.

"Why not? You just have to hold onto its back."

"You'd slip and fall off."

"*I* wouldn't."

"Birds have slippery backs."

"So do horses and cows, stupid."

Sehwa was obstinate, and I didn't know how to set her straight. Whenever I said that people couldn't ride on birds she called me "stupid." Well, I had other fears about birds as well. I once heard from grown-ups that a kite had snatched away a baby. Therefore, it was all I could do to keep this information from Sehwa, and keep insisting that birds have slippery backs.

Birds were a great nuisance in those days. Such great hordes of birds appeared that they had already covered the fields and were invading the woods in back of Uncle's house. From the time the birds began to appear in enormous flocks, grown-ups had anticipated trouble.

"First the war, and now the birds. Oh, they'll kill off all the trees."

People said it was the first time birds had ever come to that hamlet. They also said that in the next hamlet old pine trees had all withered up from incessant bird droppings the year before. I heard that a proper amount of bird droppings made the best manure, but too much destroyed the trees. The poison in the bird droppings first turned the leaves dark green and then made them shrivel.

"It's a bad omen for trees to die because of bird droppings," everybody said.

The invasion of birds was disastrous for me, too. I was ordered to scrape up bird droppings from trees and deposit them on the manure heap whenever I had nothing else to do. It was a detestable chore.

I couldn't help wondering why some bird droppings were white. I never saw other animals produce white excrement. How could birds do it?

Bird dung dropped on rocks looked like light and dark watercolor paints squeezed out on a palette. How could birds manage to produce such droppings? That, I thought, was what made birds dwell in the sky. Land animals such as goats and rabbits drop glossy black dung. People sometimes produce watery feces, but never white.

Anyway, I had no choice but to take a straw basket into the woods, scrape off bird droppings, and pile them on the manure heap. In this dense woods of white pine and junipers, some evergreen oaks rustled with dry leaves. The woods seemed to my young mind to be infinitely vast and peaceful. From the high boughs of the trees birds sometimes looked down at me pensively and sometimes cawed threateningly, as if to alert their peers of the intruder.

While thus roaming in the woods, my thoughts remained wholly with Sehwa, who stayed cooped up in the house with a face wan as a wax mask. Would anyone believe that, as a child I was feeling the pain of separation that tormented me with a pain greater than death? Even if she didn't fly away on a bird, she was going to go away soon. When the grownups decided that the best thing would be to give her away to an American family for adoption, I listened breathlessly from under my quilt, pretending to be asleep. I mourned her going away even more than if I had been the one to be sent to a faraway country. Why did her father die, and where was her mother? I didn't have the courage to beg my parents to let her stay with me, so I roamed the woods wishing I, too, would become an orphan and be sent away with her.

"Do you like scraping up bird droppings?" Sehwa sometimes asked, wonderingly. At such times I said nothing and quickly walked away from her. Nobody could have known how ardently I wished for some calamity to overtake our family before Sehwa left us—a calamity so great that it would destroy us, like the bird droppings were doing to the trees. I felt that it would seem like we were happy to see Sehwa go if all were well in our family and yet we made her leave. To compensate even in a small way for her unhappiness, I needed to be swallowed up by a great misfortune comparable to hers.

It was at about that time that Sehwa began asking me to catch a bird for her. One day she came up to me quietly and asked, "Can you catch a bird?" Her eyes glittered as she posed the question; they seemed to be telling me she wouldn't take "no" for an answer. But I couldn't speak at once. I thought Sehwa must be thinking of flying away, leaving me behind. I swallowed.

"Tell me. Can you, or can't you?" Sehwa pressed me. I just stood there blushing. Sehwa was impatient. "You can catch them if you suddenly flash a light on their nest at night. Then they become dazed," she continued.

I didn't see any way of extricating myself from the task Sehwa had set for me. I didn't have the courage to ask her what she was going to do with the bird after I caught it. She would certainly say that she would fly away on it. The reason I decided to do her bidding in spite of my fear was to make her understand that she couldn't fly on birds. I thought it might make her a little less unhappy if she came to understand this.

That night Sehwa and I went out to a tree in which there was a birds' nest.

"Are you sure you can do it?" She whispered into my ear, even though there was no one else in the woods.

"Yeah."

My breath came in short gasps. In the dark I could only hear the birds' sleepy cooing. With a flashlight hanging from a string around my neck, I grabbed the tree. How can people ride birds? I thought it would be easier to ride the strange birdlike animal with the human face I once saw engraved on an old roof tile. But Sehwa didn't say anything; she just watched me breathlessly. I must have looked like the tree sloth that is said to inhabit the Australian forests. I climbed up the tree slowly, like that tree sloth, so that the tree wouldn't shake and frighten the birds. I put enormous strength into my groin and groped with my soles for footholds. But my legs shook violently, and I kept thinking I might slip off at any moment.

"You're almost there. It's just a little further up," Sehwa whispered from below. I bit my lip. The further up I went, the more the tree was liable to shake, so I had to move very carefully. One step up, another step up. I was getting quite close to the nest. By now my brow was wet from sweat. It felt as though the branch I was standing on was going to break. I was terrified. Telling myself I needed to calm down, I stretched my hand, took hold of a bough, and pulled myself up.

"That's right. It's right above you." Sehwa's voice sounded as if it was coming from a mile off. I looked up to see the nest right above my head, but my arms and legs were shaking uncontrollably. A groan escaped from my throat. I threw my head backward and looked at the nest. That same instant a dark object struck my eyes, and a loud flapping hit my ears. My eyes felt like they were on fire, and I was overwhelmed by a vision of the black birdlike animal with the human head that I once saw engraved on the roof tile Uncle brought.

"Aaack!"

My head whirled and I fell into a bottomless pit. Then I lost consciousness.

I regained consciousness when I smelled thick bean paste. I looked around to see that I was in my room, and I also dimly saw my mother sitting beside me under the electric light. When I tried to sit up, Mother held me down by pressing my shoulder.

"You mustn't move. You must stay just as you are until we can get to the hospital tomorrow."

Only then did I feel the stinging pain and hotness in my forehead.

"What's that smell?" I murmured.

"We put bean paste on your wound. Why did you climb the tree in the dark? You could have gotten killed!"

I felt my forehead and found it was bandaged. Oh, yes. I had fallen out of the tree. Then I vividly recalled the moment. I felt both angry and ashamed about falling out of the tree without even catching the bird. But more than anything else I was worried about Sehwa. My worry took a definite shape when I saw her the day after I came back from the hospital. It had been decided she would leave us the following day.

Sehwa cast a quick look at my bandaged head but didn't come out of her room all day. I kept fretting and fidgeting; I didn't mind getting hurt so much as I was afraid Sehwa would laugh at me for being unable to catch the birds. I was afraid she'd go away laughing at me.

I felt helpless, and like a coward. I roamed the woods, trying to force myself to accept the inevitable, but to no avail. I couldn't help continually blaming myself for having been an idiot who couldn't even catch a bird.

That night I went outside pretending to go to the outhouse. "Hey, come here." The voice addressing me in the dark was Sehwa's. I crept towards it. Sehwa was standing with her body pressed against one side of the barn. My body shook violently, as if I had committed some heinous crime. I became more tense than when I had climbed the tree to catch the bird. My legs felt paralyzed. Her face, illuminated by the pale moonlight shining through the clouds, was the color of lead; the opaque, colorless face made her look like a child shaman. But it wasn't because of her face that I was terrified. I stood there silent before her because I didn't know what to say.

"Were you hurt badly?" she asked.

"No." I shook my head, even though the doctor had said the wound could have been quite serious, and that there would certainly be a scar.

"Does it hurt much?" she asked in the same tone.

"No," I said, truthfully, because I only had periodic stinging pain. Even that much conversation made me breathless. Sehwa felt like a stranger. I saw something shining in her eyes when her face turned to me.

"I'm leaving tomorrow."

The voice seemed to come from far away, like some echo from the woods. Then that known fact became a totally strange idea. I smelled a sickly fragrance, like that of straw rotting, from somewhere. I breathed hard and felt suddenly feverish. Of course I knew only too well that Sehwa would be leaving the next day.

"For where?" I inhaled deeply and asked again: "Do you know where they're taking you?"

"No." Sehwa dropped her head.

I wondered whether I had better tell her what I had heard

from the grown-ups: You're going to be sent to America for adoption. But I couldn't utter a word.

"I waited for you a long time," Sehwa began, and then just stood there staring at me. I grew more nervous. I tried to wet my lips but my tongue was dried stiff.

"Go on," I managed to say at last.

"I have nothing else to give you."

"What's that?"

Sehwa held out something she had been holding in her hand. It gleamed in the moonlight. I looked carefully at the object in her hand. It emitted a strange sheen.

"Here. Take it."

Sehwa's long, thin fingers touched mine. I stood there transfixed, like a porcupine touched by a magnet. Then I felt a strange sensation on my lips. It lasted no more than a second. Sehwa's lips were warmer, smoother, and more moist than mine. But it was when her hand, not her lips, touched me, that I felt astonishment. Before I recovered my senses Sehwa had already left me and was rapidly crossing the yard. I stood there immobile for a long time. Then I raised my hand to see if the bandage was in place, and realized that I was holding something in my hand. It was that lump of burnt glass. Sehwa had searched the rubble at the site of her burnt house, and picked up the charred remains of the doll that went to sleep when laid on its back.

Sehwa left the next day. Appearing to be totally unaware of her effect on me the night before, Sehwa even smiled brightly as she bade me goodbye. Her steps never faltered as she walked away, led by my uncle.

At first it didn't occur to me that I could go see Sehwa at the orphanage. But as the days went by and my wound healed, my yearning to see her again became more intense.

I still remember the dull clang of the orphanage bell. Sehwa appeared only after the bell had rung for the second time. I was at the point of giving up and going away when she finally came into sight. Even though her hair was tied on either side of her head and she was wearing a skirt with suspenders, I recognized her at once. Sehwa gave a casual glance toward the wall where I was standing, and seemed to sense instinctively that I was there. She darted up to the wall.

"How did you get here?" Sehwa asked, blushing. I could see that she was glad to see me. I didn't know what to say, so I just smiled sheepishly, and then asked, as if I had come to settle that point: "Are you still thinking of flying on a bird?"

Sehwa stared at me for a long time. Her face relaxed when she saw me smiling, but I did not miss the dark shadow that had momentarily hovered over her face. That made me wonder. Sehwa had always been so sure of being able to fly on a bird, and I had expected the usual response from her.

"I'm sorry about that." Her glance lingered on my forehead.

"Oh, no. That's all right. It's all healed."

I truly didn't want her to be the least bit disturbed about my wound. But her face was growing more and more clouded.

"I'm sorry I asked you to catch birds. I knew I couldn't fly on a bird. How can people ride birds?"

I didn't understand. Why was she saying that now? And there was rebellion in her voice, too. I couldn't easily adapt to the change in her, and felt the strength draining out of my body.

"I knew it all right. People can't ride birds. And my dad's dead and my mom's . . . "

Her voice was tearful, and before she could finish she began sobbing bitterly. Her shoulders shook violently. I couldn't think of anything to say. Not even a word. My forehead stung, as if the wound had opened again. I never expected to hear such words from Sehwa. Something tumbled in my head with a loud rumble. She was still sobbing.

"You're a fool. You don't know anything," Sehwa said between sobs. I was always a fool to her: I was a fool when I said people couldn't fly on birds, and I was a fool when she said people couldn't fly on birds.

Just then a middle-aged man came out of the building and yelled at us.

"What's going on over there?"

I jumped down from the stone I was standing on and took a few backward steps. As the man's rapid steps approached the wall I ran with fright. I could hear the man bellowing at Sehwa from inside the wall.

"You little chick, you're at the game already?"

I ran. My throat constricted and my body shook even more violently than it had at the treetop. Why had I wanted to see Sehwa once more? I couldn't make sense out of anything. My head whirled round and round and my legs tottered. The dark bird that I had seen when falling from the tree flitted before my eyes. I felt like a person being hunted down in a blind alley. I was drenched in cold sweat, but I kept on running. I felt that if I stopped I would sink into the earth. I didn't mean to extract that confession from Sehwa. Her words rang in my ears. My throat felt dry like an earthen tube in a hot kiln. Oh, what was going to become of her? My eyes stung and my heart felt like bursting. Feeling nauseous, I flopped down and vomited. Making sounds like a croaking heron, I threw up everything in my stomach. Chill and fever attacked me at once. After vomiting till only bitter gastric juices came up, I got up and saw that the sun had already set. I began walking again without any sense of direction.

I reached the woods, not knowing what made me go there. I looked up at the tops of the trees. I couldn't see anything very clearly and I felt dizzy. I tried to shout something, but the words stayed trapped in my mouth. Finally, I looked up and screamed, with the last remaining strength: "Come down here at once, you hateful creature!"

Falling down, I suddenly thought that a great halo of light was moving towards me, a dazzling, gigantic mass of light. Or perhaps it wasn't light at all, but a corner of the sky. I opened my eyes wide and looked. It was a huge bird—a great, dazzling bird, alighting softly on the grass. I picked myself up and went to her. She seemed to be quietly awaiting someone's approach. Her clear eyes shone powerfully but softly. I didn't show a speck of fear.

Without any hesitation I grabbed the bird's neck and climbed up on her back. Far from being slippery, it was as cozy and comfortable as a vast meadow. I wrapped my arms around her great neck, which fit snugly into my arms. I stretched my legs and pressed them to her chest: she didn't offer any resistance. Then I was about to fall asleep, warmed by her body, when a chilly wind struck me. I looked around and saw that we were high up in the air. Whenever her mountainous back heaved, her slopelike wings parted the air. Far, far below I could see rivers flowing, like baby water snakes swimming. But what had happened? The great bird had now turned into a small cormorant. I looked at myself again. I was still riding on the bird, but I was a glass doll.

I was discovered lying unconscious in the woods the next day. The long spell of illness that followed prevented me from going to school the next year, and I frittered the time away at home. But I never told anyone what had taken me to the woods that day. I couldn't. It was right after my visit there that the orphanage was bombed. I didn't betray any special emotion, even when told of Sehwa's death.

I never told anybody about the great white bird, either, even though it remained distinctly in my memory. I didn't think I could talk about it to anybody.

Later, at Yonsei University, I learned Chuang T'zu from Professor Ku Bon-myong. Prof. Ku, who was small of stature and had a boyish face, always walked up to the platform with slow steps and opened his book on the lectern. The first day of the class he began chapter one, "Free and Easy Wandering."

"In the northern darkness there lives a great fish. Its name is *Kun*. It is so huge that nobody knows how many miles it measures. This fish is sometimes transformed into a bird, and the bird is called *Peng*. This bird is also so huge that no one knows how many miles it measures across. When she flutters and soars in anger, it is as if the sky is covered with clouds." While translating thus for us, Prof. Ku looked out the window at the signs of early spring and laughed heartily.

The professor's words struck a chord in me. Yes, the great bird called *Peng*. Although we can't ride birds in reality, *Peng* can carry us on its back anywhere between reality and dream. So, it is only those chained fast to reality that can't fly.

"Now, read the passage again carefully and try to interpret it for yourselves," the professor said. I felt my chest heaving with exultation and my eyes clouding. Something welling up from the depth of my heart warmed my eyes.

I wrote this in 1981 and published it in the second issue of the literary magazine called *Writers*. Two years after that I had a chance to travel around the world. Jakarta, Indonesia, was included on the itinerary. I went to Hong Kong via Korean Air Lines, and then from Hong Kong to Jakarta via Garuda. Garuda is the name of the Indonesian airline, and it means "eagle" in Indonesian. I also flew Garuda from Jakarta to Pekanbaru, capital of Sumatra, and from there to Singapore. That made a total of three times.

"Nasi?" the hostess on one flight queried, in the course of handing out food trays. I looked at her uncomprehendingly. She quickly asked, "Rice?" Nasi was "rice" in standard Indonesian. I nodded and sank into thought, chewing on the long-grain rice of Southeast Asia.

Garuda. Eagle.

I was at last riding a bird after all these years. It felt to me not like a complicated piece of machinery, a product of contemporary civilization, but like a real live eagle. It was a bird. Whether because the Garuda shook on account of atmospheric conditions, or because I felt the urge to say something to Sehwa, nasi kept falling off my spoon and spilling over my knees.

3

I noticed with great interest a few days ago a microscopic photo printed in a daily paper of a mosquito sucking blood from a human being. The article accompanying the picture explained that it had been taken by a Swedish science photographer who killed the mosquito with insecticide spray at the moment the mosquito pierced human skin with its proboscis. Then the mosquito legs were affixed to the skin with glue, and the patch of skin removed and frozen with liquid nitrogen. The mosquito in the picture looked like an extraterrestrial creature, with stiff scrawny legs and eyes like focal lenses, its sharp sucking proboscis stuck firmly into the human skin. While looking at the photo, I remembered an event of a short while ago. Sometimes I confuse reality and unreality, so much so that recently I have even come to wonder whether Chuang T'zu's speculations in his "Discussion of Making All Things Equal" weren't all based on my case. Well, of course all great wise men's thoughts are profound. Chuang T'zu said he once dreamed he was a butterfly. Then he woke up to find he was a man named Chuang T'zu. That made him wonder whether he was a man who dreamed of being a butterfly, or a butterfly who dreamed of being a man.

Anyway, after much rambling speculation I reached the conclusion that I can have definite, realistic thoughts, at least where mosquitoes are concerned. I can still recall every minute detail of events that took place that morning, and can describe everything that happened in photographic detail. It is well-known among my friends that I dread mosquitoes. One summer I went swimming at the beach in Pohang, and, even though it was boiling hot, I covered myself with all the coverlets in the room, and spent several sleepless nights like that. The mosquitoes at the seaside were so powerful that they could even penetrate layers of blankets. And, when flying, they made sounds similar to those made by the Kamikaze planes I had seen in a televised movie. Whenever I heard that buzzing sound, I shuddered and felt like screaming. So, I had every reason to be horrified by the photograph of the dead mosquito printed in the newspaper. And it occurred to me that I could now, at last, write about a certain mosquito.

My divorced wife and I had two daughters. The younger one always had mosquito bites every summer. Of course there are plenty of mosquitoes everywhere in the summer, and plenty of people get bitten by mosquitoes. But my younger daughter seems to attract insect bites. She is of a very emotional and competitive nature, so that when I teased her, saying, "I think mosquitoes hate you," her lips pouted petulantly. But when I corrected myself and said, "Oh, no. I think mosquitoes love you," her face still didn't clear up. Anyway, whether it was because mosquitoes loved her or hated her, she suffered terribly, and it was painful to watch her. This little girl complained about her suffering, but she seemed to be smoldering with a nameless inward fury as well. Her body, swollen red all over with mosquito bites, reminded me of an ancient Indian deity whose body glowed red because of suppressed passion.

It was because mosquito season had again arrived that I was suddenly seized with a longing to see my children. With that sudden longing came the recollection that there was a promise I hadn't kept. Even though it was a promise made long ago, I decided that I would try to fulfill it even at this late date, not so much for the sake of my children as for my own conscience. I went into the first toy shop that came in sight and asked for a pencil sharpener.

"For that you'll have to go to a stationery shop," the pale-faced sales clerk said, standing beneath the shelf neatly arranged with drumming bears, rolly-pollies, toy revolvers and so on. I smiled vacantly and nodded.

"Do you know where there's a stationery shop around here?" I asked, wondering whether there would be any meaning in bringing them something so insignificant, even if a stationery shop could be found.

"Maybe somewhere over on the other side," the clerk said vaguely, pointing across the street. But that didn't seem a likely area for a stationery shop; a handcart selling oysters and sea squirts, a draft beer house and a drugstore came into view. Anyway, the promise was already two years old. The girls wanted a pencil sharpener then. I had also wanted a pencil sharpener when I was a kid: you put a pencil into a hole and turned the handle and out came the shaved wood looking like a flared skirt. One generation later, my children wanted one, too. I thought of telling them it was a stupid thing, but remembering my own childhood, I didn't. The time I had wanted a pencil sharpener was while the ravages of war lay scattered all around us. The war itself was over but its traces were still visible everywhere on our land, so that whenever I walked, I felt as if I were walking on bodies lying there in wait. I also had the feeling that dead men were peeping out at me through the bushes and the tall grass. And there were caves and holes gaping at me from mountain slopes and grounds—caves and holes left by men who could not use them any more.

I walked slowly, climbing up the overpass and crossing over to
the other side of the road. I thought perhaps I had left work too
early. On the overpass I asked a passerby what time it was. He
stopped to look at his watch.

"It's twenty to twelve."

I realized, before he finished telling me, that I too had a
watch. I had had a watch since the day before, when I had gotten
an advance from my company, and used half the money to buy it. I
was always careless about time, and had so far managed to live without a watch. Well, to be exact, I had managed without a watch since
the watch I received from my wife as a wedding present got stolen
on a bus. I never wanted a watch, and I didn't feel any particular
need for one, but when I recalled that the girls would be coming
out of their school exactly at noon, I had hurriedly gone to a jewel-
ry shop and bought one, lest that important time should slip my
mind. But perhaps I'd have asked the time even if I had recalled
having a watch, because it was the reality of time that I needed to
be convinced of.

There was still a quarter of an hour left. What could I do in all
that time? Oh, yes, I could buy a pencil sharpener. That's why I got
the advance, after all. I walked slowly, carefully checking the signboards. I could walk around the streets for a quarter of an hour
looking for it, and at five to twelve I could recross the street and
head for the school. It did occur to me that there was bound to be
a stationery store near the school, but I wanted to get to the school
exactly on time. Looking for a stationery store was just an excuse
for hanging around the street. It was a promise two years old. And
growing children change so rapidly. The girls might even be disgusted to be reminded of their puerile desire. Perhaps it would
even remind them of my unreliability, and my stature as their
father would diminish even further in their eyes. But a promise is a
promise, all the same. Even if I ignored it this time, I would still be
reminded of my having broken it from time to time. Well, it was
stupid to feel so much anxiety on account of a mere pencil sharpener, but that's what I am like. Come to think of it, I have broken
countless promises, ranging from simple appointments to the
solemn vow to love and cherish someone till the end of my life. I
know there's a saying that promises are made to be broken, but
I've really broken too many. If so, why was I so bothered by this
insignificant promise of a long time ago? Well, it may have been
because it was my last promise to my little girls. Perhaps because I
had not fulfilled it, my girls didn't ask me for anything any more.
Yes, I knew that only too well. And two years had passed. I won-

dered if there were no stationery stores in sight because this is not happening now, but two years ago? I had the feeling that I was walking the streets of the present with my past self.

"Excuse me, what time is it?" I asked a man standing in front of a hardware store, who seemed to be waiting for someone. The young man lifted his left arm to show me his bare wrist, and dropped his eyes to mine. Smiling in embarrassment, I lifted my arm and looked at my watch, tilting my head left and right, as much as to show him that my watch was out of order. The dial of my watch indicated ten minutes to twelve. On other days I'd have been fidgeting at my desk at that hour, waiting for the beginning of the lunch hour. I recalled that a few days before, at just about that time, a colleague in the office talked about "nihilistic" monks. "Is there a nihilistic sect in Korea, too?" someone asked my colleague.

"I'm not sure," he had answered.

"I heard that the sect exists in Japan," someone else chimed in. "Oh, I think I heard that, too. They're supposed to wander around playing wooden flutes and wearing hoods over their heads, like those worn by convicts."

"That's right. And they have no fixed abode."

The conversation had then petered out, like all conversations on subjects that didn't concern us directly.

I sat down on a stool in front of a general store. Why had I excused myself from work so early, and even taken a taxi here, when there was so much time? I ordered a soda. "Is there a stationery store nearby?" I asked of the shopkeeper who brought out the drink. He gazed at me blankly for a moment. I looked at my watch again. Seven minutes to twelve. Now I only had to hold out for a couple of minutes longer.

"I don't know," the shopkeeper said and went back into the store.

Without bothering to use the cup, I gulped down the bubbly soda. At first, my throat seemed to contract, but soon the soda ran down smoothly. I didn't bother to reflect whether the feeling was pleasant or unpleasant. I wasn't concerned about the pencil sharpener any more. Why was I hanging around this area in the middle of the day, anyway? What burning desire overpowered me early this morning, obliterating everything in sight and driving me to my children, as if they were the only reality in the world? It was more than a year ago since I had last seen them. That time, the girls said, as they were leaving, "Daddy, could we have a picture of you?" I had never imagined my daughters would think seriously about being parted from me. "For what?" I had asked, gazing at their faces. The younger one smiled shyly and said, "So we can look at it when we miss you." I thought then, "That's what it's like to raise girls," and felt a surge of affection, but it also gave me a sense of resignation, as if separation from them was now an unalterable fact.

I often think about the meaning of meetings and partings. Why are there meetings and partings in life? Is it true, as they say, that it is meetings that give meaning and value to life? If so, aren't partings the conclusion and perfection of meetings? Anyway, I didn't give my daughters my picture. I marvelled at how fast they are growing up, and I asked them why would they want a picture when they could come and see me anytime? The children went down the slope, holding their mother's hands. When my wife said, "Aren't we going to bid Daddy good-bye?" they turned around and bowed. I gazed at their backs, standing at the gate of my house perched on a hill. The children went down the hill with bounding strides, as if conscious of my eyes on them. But they didn't look back. Maybe that, too, was because they knew I was watching them. The slope was steep, so steep that I was worried it wouldn't be safe in winter when it snowed and froze. I seemed to remember looking down at them from far above. It was before they were born. "I'll go and gather flowers for you," I had whispered in my wife's ear at the time. In reality, I just wanted to let her sleep undisturbed. I sneaked out of the hotel room and walked around, inhaling the early morning air. I just couldn't lie still, with the consciousness welling up in me that I had at last caught happiness in my net. I thought I'd cool myself a little by inhaling the cold and clear early morning air. I went up a wooded mountain, trying to make myself as inconspicuous as possible. It was late October and there were no flowers on the mountain. I trod over the icy dew and just kept climbing. I was sure I could get back to the hotel before my wife woke up. I continued walking up and up and suddenly I found myself in an expanse of forest. Wandering there, I saw my children; they had much more distinct features than real children. They waved their tiny hands at me.

After they were born, I studied their faces intently from time to time. I thought that I ought to etch those faces in my head sharply, so that if I had been a sculptor I could reproduce them exactly, whether on clay, marble, or metal. I was certain to die before my children, and it is the duty of those destined to die earlier to carry with them the exact images of those they leave behind. The survivors can at least refer to photos, but the dead can only carry pictures in their minds.

Some soda spilled and wet my shirt front. I frowned. I had even polished my shoes that morning. I couldn't leave a shabby image of myself with my children, after all.

The sun now shone from straight above. It was time for me to go to my children. It wasn't because I hadn't given my children my picture. When I told my divorced wife that the children had asked for my picture, she laughed just the way she used to while we were married, and said, "They needn't have asked. We have your photographs at home." Laughter hovered around her face even after she stopped speaking. My wife had a way of laughing spontaneously and artlessly, so that it sounded like the sudden twitter of a snipe. I was always enchanted by her laughter, and I tried to evoke it as often as I could. Anyway, when I realized that I was to enjoy that laughter rarely or never, I feigned nonchalance before her, like on that morning I went home after spending a night with another woman. Well, there's no need to talk about that now.

I hurried to the school. No one who saw me then would have suspected that I had been so anxious to kill time a moment ago. I strode like one who was going to work for the first time after many months of bumming around. I wished the distance to the school were greater, so that I could walk even faster, but the school appeared almost immediately. It looked more like a warehouse than a school, because several wings had been added to the original building one after another with the progressive increase in the number of students. I, my former wife of ten years, my brothers and sisters and those of my former wife, all got our education in that school. And now our next generation was undergoing the same process in the same place. When I thought of this repetitive cycle, I suddenly thought that children were like dried herring. Regarding the school as a kind of concentration camp or warehouse must come naturally to those who have experienced war.

Suddenly it became noisy. The second and third graders were dismissed from school. The noise billowed out like clouds of smoke, or like a cloud of dust rising from a bombed building. Children burst out from the building, dispersing helter-skelter, like people driven by the warning sirens in a civil defense exercise. I thought I must be a fool for thinking that I could spot my daughters in that crowd. My eyesight was miserably poor. I hoped my children would see me and come to me. My passive posture was painfully humiliating to me, and made me feel like a criminal fleeing from the law, or a beggar asking for alms. The children looked like an angry crowd to me. I thought they were all waiting for some catastrophe to erupt and turn the world upside down.

"Hi there, what class was just dismissed?" I asked a girl coming out of the gate.

"Third grade." The girl answered reluctantly, eyeing me doubtfully, as if suspecting I might be a child kidnapper. It was the grade my older daughter was in. I stepped close to the gate and stood where all the children who came out could see me. My older daughter was in third grade and the younger one in second grade. They always went to and returned from school together. Two days a week third graders were dismissed an hour later than second graders. I had heard that my second grader always waited in the yard for her older sister's class to finish and went home with her sister. She did so even on cold winter days, although she sometimes cried because of the biting cold. When I heard that, I thought that the two girls were destined to share both joys and sorrows in their long voyage through life. "Blood kin," I muttered to myself. Then the meaning of that common phrase struck me forcibly. How could I be such a fool as not to have realized the meaning of a blood tie?

"Daddy!"

This surprised exclamation woke me up from my reverie. To be sure, the children saw me before I saw them. The older one had her hair brushed back and tied in a ponytail, which made her look older, and the younger one's hair was down to her shoulders. They were both wearing dresses, and had sneakers on their stockinged feet.

"Hi, how have you been?" I greeted them, putting my hand on my chest to still the nameless surge of emotion inside. The children just nodded in response. Both looked thinner than I remembered, but their lips were as cherry red as ever. I don't mean to suggest that they looked sexy. I just use the expression because one spring the girls begged me to plant a cherry tree in the yard. But I ignored their plea. Not only was the yard not big enough for a cherry tree, but I also didn't like the thick foliage of cherry trees. It was after that incident that I began to think my daughters' lips were like cherries. But the children did not forget their wish easily. Even after the spring was over, the younger one kept asking me, "Will you plant a cherry tree next spring, daddy?" No doubt they were growing a cherry tree in their hearts, as their tree of hope. That's why I always think they have lips like cherries. All of us can reap only what we've planted. I regard their having cherry lips as an indication that they have yearnings and desires. And I found a secret joy in the thought that I alone can detect this evidence of their vital hopes.

"Well, you must be hungry, girls. How about something to eat?" I suggested.

"Eat what?" Their eyes shone.

"How about Chinese noodles?"

The two exchanged glances, with their hands still in each other's, and nodded their assent. I started walking towards the Chinese restaurant that I had noted before reaching the school. Walking together with my daughters felt like a dream. The familiar street, myself, the children, and even the world itself seemed to me to be a dream. I felt as if we were all walking into a mirage. Hadn't I, perhaps, first learned to walk on some other planet? I remember hearing that the North Star was 1,090 light-years away from the earth. So the light of the North Star that we are seeing is the light that came from the time of Koryŏ Dynasty. In the same way, it could well be that our reality today is the reality of a thousand years ago. In other words, I was wishing that the reality around me was not "the true reality," because I was afraid I couldn't avoid running into it. Also, I have always thought that each of us must have a star as our original hometown. The star called the earth is nothing but a preposterous island. Suddenly, I pitied my daughters with all my heart. They will have to remain on this planet long after I pass away. That must be a dreadful punishment. The girls were walking up the steps leading to the Chinese restaurant. I didn't say anything to them; to tell them that I missed them or to ask them if they missed me would only falsify our true feelings for each other. The girls were also silent. The staircase was squalid and dark. Some people hold that the ties in this life are extensions of ties in our earlier lives. Going up those dark steps, I thought that I really must have had ties with my girls in our earlier existence. I seemed to recall walking down a dark, squalid pathway with those girls in one of my former lives. Yes, I did. And in that former life we had also stepped into a place reeking of oil and Chinese noodle sauce, just as we were doing then.

"Let's sit over there by the window," I said. As it was still early for lunch, the restaurant was only sparsely filled. The children went to the table by the window and sat down opposite me, taking down their satchels from their backs. I knew the girls loved Chinese noodles; all children love Chinese noodles. I've often seen children of my daughters' age eating Chinese noodles alone in Chinese restaurants, with the daredevil air of doing something forbidden.

"Shall I order Chinese noodles and fried dumplings?" I suggested, but there really was no need to ask. The children just opened and closed their mouths in embarrassment, and looked away.

"You decide, daddy," they said.

"How can I decide what you want to eat?"

"But you can."

"Would you like meat sauce with your noodles?"

"No."

I ordered Chinese noodles with regular sauce and some dumplings. The waiter brought each of us a cup of water. I split the wooden chopsticks and gave each of the girls a pair. The sun shining obliquely through the window made them look mature for their age. The girls didn't start any conversation; I thought they might be asking themselves why they had to have reunions with their father in such queer fashion.

"How're you doing at school?"

It was the last question I wanted to ask my daughters. I never wanted them to excel at school. I just wanted them to find their own ways of life and travel those ways truthfully, without falsehood and affectation.

"You know, this girl is an honor student," the younger girl said with an exaggerated elation, pointing at her sister. She seemed to be proud of her sister's achievement, and at the same time ashamed of her own lack of distinction.

"That's very good. But it's not proper to refer to your sister as 'this girl,' is it?"

"Oh, sorry. Sorry. Sorry."

For a moment I remembered the pencil sharpener and felt guilty. But they didn't look as though they were accusing me of anything. However, even if they had forgotten that particular item, the fact remains that I had reneged on my promise to them. That disappointment was certain to exist somewhere in their world, as we know from the principle of conservation of energy.

"So you didn't get to be an honor student?" I asked the younger one, and smiled at her sister. The older girl dropped her head a little as the younger one said "No" in a low voice.

"It's because she goofed on the music exam," the older girl said, defending her sister. The younger one shrugged her small shoulders and stuck out her tongue. I touched that tongue with my fingertip and she withdrew it at once.

"Why? You took music lessons, didn't you?"

"You know, I really don't get this time thing," she said sullenly. I remembered that she, unlike the older girl, had a great deal of trouble with her music lessons. She struggled hard with it for some time and then gave up, then started again from the beginning, struggled with it, and finally gave up again. The older girl was already into Bach; that is, she was while we were living together.

"Why don't you ask your sister to teach you? You ask your sister to help you, and you'll do well in the next exam, okay?"

"Okay." The little girl enunciated clearly and turned to her sister with a smile in her eyes.

"You'll help me, won't you?"

"Of course. Have I ever refused to help you?"

The younger one looked at me shamefacedly, as if she had been rebuked.

"So you help her a little more," I recommended.

The younger one regained her color at once. "Do: Just one more time, okay?" The older girl blinked in consent and nodded a couple of times for assurance.

"Thank you, dear sister!"

The younger girl stretched her hand and rubbed her sister's cheek with it. The older girl leaned back away from the hand but didn't look displeased. I was the one who was really grateful. The thought of the pain the two little girls must have endured because of their parents' divorce made my heart heavy. But they didn't look sad or unhappy. There were many nights I had conjured up their faces distorted with sorrow and resentment.

"What are you doing these days, Daddy?" the older girl asked. I became confused. What was I doing these days about what? I thought she was asking not just about what I was doing by way of work, but also about what I was doing about their unhappiness.

"Oh, I'm working hard, too. I work at my office and I write, too," I enunciated with difficulty. I despised myself for giving such an evasive answer. The girls looked at me thoughtfully. There was no way of explaining to them about what it means for me to write. I often thought I might be happier if I didn't write. I also tormented myself with the thought that I have not written anything worth reading, but I always scribbled, as if it were a habit I brought with me into the world. To be sure, they had asked me once, "Daddy, why do you write?" At the time, I turned my face to look up at them from where I lay on my stomach with a pillow under my chest. I was at a loss for an answer. I thought that when they grew up I could discuss it with them. So I just answered, jokingly: "It's to earn money." I knew only too well that there was no chance of my earning any money from writing. But how could I say that everyone has to do something and that I had nothing else to do?

Our conversation came to a halt because the waiter brought
three bowls of Chinese noodles and one platter of fried dumplings.
We all began to mix the noodles and sauce. The older girl, who
had a round face and plump body, looked like a crab waving its
claws as she moved her chopsticks, and the younger girl, who had
an oval face and slender body, like a lobster.

"Now, let's eat," I said.

We all began eating. As we ate, I was seized by a complicated
emotion. Isn't it unbelievable that after this simple meal each of us
had to go back to his or her life?

"I can't eat very well, because my teeth are loose," the older
girl said, and opened her mouth wide for me to see. One of her
teeth was missing.

"Oh, are your baby teeth coming out? You'd better eat carefully with your molars."

"Once she said she bit something hard while she was eating
and found it was her own tooth," the younger girl said. I told the
girls that they have to pull out loose teeth quickly if they want to
have even teeth.

"But, Daddy, your teeth are uneven, too," the younger girl
protested. The girls giggled. We continued eating, pretending to
be preoccupied with the act, conscious that what we really needed
to say was too momentous to be brought up casually. Had one better leave unspoken what cannot be solved? When we were almost
through with the meal, I noticed that my younger daughter was fidgeting.

"What's the matter? Are you itchy?" I asked, and immediately
recalled her tribulations with insect bites.

"Yes, it's scratchy." The small girl's face twitched.

"It's not scratchy, it's itchy," her sister corrected her.

"Let me see. Is it a mosquito bite? Show me."

I went round to the other side of the table, squatted down and
observed the spot her fingers were scratching. On the bare skin
between her stocking and panties there were a number of big red
welts. These swellings, which stood out like embossed carvings,
looked like the flesh of some red fruit.

"Use mosquito incense. And a mosquito net, too," I said, coming back to my seat. But I knew that all such devices were useless.
We always used to use mosquito incense and a mosquito net, but
the child was sure to get mosquito bites anyway. Some summers her
whole body got covered with mosquito bites and then with scabs. It
made her look like a rock covered with barnacles. There was nothing to do but to pray for the summer to pass quickly. Now, the

painful summer was beginning on her thighs. It made me furious to think that her little body was going to be bitten, swollen, runny and scabby all summer long, without her being able to fight back in any way. Of course I was aware that my fury was directed not so much at the mosquitoes as at myself. Rage seethed in a foamy, stagnant pool inside my chest, where rotten fish, rotten frogs, and rotten earthworms swirled in a confused mass, and innumerable wriggling eels danced.

When we wiped our mouths with our napkins, it was time to say good-bye. I felt as if I should tell them about having hope for the future and a positive attitude toward life and so forth, but nothing came out of my mouth. I felt it would be hypocrisy to go back to the office tomorrow and start working again. I stood up with a heavy heart. What a strange way to end this midday meeting. I became confused and had difficulty holding my head up. I had accomplished nothing in the meeting, and only showed the children what a totally weak and crude human being I was. The children wouldn't have a chance any more to beg me to plant a cherry tree. They wouldn't be able to cry out, "Daddy, Daddy, kill that mosquito," as they were being bitten. Instead of all these they were given that incomprehensible thing called "separation." I thought I must not prolong this parting. I must extricate myself from this mire of contradictions. I must escape since I could not solve the problem. I realized that my legs were shaking as we descended the staircase. How far should I flee? When we stepped into the broad daylight, my head went blank, as if my brain had been bleached by the white light. The street rose up before my eyes.

"I have to go back to work," I muttered gloomily. The children stood as still as mannequins. "You mustn't get sick. Stay healthy, all right?" I felt stuffy and my words came out in gasps.

"Yes, sir," the girls replied in unison. I then retreated hastily, guiltily.

An endless blank engulfed me, and fatigue and ennui assailed me. When I looked back a little later, the girls were no longer in sight. My heart pounded loudly. I took tottering steps. I must escape to the end of the world. I must insult, abuse, accuse and laugh at myself. I knew then where I was going. I was going to a tavern. But I knew well enough that liquor could neither save nor damn me. Then why drink? Let's say it's to wash out the mosquito from my head.

If only I could figure out to a certainty how much pain I'd have to inflict on myself, that would already put me half way to salvation. I trod on. Concepts such as universal order, *Idea,* "Li" and "Chi"

raced through my brain. What were they, really? Were they like
those petals of azalea that the poet strewed on the path and asked
his lover to "crush lightly" on her way to another lover?

Once upon a time there was a girl named Sehwa. She was a
young girl, younger even than my daughters are now. But the girl
died. Even when other children rushed to the beach in a group,
this girl and I played alone together. We played "doctor and
patient." We took off our clothes and pretended to examine each
other. We found each other perfect. On the beach she parted her
legs and sprinkled sand on her crotch. We giggled with a grown-up
air. But soon after that she died, without having had a chance to fly
on birds. She died without leaving any trace of herself. She died
for good. It was towards the end of the war.

I don't remember how much I drank that day. I only think I
heard the tavern hostess asking me, "Do you remember Sehwa?
She was pockmarked." "She was?" I had said. "Yes, she was. She
died in childbirth," the hostess had clicked her tongue in commiser-
ation. "That's right. She's dead. Because we're alive," I had muttered and gulped down my liquor. By early evening I was dead
drunk. But I still had to flee. I staggered out into an unfamiliar
street. It looked as if the ground, the whole earth, swirled. All faces
looked alike. "There was a girl named Sehwa. Once upon a time,
that is. She died at the age children play house," I shouted. I tried
to recall her face but could not. Her face was lost in oblivion, just
as surely as that long-ago time in which she lived. Walking on, I
thought that time is a tomb. My daughters, my wife, all disappeared into time. An old childhood friend walked out of the tomb
of time. Was I bewitched by the meaning of separation? Was the
whole of life no more than playing house? I sang aloud, to a popular tune: "Once upon a time, we lived. That time is now. We lived
happily in a tomb." My legs shook as if I really were a ghost, but my
tears wouldn't flow. I arrived at a cemetery, the joint cemetery of
time. A woman blocked my way.

"Looking for someone in particular?" the woman said.

"I'm scared. Scared. So I'm looking for a girl named Sehwa."

There was a short silence. The woman looked into my eyes. I
fretfully searched for a way to let her know I was in earnest. I wanted to sink into the tomb of time and go to sleep, pillowed on the
soft skeleton of my dead childhood friend. I took out the advance
pay I had gotten from the company and waved it before the
woman, as much as to say, "Will this convince you of my earnest-
ness?"

"Come."

She smiled a skeletal smile. Led into a grave, I flopped down with the relief and the despair of having arrived at a place from which there was no escape.

I was groping along a passage leading to a tomb. From somewhere a faint light seeped out. Chewing the uncooked rice that the funeral parlor people had put in my mouth while preparing me for burial, I walked the interminable passage towards the light. Someone suddenly appeared out of the darkness and stopped me. He asked me who I was; I couldn't remember. I grinned sheepishly but his face didn't relax. "You can't die until you find out who you are," he declared. My bosom heaved with the sorrow of not being allowed even to die. A vague, shapeless fear engulfed me. I must die by all means, even if I had to climb on top of Sehwa and fuck myself to death.

The next morning I found a mosquito. I woke up naked and paced about the room without putting my clothes on. The empty room really did look like a tomb. I paced about like a sleepwalker. What had happened? What had happened yesterday, and what had happened to my life? Everything was hazy. The strange planet I was on was smoldering to death, emitting a thin light that would be caught by beings on other planets hundreds of years from now.

A mosquito alighted on a wall. I approached carefully and studied it. The mosquito's belly was as red as a finger hit by a hammer. I swatted the insect hard with my palm, pasting it to the wall. Wasn't it odd that the mosquito that had sucked my blood so ferociously the night before could die at one stroke of its victim's palm? I laughed. I stood there gazing at the mosquito, forgetting my naked state.

The Sunset over My Hometown

~~

Yi Mun-ku

Yi Mun-ku, born in 1941, is a writer of distinctive color and flare. Born as a scion of an old and honorable family clan, his family fortunes dwindled progressively until he had to earn both his livelihood and tuition as a college student. Soon, he quit college to work at construction sites and did any other work that came his way to eke out a precarious living. His first novel, A Long and Bitter Dream, *was based on his experience as a day laborer clearing a cemetery for apartment construction. Not long after he debuted as a writer, he decided to move to the country—no doubt partly because he was disgusted with the way things were turning out under the military dictatorship—and stayed there for more than ten years. Of his two short-story collections, the famous "My Neighbor Mr. . . ." series contains vivid first-hand sketches of life in Korean farm villages in the grip of modernization fever. The stories are told with keen satiric humor. Yi's native Ch'ungchŏngdo dialect is utilized to great hilarious effect.* Kwanch'on Essays, *on the other hand, are based on the memory of his own childhood and the life of his old neighbors who were not very successful in riding out the wave of change. As befits the descendant of the grandfather he depicts in "The Sunset over My Hometown," he is deeply interested in the traditional cultural and intellectual heritage. His two full-length fictional biographies of historical figures attest to his interest in the spirit of Korean ancestors and the kinship he felt for eccentric geniuses who would not and could not conform to the norms of their societies. Writing on the most eruditely classical as well as the most crudely vulgar subjects, Yi has cut a unique niche for himself in Korean literature.*

"The Sunset over My Hometown" (1972), the first story in the Kwanch'on Essays *collection, is Yi's most straightforwardly autobiographical story. It is a loving recollection of the author's old grand-*

father who tried to uphold the crumbling ways of life of his ancestors in
the face of rapid modernization taking place all around him. The story
evokes nostalgia for the old way of life that had already become rather
absurd in the author's childhood but which had peculiar grace and
charm.

I was visiting my hometown for the first time in over a decade. As
I had no relatives left there, I was taking the trip solely for the
purpose of paying my respects at the ancestral graves. It was the
first time in my life that I visited them at the solar new year. It is
true I felt slightly uncomfortable about paying homage at my
grandfather's grave at the beginning of the solar new year, as he
had always strongly disapproved of the custom of celebrating the
solar new year, which was introduced by the Japanese. However,
being tied to my job, I had no choice but to take the solar new year
holidays, since none was given at the lunar. But while I was riding
the train, I was conscious of committing an act of serious impiety.
My grandfather was the only ancestor I knew, and the one who
kept the family line alive through those turbulent and difficult
years.

That meant that to me my grandfather, rather than my parents
or siblings, stood for my family line. Grandfather was a man of the
Yi Dynasty, and the living embodiment of the spirit of my ancestors. He and only he will remain that for me forever. To be sure,
for love and affection it is my mother whom I miss most tenderly,
but it is my grandfather whose teachings I honor above all others',
so I felt I had to pay my respects first of all at his grave.

The train ride tired me out. I had chosen the third of January,
thinking that by then people would have finished visiting their parents and the train would be less crowded, but I was wrong. Anyway,
I got off the train in my hometown station late in the afternoon. It
had begun to rain as the train rounded the bend of the village of
Kwanch'on, my hometown, which is located at the entrance of the
town of Hannae. The rain was an indication of how warm the winter was. The rain and the sight of the hills of my childhood tugged
at my heart and made me sentimental.

I had been standing at the train window, staring at the hills
and houses of my hometown. Part of me was excited, but another
part of me was lonely and gloomy. Nothing looked the same as it
did in my childhood. Was it so hard for something just to remain
the same?

The change that smote my heart the hardest was the disappearance of the giant pine tree. A chimney belonging to a slate-roofed sundries store standing where the pine tree used to be was stretching its impertinent cylinder towards the sky. Thirteen years ago, just before I left my hometown, the needles of the pine tree were beginning to turn yellow and its branches were beginning to die off. But to think that such a sacred tree which had stood guardian over the village for more than four hundred years with its noble form had been razed and disposed of made my heart boil.

I still remember vividly the day in my seventh year shortly after the feast celebrating my mastery of the "Thousand Characters." I had accompanied Grandfather to the embankment and watched the tide rushing in with such force that it looked bent on sweeping away the whole village. The sun was spreading its evening glow on the waves, and gulls and other sea birds were filling the air with their songs. The railway stretched endlessly along the embankment, and the new highway, whose pebbles glistened white in the evening sun, curved out of view. The pine tree was standing close to the railway and the expressway on a turf-covered mound that had no other tree on it.

On that day, Grandfather caressed the trunk of the pine tree, which required four young men to link their fully spread arms to cover its circumference, and said, "My child, this pine tree grew from the cane of Grandfather T'ojŏng, our ancestor, who stuck it here while taking a walk one day. Legend has it that Grandfather T'ojŏng predicted that when an iron horse runs past the tree we, the Yis of Hansan clan, would have to leave this town. Maybe I ought to have left the village and moved to somewhere else when the iron horse began to run. That might have averted some of the misfortunes . . . "

I still remember Grandfather's words of that day very clearly. It was the first piece of legend I heard about the pine tree. Frankly, I didn't give much credence to the legend of a walking cane turning into a huge pine, although I had heard Grandfather talking about the many supernatural feats that Grandfather T'ojŏng performed and could understand his reverence and admiration. Be that as it may, the pine tree was the king of all the trees in the village, and no other tree even remotely compared with it either in size or imposing dignity. Looking out the window at the familiar and strange sights of my hometown, I noted mentally that the tree had disappeared without a trace and that I was riding that iron horse which an ancestor of my clan had dreaded as a messenger of the demise of the family line.

I found myself murmuring, "The place is depraved now. How

the pine tree must have suffered from the shrill whistle and smoke of the train that ran many times a day, and almost constantly during the summer, since this area became a swimming beach!"

The disappearance of the pine tree was not the only reason for my gloom. The run-down appearance of my old house affected me even more acutely. Even in that momentary glimpse through the train window, I could see that the house, which was so elegant and spacious that passing strangers often mistook it for the head family's house, had become dilapidated and shabby.

Houses built without any regard to dignity or beauty were scattered around the village in great disorder, so that only the ridge of the thatched roof of the inner quarters of my old house retained some vestige of old elegance. Even my old house was quite run-down, so that the delicate roofline of the men's quarters had become blunt, the ivy that used to cover the wall had grown straggly, and the trees standing like palisades along the kitchen garden had lost their look of thriving vigor. The whole village looked confused and shabby.

A man without a hometown. I could not help feeling that I was a man without a hometown. It was true that I had neglected to visit my hometown for over a decade, as I had no tie left binding me to the place except the graves of my ancestors. Nonetheless, I could not but feel lonely and miserable to see it in such a state of deterioration.

I deemed it my first duty to pay respects at Grandfather's tomb. The tomb was located on the slope of one of the hills owned by my clan, near the shoreline village called Koman, at about twelve kilometers' distance from Hannae. It was a remote place without public transportation, so I had no choice but to walk there. As it would be impossible to walk there and back in the remainder of the day, I would have to stop over at a house in the village. Though I had not visited my hometown for a long time, I was sure that everyone in the village would willingly give me a night's lodging. I decided to stop over at a relative's on my mother's side. That decided, I could use the time until nightfall to saunter around. But it was not entirely to kill time that I walked over to my old neighborhood.

It was more to look at the familiar haunts of my childhood and note the contrast between their former shapes and their present state. I was trying to convince myself that I had a hometown, even though I live far away from it and it had changed sadly.

Stepping out of the station building, I had to get hold of a plastic umbrella. The rain hitting the plastic dome of the umbrella underscored the hollow feeling inside me, intensified by my empty stomach.

The village of Kwanch'on was in the outskirts of Hannae at about ten minutes' walk from the center of the town. At the entrance of the village, three thatched-roof houses used to stand apart, across the new highway from the village. One of them was a sundries store selling candies and matchboxes, run by a couple who used to own a tavern. The hovel facing it was a blacksmith's, in which the one-eyed blacksmith was seen all day pumping the bellows. A little way from the two huts was a dark hovel that was a tavern run by Chang Chungch'ŏl. In the kitchen of the hovel wine and snack trays were prepared, and in its tiny yard an unlicensed barber ran an open air barbershop, frequented by vendors doing business at the market. Beside an electric pole, halfway between the tavern and the blacksmith's, stood a sooty cylindrical drum, which was used as a dyeing cauldron. Clothes, linen and other fabrics sold in the market were dyed in it, with the wood gathered on the mountain used as fuel.

But none of these remained. Where the sundries store used to be now stood a neat and bright new building, boasting the signboard, "Kwanch'on Barbershop." The smithy had also disappeared, and in its place was a cement-block house, which seemed to be inhabited by a middle-class family. The hovel that used to be the tavern had a slate roof now, and its plank wall had traces of blue paint and was hung with posters proclaiming anticommunist slogans and expostulating increased consumption of wheat flour to alleviate the rice shortage. And it had a signboard made of a narrow strip of wood that said, in disorderly handwriting, "a sales agency of the 13th district of the Ch'ŏn'il Rice Wine Distillery." From the tin chimney jutting out of the barbershop window white smoke was billowing, and a few unfamiliar faces studied me through the windowpane in surprise and wonder, but no familiar face appeared. I felt like a stranger there, even though I grew up and lived there for eighteen years and regarded the whole village as the outer yard of my house!

I turned into a narrow alley of dark red earth that branched off from the highway. I reached the orchard in no time. I felt breathless with anticipation as, right next to the orchard, at the end of its gardenia hedge, was the three-hundred-square-meter garden patch that supplied many generations of my family with vegetables and which I tilled with my own hands until I sold it off with the house just before leaving my hometown. The alley, whose frozen surface the rain had just melted, was slushy, and dampened my nostalgia. The brook, which became a clear stream as soon as there was the least bit of rain, had dwindled to a mere ditch, and alongside it shabby cement-block houses stood in a row. It was just like any other rural village.

On reaching the former garden patch of my house I darted in, stepping on the barley stubbles that were sprouting new shoots. At that moment I stopped short, transfixed.

I beheld Grandfather leaning on his cane and gazing down at the tomb he had prepared for his burial. He was standing in his usual stooping posture with his white beard blowing in the wind, his horsehair hat over his headband and his eyeglasses case dangling from his belt under his silk jacket.

I came back to the present after a while, like one coming out of a trance. Then, sighing deeply, I turned my steps towards the Dipper Rocks.

I had had a momentary illusion that I beheld my grandfather as I used to see him almost daily in my childhood, an indelible and peculiar form characteristic of the old man.

I climbed the nearest of the seven rocks that formed the Dipper Rocks. The square level rock was one of my childhood havens, on which I used to take short rests while picking melons or steaming millet. I took out a cigarette and lit it. The rain continued to spatter on the plastic umbrella. The rain beat down the evening smoke of burning pine needles from the chimneys of the thatched-roof houses among the grove of dwarf pine at the foot of the Owl Mound, so that the smoke spread out like mist instead of puffing up as on clear days.

I began to examine the Dipper Rocks one by one. Being huge solid rocks, they remained in their place, forming the shape of the Big Dipper as they always did. The smallest of the seven rocks, which was closest to the road and therefore used more frequently by the village urchins, retained its jeep-like shape, and the one shaped like a toad was still crouching as humbly as ever. The third largest rock, which looked like a tiger in repose, had retained its stateliness, although the bush surrounding it had become thinner. The bush still had the two lacquer trees and wild rose vines and various creeping plants, and was inviting birds as in the old days.

The site that had been chosen to be Grandfather's tomb, which was located right below the tiger-shaped rock, was always covered with a beautiful coat of turf while my father was alive. Father, being an eminently filial son, must have seen to it, just as he had special treats prepared for Grandfather on the first and the fifteenth day of every month, saying that one should fulfill one's filial duties while the parent is still alive, not after his demise. The burial site was one chosen by Grandfather himself, who had a tomb built there while he was alive. Having had no hobbies and desisting from alcohol and tobacco all his life, Grandfather often came to look at his false tomb on long spring days, to make sure there were no weeds or rat holes. He stood there leaning on his cane, tenderly gazing at what was to be his tomb. Seeing him at those times, I used to be overcome by a feeling of solemnity, which remained with me all these years.

In my childhood the garden patch was thick with berry plants and herbs. A weedlike plant that yielded sweet edible berries when ripe grew in profusion on the mound of Grandfather's false tomb, so that I became chestnut brown from the sun, playing with my pals on the rocks all day long on late spring days. On such days Grandfather also came to the rocks leaning on his cane, and our housemaid Ongjŏmi, who was a strapping girl and who could collect in the same amount of time twice as many edible herbs as the other girls in the village, gathered herbs in the barley field at the foot of the rocks.

Ongjŏmi was an affectionate and generous girl. She was the daughter of a bond servant belonging to my maternal home, whom Mother had brought over as part of her dowry when she got married. My maternal grandfather had served as a low-level official of the Bureau of Military Affairs and was a government doctor, who later returned to his hometown to take up residence there. The female servant had run away soon after she came to my home, and after having had a series of lovers, settled down as a tavern proprietress. Ongjŏmi is her daughter by a widowered former husband of another servant girl. She got her name meaning "Earthen jar" from having been born among rows of earthen jars in an earthenware shop. Ongjŏmi came to live with us when she was seven. Her mother had left her with my maternal grandparents, who gave her to my mother. My mother was always full of praise for her, as she was tender-hearted, clever and good at all kinds of manual work. Because of her generosity she was very popular with all the beggars, mendicant friars and lepers. Our field hands also eagerly helped her carry water jars and fire logs and anything else she might ask for or need.

I remember how my mother used to make me laugh by mimicking Ongjŏmi's accents. It was Grandfather who taught her manners and decorum. Grandfather could discern people's character at a glance, so he saw promise in her from the first and decided to teach her.

"How old are you?" was the first question he put to her when she was brought to our house.

Ongjŏmi, who was never taught to be respectful to her elders, answered fearlessly.

"My mother always chided me for being only six. But that was last year, so I don't know how old I am now."

"You mean you don't know your own age?"

"No. Someone said I'm now seven, but someone else said I've eaten up a year so I'm five now."

"What silly talk. So, does that slattern mother of yours come to see you from time to time?"

"Yes. The last time she came to his lordship's house she was wearing a fake silk skirt, and had her hair all done up in curls. She looked awfully pretty."

"Does she drink as much as ever?"

"Yes. She got drunk the other day and got thrown out by my father in her underwear."

"Oh, shame!"

Grandfather didn't ask any more questions. It wasn't because Ongjŏmi's answers embarrassed him, but rather because she called my maternal uncle, who was a dissolute rake, "his lordship." It was the most natural form of address for the girl, but it was an irreverence before Grandfather. However, Grandfather swallowed his displeasure and asked her name.

"What's your name, then?"

"I'm called the first one."

"The first one? Then, don't you have a name yet?"

The girl didn't understand the question because she thought she'd given her name.

"Well, I heard that your mother gave birth to you behind a row of earthen jars. Let's call you Ongjŏmi, Earthen Jar, from now on. Yes, that should do."

That's how she got her name Ongjŏmi. And that became her official name as well.

Ongjŏmi was sensitive to her elders' moods and affectionate and generous to children, even though she often broke dishes and was a chatterbox. Whenever she came back from her herb gathering at the garden patch where she saw Grandfather lingering around his false tomb, she would report to my mother at the top of her voice, dropping her herb basket noisily, "Ma'am, I suppose his lordship is having springtime blues."

"Goodness! When is the girl ever going to learn to talk sense?" Mother would say and put down her sewing, to go and see if Grandfather had come to some mishap.

"I think his lordship is worried about his false tomb."

"That's enough. Go and do your work," Mother would say, breathing a sigh of relief, and ask, "What have you got in the basket?"

"Oh, platycodon and arrowroot, his lordship's favorites. My, the day sure is long. 'The ferry's leaving, its double horns ringing through the port . . . '"

Ongjŏmi would murmur the popular song she'd picked up from somewhere, squatting down in front of the stove and sorting the herbs. She was approaching her mid-teens then and must have been entering her adolescence.

"Oh, yes, he must be worried. He's been looking all over for his burial site," Mother would say, half to Ongjŏmi's back and half to herself. Mother understood Grandfather. Grandfather had consulted every geomancer in the area, and climbed numerous hills far and wide. He had traveled to all the famous hills and mountains in the county, hills where his famous ancestors were buried, but the auspicious place he found at last was right in the garden patch of his own house.

Grandfather took such good care of his tombsite that even I, young as I was then, felt compelled to express my interest.

"Grandfather, how can this be an auspicious site? It's just a piece of red earth overgrown with thorny bush," I remarked one day when I saw him bending over his false tomb.

Grandfather, whose hearing was much better than his sight, returned, "Well, look at those rocks. Aren't they arranged exactly like the stars in the Big Dipper?"

Unconvinced, I pursued: "But why do you want to be buried in a garden patch? Do you like dying?"

"Oh, it's all the same. To be waiting for death doing nothing day after day, or to die early and take my place under the turf . . . "

I didn't know what to say.

"Oh, how stupid of me to be talking to a child like this!"

"But why below the rocks? Other people bury themselves on the mountains."

"These rocks and myself are four to one."

"What do you mean?"

"Well, do you know the expression, 'Extract one litre from four'?"

"No."

"How shameful. You've finished the "Thousand Characters," and yet can't figure out the meaning of such a simple phrase?"

I hung my head.

"Listen. Do you know that four kilos of cotton blossoms yield one kilo of cotton wool?"

"I know cotton blossoms come from cotton plants after you squeeze out the seeds. And cotton wool is made from the cotton blossoms in the wool mill."

"Have you not heard the herb doctor say four kilos of water ginseng is equal to one kilo of dry ginseng?"

I wasn't sure I had.

"What those phrases mean is that something, when refined, is reduced or condensed to one fourth of its original volume."

"Then four kilos of barley must be equal to one kilo of rice?"

"Shame!"

"Shame!" was an exclamation of disapproval Grandfather used all the time. He used the word alike to reprove the inferiors and to chide me for stupid and selfish words or deeds.

At the time Grandfather was a hoary-haired old man of eighty-nine. Old and frail, he was holding onto life tenuously, but he was always calm and dignified as befitting his venerable age. I suppose, since he knew that he was one with the rocks, he must have known what properties he had in common with the wind and rain and other natural elements.

On that day the rocks seemed not merely material objects but sacred embodiments of Grandfather's spirit and will, or at least venerable symbols of his soul.

I stepped down from the level rock and approached the tiger rock, below which was Grandfather's former tomb. It was where numerous pheasants and wild pigeons alighted on rainy winter days. Pak Ch'ŏlho, who was our field hand for five years, could catch pheasants and wild pigeons easily, by burying a trap inside the manure heap or laying poisoned bait. I, who used to eat at the same table with Grandfather, heard him say time and again, "Though the world has changed, some distinctions must be observed. Pheasants are dish for the *yangban,* and pigeons are food for the commoners and servants." He seemed to be dreading that I might eat pigeon inadvertently.

I had moved Grandfather's grave to our ancestral hill before moving to Seoul, and sold the garden patch together with our house to a Mr. Kim, a railway official. Judging from the scattered heaps of dried potato vines, sweet potatoes seemed to have been planted and harvested on the gravesite. I realized belatedly that the rain had stopped. After the rain, the wind was biting. I thought I had better get to the town before it got darker and colder. But my legs were carrying me up the rear hill of my childhood, past some shabby houses. How lucky it was that we had moved the tomb. Half a dozen cement-block houses stood huddling around the Dipper Rocks. The houses had no walls, and garbage dumps and chicken and duck coops were scattered around them. I had moved the tomb, as dirt and waste would seep into the tomb once houses were built around the garden patch. None of the houses had drainage, so there were stinking puddles all around the Dipper Rocks and the former site of Grandfather's tomb, and the outhouses cluttered the area like ugly and stinking scabs.

As I climbed up the hill, more and more of my old house, in which I spent eighteen years of my life from my first birthday, came into view. Three eighty-seven Taech'ŏn-ri, Taech'ŏn Ŭp, is the address of my house where Grandfather breathed his last and where Mother also passed away after putting up a hard struggle to maintain the declining household. I sold the house over to a stranger. Comprising about eight hundred square meters of land and standing on a little more than two hundred square meters of building space, the house had a main part and two parallel wings stretching at right angles from either end. The house, which faced south and had a natural storage place to the rear of the building, still retained some of its old dignity and elegance. However, the palisade of trees that made up the hedge of the kitchen garden and the twelve chestnut trees standing outside the rear wall looked old and worn. The paulownia tree remained in front of the main gate, but the gate looked narrower, on account of the new chicken coop and pigpen taking up some of the space of the entranceway.
I looked into the yard. Are those the peony and plum trees of my childhood? And are those the apricot and gardenia trees that Mother used to tend? It was hard to believe, but they seemed to be the same trees. The inner yard with the well in the middle looked bleak and untidy, but the trees were still standing. The persimmon tree, from which every year we harvested several hundred persimmons that were peeled and hung to make dried persimmons, and the jujube tree beside it, had grown higher than the roof, so I had to stand on tiptoe to get a good view of the yard. And I recalled another persimmon tree that yielded enough fruit in the autumn to last the whole winter but which had died before we moved away. I don't know who had planted the tree. Nor did I know who put the wedge-shaped rock at the divide of its two main branches one January Full Moon Day. The placing of the stone, which we called "wedding," in a crude sexual analogy, was done on January Full Moon Days, so that the branches would spread wide apart as they grew. After it withered I hewed it down and fed it into the stove. Mother breathed her last, after suffering from asthma for more

than half a year, early in the August of my nineteenth year, when I
came home for the summer vacation. I firmly believe that the persimmon tree died at the same moment. When we came home after
burying Mother, we discovered that the tree, which had boasted
dark green foliage and innumerable young fruit only a few days
before, had suddenly withered. The leaves had all shrivelled up,
and the dried and shrunken little persimmons fell in showers at
the slightest wind. All my relatives and many villagers agreed that
the tree must have died suddenly, immediately after Mother's
demise. It didn't revive even after the first anniversary of Mother's
death. On the contrary, it withered completely, and the dead
branches broke with a snap at the merest touch. Village people
said that the tree reminded them of my mother. It was an indirect
suggestion that I should cut it down. I also felt that I could not
leave my hometown with the dead tree that lived and died with
Mother still standing. But people also told me that cutting down or
moving garden trees provokes the wrath of the tree god, so if you
cut down a garden tree you must stick a sickle or a knife in its
stump to prevent a mishap. I was never one to ignore people's
advice. But I remember vividly what copious scalding tears I shed
while splitting the logs into firewood.

   Now, in the place where the persimmon tree used to stand was
a straw mound. The cherry tree beside the storage platform and
the pomegranate and peach trees standing to its left were all still at
their former places, and their previous owner gazed at them sadly.

   While the maintenance of the house was under my charge, I
wished I could live in a small cozy house, weary from having to
clear the endless piles of fallen leaves in the fall and to scrub the
numerous floors and verandas in the inner and outer quarters. It
may be a sad fulfillment of my stupid wish that all the property I
now own under the Heaven is a tiny apartment entirely devoid of
earth. The west wing of the house, which used to contain the barn
and the storage room, seems to have been turned into a separate
living quarters and let to a tenant. The flowerbed in front of the
men's quarters, which used to have fragrant plums, roses, lilies and
orchids and in which we also planted mint and other medicinal
herbs, has apparently been long since turned into a vegetable garden.

   The servants' quarters, which in our time was inhabited by
Taebok's family, became a separate house with a tile roof, and it
now had a nameplate of its own. The rice paddies, which stretched
from the tip of our yard to where the new highway was running
and which never needed irrigation, had all disappeared, and in
their space red tile- or slate-roof houses were standing randomly.

Originally, all the land from our house to the new highway was ours, and the railway ran just beyond the highway. But the land was now divided into so many houses, and the giant pine tree that stood guard over the fertile land had yielded its place to a cement-block store and a stone post with a "Provincial Boundary" sign in yellow paint, which stood like a sinister sentinel. Beyond the railway was the sea. Along the shore, village urchins used to play stark naked from spring to autumn. At ebb tide the far horizon glittered azure blue, and at full tide the water came almost up to the top of the embankment that was connected to the railway tracks. Gulls and herons hovered above the embankment, and along it chimneys from the salt farms baking fine-grain salt exhaled smoke that looked like sea mist. Anglers throwing for trouts used to line up on the embankment like herrings on a string, and on days when the sailboats brought in fish the fishermen's chants filled the air with melodies sweeter than the songs of the sea birds. But even the sea had disappeared. The shore was converted into paddies. The proverb, "The mulberry grove has become a blue sea," must describe just such cataclysmic change. The embankment stretched for more than six kilometers. The shore of fine sand on this side of the embankment, on which we played as children as if it were our own backyard, had turned into rice paddies with distinct boundaries. The roads between the paddies had crisscrossed prints of oxcart and handcart wheels, instead of being strewn with clams and gobies as of old.

Waking up from the reverie, I saw that the cloud had vanished and the sky and the field and the village were all covered with the glow of sunset. I prepared to climb down the hill. The temperature had dropped steeply.

There must be quite a few of my old neighbors still living in the village. But I could not drop in on them casually, for old time's sake. After addressing them all my life in the plain form as social inferiors, regardless of their age, I was at a loss as to how to address them now. It was a serious problem. I decided not to go around visiting old neighbors. Frankly, I was hoping I wouldn't even run into any of them by chance. It was only after making up my mind on that point that I turned my steps towards the village.

Until the day of my departure I had never used the honorific form to anyone except the elders in my family clan. It was by Grandfather's express order, and a habit I'd picked up naturally in the course of my childhood. To those men who were old or middle-aged, I used *sŏbang* after their surnames as a form of address for social inferiors, and I always addressed men in their thirties or younger by their given names. The women of the village I called so-

and-so's mother or so-and-so's aunt. That would be an unbearable impertinence in modern times, but in those days it was the most natural thing for them as well as for me. Grandfather insisted that since most of the villagers were servants of our clan members, plain form was the fitting mode of address. A consequence of Grandfather's class consciousness was that I had no friends throughout my childhood. I tried hard to make friends with the village boys, but they shunned me strenuously. In our village there were about a dozen of my contemporaries, but they all dreaded Grandfather as much as their parents did. I tried to ingratiate myself on them by trying to join their sleigh rides and tipcat games and giving presents of kites and tops I made, but they refused to make me one of their gang. Even so, from time to time Grandfather found out about my attempts to befriend them and admonished me, which made me lose my appetite and toss and turn in bed in trepidation. Grandfather never flogged me himself, but he would say, "For shame! I'll tell your father to give you a whipping." It was the most dreadful threat. But he never really ordered my father even to give me a scolding. It was from Ongjŏmi's telling on me that Grandfather got wind of my following the village urchins around. One of her favorite amusements was to see Grandfather lecturing me.

"Fie, did you play with those vulgar children? If you want to be chums with those commoners, why did you learn letters?"

I had no answer for that.

"What a pity you're always itching to play outdoors. Don't the phrases 'Seeking a quiet place to dwell' and 'To take a walk to dispel anxieties' mean anything to you?"

"But they ask me to play with them!"

"If you make companions of those vulgar children, you'll become vulgar like them. I warned you for your own good, but you never pay any attention."

Grandfather's reprimand was loud enough to be heard in the inner quarters, and I had to hear him out, hanging my head and crouching guiltily.

My conscience hurt me for the innocent lie I told Grandfather and made me gloomy afterwards, but I simply could not tell Grandfather that it was I who sought the boys out.

In all my years in the village, the village children never came to my house to ask me to join them in their games and expeditions, not even once. It was because from early on the children's parents, knowing Grandfather's views, had told them not to play with me. Even in elementary school, the village children reluctantly let me join their games if there were children from other villages in the group, or let me walk to and back from school with them if I ran into them by chance. Such constraint continued even after the elders in my family all died, so there was always an invisible chasm between them and me.

The Korean War broke out when I was a second grader in elementary school. The war wreaked havoc on my family. Grandfather's demise was a sorrow not just for my family but for the whole village, as it meant the loss of its revered spiritual patriarch. From the war I learned the precariousness of human affairs. I also learned, from the fact that the children kept avoiding me even after Grandfather had passed away, that not even cataclysmic changes can break ingrained mental habits. At any rate, it was embarrassing and inconvenient not to have friends even as a middle school student. I once aired my grievances to Mother. But she didn't sympathize with me.

"How can that bother you? There aren't any kids in this village worthy to be your friend. They don't want to mix with you because you're an excellent student and superior to them in every way," was what she said.

It was true that I was good at my studies. I had passed the entrance exam to middle school with the highest score, in spite of the difficult situation at home. Of course I was excited about it for a whole year.

Anyway, even though I was unhappy to be lonely, I didn't fret too much about it or feel like an outcast, since I knew it was a result of Grandfather's maintaining a strict class distinction in an effort to preserve the family dignity. As I suffered many quirks of fate from early on, I had learned to take things as they came.

I was shivering now as with an ague from the icy night wind blowing downhill. The earth crackled under my feet, its surface having frozen over again after melting in the rain. I hurried down the hill. But I was still reluctant to head straight to the village. I had not looked my fill at my old house. I decided to take the narrow alley that used to stretch from the top of the hill to the yard in front of the men's quarters.

Nothing in my old house—neither the yard trodden for two decades by its former masters; the well famous for its divine-tasting water; the rock beside the well that was an ideal place to bend over and have someone pour the cool water down one's back; the trees that were listed on the deed among the items to be transferred when the house and the garden patch were sold—not one of them seemed to recognize the return of its former master. No one was visible in the yard, and only the pigs oinked in their pen and a few chickens trotted across the yard. Perhaps the whole family was at dinner, judging from the clinking of metal coming from the inside. The wide veranda of the men's quarters still had a wooden floor, but instead of the bright and varnished look of yore it looked dark with ingrained dirt and was coated with dust. The ceiling above the floor had rat piss stains here and there, and the rafters under the eaves and the swallows' nest beneath the girder was thickly covered with cobwebs, a telltale sign that swallows weren't nesting there any more.

According to Grandfather, all the principles of geomantic philosophy were observed in building the house. It had the rear hill shielding the house from the back, and the paddies in the front serving as the felicitous bird of geomancy. It had proper protective formations on the left and the right, and its shape was a combination of the most auspicious layouts—in sum, a beautiful, spacious structure erected upon solid foundation.

"It is a superb house. It has good light, gentle wind and good water. Be sure to take good care of it after I take my place under the turf," he used to say. "Take my place under the turf" was his euphemism for dying. "I'm old and my faculties have decayed, so I'd have nothing to worry about as long as my modest barn doesn't become empty. But these troubled times make me uneasy," Grandfather used to say, and smile desolately. My family's finances had been declining ever since my great-grandfather resigned his post and retired to our hometown.

I had a momentary illusion of seeing Grandfather a while ago near the place that used to be his grave; I had another illusion of seeing him on the veranda of the men's quarters, and couldn't help shedding tears. Grandfather always had two rush mats spread before him on the veranda outside his study, and underneath the signboard that said "The fish soars out of the sea to the Heavens" in his bold calligraphic hand were hung his rattan muffs, which provided ventilation inside the sleeves in the summer, a woven reed rainhat, and his back scratcher. I played with the last item, being amused by its funny shape. On top of the square table that stood at the end of the veranda and which served as his desk lay an inkslab, calligraphy brushes and two feather fans. The three-tiered paulownia chest with the engraved plum tree decoration was relegated to a dark corner, being old and worn, and his cane used to lie lengthwise on the veranda. Recalling all these as if they were objects glimpsed in a dream, I stood there absently under the darkening eave, like a stray traveler who didn't know which way to proceed.

I recollected myself, espying through the door between the living room and the kitchen of the men's quarters flames flickering in the stove heating the floor of the men's study. Inside that door was the kitchen of the men's quarters, which had a huge iron pot hanging over the floor-heating stove. As we never raised cattle, the iron pot was not used to cook cattle fodder but simply to heat water. It was also used at times for cooking bean pastes and fish juices and for hardening bean curds, buckwheat cakes, and corn and pumpkin candies.

As soon as smoke began to seep out I could tell at once what was being burned for fuel. The pleasant smell told me they were burning bean pods and millet stalks. That smell, which I hadn't smelled for over a decade, suddenly brought on a keen nostalgia for the days I fed bean pods and millet stalks into the stove. Even though I had to till the land then with my own hands, I have much stronger nostalgia for those days of my adolescence than for my childhood in which I was fed with delicacies and pampered by all the villagers, including the hoary-haired old men who called me "young master." I recalled the various odors that used to come from the stove of the men's study. We made buckwheat jelly only now and then, but the smell of bean curd congealing and the corn or pumpkin candies hardening were smells that had seeped into every part of my body. We made candies every year after harvest, as soon as the ancestral offering was over. From candies we got the syrup for feast days such as the New Year or Grandfather's birthday, but more importantly they were made into snacks for Grandfather who neither drank nor smoked. Grandfather had the hardened glutinous candies in a jar in the closet of his study, so that his grandchildren always hankered after the candy jar in his closet. Mother never allowed his closet to run out of snacks, just as she made sure a fresh bowl of rice water was placed on his stationery chest every evening.

Mother was famous for her culinary art, and she was a proper and pious daughter-in-law as well. So she prepared for her aged father-in-law all seasonal and timely food and snacks. She cooked abundant rice cake soup in early January. For the January Full Moon Day she cooked glutinous rice flavored with caramel water and many kinds of nuts, as well as various kinds of cool drinks and nuts for cracking and crunching according to custom. Throughout the year she cooked gruel with seasonal specialties and several kinds of cakes and pancakes; she stewed chicken in the peak of summer and cooked red bean paste at winter solstice. And she never failed to broil seasoned meat on a day in December when it was customarily eaten. On the days Grandfather took outings, I always went through his closet to filch snacks. His closet contained not only honey and candies but glutinous rice cakes and fruits and nuts. In the spring and fall dried fish fillets and dried shellfish were found. And the various medicinal herbs served to refresh my mouth in the summer. I didn't always have to steal, as Grandfather often called me in to share his delicacies, and I could also buy candies and fruit easily with the pocket money Mother gave me. But my appetite was ravenous then, and filching just so much of the food as Grandfather with his poor eyesight wouldn't notice was a special thrill as well. Before I began studying the "Thousand Characters" I used to fret and beg Mother for snacks sitting on the living room floor, loud enough to be heard in the men's quarters. It was a trick to draw Grandfather's attention. At those times Ongjŏmi would goad me on, whispering in my ear, "Sob a little louder."

Sooner or later, Grandfather would call out from his study: "Why is he crying? Has he got a stomachache or something?" Then, it was sure to be followed by, "Here, give him this medicine."

At that, I'd get ready to run, as there was nothing I hated more than taking medicine.

"Oh, your lordship, he's not sick. He's only crying for candy," Ongjŏmi would retort instantly, in her loud voice.

If I was lucky, Grandfather would respond, instead of exclaiming "Fie," or "Shame!," "Well, let him come here." Then I'd enter his study sheepishly, to find him waiting for me with a chunk of pumpkin-flavored glutinous candy rolled round his silver spoon. Biting off the chewy candy from the spoon was the most delicious fun in the world! But Grandfather became less generous to me when his great-grandson became a toddler.

It was when I was seven and my nephew was three. I had mastered the "Thousand Characters" and was beginning the "Children's Primer." My nephew had supplanted me as the recipient of Grandfather's treats while I was studying the "Thousand Characters." So I had to devise ways of worming them out of Grandfather. One method was to make my nephew cry, so Grandfather would pacify him with treats, and share in the spoil. Another trick was to teach the toddler obscene words and make him babble them in front of Grandfather. As the old man could hardly scold or reason with the toddler, he would give him treats and send him away. It succeeded every time.

I would enter Grandfather's study with my nephew, and he would blurt out the words at the top of his voice, clapping hands. For example, he would point at Grandfather's topknot visible through the diaphanous horsehair headband and hat and chant, "Look, look, Grandfather has a cock on his head. A cock on his head!"

Then Grandfather would cough a couple of times, pretend to yawn, and turn to open the closet door. Each time, the contents of his candy jar would dwindle. After a while my nephew would put on the act without my prompting, so I could snack on the candy without putting myself through any trouble.

Smoke was rising not just from the stove of men's study. I noticed smoke curling up from the chimney of the outer quarters beside the gate as well. The color of the smoke from that chimney revealed that the fuel was dead grass and fallen leaves raked from the hills. The outer quarters was originally a tin-roofed separate building with two rooms and a gate of its own. The field hand occupied one of the rooms where we also stored grain sacks, and the other served as a dry storage. So the latter was never heated, and rarely if ever lit up at night.

Today, however, that room was clearly being heated. That meant people were sleeping in it. The railway officer's family couldn't be that large, so the room must have been rented out. I wondered what kind of people were inhabiting that room. I recalled that the room had a papered floor and was kept clean at all times, but it always gave me a creepy feeling. It was because of the kind of things being stored in that room. I walked away, remembering what were in that room. As a child I tried to avoid going into the room. I was always on guard lest grown-ups should tell me to fetch something from the room. If I had to enter the room for any reason, I tried to take someone with me, even if it were only my toddler nephew. The room used to be filled with a variety of objects. There were sheaves of medicinal roots and plants, a dark offering table, the table for the incense burner, and a full set of ritual wares. There were also great piles of genealogy books and many other books, and the engraving press for book covers. But it was not these that gave me the creeps. It was the coffin covered with a hemp cloth that lay in the innermost part of the room that made me shiver. On top of the coffin was a big bundle wrapped in a huge hemp sheet. It contained the whole set of Grandfather's shroud and the mourning apparels for family and servants and funeral accessories. They were there because Grandfather was in his late eighties and could pass away any day. I dreaded the sight of the coffin and the bundle of shroud. The sight of a funeral procession passing on the highway, preceded by a hemp banner and with a black-bordered funeral tent fluttering in the wind, was not an uncommon one. When I met them, I shuddered and tried to shake off the sinister feeling.

The Korean War wrought havoc on my family. The war

brought disaster to innumerable families, of course, and ours was one of the most severely hurt.

In December of that year Grandfather passed away. He died an unhappy man, who suffered the supreme misfortune of seeing his son and oldest grandson die before him. A straw mat and a bamboo staff lay on the veranda of the men's quarters for three years, and the inner long coat of hemp hung limp from the wall like a hanged corpse. They were my ritual garments and accessories for making offerings to the dead.

I was the only one among the surviving family who wasn't present at Grandfather's deathbed. I had been sent to a relative's to escape the war. Grandfather didn't pass away from a lingering or sudden illness. I suppose the atrocious misfortunes he suffered in his final days made him let go of the thread of life. He was ninety. His last words were, "Please take care of our genealogy books."

That was all. Genealogy. I suppose, for an old man who tried to uphold the family pride and dignity even in the midst of decay, the book of family genealogy was more valuable than titles and deeds to the houses and land.

Now, living in my tiny apartment, I am holding onto the genealogy books whose information hasn't been updated since Grandfather's time, as the most precious family heirloom. When I miss Grandfather, I leaf through the seven volumes containing the genealogy of the whole branch of our clan. I often have the illusion that I can smell Grandfather between those old leaves.

It wasn't as if Grandfather was well-versed in genealogies of prominent families, or that he was a snob. Our clan doesn't boast many prime ministers and ministers, but my ancestors served in the king's government generation after generation. Grandfather always felt guilty that he remained a private scholar, and deemed himself unworthy of his ancestors. At any rate, he honored his forebears and tried to conduct his whole life in accordance with the dignity befitting the heir of such an honorable clan.

It was he who changed the name of our village from Kalmŏri to Kwanch'on, meaning "the village of horsehair hats." Traditionally, of course, only the scholar-literati class was allowed to wear horsehair hats. Now, even natives of the village are more familiar with the name of Kwanch'on than its original name, Kalmŏri. Just as nowadays most people know where the town of Taech'ŏn is but few know Hannae, the town's old and purely Korean name with the same meaning.

Grandfather never took off his headband and inner hat during the day in all his ninety years of life, and he never went barefoot even in the most sweltering heat. It was because of Grandfather's strict adherence to decorum that Mother could never wear the convenient bloomerlike trousers most women wore for work-clothes and Ongjŏmi could never cut her hair short. It wasn't that Grandfather expressly forbade them. It was just that the women never dared do anything they knew Grandfather would disapprove.

Grandfather's sobriquet was Nŭng'ha. Born in 1861, he was the son of the prefect of Sangju and grandson of the mayor of Kangnŭng. But he didn't take the state civil service exams. I heard that it was because by the time he was old enough to take the exam all the elders in the clan had resigned their offices and came back to their hometown to live in retirement, and, with the family circumstances declining, he simply didn't have the determination to study for the exam. He blamed the decline and fall of the country as the reason for his remaining a private person, and he deemed himself unlucky. He was a true conservative who honored his ancestors' way of life, and he disapproved of his eminent kinsman Yi Sangjae, one of the leading exponents of modernization and reform, for abandoning his ancestors' way of life. Disliking modernism, he took the position opposite that of his distant cousin.

The only office Grandfather had held was the chancellorship of the Hwa'am Academy, which was located in Okkye, in the nearby county of Ch'ŏngna. He was already in his eighties as far back as I can remember, but palanquins used to come to our house to take him to the academy at spring and autumn ritual offering times. Grandfather didn't reside in the academy but took care of all the business from his study in our house. So, servants belonging to the academy walked the six kilometers to my house to consult his opinions and get his seal of approval on documents. However, when I was old enough to know what an academy was, Grandfather had in fact resigned his office, using his old age as an excuse. The academy had survived all kinds of interference and insults from the Japanese during the occupation, but it was powerless before the tide of modernism and the spread of modern educational institutions. I suppose it was that, rather than his old age, which was the real reason Grandfather resigned his chancellorship. I don't know how well he discharged his office. I simply don't have enough information to form a judgment on that point.

The servant of the academy who came to my house most often was an old man of about sixty. He wore a woven bamboo hat, straw shoes, no coat over his shirt and trousers, and carried a pouch. When he met me at the entrance of the village or beside the highway, he would repeatedly bow low and greet me with, "Young master, is his lordship home?"

"Yes, he's in the study," I'd respond.

One time, I came home with him, rushed into Grandfather's study, and said, "Here's a guest for you."

"What guest?"

"An old gentleman," I said.

Later I was reprimanded for having called him a guest and a gentleman. Grandfather always greeted him, "Oh, is that you, Subok?" as if the old man had been a mere child. It was much later that I learned that the old man was a bond servant belonging to the academy. Grandfather greeted the young servant from the academy with "Oh, is that you, Subok?" as well, so I began to wonder about the appellation of "Subok." Do all menservants in the academy have the same name, "Subok?" I thought up all possible combinations of the letters "su" and "bok" among the thousand characters I'd learned, but could not get a handle on the problem. It was rare that so many people had the same name in one village. Considering that my own name was changed several times on account of there being children and relatives with the same name in the village and clan, it was odd that all the servants of the academy had the same name. So, I finally asked Mother, "Are all the servants of the academy named Subok?" My mother answered casually, "Of course they're subok while they serve in the academy." Only then did it occur to me that "subok" was not a proper name but a word made up of the "su" character for "to keep" and the "bok" character for "servant."

Grandfather's authority was absolute to the servants of the academy. He was also the living law of the entire village and its vicinity. Not only was he descended from the most prestigious family line in the area and officiated at the ritual offerings at the academy shrines, but he himself was also such an embodiment of scholarly dignity and decorum that not only commoners but also *yangban* paid him the utmost respect.

As I said, Grandfather was eighty when I was born, so I could have had only a very partial picture of the old man in his retirement, and that seen through a child's eye. But I can't help regarding him as the greatest influence on my life, and a person whom I cannot forget even for a day. Was it because I was the only one of his grandchildren who tried to uphold his teachings and precepts? It is true that my father, who had chosen the path opposite Grandfather's long before I was born, defied and disregarded those time-honored precepts.

Of course Father's choice was not from any personal disrespect for his father, nor did he hold the ancient precepts worthless. Father was a man of such filial loyalty that if Grandfather had demanded his life he would have gladly given it. But Father chose a different ideology for himself.

Father seemed to set little value on his *yangban* descent. Of his family line he valued only the fact that there have been a few scholar-officials of exemplary probity. He never tried to sell his *yangban* descent, nor did he complain about the lack of inheritance from his ancestors. Neither did Grandfather, but Grandfather was not in a position to complain, as it was he who had wasted a substantial ancestral legacy. He had inherited from his father, who had been the mayor of Kangnŭng, real estate of considerable value, which he had sold off bit by bit, to speculate in the grain market during the Japanese occupation. Father, in contrast, had financial acumen. He was a legal scrivener by profession, but he was also the owner of several fishing vessels and many tracts of salt farm until a few years before my birth.

However, around the time of national liberation, or rather from the year of my birth, Father became a revolutionary. He denounced the class system as a pernicious evil, and devoted himself to fighting for the advent of a society in which the indigent masses would become the masters. Father made speeches on every market day, on the sands of the Hannae shore or in the market squares. I heard that he was an eloquent orator who won the enthusiastic admiration and support of farmers and laborers. It was many years afterwards that he became affiliated with the South Labor Party. Naturally, a rift grew between Grandfather and Father. But, although Grandfather disapproved of Father's thoughts and activities, he did not try to stop him. Perhaps he felt powerless to stem the irresistible tide of history that had forced him early on to lead a retired life.

By the time I mastered the "Thousand Characters" and was learning the "Children's Primer" from Grandfather, Father spent more days in jail than at home. He wasn't a scrivener or a shipowner any more; instead he was only a small-scale farmer barely managing on the little plot of land that fell to his share after the land reform.

My boyhood was thus spent in two totally different worlds. The men's quarters of my house had two big rooms. The inner study was the haven of Grandfather, who spent his days sitting upright at his desk, with his back to the closet that contained the snacks I hankered after. The room was also a haunt of all the surviving ancient scholars of the Yi Dynasty, in which they whiled away their time lamenting the state of affairs in the country and the mores of the times. The other room was Father's drawing room. Grandfather's room bustled with decrepit old men who could bare-

ly walk leaning on their canes. Mother often said, after taking meal
or snack trays to Grandfather's study, that the stale smell those old
men gave off was suffocating.

Father's guests were even shabbier than Grandfather's. Most of
them were indigent villagers whose existence Grandfather never
bothered to notice. They gathered in my house as soon as they'd
eaten supper. There were the village firewood seller, the blacksmith, the former ferryman turned salted shrimp vendor, the
laborer on the salt farm, the carpenter, the tinman, the mill worker, the grain middleman, and so on. They were daily guests. In
addition to them, there were numerous stray visitors who made our
house their temporary lodging, sharing our field hand's room for
one night. They were mostly traveling salesmen or itinerant trades-
men, such as the salt vendor, the candyman, and the fortuneteller.
If it weren't for the fear of police raids, our house would have overflowed with guests day and night. Father's guests called each other
"comrades."

Such behavior of Father's may have provided an added incen-
tive for Grandfather to raise me, his grandson, in the traditional
way of life. Teaching me the "Thousand Characters" may have
been his way of inculcating in me reverence for classical learning
and the classical way of life. Anyway, it seemed to give him solace to
teach me the Chinese characters. The text used was the thousand
characters written in his own calligraphic hand. He had transcribed them in his youth for the instruction of his posterity. At
first I was his only pupil. But I made no progress. I just didn't have
any interest in what I was taught. So, Mother suggested that I have
some companions to study with. But Grandfather wouldn't listen.
"How can I let him have commoners' children for his school fel-
lows? That's unheard-of!"

However, as I continued to be bored and inattentive,
Grandfather at last decided to give me some school companions.
So, two of my contemporaries in the village, Chunbae and
Chinhyŏn, were invited to share my lessons. They were children of
people who had moved into the village from elsewhere. They were
chosen because Grandfather couldn't bring himself to teach
descendants of former slaves of the clan and official clerks of yore.

The lessons were conducted in two daily sessions, from ten to
twelve and from two to four or five. The two children came on the
first day with their textbooks printed on cardboard paper bought
from the market. And they each had in the textbook a bamboo
stick a foot long, for the convenience of pointing at each character.

Needless to say, the lessons flew on wings from that day. We
were so excited about playing together afterwards that we were

eager to get through the day's lesson as fast as we could. After the lesson was over, we went up the mountain or ran out to the sea and played until darkness forced us to return home. To the rear of my house was a small hill covered with baby pines. To the front, there were rice paddies bordered by overgrown bushes. Further down there were the new highway and the railway, and then the sea. Grandfather gave us short breaks during lessons, but they were no fun, as we had to return to the study the minute Grandfather called out my name. So, we began to devise tricks.

One of us would say, in the middle of a lesson, "Sir, I need to pee," and pretend to loosen his belt.

"My, you boys relieve yourselves much too often."

We would hang our heads.

"Don't eat salty food. It's because you eat salty food that you drink a lot of water and have to go to the outhouse so often."

We'd hang our heads even lower.

"Well, be quick about it."

Then all three of us would rush out together. Grandfather's eyesight was extremely poor, so if we were swift and quiet he could easily be hoodwinked. And he never used the rod on us. He said that as he was teaching the boys for the sake of teaching his own grandson, flogging would be unjustifiable.

Grandfather seemed to find much pleasure and comfort in teaching us. Before, he had to spend all his days sitting in the lotus posture and recall, with eyes closed, memories of the past or his favorite passages from the books he'd read in his youth. So, scolding, cajoling and exhorting three urchins must have been an excellent pastime and exercise for him.

I was way ahead of my companions in learning. There were two reasons for this: one was that I had a few days' head start over them, and the other and more important reason was that we had different textbooks.

My textbook, which was in Grandfather's calligraphy, did not have the meaning and pronunciation annotated in Korean. But the text my companions used, which was a commercial publication, did. Of course, none of us could read any Korean, but it did make a difference. I committed to memory the meaning and pronunciation of the characters as they came from Grandfather's lips, but the other kids went over the text with their parents at home. Now, Grandfather's Korean was more than half a century older than the one used in the textbook. So, all I had to do was to memorize the meaning and the pronunciation as they were given to us by Grandfather, but my friends got confused between his instruction and what their parents read to them.

Anyway, we managed to get through the meaning and the pronunciation of the thousand characters in a few months, and then
we memorized the whole thing from first to last and again backwards from last to first. A few days later, we moved on to the
"Children's Primer" and could easily recite phrases after
Grandfather, imitating his melodious intonation.

After reading a passage, Grandfather expounded the meaning
in a way we children could understand, using analogies. It was
much more interesting than merely learning the characters.

However, the lessons involved other responsibilities for me,
which made me want to grow up quickly. It was Grandfather's firm
conviction that one must practice the precepts one has learned.
So, he made up a list of things I had to do as a student of the teachings of the classical sages. That meant I had to get up at four
o'clock in the morning, regardless of the time of year, and perform
the duties assigned me.

Getting up at four, I washed my face in cold water—
Grandfather forbade the use of warm water, for the reason that
warm water made one lazy and effeminate—and went to
Grandfather's study to pay my respects. I made a deep bow before
him and then, kneeling before him, asked after his health.

He responded with, "Oh, yes, have you slept well, too?" The
next task was to clean his brass stool and spittoon. From the time I
began to perform this drudgery, Ongjŏmi grew even more kind
and affectionate to me, because cleaning those items were her
most detested chores. Cleaning the stool wasn't all that bad. But
pouring out the contents of the spittoon and scrubbing it clean
was an abominable task. After that I scrubbed the floor of the study
with a wet mop. Only then did dawn break. Then, until sunrise I
had to recite, kneeling before Grandfather, the lessons of the previous day. As there were guests staying in either or both of the
rooms of the men's quarters most of the time, I had to be especially careful not to slip or falter. The guests listened breathlessly, and
most of the time I got through that part without a single mistake.

"What do you think?" Grandfather would ask his guests, and
they delighted him with unstinting praise. Grandfather's teaching
extended to dietary matters as well. He began to warn and exhort
me about which food to desist and stay away from when I began to
learn the "Thousand Characters." When we reached the phrase
"Among vegetables mustard and ginger are the most precious," he
explained, "People are apt to take vegetables for granted, and prepare them without much care and eat them without much
thought. But a gentleman must be careful about his diet, and it
begins with vegetables. You must remember this phrase and never

eat vegetables that are not seasoned with mustard and ginger. Just as you must remember that the gold that comes from Yŏsu and the jade from Kon'gang are the most precious among ores and stones."

"I see, sir," I would reply, automatically as I did to all his other admonitions.

"Remember, even when you eat outside home you must not touch anything that isn't seasoned with mustard and ginger."

So, for years afterwards I tried awfully hard to avoid eating kim-chi and seasoned herbs when eating at other people's houses. Even today I often recall that phrase at mealtimes. In those days there were many celebrations and feasts in our village. One late autumn no less than five weddings were celebrated in Kwanch'on. It was an unwritten rule that any house in the village that held a feast should send a table loaded with food to Grandfather. That was the tribute villagers paid to the oldest and most venerable elder of the village. The table was usually carried by two sturdy youths and placed on the veranda in men's quarters.

"Who sent this?" Grandfather would ask the men, but before they could answer, Ongjŏmi would say, swallowing, "The herb doc-tor's daughter's getting married."

Grandfather would dismiss the men with, "Please convey my appreciation and good wishes."

After they left, Ongjŏmi would draw away the cover, and Grandfather would ask her what kinds of food were there. Ongjŏmi would call out the names of the dishes one by one.

Then, with a face that plainly said he didn't expect any of it to have been prepared right, Grandfather would take a sip of the cool beverage made with dried persimmons soaked in cinnamon water or sweet fermented rice in juice and would exclaim every time, "Shame! Do they call this food? You go ahead and eat them and return the table." That, of course, would make Ongjŏmi and me to grin from ear to ear. Grandfather was that particular about food.

Father was the opposite of Grandfather in that as well as in many other respects. He ate all kinds of food with anyone. And he didn't even scold me when my diet grew more and more unbal-anced, like Grandfather's. And he seemed unconcerned about my excessive timidity before strangers, arising from implicit obser-vance of the Confucian precept of deference to elders. In fact, even to this day I shrink before people. I would fain be invisible, if possible. I realize now that such extreme deference is of no use, either to myself or to anyone else. Of course it might be argued that it is because the times are wrong that such virtues have become worthless. But I'm inclined to think that even in the old days that precept took away from many men due recognition of their merits. It is sad that timid people like myself have to serve other people's needs all the time and never get our just deserts. Humility brings no satisfaction of any kind to a man like me who is not destined to be a saint. I find it hard to understand that I inherited none of my father's bold disregard of traditional forms. It is certainly very unfortunate. Father's way of thinking was diametrically opposite that of Grandfather's. He always did what would make Grandfather shudder. If, on his way somewhere, he happened to hear of a rice planting or harvesting carried out by numerous villagers, he would always drop by, donate some money towards the purchase of rice wine, and join in the drinking. No matter how busy he was, if a farmer saw him pass by and invited him to share his snack, he'd stop by, take a spoonful, and exchange greetings. The only things Grandfather and Father agreed on were that offerings to our ancestors should be observed with the utmost care, that no member of their family should go near either a Christian church or a Buddhist temple, and that offerings should be made every year to the gods on the first Horse Day of October. The latter practice was a carryover from the time Father used to be a shipowner and had to propitiate the spirits of the sea. There were other minor things, too, on which they agreed: women should never enter the men's quarters; men should use separate facilities from women and children; no man should even go near the kitchen, except servants; everyone, including children, should be decorously and formally attired at all times, even in hot summer; and men should never speak with women outside their own family and should never go near the village well where women work and chat. In everything else, they had different ideas.

It is true that Father was even more conservative than Grandfather in some respects. But he had the boldness and tolerance that Grandfather lacked. For an organizer of an underground network those must have been necessary and appropriate traits. However, to his children Father was strict to the point of severity. And, unlike a man who was in constant danger of being arrested, jailed and tortured, he was always calm and dignified and never acted flustered even during crises.

I stood in constant awe of Father. It might be more correct to say that I was terrified of him. Though famous for his eloquence, he was always taciturn at home. It was this taciturnity, composure, dignity and courage that I noted in his bearing much more than generosity and tolerance, and it inspired in me a reverence akin to fear. Once, Father spent close to a month in jail. It was one of the many times he was in jail, so I've forgotten the incident for which he was arrested and detained that time. Anyway, I carried his meals to the police station twice each day. Depending on the offence charged, sending in meals to prison could be forbidden. During those times we had to bribe the prison caterer to prepare special meals for Father. But in this instance there was no interdiction. So, I carried the heavy, steaming meal trays to the prison twice a day. After bringing the meal tray, I waited for Father to eat the meal in the presence of the policeman and then returned home with the empty dishes. With two trips a day to the police station, the days flew by quickly. I wasn't afraid of the policemen. On the contrary, I felt pride in the fact that I was the son of a prominent political prisoner.

It was Father I was afraid of. Seeing him talking and laughing nonchalantly behind bars filled me with dread. His dauntlessness in the face of imprisonment and even worse dangers and affliction struck fear into me. I quailed to think of his convictions that made him unafraid of death. On the day of his release, he stepped out of prison with brisk steps, his health having been preserved thanks to the meals I had taken him. Heading home, he took my hand that was still holding a warm meal tray, and said, "Have you been obeying your Grandfather like a good boy?" I don't hesitate to say that that was the decisive moment of rupture between myself and Father. The fact that he never acknowledged, even by a word, my taking the trouble to carry the heavy meal trays to him for a whole month, was consistent with his principle of bringing up his children strictly. But he seemed so heartless that it aroused in me a feeling akin to terror.

It was followed by another incident that made me even more terrified of Father. I think the two incidents made me the timid, shiftless and insignificant person that I am, both at home and outside. The second incident is more significant than the first, in that it was connected with Father's first and only attempt to teach me something. It lasted maybe about an hour. Father must have had some spare time that day. He had Grandfather's calligraphy table brought into his study and called me in. It was a spring day, and a drizzle that nurtures the new leaves was falling outside. The time was around eleven o'clock, so it was the ideal weather and time for studying quietly.

First of all, Father bade me rub ink on the ink slab. I performed that part all right, thanks to having rubbed ink for Grandfather from time to time. Father explained to me how to rub ink to an appropriate thickness without splashing it all around, showed me the best posture for calligraphy writing, and taught me how to hold the brush, how much strength to apply, and how to

turn the brush. Then, he told me to practice the horizontal stroke
a dozen times on the white-painted board used for the purpose.
With beads of perspiration forming on my forehead, I did as bidden with shaking hands. Father's breath on my neck sent chills
down my spine. I don't think even a born calligraphic genius, if his
heart was trembling like mine, could have executed those strokes
much better. Whenever the brush faltered, I saw an abyss opening
before me. But the trial didn't last long. Thunder struck pretty
soon: "How can a child's hand be so stiff? You're not fit for anything but fieldwork."

Oh, how can I forget the despair of that moment? Father's
words were scarcely more than a muttered lament, and weren't
even heard by Grandfather in the other study, but it was more terrible than thunder to me. When I recovered my senses, Father had
already left the room. I hadn't even heard a visitor calling Father
out. I was unutterably ashamed and hurt, but for the moment I was
relieved to escape the trial, so I hurried back to Mother's room.
How grateful I was to the visitor of that day!

From that day I hated myself for being such a dullard. I felt
mortal shame. Father didn't seem inclined to teach me calligraphy
again after that day. But for many days afterwards I practiced calligraphy in secret, on newspaper spread in the closet room at the end
of the corridor. I felt I had to get over my shame and humiliation
by earning Father's approval. But I gave up the hope soon after
that. The atmosphere of my house, which was filled with danger
and uncertainty all the time, didn't allow me even that much spon-
taneous exertion. But it was a desperate battle I had with the brush
while it lasted.

It is on the strength of those few days' intensive practice that I
sometimes write posters of programs and agendas with brush and
ink for conferences and such.

Before rounding the bend beside the gardenia hedge of the
orchard, I halted a moment and took one last look at my old
house. The sun was about to rest its tired body on the western top
of the Dragon Ridge, and the smoke from the chimneys, which
had been veiling the twilight, had mostly subsided, and was just lingering under the eaves. I then turned my eyes towards the Dipper
Rocks, hoping to catch another glimpse of Grandfather, but his
image was gone. However, I felt as if Grandfather's spirit was hovering over his former grave, which he had so treasured as his eternal
resting place. "Goodbye, dear old house," I whispered inwardly,
looking at it for the last time. The sun was sinking behind the western ridge far beyond.

The Mural

_~_

Kim Yŏng-hyŏn

_Kim Yŏng-hyŏn, born in 1953, stands for a whole generation of intel-
lectual dissidents and idealists. The military regime of South Korea,
which lasted from 1961 to 1992 with only a half-a-year break following the assassination of President Park Chung Hee, produced numerous student dissidents and "democratic warriors," who experienced
brutal repressions under the military government. Some of them were
able to turn the records of their persecution into assets for their political
rise, but most of them had to live with lingering physical and psychological aftermaths and the distrust of the public who considered them
as threats to established order. Kim Yŏng-hyŏn, a former philosophy
major at Seoul National University, said that the experience of having
lived under military dictatorship distorts the human personality, which
becomes overly defensive, timid, self-righteous or compromising. So,
Kim is a trustworthy chronicler of the lives and consciousness of those
whose causes have disappeared and whose lives must be reconstructed
out of the debris of their youthful and idealistic dreams._

_"The Mural" (1994) presents a central character who is rather
like the author himself. He is an artist whose aesthetic interest lies with
the internal and eternal aspects of humanity but who has been compelled by the historical reality to join the struggle for social justice. The
mural of the retreat center he paints indicates how the author yearns
for a Jesus who can suffer and grieve with humanity, instead of a triumphant and transcendent divinity. The story has a special meaning
for Koreans who lived through the dark years of military dictatorship
when just leading a normal life constituted compromise with injustice
and insensitivity to the wrongs all around them._

W hen the train made its way out of the station, the view began
to change almost immediately. Run-down houses along the
train track with television antennae jutting out on low roofs; ball-
shaped industrial water tank; tall, thin chimneys emitting smoke;
the construction site of an apartment complex, work on which has
been suspended for some time; signboards of shabby inns commonly seen around train stations; dirty ditches that meander
through indigent neighborhoods . . . These and other uncouth
sights came and then passed as the train moved, like images in a
slow-motion video. A gloomy winter sky overspread that shabby
landscape like a worn blanket.

When the train began to accelerate after emerging out of the
city, Chaesŏp folded the newspaper he had been inattentively
glancing through, dropped it on his knees, yawned, and looked
out the window with watery eyes. The snow that had fallen a few
days ago had still not quite melted, so patches of it remained in the
shade between houses and mountain valleys, like scabs. Beyond the
plank wall of a shanty house beside the track, Chaesŏp could see a
young woman in the yard and a thickly clad toddler sitting on the
veranda. The baby gazed at the train as it flitted past noisily, but
the young woman went on spreading laundry and didn't pay any
attention to the train. When the train was completely out of the
city, houses became scarce and instead a wide plain, a desolate
mountain, and a creek came into view. They spread out and receded from Chaesŏp's view, like objects on the surface of a continuously opening folding fan.

Along either side of the creek that kept hiding behind the low
hill and then reappearing with a glazed surface stood rows of leaf-
less poplar trees, like newly drafted soldiers at attention, with the
cold winter wind whipping their bare branches mercilessly. But
warm rays of the winter sun streamed in through the train windows, so bright that Chaesŏp had to squint to protect his eyes.
Moreover, because the radiator was turned on to full capacity, the
air was stuffy, even though it was still early morning.

As the view changed from urban to rustic, his life, which had
been oppressing him with an unbearable weight up to just an hour
ago, began to take on an atmosphere of unreality. The faces of his
landlady to whom he had said good-bye earlier that morning, of
his wife who left home some time ago, of his pals with whom he
drank until midnight last night, and of his friend Pak Myŏngho
and his girlfriend Yŏng'ae, and the alleys and streets he walked
every day all became blurred and dim, like objects in a faded photo
in a worn-out frame. But Chaesŏp's head was still filled with many

problems, and a gloomy oppression weighed on him. So, he felt depressed, guilty and uneasy, all without a particular and clear reason.

After gazing out absently for quite a while, Chaesŏp stood up and took out a book from his backpack on the overhead rack. It took some maneuvering to extricate the book from the backpack crammed with painting tools and clothes. Then he sat down again. It was a paperback novel.

Having come upon the book in a corner of his bookshelf, he had been reading it for the past few days, but without much concentration. His head was all in a confused muddle, so he had not been able to make much progress. On the front cover was printed the title *And Never Said a Word* in small letters. Chaesŏp thumbed through the book, but couldn't remember where he'd left off, so he just picked a likely passage and began reading.

The scene he began reading described Fred, the hero who worked as a telephone operator in a church-related organization, meeting Kate, his wife, and going to a cheap inn with her. The novel by Heinrich Böll depicted the inner consciousness of a middle-aged couple leading gloomy and painful lives in destitute and hopeless Germany after it was defeated in the war. Chaesŏp had the illusion that he was just like Fred, the timid and nervous hero in his fifties. And it occurred to him that you could not expect much from life after all. But, being as much absorbed in his own thoughts as in reading, he kept losing his place in the book.

"Would you care for a piece of this?"

Chaesŏp came to himself at hearing these words, and looked at the man sitting next to him. He had been there from the first, but being preoccupied with his own thoughts, Chaesŏp had not paid him any attention. The man, who looked to be in his late fifties, was wearing a formal suit with a necktie, but the suit was obviously old, as it had wide lapels and the sleeves were threadbare at the wrist. His hollow-cheeked face was deeply furrowed, and his hair was grey, with even strands of black and white. Long-nosed and innocent-eyed, he looked guileless. On a newspaper spread out on his lap was a bunch of sliced laver rolls of rice.

"Oh, no thank you," Chaesŏp said courteously and with deliberate stiffness, lowering his book and smiling lightly. The tone of exaggerated politeness was meant to discourage any friendly overture, as he was in no mood for small talk with a stranger. Even though he felt gloomy and uneasy, Chaesŏp wanted to be left alone to his own thoughts. That was why he left on this journey in the first place.

"Where are you going?" the man asked, not sensing his mood.

"To T'aebaek," Chaesŏp responded, even more stiffly than before.

"To T'aebaek? Then you must change the bus at Chechŏn. What takes you to Taebaek?" the middle-aged man asked, surprised at hearing Chaesŏp's destination and looking at him with curiosity.

"Well, I'm just going there to . . . rest a bit," Chaesŏp returned, barely concealing his irritation and resenting the need to observe even that much etiquette. Then he returned to his book with exaggerated eagerness. Where was I? Oh, yes, Fred borrows money from the priest for his wife and children. With a part of that money he drinks at a pub and plays the slot machine. He wanted to return to his wife and children, but in the hovel of his rented room there was no space for him. He had been a wireless operator during the war. He was a good man, but there was nothing he could do to better his lot.

"You're going to T'aebaek to rest? Won't you have even a bite? Well, going to T'aebaek of all places for rest! One of my daughters lives there. Believe me, that's no place for a rest," the middle-aged man said, munching on the rice, as if talking to himself.

"You don't look like a miner. I can tell a miner at a glance. Well, I used to be a government clerk until quite recently. A white-collar worker, that is. It was only a small town hall, but everybody in the town knew me. Then I got my retirement money and went to live with my daughter in Seoul, but my son-in-law's firm went bankrupt . . . "

The middle-aged man began to unfold his life history, as if he thought he met just the right person for conversation. Chaesŏp pretended to listen to him and tried to return to his own thoughts. What was I thinking about? But he wasn't exactly thinking about anything. He was following a vague image, or an ineffable feeling. The feeling was rather painful but there was something delectable in it, and also something searing.

Then it occurred to him that he himself didn't have a clear idea as to why he was going to T'aebaek. Going there to take a rest . . . well, that wasn't totally untrue. And he even had a definite purpose for going there, too. It was to paint a mural on the wall of a new building of the retreat center there. The priest who was the director of the center was a friend of his friend Myŏng'ho. He wanted someone to paint a mural on the front wall of the building he had managed to have built. Chaesŏp wasn't asked by the director himself. The director had asked Myŏng'ho, but Myŏng'ho was busy with something else, so he had suggested that Chaesŏp do it.

Myŏngho had also made it clear that the center probably couldn't pay him anything for the work.

Chaesŏp had some experience in mural painting. In the '80s, under Pak Myŏngho's direction, he and a bunch of his friends had painted a huge mural over thirty meters high on the wall of a factory. They had worked on it for a whole month in the summer, and then one day someone had smeared white paint all over it. He had stood there aghast, feeling all strength draining out of him. Later on he found out that it was the work of the district office, acting under the order from the police which took issue with the subject of the painting.

That incident led to a legal battle over the freedom of artistic expression and illegal installation of art between the artists' association and the authorities. It ended without a verdict, as the factory owner withdrew his suit under pressure. Chaesŏp felt disappointed that his efforts of so many days could disappear in a flash, like a bubble.

But Pak Myŏngho's concept of art was different from his. Myŏngho held that no work of art can last forever, and that an artist should work for his own times. He valued art "as a weapon in the war for building a better society," as he put it. So, he valued such propagandistic works as murals and paintings on cloth draped over buildings more than delicate and elaborate studio paintings. His pictures, therefore, had a strong social message and exuded power and fury.

Chaesŏp and Myŏngho were close friends in their college days and went on painting expeditions together. So, Chaesŏp knew Myŏngho's thoughts better than anyone else. At times he was influenced by his friend and worked with him. Pak Myŏngho painted caricatures for underground papers and with his juniors from the same college did huge banners to be draped over buildings at demonstration sites. He was tall and gaunt and grew a beard. He was slightly consumptive as well. Chaesŏp understood his friend well, but he didn't share his beliefs. In fact, his view of art was almost diametrically opposed to that of his friend. It was not just his love of painting that prompted him to choose the college of fine art despite his poverty and parental objections. It was because he wanted to devote his life to creating something permanent and unchanging in this changing and evanescent world, as did the great masters before him. If he wanted to serve the needs of his times, there was no reason for him to choose art over technology or practical science.

That was Chaesŏp's view of art. But he was also sceptical about painting pictures that would hang in a corner of a gallery, waiting to be sold to rich women. It would be a miserable thing indeed if he were to paint for the rich collectors. He thought his task as a painter was to paint the eternal shadow hidden within human beings and things and at the same time to convey the virtues and pains of his own times. He would have to find the way to give them shape all by himself.

Though he had not yet come to a conclusion about the nature and purpose of art, he accepted, after only a short hesitation, Myŏngho's suggestion that he do the mural for the retreat center in Kangwŏn Province. It was because he had a strong urge to get away from the feeling that reality was closing in on him from all sides.

The work itself was obviously not going to be a lucrative one, and he didn't expect it to bring much artistic satisfaction, either. What could one expect from painting the wall of a nameless retreat center deep in the mountains of Kangwŏn Province? Taebaek was as remote a place from Seoul as can be, and he had never been there. But he decided not to regret his decision to go there. There is a kind of inevitability behind every choice, he thought. We think we make choices, but it is only an illusion. That thought made him feel at ease. In any case, the commission gave him a good excuse for getting away from his life.

Chaesŏp felt he had become reckless and exhausted lately. His wife, who had been having spells of insanity ever since their only daughter Sŭng'hi died two years ago, finally left him. At that time he had been preparing for a joint exhibition with Myŏngho and several other friends, so he had been as good as living in his studio. The exhibit, which was to be titled "Torture," was devoted to reproducing in painting the pains of the victims of military dictatorship. He worked hard for the event. He kept on working even after hearing that his wife had left home. He was not exactly close buddies with his friends who painted protest pictures, but he liked the exhibit. Nothing could bring out human vulnerability like torture.

His contribution to the exhibit included a painting of a man screaming and howling in abysmal darkness, with three men surrounding him. Even though all of them were tense, there was also a feeling that each was acting out a part imposed on him by inscrutable fate. The three torturers had the face of a devil, an angel and a man. They were standing around the howling man with stony and slightly sad expressions, like surgeons around an operating table. Only the man with the human face had his face and body slightly averted, as if to avoid looking at his alter ego.

Fear was clearly written on his face. Except for the screams of the victim, the room was sunk in heavy silence.

His friends said that Chaesŏp was clinging to work to forget his sorrow. But Chaesŏp knew that his devotion to work was a calculated one. He had known that his wife would leave home someday. In fact, in a way he may have been hoping that she would. Their daughter's death meant the end of their relationship, and despair of life for both of them. Chaesŏp, grown extremely irritable, had often quarrelled with his wife who had become hysterical. They thus tortured each other, and they both became exhausted.

In the meantime, Chaesŏp had an affair with Yŏng'ae, an aspiring artist who dropped into his studio from time to time. She wore fashionable clothes with frills and ruffles and had big earrings. And her metal bracelets jangled unpleasantly. She was stylish and good-looking but also vain and frivolous.

Chaesŏp, however, told her he loved her, even though he despised her in his heart. They made love on a mattress behind the movable partition in his studio. Yŏng'ae knew that Chaesŏp had conflicting emotions about her, and she partly pitied and partly despised him. She had an aversion for the complicated type like him.

Pale sunlight darted through the window of his studio, like spent arrows. Lying in that sunlight he used to puff on cigarettes, picturing the faces of his sweet little daughter Sŭng'hi and his wife. Smoke from the cigarette spread in the room like ink dropped in a pail of water. Scattered paint tubes and canvases also came into view. Beside him, Yŏng'ae was humming on the mattress with a towel thrown on her bare torso, clinking her metal bracelets. And the thirty-eight-year-old man lying beside her puffed on his cigarette with a tense and irritated face . . . All these images passed before his eyes like a scene in an oppressive dream.

It was then, while lying on his stomach beside Yŏng'ae and smoking a cigarette, that he hit upon the thought of going to India. It was like beholding a mirage while struggling not to sink in a swamp. Why India? He couldn't tell for sure, but perhaps it was from a longing for something fundamental, something free from the trappings of civilization. He wanted to extricate himself once and for all from the tattered garments that had been thrust on him by life, like a butterfly sloughing off its coils, and soar up lightly, freed from all the uncertainties and guilts and misgivings. He yearned to go to India, even though it might be a painful and poorly funded trip, or maybe because it was bound to be a painful trip. He recalled a passage from "Wandering Through India," a travelogue written by a Japanese named Fujiwara. It said:

With every step I saw myself. I saw the falsity of the world I've
been taught to accept. But I also saw many beautiful things as
well. I saw many lives nesting on a colossal banyan tree. I saw a
huge raincloud forming behind the tree. And the fierce elephant
charging at men, and the triumph of the boy who subdued the
elephant. And the tall forest which took the boy and the elephant
in its bosom. The world was good. The earth and the wind were
wild. The flowers and the bees were beautiful. I walked on. I saw
the people. They were destitute and ugly. They were miserable.
They were humorous. They were gay. They were noble and they
were rough. The world was good.

After making love to Yŏng'ae, Chaesŏp smoked a cigarette and
pictured huge banyan trees and colossal rainclouds and elephants
and humans in rags. It didn't have to be India. It could be a place
he'd never heard of, as long as it was someplace that would enable
him to face his true self. He wanted to see face to face the essence
of life hidden somewhere deep down behind the fleeting,
ephemeral phenomena.

The exhibit met with a moderate success, but he could not
throw off the garbage that was weighing down on him. He heard
that his wife had stayed with a number of friends and then recently
entered a prayer house. At the evaluation meeting after the exhibit, he finally let go of all his restraint. He got deliriously drunk,
threw up in the salon, and screamed and yelled at his friends.
Thrusting his face close to Myŏng'ho's, he raved, half accusingly
and half pleadingly: "Look, Myŏng'ho, you're the noble champion
of the people. I'm garbage. Do you hear? I'm trash. Stinking, rot-
ten-to-the core trash. I'm . . . Yes, look, Myŏng'ho, look at the face
of human trash. I loathe myself!"

He raved on. At last he ended up sobbing like an ox from self-
pity.

"Don't be too hard on yourself," Myŏng'ho had said gently but
firmly. Chaesŏp cried for a long time.

When he awoke the next morning, he felt like he was sitting in
a tub of shame and torment. Rough wind swept through his body,
as if his flesh, heart and soul were all riddled with holes.

It was then that Pak Myŏng'ho suggested he do the mural.
Maybe Myŏng'ho was trying to give him a chance to get away from
the city to recover from his fatigue and sort his life out in the
mountains, far away from familiar scenes and faces. After thinking
for a few minutes, Chaesŏp had nodded consent. The work itself
sounded attractive, and the word "retreat center" sent a ripple of
classical piety through him. There was nothing to hold him in

Seoul, so he packed his things and left the very next day, which was today.

He didn't want anybody to know that he was leaving for a retreat center in T'aebaek. Of course he didn't tell Yŏng'ae. He was a little bit worried that his wife might return and want to contact him, but he thought that his absence might be what she needed for the time being. So, after deliberating for a little while, he recorded this message in the answering machine:

"I'm not home. I'm leaving for India." Then he hesitated a bit, but concluded with "Thank you."

He thought of saying "I'm sorry," but said "Thank you" instead. "I'm sorry" suggested something unfinished, and he didn't want to feel that he was leaving something unfinished. "Thank you" also sounded inappropriate, but he decided that he needn't worry about such minute details and left for Ch'ŏngnyangni station to board the ten o'clock train to Ch'echŏn.

He must have dozed. He awoke to see the train passing through a tunnel. His middle-aged seatmate was fast asleep, with his head on one shoulder. Chaesŏp yawned until his jaw almost fell out, and stretched himself.

It was nearly two o'clock when the train pulled into Ch'echŏn. Chaesŏp took a taxi from the train station to the bus station and got on a bus to T'aebaek. The February sky was lowering with rainclouds, but luckily the wind had subsided and it didn't feel too cold. Buses ran at frequent intervals to T'aebaek. Perhaps because it was a weekday, the buses were almost empty. Chaesŏp took a seat in the first row on the right-hand side, opposite the driver. He had eaten a bowl of instant noodles in Ch'echŏn, but he still felt a bit hungry.

The driver, a gaunt young man, was wearing dark green sunglasses. He was playing a cassette tape of popular tunes at full volume. Because the cassette player reversed automatically, the same tune came on over and over again. The driver, however, sang along elatedly and was not about to change the cassette. He wasn't paying any attention to how the music might affect his customers. Chaesŏp felt a motion sickness coming on, what with his hunger and the headache brought on by the blaring music. But he didn't want to ask the driver to turn the cassette off, so he just put up with it.

The dried-up winter landscape in monochrome of rusty brown seen through the bus window looked desolate, with only a scant presence of humanity. As the sun sets quickly in the mountain region, the afternoon sun was already declining weakly on the brown hills. The empty bus and the hackneyed melodies. And the hunger and motion sickness. All these combined to make Chaesŏp feel that he was being pushed out of the world.

It occurred to him that no happiness fell to his lot during the past few years. It might have been a little different if his daughter had been alive. Sŭng'hi was a sweet little girl. She had said, with her lisping accent, "Daddy, I wanna doggie." And there was another death as well. It was his friend Chŏngmin's. He had committed suicide. Chŏngmin's death was a great shock to the whole circle of his friends who had engaged in antigovernment protests in school days. Chŏngmin left a letter in which he stated his utter confusion and despair occasioned by the political betrayal of one of their school seniors, who had been their hero. It also stated that he was trying to figure out how he could save his life from utter meaninglessness, and that the more he lived the less sure he felt about being able to wrestle with it.

The deaths of his beloved child and of the friend who left him many unsettling questions made him incapable of feeling joy. His self-image, when he thought about it, was devoid of light-heartedness and gaiety. And he thought that life was made up of a much greater portion of unhappiness and only a little bit of happiness, and to live meant to ford the swamp of misery by jumping precariously from one lotus leaf called happiness to the next.

"I can take it if there's to be no revolution after all. But I can't stand it if there's no absolute value for which I can dedicate my whole being," Chŏngmin had once said gloomily, during one of their drinking parties. Chaesŏp recalled Chŏngmin's deep brown eyes, which used to glow with enthusiasm.

Chaesŏp opened the window a slit and lit a cigarette. Wind raced past the bus with a loud wail. It seemed to suck away the cigarette smoke as well.

"What have I been devoting my whole life to, till now? Or, was there ever anything in my life I wanted to devote my entire being to?" Chaesŏp mourned internally. "But what does it matter if there isn't any such thing!" he muttered to himself with abandon. Then he felt a little better. He tried to think about the work ahead. How many days would it take? And what should I paint? These thoughts enabled him to lessen his gloomy and oppressive reflections a little. It was a blessing that he had work that demanded his immediate attention.

"I'll forget everything. I'll forget it all and think only of the painting while it lasts," Chaesŏp said to himself repeatedly, like one trying to exact a promise from himself.

The bus made only a few short stops and rattled on. He had thought Taebaek was quite near Chechŏn, but it was already dusk when the bus arrived in T'aebaek. It was not only getting dark, but rain began to scatter. The retreat center was still four miles away. Chaesŏp inquired about a bus going there and found out that the next one would be leaving in about an hour. He thought he'd eat first and went into a small eatery beside the bus depot.

It was quite dark when he came out of the restaurant. Mist had descended in the meantime and completely covered the mountain city. Shouldering his backpack, Chaesŏp sauntered over to the bus depot. Even though a small hillside town, Taebaek was brightly lit up with neon signboards.

The bus came about a quarter of an hour later. Chaesŏp quickly hopped on the bus, sat in the front row, and asked the driver at the top of his voice: "You know the retreat center, don't you? Please drop me off there."

"All right," the driver said in a playful tone, casting a glance at Chaesŏp.

"How long does it take to get there?"

"Oh, not long. Twenty minutes, maybe?"

Chaesŏp unslung his backpack, hugged it tightly, and looked ahead. He could see the mist moving rapidly in the darkness lit up by the headlights.

There were only a few passengers in the bus, all sitting toward the front.

"It's quite misty, isn't it?" Chaesŏp made small talk with the driver, having recovered a little of his spirit.

"Yes. It didn't used to be this misty, but ever since the dam was built over there it's misty all the time. Is this your first time here?"

"Yes."

"Well, this road didn't used to be paved. Before it was paved, it took some work to negotiate it in the mist. Sometimes a wild animal jumped out at you out of the mist, so it was awfully dangerous."

Chaesŏp thought the driver, who looked like a bluffer, was exaggerating, but he also thought it quite possible. A truck appeared ahead, running towards them with its blinking lights on.

"Are there many visitors to the retreat center?"

"Well, not so many in the winter. But it seems to attract quite a few people when it's warm. I heard that the director is an interesting person."

Chaesŏp nodded, to signify he understood as much. He thought it was fortunate that the bleak landscape was covered over with mist. The mist soon turned into a fine drizzle. Raindrops rolled down the windows on the outside. The road, the trees and rocks glittered with rain in the headlights as well. Chaesŏp had the illusion that he was penetrating a fantastically remote corner of the world.

"Well, here we are. The retreat center's down that valley," the driver said, bringing the car to a stop and pointing to the darkness outside with his finger.

"Thank you," Chaesŏp said, and quickly jumped off the bus with his backpack.

The bus started again. The red taillights of the bus disappeared, as if they had been sucked in by the mist. Chaesŏp found himself standing all alone in the darkness. It was the first time in a long while that he was alone in the darkness. The fine drizzle kept falling. It felt cool and refreshing against his face. The rain slid down his skin caressingly.

Shouldering his backpack, Chaesŏp began walking in the direction indicated by the driver. When he crossed the bridge and turned into the valley, the noise of a running brook assailed him. Mixed with the noise came the ringing of bells, a sound that seemed to have flown out of some deep abyss but one that nevertheless had a clear and distinct resonance. Chaesŏp looked up to see a number of lights looming up in the mist and rain from the other side of the dark valley. He quickened his steps towards the lights.

After walking the uneven path for quite a while, he came upon the retreat center, which stood like a citadel. He was to learn later that the retreat center had the imposing look of a citadel when seen from below, as its buildings stand on the slope of the hill in tiers. It may have looked even more imposing that night on account of the darkness.

The dark wooden building he came upon first had a single incandescent light hanging at the tip of its dripping eave. The light dispelled the darkness a little bit. Standing under the light, Chaesŏp wondered where he should go. Deciding that the wooden building must be the main hall, he began walking towards it. The wooden stairs that led up to the building were slippery from rain. A man who had been walking down the stairs politely stepped aside to let him pass.

"Can you tell me which is the office?" Chaesŏp's voice was tense as he asked the man.

"Yes. It's right over there," the man, whose face was hidden in a shadow, answered politely, pointing to the top of the stairs, and went down the stairs.

The office was on his right as he reached the landing. Anybody could see it was the office, as indicated by the bulletin board with many notices beside the door. The notices were about rules to be observed in the center and contained announcements. There was also the schedule of buses to town.

Dim fluorescent light seeped out of the semitransparent glass of the door. Chaesŏp softly pushed open the sliding glass door, trying not to make any noise. There was a small desk in the office, and to the rear of the desk was a worn sofa set, big enough to seat six to seven people. A young man wearing spectacles was seated at the desk, writing something in the notebook on top of it. On the sofa, a woman who was clad in a black one-piece dress and black stockings and looked about thirty, was talking to a couple in their late twenties.

"How are you?" Chaesŏp said, smiling awkwardly.

"How are you?" the young man returned, without taking much notice of him and going on with his work. Chaesŏp could tell that he was quite used to unexpected visitors. Chaesŏp stepped into the office, closed the door, and said, "Where can I find the director?"

The young man looked up from his notebook to study Chaesŏp.

"May I ask who you are?" the woman in black dress rose from her seat and asked, smiling. Chaesŏp's hair and eyebrows were wet. He responded with a faint smile. She didn't look like a nun, but piety emanated from her.

"Oh, I'm . . . My name's Do Chaesŏp. I came here to paint a mural for the director."

"Oh, so you're the painter. The director told us you'd be coming," the woman said, with a smile of warm welcome. Chaesŏp, who had been worried that he might not have been expected, felt relieved.

"Please sit down," the woman said, making room for him on the sofa.

"Thank you," Chaesŏp said, and sat down, unstrapping his backpack and hugging it. The backpack was wet also.

"I'm sorry to tell you that the director's not with us at the moment. But don't worry. The general manager knows all about it. If you'll wait just for a moment, we'll fetch him. I'm called Kim Maria. But please excuse me for a minute. I have to exchange a few words with the gentleman and lady here," the woman said lightly and amicably, with just a hint of childish prattle.

"Oh, of course. Please go ahead," Chaesŏp said, and looked around the room to avoid looking at the others. The room had little in the way of decoration, except for a wooden cross and a few knickknacks in one corner, and there was a door leading to another room on one of the walls.

Chaesŏp pretended not to pay attention to the conversation, but he was listening all the same. The young couple, who turned out to be a Protestant missionary and his bride on their honeymoon, had come to spend the night, but as there was no vacant room they were inquiring about the bus going to T'aebaek. It was quiet all around, and the sound of wind and rain seemed to heighten the stillness. Through that stillness came the sound of a hymn sung in low and harmonious voices.

In a little while, a man in crew cut and wearing a wind jacket came in, exposing all his teeth in a big smile. He had thick eyebrows and looked to be in his early forties.

"So you're the painter?" he asked, extending his hand for a handshake. His hand was cold, perhaps because he had just come in from the outside.

"Welcome, welcome. We've been expecting you. We had a telephone call from Mr. Pak this morning. I'm An Ch'angsu, the general manager here. My Christian name's Peter."

"How are you? I'm Do Chaesŏp. Is the director on a long trip?"

"No, he's gone to Seoul for a few days for medical treatment. He'll be back soon. Have you had dinner yet?"

"Yes," Chaesŏp said promptly because he wanted to go to bed at once.

"Oh, I see. Well, we hope you can begin the work from tomorrow. I'll show you the building and the wall tomorrow morning."

"I asked for the paint and brush to be ready."

"They're ready. We fixed the construction ladder for you to use as well. If there's anything else you need, just tell me."

"Thank you. I'll take a look tomorrow."

"Sister Maria will tell you about the rules in this center. This is not a monastery for priests and nuns but more a retreat center for lay people. We welcome people of other religious persuasions as well. Would you please excuse me now? I was leading the evening chapel."

After the general manager left, Chaesŏp felt as if everything was already familiar to him. Then the tension left him and fatigue rushed in in its place. He suppressed a yawn with difficulty.

"Excuse me, but . . . " Chaesŏp said, to remind his hostess of his presence.

"Oh, I'm sorry. Please follow me. I'll take you to your room," the woman in black dress said, standing up.

Chaesŏp picked up his backpack and rose to his feet. Kim Maria took out a folded quilt cover and pillowcase from a chest of drawers standing in one corner of the room and led the way out.

The rain had thickened in the meantime, and the wind was blowing, too. He could see the rain scattering around the electric lamp like water pouring out of a watering can. The rain blown on the breeze struck Chaesŏp's face and neck and made him refreshingly cool.

"You're here to work for us, but I hope you'll observe our timetable. That'd be mutually convenient. Although it's not compulsory," Kim Maria explained, rather in the tone of a soliloquy. Her black dress was absorbed by the darkness, and only her fair neck showing through the tress of her bound hair stood out. Chaesŏp felt momentarily flustered, an old forgotten longing reviving in him. He recalled his wife who had left him. Then the image of Kate, the heroine of *And Never Said a Word,* overlapped that of his wife. The thought of his wife aroused pity and guilt in him.

"We rise at half past five. The morning prayer is at six. Breakfast is at seven-twenty," Maria enumerated rapidly in a businesslike tone. "This room is the main chapel. It also serves as our dining room. The kitchen's over there. That wing is the women's quarter, so you'd better not go there at night. And there are families staying here, too. And we have long-term residents as well."

A low structure with a thatched roof stood along the long stairway, and a number of buildings stood on the slope. They went to the building at the very top. It looked like a roughly built two-story cement building. There were many small rooms on the first floor, and on the second floor were two large rooms. Maria led Chaesŏp to one of the big rooms on the second floor.

"Here we are. You'll be sharing it with a few of our guests, but they won't bother you. Well, good night, then," Maria said, handing the quilt cover and pillowcase to Chaesŏp and smiling lightly. Then she stepped down into the darkness and rain. Chaesŏp watched her receding back and then slowly slid open the sliding door and stepped into the room.

The room had a coal briquet stove in the middle and had rush mat flooring. It was about thirty square meters in area, and three people had already spread their beddings and were either sleeping or reading. The fire in the stove must have died out since the room was just as cold as outside. Nobody paid any attention to Chaesŏp, so he took a folded mattress and quilt from the pile in a corner and spread them. Then he took out the toothbrush and towel from his backpack and headed for the washroom. The water was so cold it made him shudder.

Returning to the room, Chaesŏp put the covering over the quilt and snuggled under it. Then he thought about the events of that day. It seemed as if a long time had elapsed since he left Seoul. The sound of the bells that he had heard at the entrance of the valley came again. The bells were signalling the end of vespers. Chaesŏp felt utterly insignificant and small, a lone castaway in a strange world. A misgiving squirmed in his breast. But being tired out from the long journey, he fell asleep quickly.

When he awoke the next morning, day had not completely broken yet. He heard a bunch of sparrows chirping somewhere. His head felt completely clear. Putting on his clothes slowly, he came out of the room with his toiletries.

The rain had lifted, and it was a clear day. The sun had just risen and with its long oblique rays was illuminating the trees and buildings wet with the previous night's rain. Smoke from the main building was scattering in the chilly wind. As the building he slept in was located highest on the slope, he could see the whole layout of the retreat center at a glance.

"Did you get a good night's sleep?" someone accosted him from behind.

Chaesŏp looked back to see a bald-headed man with a towel draped around his neck. The man looked about forty and was smiling. He seemed to be in glowing health, perhaps because of the steam rising from his head and face. He must have just washed them.

"You arrived last night, didn't you? I'm one of your room-mates"

"Yes, hello."

"You had quite a big backpack. I suppose you're going to stay a while?"

"Yes."

"I'll be leaving soon. I've been here a week already."

"Is that right?"

"It'll be breakfast time soon. Let's go down together."

"Good. Thank you."

The light conversation was pleasant to Chaesŏp. When the man went back to the room, Chaesŏp stretched himself once and then slowly walked to the washroom.

While walking to the main chapel, the bald-headed man told Chaesŏp that he was a writer, that he had come there to plan his next novel and to give his brains a rest; that he had slept the whole time he had been there; that it was his conviction that laziness is the mother of creativity; that he felt like an alien because everybody there was diligent; and that he was not in the least interested in religious questions. Chaesŏp listened to him inattentively, but nodded and grunted to show his sympathy and agreement.

Approaching the main chapel, they could smell the mouthwatering aroma of cooking rice. The main chapel was already filled with people. It looked like they had had morning prayer there. The thirty to forty people gathered there consisted half of men and half of women. They belonged to all age groups, and there were children as well. The main chapel had wooden floors and was very simple and spare. A small copper cross and a large Bible with old typeface were on the altar, and there was a fireplace with burning logs on one wall.

"Good morning," someone greeted them inside the doorway. It was a lame man, who was arranging the wooden tables with a few others. When the low tables were placed in rows, people grabbed cushions and sat down in front of them.

Chaesŏp sat on the same table with the bald-headed novelist. The general manager saw them and came over to sit with them.

"Good morning, Mr. Do. Did you sleep well?" The general manager smiled, exposing his white teeth as he did the previous night.

"Yes. Thank you."

"You weren't cold?"

"How couldn't he have been cold? The room is unheated. I have to cover myself with two quilts to fall asleep," the novelist answered for Chaesŏp, half jokingly and half complainingly.

"Well, the fire must have gone out in the stove. I guess some people would rather freeze than bother to light the coal briquet stove," the general manager responded, still smiling.

The food was served. The rice was half barley. Soybean soup, kimchi and seasoned bean sprouts were all the side dishes there. But Chaesŏp was ravenously hungry, so his mouth watered the whole time the grace was being said. When the grace was finished, the general manager stood up and said he'd like to introduce a newcomer.

"We have a painter with us. He'll beautify the chapel you built with your sweat," he said and made an eye signal for Chaesŏp to stand up and say a few words of greeting. Chaesŏp stood up blushing a little and made a bow.

"Hello, everyone. I'm Do Chaesŏp. I'm afraid my gift's not equal to the important task ahead. I look to you for help and encouragement. Thank you."

Everyone clapped as a gesture of welcome. Then the meal began.

"I wish you all good appetite. If you want more of anything, just ask, all right?" the general manager said.

"Oh, it's awfully nice to meet a fellow artist in a place like this. Now I have someone who'll understand my laziness," the bald-headed writer said with an exaggerated seriousness, and a hint of raillery. "Fellow artist" sounded droll when he said it.

"Oh, I suggest that Brother Yunbae lend a helping hand to Brother Chaesŏp now and then. I think Brother Chaesŏp could use an assistant," the general manager suggested good-naturedly.

"Oh, you're going to make me an errand boy!" the self-proclaimed novelist said with a chuckle. "All right. I must do something to earn my keep here. And I'm good at painting, too. I was in the fine arts circle in my high school days. My fine arts teacher always praised my work very highly."

"Good. I'm very lucky," Chaesŏp said, even though he was worried that the novelist might be a hindrance. It was true, however, that mural painting did require an assistant.

When people dispersed after breakfast, the general manager led Chaesŏp and the bald-headed novelist named Hong Yunbae to the building where the mural was to be painted. The building stood somewhat lower on the valley, slightly to one side. It was rather an ordinary two-story cement building. The only noticeable features were a rather stylish flight of stairs leading to the front porch and the mosaic glass windows girding the cross tower.

"Well, this is the building. I know it looks rather makeshift, but it was built entirely by our own hands," the general manager said. "As you've just seen, the main chapel is much too small when we have a large number of visitors. So, we built this one. In spite of his advanced years, the director himself carried cement and pebbles when this was being built. 'Labor is prayer and prayer is labor,' is the priest's motto. I think he regards this building as his last achievement. So he feels a special attachment to it."

Chaesŏp and the novelist listened to him, circling the building after him. The whitewashed wall still gave off a faint smell of thinner. Tall white pine trees cast their shadows on it.

"That's why we asked brother Pak Myŏngho to paint a mural.

We had hoped the mural would be finished before the chapel opened. It was lucky that brother Myŏngho recommended you to us."

Chaesŏp felt tense as he listened to the general manager's explanation, so tense that he felt an urge to pass water. He had expected a much simpler job. But it seemed that what was expected was not a merely decorative wall painting. And to tell the truth, Chaesŏp had never painted religious pictures before. He thought he should have either refused or have come better prepared. But he kept silent and just continued walking behind the general manager.

"It's this wall," the general manager finally said, stopping in front of a wall. Chaesŏp took a few backward steps and looked at the wall. Fortunately, it was not very big. It was about five meters wide and eight meters high. So, if he left about two meters' margin at the bottom, that would leave him five by six meters of canvas. The other sides wouldn't need painting because their views were blocked by the hills. Chaesŏp nodded, frowning slightly.

"How long do you think you'll need?" the general manager asked. He looked somewhat cold and stern when he wasn't smiling.

"Well, let me think," Chaesŏp said, and stood thinking. First, he would have to decide on a subject and then do the base painting. If that went well, painting in colors was rather mechanical work. As wall paintings should be conspicuous from a distance, it didn't need delicate brushwork. The question was how to paint a picture that would blend well with the surroundings and yet stand out clearly. "Well, it's winter, and the days are short, and the weather is irregular, too, so . . ."

"Of course. Please don't overexert yourself," the general manager said, flashing his polite smile, and began to move away.

"Well, the only wall painting I know is the doodling I used to do on my neighborhood walls. As children we had our own symbols and metaphors that grown-ups couldn't figure out. Isn't that so? Don't you think those were the best wall paintings?" the novelist said with a pedantic air and chuckled to himself. But far from being amused, Chaesŏp was feeling stress from thinking about what he should paint to cover the big blank.

"Well then, see you both later," the general manager said at a parting of the paths and took the way down. Chaesŏp went back to his room and took out a sketchbook and a drawing pencil from his backpack. The novelist slipped under the quilt, saying he had to work out an idea for his novel. It was obvious that he was going to take a nap. Because a companion would only be a hindrance at that stage, Chaesŏp left him alone and went out.

Walking back to the new building, he sketched the outline of the structure in his book and then slowly climbed the rear hill, from the top of which the vista of the whole complex could be seen.

For a few days after that Chaesŏp sat atop the rear hill and thought about what to paint, listening to the rustling of the dry leaves in the wind. Along one side of the valley much lower down, he could see a strip of ice and occasionally heard a distant noise of airplane engines from high up in the sky breaking the silence. Otherwise the stillness was totally undisturbed.

Several days passed quickly. During that time, Chaesŏp went up the hill in the morning with his copy of *And Never Said a Word,* and in the afternoon took long naps, just like the bald-headed novelist, from an incomprehensible fatigue. As he grew accustomed to the life in the retreat center, he felt as if he'd been living there for a long time. People didn't look at him with curiosity anymore, and made light jokes and small talk when they ran into him. The days were totally uneventful.

If Chaesŏp gave any indication that he was in creative agony, it was to grow his beard. He didn't grow it to exhibit his creative agony; it was rather from laziness and indifference, but people seemed to take it as a mark of his artistic anguish. But he didn't care what people thought.

It was true, anyway, that he was in serious agony, not only in the mornings when he was up on the hill projecting mental pictures on the blank wall, but also while he was lazily napping in bed, visualizing pictures.

What should he paint? It could be a simple question. The range of subjects for religious paintings is small. The building and the surroundings further restricted his choice. So, all he had to do was to depict a religious subject to blend in naturally with the environment. The subject could be any of the scenes in the Bible. People tend to accept an artist's choice of subject on the authority of art.

However, Chaesŏp could not just proceed. Perhaps it was because somewhere in his heart there was something that made him refuse all conventional and commonplace ideas. He recalled Dürer's *Martyrdom of the Ten Thousand* and *Lamentation of Christ.* Dürer's paintings were full of cruelty and horror, but there was also a childlike playfulness and gaiety in them. Jesus Christ, symbolized by passion and victory, death and resurrection, and humanity and divinity, was a huge contradiction. It may be that Renaissance artists intuited the essence of art and the meaning of life in that very contradiction.

But it seemed to Chaesŏp that a mural for an outer wall should depict triumph rather than suffering, resurrection rather than death, and divinity rather than humanity. Those would harmonize better with the grave, reticent and somber atmosphere of the retreat center. It would make people's hearts heavy to always behold suffering and pain depicted on a wall, even if the painting was full of reverence and gratitude towards God. A mural in a retreat center shouldn't be like a picture in the "Torture" exhibition.

But Chaesŏp felt quite unequal to painting a solemn and holy picture. He knew that even though he might manage to do that, it would not be something genuine, inspired from the depth of his being. He was too used to the internal landscape of suffering. He knew unhappy, suffering, despairing humanity far better than triumphant and holy humanity, and it seemed to him suffering was closer to man's basic condition.

The other problem for him was how to harmonize the transcendent nature of religion with the world of mundane reality. For Chaesŏp it was not only a question of the mural but also of religion as a whole. To him religion was not a matter of whether you can accept its creeds but a question about the ultimate nature of this world in the face of the meaningless flux of visible phenomena, and about the existence of individual human beings. It seemed to him that a world that completely transcends reality would also be a gloomy, mirthless place. Without the energy and conflicts of ordinary humanity, religion could only be an opiate of the people, as the communists insist. Even though it was to decorate the wall of a religious building, Chaesŏp wanted the picture to reflect reality to a degree.

The rear hill was completely deserted, and silence brooded on it heavily, disturbed only by the rising mist. Smoking was forbidden in the center, so Chaesŏp smoked on the hill. While sitting on a rock and inhaling a cigarette in the heavy silence, Chaesŏp felt a fathomless loneliness penetrating his heart. The image of his wife loomed before him. Where was she now? Perhaps neither of them were to blame for the breakup. It may be impossible for fickle humanity to live a whole life on love alone. The thought of his lonely wife, wandering somewhere like himself, smote him.

To shake off that gloomy thought Chaesŏp opened the book

randomly. Fred followed the blond girl and the idiot child and was having coffee and cookies in the bakery. His wife Kate, after confessing to the priest, went to the same bakery to buy cookies on credit. They were lonely people. To be more precise, they were people whose flesh and bones were saturated with loneliness. But then, who isn't lonely? Even Christ wasn't an exception. It may be that Christ was the very incarnation of loneliness. If he were a god . . . a god who had to come down to the human world and act out a drama whose conclusion he already knew through and through? A drama, moreover, that was so very painful! A colonized subject of the Roman Empire, a penurious young man from Nazareth aged thirty-three!

On the fifth day, Chaesŏp began drawing on the wall. First of all, he asked the ladder to be brought to the wall. To move the construction ladder from the empty lot right behind the building to the front wall was a much bigger job than he'd thought, and required nine people to struggle for several hours.

When the ladder was put in position, Chaesŏp swept the wall clean with a broom, and began to mix paint. The bald-headed novelist stayed by his side, lending him a hand with an excited face and talking incessantly.

"I once dreamed of becoming a painter," he said, stirring the pail of paint with a rod. "Do you know *Jean Christoph* by Romain Roland? The central character was a musician. I forgot all about it, but just remember one passage. 'Even shadows have colors.' That's the passage. Well, what do you think of that? Isn't that just profound? That shadows have colors? So, have you got it all in your head?"

"I'm not sure," Chaesŏp returned gruffly.

As a matter of fact, he didn't have a clear picture in his head yet. It was true that he had a vague image forming in his heart, but the picture was not clear yet. However, he thought that he'd better begin. He was worried that he'd been idle for too long. He thought that once he began, the picture would shape itself somehow. Anyway, an outdoor mural fades in a few years.

"Forgive me if I've been impertinent. But you could just give me a hint, since I'm to be your assistant. It's bound to come out anyway," Yunbae said, with a slightly hurt expression.

"I'm thinking of doing a Christ in the wilderness," Chaesŏp said somewhat irritably, mixing paint for the base picture.

"Christ in the wilderness? Christ in the wilderness!" Yunbae muttered to himself as if it was something completely out of his expectation.

Chaesŏp had tossed that out more to take care of Yunbae's curiosity than because he had clearly settled on it, but after he had said it, he realized that that was exactly the picture he had in his heart. That's right. Maybe that's exactly what I've been groping for.

Christ in the wilderness. A young man in rags walking with bowed head buried deep in thought, on a wilderness brightening up with a white strip of light rising from the far horizon. His eyes shining with infinite pity and tenderness for humanity, and fear of the approaching cruel death, and loneliness in a wilderness wide as the universe in a silence deep as the ocean. A white strip of morning light, and deep and heavy darkness brooding on top of it. A few small trees with bare branches. And stones that are just beginning to be visible. Yes, that was the picture that rose before his eyes with his answer to Yunbae's question.

"Do you believe in God?" Yunbae picked up the conversation again.

"I neither believe nor disbelieve in Him," Chaesŏp returned dryly after a brief thought.

"I'm an atheist. I don't care whether God exists or not. And I wouldn't be too keen about going to Heaven even if there was one. You want to know why? I'd be bored stiff in a place where there's neither pain nor conflict. How about you?"

"I never thought about it," Chaesŏp answered carelessly, absorbed in his thoughts about the painting.

"Anyway, I'm glad to lend you a hand. I've been bored, frankly, you know," Yunbae said with a slight smile, as if to lighten up the conversation.

After lunch Chaesŏp took out his paint-stained overalls from his backpack. And he put on his hiking cap with the blue border, and draped a towel around his neck. Then he put on his white gloves to complete his transformation.

His work clothes seemed to remind people that they indeed had a painter among them. Maria also seemed quite struck when he went over to the kitchen to borrow a basin.

"Oh, you're going to begin work now?" she said with a bright smile.

"Yes, I guess so."

"Oh, I envy you. Although I'm as good as blind when it comes to painting."

"Well then, maybe I'm one-eyed."

Maria giggled merrily at his inept joke. Her laughter rang in his ears even after he returned to the wall. He felt his heart which was heavy with the thought of "Jesus in the Wilderness" lighten up considerably.

Yes. What piece of art can be immortal? Anything made with a material is bound to perish some time or other. And I can't live here forever. If I concentrate on it, two weeks should be enough. Yes, I'll finish it in two weeks. Maybe my wife's back home. My wife. In our courtship days she used to move me to tears. How many ardent letters we wrote each other while I was in the army! And when we got married, how happy we were, even though we were poor. She used to grow rose mosses, garden balsam and morning glory on the terrace of our rented room on the second floor. Maybe it's all my fault that we became estranged like this. Maybe Sŭng'hi's death was just an excuse. I wavered without any reason, and Sŭng'hi's death was a consequence rather than the cause of my wavering.

It didn't take him long to paint the base picture. He filled the entire width of the wall and left two meters' margin at the bottom. It was partly because the bottom part of the wall is apt to become soiled, but, more importantly, because the proportion of the entire wall was not suitable to the picture he had in mind. It took him two days to paint the base picture with light grey paint. While Chaesŏp was filling the sketch with paint, Yunbae watched, sitting on the slope of the rear hill smoking in stealth, offering occasional comments. Sometimes his comments were quite perspicacious, so Chaesŏp thought he might really be a writer after all.

"I just had a brilliant idea," Yunbae said one day. Chaesŏp went on with his work without looking back.

"I'm going to make you a character in my fiction."

Chaesŏp almost broke out laughing. But he just smiled.

"As a tragic artist, I mean," Yunbae pursued, not minding Chaesŏp's lack of reaction.

"Tragedy emanates from your whole being. And from your painting. You are, in short, the kind of man for whom the world isn't a fitting garment."

There was a short pause and then he added, "Of course most people here are of the kind."

Snow began to fall when he almost completed the base picture. The snow, which covered the whole valley, put a stop to his work. The valley lay hushed in perfect silence under the blanket of snow, and only smoke from the chimneys signaled human presence. It was a pure sight inspiring piety. Peals of bells announcing meal and prayer times spread over the quilt of snow eight times a day. Two days passed thus.

The snow lifted on the third day. The sun shone radiantly, and the water dripping from trees and buildings made a lively sound. The retreat center seemed to wake up to life again, and it felt rather noisy to Chaesŏp after the silence.

He resumed his work. First, he painted in the base color of the sky and the wilderness. Because it was to be finished with another coat of paint later on, he painted the sky dark blue and the wilderness bright orange red. And he drew the outline of Jesus's profile in black. Because the wall was wide and the ladder was not tall enough, it was awfully hard work. Moreover, the paints were water-based, so they took a long time to dry. After painting the base color, Chaesŏp began painting details and putting on finishing colors. The top rim of the sky was painted over with nearly black tint, and he made the sky progressively lighter as it dropped to the horizon, until the horizon was almost the color of the deep sea. It was difficult to paint the sky of dawn. It could easily be mistaken for dusk. To catch the exact color of dawn, Chaesŏp went up the rear hill one early dawn and observed the sky until it became completely light.

The color of the wilderness would have to harmonize with that of the sky. Chaesŏp painted the lower rim of the wilderness nearly black as well, and made it progressively lighter as it ascended to the horizon. And he also added light paint to the tips of the few sparse trees and the pebbles. Then he made the horizon a long strip of white light, as he had originally intended. Because both the sky and the wilderness were dark, the white strip seemed to divide the canvas in half.

Chaesŏp looked possessed. His face and hands were heavily soiled with paint, and his unkempt beard made him look like he'd never shaved in his life. His eyes sometimes looked vacant and sometimes keen, and tacitly forbade other people's approach. He was never given to much talk, and now he almost never talked. In other words, he was growing obsessed.

The other people left him alone. They were all people who had experienced insurmountable problems in life, and they were all each in his or her own way estranged from the world. They all looked peaceful and amiable, but you could hear wrenching prayers at night. Sometimes sobbing and wailing rose from every

dell in the darkness. But the next morning everyone looked peaceful and tranquil.

In any case, they were kind and understanding. They let him
eat by himself in a corner. Or rather, they didn't intrude on his
chosen corner. It lay between the fireplace and the altar. The meals
were always simple and eaten in a pious atmosphere.

"How's it going?" Maria would sometimes ask lightly as she
passed by.

Chaesŏp just smiled in response. Only Yunbae kept on offering
unsolicited comments and soliloquizing by his side. Sometimes he
did chores for him like fetching water, but most of the time he just
loafed, carrying on a monologue. He would mutter, for example,
"Well, I'm impressed. I didn't know that you can depict human
agony simply by using color." Or he would say in a challenging
tone, "If there is a God, what do you think he can do for us at this
moment?" Then he would answer his own question: "Well,
Nietzsche declared, in *Zarathustra,* that God is dead. But I think
God died much later, in our age. Only think. If God existed in the
Mesozoic era, what do you think he could have done for the
dinosaurs? What indeed! But this is another age of dinosaurs. So
there's nothing he can do on earth, nothing at all!"

Then he added, with a serious expression, lowering his voice:
"Don't you think it's ironical that the collapse of socialism, which
denied his existence, hastened his demise? That's one of the egre-
gious ironies of history."

Chaesŏp kept on working, listening to Yunbae absently. But it
did occur to him that the bald-headed novelist might be a very
complex person, even though he carried on like a simple, happy-
go-lucky character. Carefully touching up a detail, Chaesŏp
thought, what a labyrinth man's internal landscape is!

As the weather continued to be clear for several days, the work
went on without interruption. Externally, it was a repetition of a
simple routine. He began working on the painting after breakfast
and kept at it until lunch. After lunch he took a little rest and then
took up the work again until sundown. Nothing seemed to change,
except the painting and the weather. It was already two weeks since
Chaesŏp came to the place, and you could smell the spring on
whiffs of chilly wind. The ice in the valley had almost melted as
well.

The painting had progressed so far that everyone could see
what his subject was. The dark, dawning sky and the red earth
tones of the wilderness in the shade of the sky blended smoothly

with the white wall; the painting was impressive without being glaring.

Now it was time to paint Jesus, the focus of the picture. At first, Chaesŏp thought of painting him in rags, but because the background was somber, he decided to clothe him in white. He made the white stand out by making the folds of the garment black. Also, he painted the side of him that didn't face the horizon dark.

The background and the figure were quite striking. Now, all that remained was to paint Jesus's face and the emotional atmosphere of the whole. It would require detailed and delicate touches to give the face the proper expression.

As the painting approached completion, people of the center came to see him work. Trying not to intrude, they pretended to be stopping for a moment on their way to somewhere, but curiosity was written on their faces.

"Oh, you're working so hard," the short-haired and bushy-browed general manager remarked, revealing his trademark smile. "We've had a call from the director. He's coming back in three days. I told him about your mural, and he asked me to convey his gratitude. He said he's impatient to see it."

Maria came by also. She handed him a dish of peeled fruit, rarities in such a remote mountain, covered with a cloth so people wouldn't see it. But the bald-headed writer spotted it twice.

"Oh, you're a lucky guy," he exclaimed, grinning. "You're the first one in this place she's paid such special attention to," he said, and gobbled up the treat ravenously.

Chaesŏp took a rest for a day preparatory to finishing the picture. After breakfast he went up the rear hill by himself. As always, the hill was sunk in complete silence, and only the tall grass rustled, rubbing against each other in the wind. Chaesŏp sat down on a rock from which he could take in the whole place and the wall he was painting. A mist was rising from the valley. The desolate feeling in his heart, which was there when he first came to the place, had considerably abated, but there was still a chill in his heart. Chaesŏp lit a cigarette and smoked slowly, inhaling deeply. A nameless sorrow and misgiving spread in his heart.

A small bird flew up and away, drawing a straight line to the next hill. The trail it cut was instantly zipped up by silence, which hovered in the air for a long time.

If he worked at full speed, he would be able to finish the mural the next day. He must bring to life the figure of young Jesus Christ who, after shivering all night long with the cold and loneliness that penetrated into his bones, was walking in the wilderness into the light of dawn, soaked with dew.

What did Jesus dream in the wilderness? What did the country of his mortal self, Judea, that was a colony of the imperialist Rome, mean to him? Did he have to die, in order to reveal his glory? If it was for the salvation of mankind, what was he saving mankind for? And what was supposed to come after salvation? If he were alive today, what could he do in a world filled with dinosaurs, as the bald-headed novelist had said? Could it be that he just died, after all?

Skipping lunch, he roamed the hill, turning such questions over in his mind. It was late afternoon when he came down from the hill without having found a single answer. As he came down, the retreat center was snugly nestling in the shadow of the mountain that had just begun to spread, and the unfinished painting gleamed in the evening sun on the new building that stood on the edge of the complex.

That night, Chaesŏp woke up at hearing a commotion. It sounded like a violent quarrel, and someone seemed to be screaming. He opened his eyes to see it was still dark. Had he imagined the noise? He could have. Noisy quarrels seemed unlikely to take place in a retreat center. Reasoning thus, Chaesŏp was falling back to sleep when someone came in and shook him by the shoulder. The person called urgently, "Brother Chaesŏp, Brother Chaesŏp!"

Chaesŏp pretended he had been sleeping and sat up slowly, saying in a sleepy tone: "Is anything the matter?"

"Yes. Go out and take a look."

He was a lame young man by the name of Pak Taljin. Even in the darkness one could see that he was agitated.

"What's the matter?" Chaesŏp asked again in a sleepy drawl.

"You'd better hurry. Brother Yunbae's done something to your painting."

"The painting?"

Chaesŏp sprang up. Hurriedly putting on his clothes, he asked, "What did he do to the painting?"

"He smeared it with paint."

Chaesŏp ran out of the building. It was still quite dark, with a few electric bulbs dispelling the darkness here and there. And stars were strewn all over the cloudless winter sky. The cold night air of February struck his face. Following Chaesŏp with limping gait, Talchin explained breathlessly: "Brother Yunbae said he had to finish the painting himself."

Chaesŏp felt as if he had been hit by a club.

"The general manager found him, on his way back from the night chapel. He thought it must be you, but it was Hong Yunbae!"

Chaesŏp could imagine what had happened. But why? For what? He could guess what Yunbae's motive could be.

"Then what happened?" Chaesŏp asked gloomily.

"So the general manager climbed up the ladder, yelling at him to stop, and Yunbae missed his footing and fell down. He hurt his head!"

The two ran toward the new building, talking breathlessly. Unlike when he walked at a normal pace, Taljin limped badly.

The new building appeared before them, brightly lit by an incandescent light. A few people were nervously pacing before the wall. Their shadows shook against the wall. As they came near, their unsettled whispers became audible.

"I think he should be taken to a hospital in the city," someone said.

"At this hour?" another objected.

"Yes. He's bleeding too much. Somebody must carry him on his back. Brother Joseph!" It was the general manager's voice. Glancing at Chaesŏp who had arrived there just then, the manager called for Brother Joseph again. In the electric light his face was blanched white and covered with sweat.

Brother Joseph appeared.

"Please carry him to the car. I'm sorry."

The bald-headed writer's face was smeared all over with blood. Blood was still spreading on the towel pressed to his wound.

"It's not really serious. It's just a cut," the general manager said reassuringly to Chaesŏp, who looked worried.

Hong Yunbae opened his eyes then. His bloody face looked villainous. He forced a smile at Chaesŏp. His bloodstained smile made him look diabolic.

"I know you," he brought out with difficulty. "You have no God in you. So you can't paint God. That picture is a fraud. A fraud, I say," he said huskily. "Your picture's full of human suffering and despair. I know. That figure up there . . . that's only yourself. Yes. It'd have been honest to make it your self-portrait. But you pretend it's the figure of a despairing God. I won't allow it." He closed his eyes, as if it was too much effort to speak. Then he muttered, with closed eyes: "God mustn't despair. You understand? I tell you, even though I'm an atheist."

The sturdy young man called Joseph hoisted Yunbae onto his back and began to descend the hill. Another man walked close beside him, pressing the towel against Yunbae's forehead. The gen-

eral manager and several others followed them down as well. They
were heading towards the entrance of the monastery where a
minibus was parked. They soon disappeared into the darkness.

Those who remained began to scatter, saying a few consolatory
words to Chaesŏp. Left alone, Chaesŏp lit a cigarette and took a
good look at the wall for the first time. Even though there was a
light nearby, the picture was in the shadow, so he couldn't see
clearly what was done to it. He climbed up the ladder.

Then he saw the part that was still wet with paint. It was Jesus's
face and his halo. Yunbae had painted in a big, bright yellow halo
around Jesus's face. And the face looked like a child's, painted in
simple childish strokes. It was rather rough, but it was a clear picture. Jesus's eyes, especially, were big and delicate. Chaesŏp could
see at once what Yunbae tried to do. Jesus's eyes were staring at the
horizon. They were not those of a suffering, despairing man but
full of exultation and challenge, like those of one who had tri-
umphed over the darkness and oppression of the night.

For a while Chaesŏp just stood there, unable to decide what to
do. The area Yunbae had painted was not large, so painting over it
wouldn't be a big problem. But Chaesŏp came down the ladder
and sat on a sandbag lying nearby. Strangely enough, he felt no
resentment or anger against Yunbae who took such outrageous lib-
erties with his work of art.

Dawn broke after he had smoked several cigarettes in a row.
Stars began to fade, and white particles of light spread in the air,
revealing the outlines of objects. Then, objects which had been a
part of the darkness began to take on individual shapes. Stones,
trees, and walls regained their proper identity. Soon, the chimney
beside the main chapel was tossing up billows of black smoke.

After observing the change intently, Chaesŏp sprang up and
climbed up the ladder.

Chaesŏp worked on the painting the whole day, like one possessed. People who came to call him to meals went back shaking
their heads when he ignored them completely. Maria came with a
bowl of gruel when lunch hour was past. She looked up at him with
a worried expression. But Chaesŏp just told her to put it down and
went on with his work.

"Brother Chaesŏp, I know what's in your mind. You want to finish it quickly so you can go back . . . " she said in a slightly shaky
voice, still lingering below. Chaesŏp halted a minute and looked
down at her. She was wearing a white jacket over her accustomed

black dress. The jacket made a bright contrast against the black dress.

After gazing at her for a moment, Chaesŏp resumed painting. Maria lingered there awhile longer, like one deep in thought, and then went away quickly.

Chaesŏp looked like a madman. His cap had fallen, so his hair was blowing in the wind, and his lips were blanched white. He had not even had a drop of water that day.

Towards late afternoon the work was nearly finished. He had completely painted out Yunbae's picture and painted his own picture over it. It was the deeply troubled face of a thirty-three-year-old man, with long hair coming down to the shoulders. Half of his face was shrouded in dark shadow, but the other half was brightly illumined by the light of dawn. Chaesŏp accepted Yunbae's idea of him looking far away at the horizon. His eyes were alight with the inner fire that enabled him to fight off the dreadful loneliness of the night before, whose rule of darkness seemed to last forever, and face the innumerable pains that lay ahead. And his jaws were thrust forward slightly, as if to show pride in his tragic fate, and a warm but confident smile played around his mouth. Nonetheless, his face as a whole was filled with the loneliness and sorrow of a young man who had many questions about his own destiny.

Chaesŏp thought of retaining the halo, but decided against it after much deliberation. His aim from the first had been to paint Jesus the son of man, not Jesus the son of God. He was convinced that "Jesus in the Wilderness" was still a young man struggling to understand his inscrutable fate. Endowing him with a halo would make the painting just another run-of-the-mill religious picture. So, instead of the halo, Chaesŏp drew a white line along the outline of his head, in the same white color as the brightest part of the horizon, enveloping the head caressingly.

The sun was beginning to set when Chaesŏp put down the brush at last. It was a mural five meters wide and six meters high. Wind began to blow from the ridge. And the setting sun gave the mural a golden glow.

When people saw the completed picture, they offered praises and prayers. But Chaesŏp felt exhausted and slightly dizzy, so he was oblivious to their compliments. His legs shook as he climbed down the ladder. When he reached the last rung, he fainted and fell down. He heard people screaming and running to him, but he lost consciousness with an illusion that he was sinking deep into the earth.

It was night when Chaesŏp came round again. And he was not in his own rushmat-covered room but in a warm ondol room. The room, which had no furniture except a wooden desk, was small and dark but clean. An ivory Virgin hung on the wall lighted by a fluorescent light, and a glass vase containing what must be artificial flowers stood on the bookshelf above the desk. From a distance came voices singing hymns. A clear bell was heard also. It was the sound of the same bells that he heard the first night he came to the place.

As he lay there breathing low, the days he spent there passed through his head like a kaleidoscope. The memory of the train ride to Chech'on seemed like a scene from a distant past. He recalled the smoke that rose from far away in the bleak winter landscape as seen through the train window. The portrait of a tired and haggard man in his late thirties overlapped on that tableau. That was himself. Over that flitted Sŭng'hi's death and his wife's departure, followed by the gloomy lovemaking in the studio lighted by the pale sun. It all seemed unreal to him. At the end of the reel appeared the retreat center soaked by a drizzle.

He felt devoid of passion, like a burnt-out furnace. His hopes and dreams had also departed. "I can take it if there's to be no revolution after all. But I can't stand it if there isn't an absolute value for which I can dedicate my whole being," Chŏngmin had said. Well, it was natural Chŏngmin couldn't stand it. He had gone to prison for adhering to that value. So he must have found it hard to keep on living when he found that such a value no longer existed.

But what about me? Wasn't I one of those who disbelieved in the existence of such a value from the first? Then, why should I feel so empty?

Chaesŏp remembered the word "India," like one recalling a long-forgotten fact. The colossal banyan tree, the huge cloud billowing behind it, the fierce elephant and the brave boy and the crowd in rags. Innumerable corpses awaited cremation or water-burial along the shore of the river, and that's another face of the absolute, something quite different from the "absolute" in Chŏngmin's book.

The wall painting was a failure. There was no aspect of the absolute in it. There was no fury for the destitute and exploited humanity, and no agonizing search for the ultimate nature of human existence. He knew his failure too well, whether or not it was perceptible to others. His heart ached with shame and a sense of failure. Yes, Yunbae was right. That Jesus was not Jesus but the portrait of Chaesŏp himself. Chaesŏp, a miserable, desiccated specimen of humanity . . .

He lifted his eyes to the ceiling.

There was a knock. And the door opened before Chaesŏp could answer. He turned his vague eyes to the door.

"Are you awake?"

It was Maria.

"Yes. What time is it?" Chaesŏp asked, sitting up.

"It's nine o'clock. Don't get up. I was going to let you sleep, but the general manager said you must have something to eat."

"Oh, I don't feel like eating. So, don't worry about that," Chaesŏp answered indifferently, rubbing his face with both hands.

"Thank you for your hard work. Everybody says the painting's unique. I don't know much about painting, but . . . anyway, I never saw Jesus with such a sad face."

Chaesŏp laughed a silent hoarse laugh.

"By the way, how is Mr. Hong?" Chaesŏp asked, remembering the writer.

"He's crazy!" Maria exclaimed. She seemed worked up, unlike her usual self. "He's not really a writer, either. He's never written a single story yet. He came here a few times before, too, but all he ever did was to sleep day and night. Someone said he graduated from a seminary and was a minister once, but I don't believe it."

Then, perhaps feeling embarrassed by her own vehemence, she calmed down a little and answered his question. "He's in a hospital in T'aebaek. The general manager says it doesn't look serious, although we can't know for sure as yet."

Chaesŏp thought of Yunbae. His bald head. His large brown eyes that gave off a hint of sarcasm. His thick lips. His face looked funny but it was only a mask worn over a complex, troubled face. He declared himself an atheist, but, come to think of it, he couldn't be an atheist. Didn't he say, with his horridly bloodstained face, "God mustn't despair. You understand?" That meant that he himself was in despair about the world.

"And I have a letter for you. I meant to give it to you during the day, but you were too intent on your work," Maria said, handing him the envelope she was holding. Then she stood up.

"A letter, for me?" Chaesŏp exclaimed in surprise. "Who could it be? Who could possibly know I'm here?" crossed his mind. Chaesŏp took the envelope and looked at the sender's name. Then he looked bewildered. On the envelope was the name of his wife, Pak Mikyŏng.

"Is it from your wife?" Maria asked with a somewhat sad and significant smile, and went out.

Chaesŏp tore open the envelope and took out the letter with tense fingers. His heart was beating. It was a familiar handwriting,

which he hadn't seen for quite awhile. He read from top to bottom
in one breath.

> Chaesŏp,
>   I called your studio and heard you say you're going to India.
> I was so astonished. But Myŏng'ho kindly gave me your address,
> asking me at the same time not to tell you I got it from him. If he
> hadn't set me right, I'd have believed you went to India. I'm so
> sorry about leaving you like that. We were both under too much
> stress. Since then I relived many scenes from our past. Do you
> remember? That time we went to the North Han River shore on
> your day off from the army? On that day, there was such a profu-
> sion of evening primroses on the shore. What can be more pre-
> cious in life than happy memories?
>   I dread asking this question. . . . And dread myself for dread-
> ing to ask it. . . . But, do you still love me? I'd like to end my drift-
> ing and return home. And I'd like to have a baby, too. I think it's
> time we let Sŭng'hi go.
>   Please give me a call when you come back from India. I miss
> you.
>   Your Mikyŏng

After reading it through quickly once, Chaesŏp read it once
more, slowly, savoring every phrase. Then folding it neatly, he put
it back in the envelope. He felt his nosebridge smart and his vision
clouding over. Do I still love her? Chaesŏp smiled faintly. Tears
rolled down his cheeks. He pictured his wife, a lonely vagabond
like himself.

It must have begun to rain. He could hear the sound of rainfall
along with the wind. After pondering for a long time, Chaesŏp
sank into sleep.

Early the next morning, Chaesŏp packed his backpack.
"You're not thinking of leaving today, are you?" the general
manager, in whose room Chaesŏp had slept, said surprised.
Smiling, Chaesŏp nodded.
"You mustn't. You're not recovered yet," the manager said, but
Chaesŏp's mind was made up. After breakfast Chaesŏp went up the
rear hill and took one last look around. The valley, to which he had
grown attached in the short time he was there, came into view.
Instead of the piled snow, it was now misty on the valley. The
retreat center lay shrouded in the mist. And on the wall of the new
building which stood on the edge of the complex, the newly finished painting was shining brightly in the morning sun, like a testi-
monial to his having been there. Chaesŏp gazed at the wall and

everything else in sight for a long time, as if to etch all of them into his memory. Then, picking up his backpack, he slowly walked towards the office. The general manager, who was alone in the office, sprang up when Chaesŏp entered.

"Are you really leaving?"

"Yes." Chaesŏp answered tersely, smiling.

The general manager looked perplexed for a minute. "The director will be coming back tomorrow. I'm so sorry about what Brother Yunbae did," he said in a tone of sincere apology.

"Oh, no. It was all right. On the contrary, it taught me some important things."

"I'm so sorry to see you go away like this. Won't you stay just one more day?" the general manager said almost pleadingly.

"Thank you so much, but I think I'd better go."

"All right. We won't detain you against your will. But you must let me see you to the bus stop," the general manager said, giving in to Chaesŏp's obstinacy. Chaesŏp nodded assent, because he didn't want to offend him by refusing all hospitality. The manager took out an envelope from the drawer and put it in his inside pocket. Chaesŏp took a quick peek over the movable partition. He was sorry he could not say good-bye to Maria. But, giving up the thought quickly, he took out something from his backpack and handed it to the general manager.

"Would you please give this to Sister Maria? And give her my thanks for looking after me."

"Oh, yes," the manager looked a little perplexed, but took the present with a rather exaggerated smile. It was a tattered paperback novel.

"*And Never Said a Word?*" the manager pronounced the title, as if reading to himself, showing his usual friendly smile.

They came out of the office and walked down the wooden steps side by side. The steps had looked so slippery on the night of his arrival. They were the steps he saw when he was looking for the office in the rain.

Most of the inhabitants and visitors had left for work, so the buildings were empty. When they left the compound, a stubbly road awaited them. Along the road, the deciduous trees that were coming to life again spread their flexible boughs, and on the ridge stood tall and straight narrow-leafed evergreens. Along the dale beside the road ran a brook, breaking the silence of the mountain.

The wall with the mural came into view through the evergreen trees. But Chaesŏp walked with his eyes fixed on the ground. The general manager was walking a couple of paces ahead of him. Each

was sunk in his own thoughts. Then, when they were past the convenience store and reached the bridge, the manager began to
speak.

"You know, the night you came, when I saw you sitting in the
office hugging your backpack, you looked so tired that I had
doubts about your being able to do the mural on the big wall."

Chaesŏp listened in silence and kept walking.

"But I soon realized how wrong I was. I was deeply moved by
your passion. It's not an ordinary wall painting you did," he said in
a deep tone, turning to look into Chaesŏp's eyes. "Even if it may be
your own self-portrait." Then he added slowly, "It is one man's
ardent prayer. The prayer of a wounded, suffering human being.
We will all make the sign of the cross at your painting. And we'll
remember you." Then, revealing his friendly smile, he took out a
white envelope from his inside pocket and handed it to Chaesŏp.
"This is just a small token of our gratitude," he said.

"Oh, no, I can't take it."

"Please. It's just a token. Sister Maria knew you'd be leaving
today, and she had it ready."

Chaesŏp tried to refuse once more, but was forced to accept it.

"I really didn't expect this. But thank you."

"It's in no way a payment. We couldn't afford to pay you a fair
fee for the work you did. I hope it will at least compensate for your
travel expenses. Anyway, I'm so sorry you can't meet the director,"
he said, continuing to walk ahead with hands folded on his back.
Wind stirred his short-cropped hair. Chaesŏp folded the envelope
in half and stuck it in his trouser pocket.

In just a few more minutes they reached the bus station.
Before long they saw a bus rounding the corner and stopping in
front of them.

"Well then, good-bye." Chaesŏp shook hands with the manager,
picked up his backpack, and quickly stepped onto the bus.

"Thank you so much, brother Chaesŏp! Do come for a visit in
the spring! You'll be most welcome!" the manager shouted at the
receding bus, waving his hand. The engine noise soon drowned
out his voice.

The bus was almost empty, just as on the day he came. The few
elderly rustic passengers sitting in the front row studied Chaesŏp
with curiosity but soon looked away. Chaesŏp took a seat in the
middle row.

He recalled riding on that road in heavy mist. At that time he
had the illusion of riding to the end of the earth. But now the road
was paved with bright and warm sunlight, which covered it like
transparent glass.

Withdrawing his eyes from the road, Chaesŏp took the envelope out of his pocket. In the sealed envelope was a cheque for 100,000 *won* and a brief note. The note in thin script just said: "Jesus be praised. Thank you, Brother Chaesŏp. May God bless you. Kim Maria."

Chaesŏp put the note and the check back into the envelope and looked out. On the sunny side of the ridge azaleas were showing pink buds, which looked ready to pop open. Chaesŏp recalled a drizzly night and a white face on top of a black dress. The short and impersonal note seemed to conceal sorrow. Then, he recalled India, with the colossal banyan trees reaching up to the sky and the huge billows of raincloud, and fierce elephants and threadbare humanity. He might encounter some or all of them in the course of his life on earth. They may also be symbols of eternal sorrow for what can never be realized.

He thought he'd call his wife just as soon as he got off the bus at T'aebaek.

The Flower with Thirteen Fragrances

Ch'oe Yun

Ch'oe Yun, born in 1953, is a writer of formidable intellect and stylistic versatility. Professor of French literature at Sogang University, she utilizes many of the modern fictional techniques in her writing, such as mixing fantasy with reality, parallel time structure, multiple versions of an episode, and so forth. Her novella, "Yonder a Flower Is Quietly Fading," is rated as one of the finest stories depicting the devastation wrought by the Kwangju massacre, which was carried out by the military strongman Chun Doo Hwan in 1980 to tighten his grip on power by showing that any resistance against his rule would be ruthlessly dealt with. Like Kim Yŏng-hyŏn, she belongs to the generation of college students whose days were spent in the oppressive shadow of military rule. "The Soiled Snowman," another much-discussed story of hers, looks ironically at the "heroes" produced by the resistance movement. The story's hero was a true hero while he put his life on the line to fight injustice, but he becomes corrupted by popular success and acclaim. Ch'oe thus exposes the germ of self-deception latent in all men. Another theme Ch'oe frequently explores is the national legacy. Most often it is the legacy of the ideological struggle that led to the division of the country and the Korean War, but sometimes it is also an older and more traditional legacy—the ethical, intellectual and artistic heritage of the Korean ancestors. Ch'oe shows that though modern Koreans seem to have traveled far from their past, there is really no escaping their national heritage and that they have to find meaningful and constructive ways of embracing their past.

"The Flower with Thirteen Fragrances" (1995) is a fable of modern times. The fairytale atmosphere of the story belies its serious message and satirical intent. A lonely youth and girl find each other and give birth to the modest-looking flower with thirteen different kinds of fragrances as the fruit of their union. The flower, having powerful *medicinal properties on top of ineffable fragrances, becomes a national craze for a time, but man's greed for money and fame kill the flower and drive its creators out of their territory and eventually to take their own lives. This jeu d'esprit should make Ch'oe Yun accessible to all readers who may hitherto have found her work overly intellectual and difficult.*

A Phone Call to the North Pole

I t was one day late in the winter of his twentieth year. Bai had been trying his hand at a variety of miscellaneous jobs in Seoul after finishing high school in his hometown. Once he tried selling dogs after he got to know a breeder of the indigenous Korean Chindo dog. Having learned to drive a truck from his uncle, he had had temporary jobs with several moving companies. Life was pretty tough then, but before too long he got a chance to set himself up in a small business of his own. It might have been a piece of good luck, but it might have been the reverse, too.

His uncle, who had left his hometown many years ago and secured a footing in the metropolis after a hard struggle, died suddenly one day. Although only six years older than Bai, his uncle had been a kind protector and friend to Bai who had no one to help him in Seoul. So, Bai inherited his uncle's small delivery truck. The dead man's passionate hope was to be an airplane pilot. He had worked in an auto repair shop for several years until he had saved up enough money to buy himself a truck and set himself up as a small-scale mover. As a way of attaining his dream, he spent endless hours taking apart and putting together auto parts. Bai had explained to him countless times that repairing cars and flying airplanes are quite different, but to no avail. Uncle's dream was to be a combat pilot, but he never managed to save enough money to enroll in a pilot training school. Besides, there had been no war since he reached an age to be able to fly an airplane. Hoping his nephew would become a shining pilot in his place, he had financed Bai's education up to high school out of his meager earnings. And whenever he succeeded in making a strange gadget out of old auto parts, he proudly showed it to Bai. Most of them were no more than mere toys that had no practical use.

"Do you know what's a pilot? It's not the brand name of a fountain pen, mind you," Uncle would say to Bai from time to time. Then Bai would respond, hoping to make him give up the dream, "You have to be born in the right place to be a combat pilot. Like

America, for instance. It is fighting a war in one country or another all the time. You can't be a fighter pilot unless you're born in the right place."

Uncle's last wish was for Bai to inherit his entire fortune, but on condition that Bai would not bury him. So, Bai cremated his uncle and scattered his ashes on the creek in their hometown. Then he inherited his uncle's truck and bits and pieces of miscellany, which included several maps, a few pairs of binoculars and a dozen compasses. Bai wasn't sure how they were supposed to help his uncle achieve his dream, but he didn't throw any of them away, and he always took the least old of the compasses with him on his moving and delivery jobs. Most of his routes, however, were familiar to him, so he never really needed the compass. Sometimes, though, when he had to drive on a deserted country road he would stop the truck and check the compass.

"Well, I'm headed north by northwest," he would say with an air of satisfaction.

He had decided to continue the moving and delivery business partly out of his need to earn his living but also out of deference to his uncle who had spent the best years of his life as a truck driver. Bai's dream was to live on the North Pole. For awhile he rented a small room in the suburb owned by a one-time customer of his and worked for a freight company. On the days when there was no work, he stayed home repairing appliances or the house. His uncle's truck always served him well and never gave him any trouble.

He passed his evenings absent-mindedly watching programs on the second-hand television set that had only two channels, or playing tapes of popular songs on the worn-out cassette player that worked when he gave it a few light kicks, and singing along with the singers. Sometimes he examined the makeshift appliances his uncle had left him. Because he suffered from a rather severe case of insomnia, he sometimes drove around the highways at night to induce sleep. His insomnia produced fantasies that grew wilder and wilder and chased his sleep clean away. He fantasized about inventing a gadget that would enable people to exchange the thoughts in their hearts over a long distance without articulating them, or a ball-point pen that, if connected to your ear, would transcribe the thoughts in your brain. From them he moved on to visions of travelling all over the world to explain the use of the ball-point pen, which had created a worldwide sensation. He pictured himself explaining its uses in many different languages without any difficulty and smiling modestly to the crowd of fervent admirers. It was often past midnight when he woke up from such wild dreams. He knew it was just a harmless pastime of a lonely youth, but he thought his dreams were far less fantastic than his uncle's.

In the evenings he sometimes recalled the faces that had left an impression on him and the girls who had made his heart beat faster at one time or another. For lack of more interesting things to do, he tried to remember the girls in his classes who were scattered far and wide, working in beauty parlors, factories and supermarkets.

One very cold winter morning he ironed and put on his only suit and threw a red muffler around his neck to brighten up his black suit. Strutting like a preposterously vain turkey he once saw in a zoo, he stalked the streets of Seoul all day long. With his frozen hands stuck in his pockets, he looked like one who was looking for a miracle or on his way to sign a very important contract. He hurried his steps, as if the miraculous chance that was within his grasp would vanish if he tarried, even if momentarily. But no miracle happened to him. Nothing happened, and no one appeared, to ease his unspeakable loneliness.

With hands pushed deep in his pockets, he observed young people vigorously walking the winter streets, bright smiles on their faces. They looked about twenty, like himself, but they were so full of energy that he imagined that even their breaths would smell fragrant. He could not believe that they were his contemporaries. Returning home in the early evening, he took out one of his uncle's maps and hung it on the wall. Then, leaning on his folded bedding and sipping beer, which was the only luxury he could afford in his life, he gazed at the map. Thus began his dream of the North Pole. When he felt bored with life he took the map down from the wall to read aloud the difficult names of the cities. Ulan Bator, Vladivostok, Sierra Leone . . . But the place that excited his imagination the most was the North Pole. Ellsmere, Eta, Tulle, Reykjavik . . . Across the vast frozen plains of the North Pole are scattered villages consisting of a few households. . . . In this way he began his slow approach to the North Pole.

Every night he walked on the plains of the North Pole alone. Lights seemed to shine from afar, but they always receded when he drew near. He was breathless and felt so cold that his blood seemed to have frozen in his veins. If I don't reach that light, I'm going to fall down on this floor of ice and freeze to death, he murmured, all the while straining to put one frozen foot forward at a time. I'll find a kindhearted Eskimo girl and marry her, he thought. We'll have a faithful reindeer and sleigh dogs, and we'll have a baby in time. When the baby grows up, I'll take him out hunting. The march on the polar plains taxed his strength to the utmost, and he woke up just as he was on the threshold of death.

Do I have to go all the way to the North Pole to have such a simple dream? he thought as he woke up, rubbing the soles of his feet, which itched as if they really had been frostbitten in the North Pole. But, as soon as he fell asleep again, he was once more on the vast polar plains, where there was neither noise, gravity, pain nor sorrow.

One day, while he was again walking on the North Pole, a telephone rang. The ringing of the phone rippled through the North Pole. There can't be phones on the icy plains of the North Pole, he thought, and walked on, murmuring, how clean the air is here, and it's so quiet that this might be the Ice Age. A house appeared in the middle of the frozen plains, and he walked inside. The phone was ringing in that house. He picked up the receiver, which felt cold in his hands, and heard a strange and muddled sound from the other end of the line. Then, he heard a delicate sigh, which seemed to be coming from quite close by. He waited, for more than five slow minutes by the polar clock. Then the phone went dead.

The North Pole woman didn't speak. But she called the next day and the day after. When he picked up the phone, the same voice said "hello," then waited. If he stopped talking for awhile, the woman also stopped talking.

Bai continued to work during the day as before. The metropolis was full of people moving from one place to another and leaving old houses for new ones. So, he received phone calls almost every morning. One day he moved several dozen oil drums; another day old cabinets and a sewing machine; on a third he took care of an evicted woman's pots and pans, and so on. Sometimes he would answer a summons and find that the moving plan was cancelled because the lease or purchase contract was broken. There were days, too, when he had no work.

As yet he knew very little about the North Pole. He had only seen a few photos, and he had watched a documentary about the life of an Eskimo couple on television a long time ago. All the same, he always fell asleep thinking of the North Pole. There was an Eskimo youth by the name of Baihagitu. He was on his way back from a long trip. He didn't even remember when it was that he had left for his journey on a fishing raft. He had planned to come back with lots of fish and fur, but the raft snagged on a reef so he barely escaped death. He even passed a whole season among sea tigers which spent their winters in the blizzard. With icicles hanging from his beard, he broke the ice with his teeth, and once even helped a female sea tiger give birth to a litter on an iceberg. Many changes took place on the North Pole in the meantime. He had left his igloo as a lad of sixteen, and now he was a young man. Checking his compass, he walked and walked towards his village, but it didn't appear. He walked on and on, because he would freeze to death if he stopped walking. It went on for no one knows how long. One white night, he met on the frozen plain a woman dragging an old and ridiculous-looking sleigh.

Green Hands

"I'll jump in front of the next car for sure," she whispered to her-self in the middle of the night from the dark side of the woods beside the highway. It had taken her a few hours to reach this spot on foot after making up her mind to jump in front of a passing car. She crouched down behind a bush around a bend, which seemed to her an ideal spot for carrying out her purpose. The bush con-tained a pine tree, whose needles tickled her cheeks and made her laugh as she crept under it. The light from the sparse pale lamps along the highway seeped faintly into the bush and reached even to where she was squatting. She had already let pass quite a num-ber of cars. Shivering in the chill of the early spring night, she whispered to herself again, "I won't jump in front of just any old car." That seemed to give her limp body a little bit of strength. From where she sat she could see far down the road. She could choose the car she liked; then she could take her time to dash out in front of it. She did not keep count of the number of cars she let pass, because she felt as if counting each passing car would make her fall deeper and deeper into a bottomless pit. I'm not afraid, she told herself for the thousandth time that night. Once, she pan-icked when something jumped out at her out of the darkness. But it was only a wild cat. And once she tripped over a stone and fell. Such small incidents frightened her.

But I won't jump in front of just any car! she repeated to her-self and bit her underlip. Her underlip was unusually full, as she had bit it often in her childhood, trying to endure her numerous sorrows. She felt chilly. Trying to rally her spirit by singing a child-hood song she used to sing in her hometown, she waited for the right car.

Her hometown was deep in a high mountain. She had neither parents nor siblings. She only had an ancient grandmother, who looked old from the very first time she saw her. She didn't know how she was born, why she spent her first twelve years in her hometown, and why she had drifted from her hometown to a small town, then to a city, and then to the capital. Each transition brought fresh unhappiness. She had been thrown out of every single job she had and just now was on her way back to her hometown. Because so many things had happened to her in a short space of time, she could not remember all of them. She always thought of her brain as a small and rather seedy box, somewhat like the colored cookie box that a distant relative of hers who had come to visit her grandmother at one time had given her. A worn and rather soiled box whose lid didn't close because it was crammed to overflowing with strings, dried leaves, pebbles and the like. She had several keys to the box of her brain, but she always misplaced them and couldn't find any when she needed them.

Deciding that she couldn't face her grandmother as a failure, she had gotten off the bus bound for her hometown. She remembered the whirlwind that shook her when she decided to take her own life. Of course she didn't understand herself why she must die. She was only sixteen. To the sixteen-year-old girl, death seemed like a sweet fairy, one that comes to you to help solve your difficult and knotty problems. She had been talking with the fairy for a long time now. The first time was when she was thrown out of the house she had been working as a maid for a trivial mistake. But she couldn't tell anyone that she was going to die because the fairy had advised her to. Everybody would laugh, as they usually did at her words. Everybody? But really, there was no one she could assign to that pronoun. Anyway, because she was going to die that night, nobody would be able to ask her why she took her own life.

She recalled her life of the past few years, like one remembering a sad dawn spent on a chilly mountain. She recalled the little girl she was looking after in the first household where she worked as a maid. On that day, she followed the child around all day long, singing along with her a children's song about the zucchini coming to visit the cucumbers and lamenting her weight, and the apple coming to visit chile peppers and screaming about their spicy hotness. It was not her fault that the child died, but her employer gave her a beating and threw her out. She escaped, clutching only the potted gardenia she had been growing on the terrace. It was not entirely because Green Hands gave the gardenia a strong mixture that its fragrance was so strong. The girl was only four years old and had heart trouble. Green Hands knew that the young couple threw her out because their grief at losing their child was unbearable.

She was thrown out of many more houses after that. And every time for reasons she couldn't understand. One time the son of the house broke down the door of her room to rush in and order her out. Another time the head of the family got drunk and beat her up. In the process the gardenia she kept with her all the time died. Then she got work in a nursery farm. That was a happy time for her. But she was thrown out again, because she cut off all the wires that were strangling the young pines, maples, boxwoods and cone pines and gave them plenty of water. After that, she worked at many hothouses and nurseries but was thrown out of every one of them.

One more car passed. But she shook her head. No, not that one. The medium-sized truck had glaring headlights like the eyes of a drunken man and rushed past the bush with an explosive sound. The gust raised by the truck shook the bush. Then the highway was silent once again.

She thought, I suppose my flesh will tear and my bones will break, and touched her plump wrist in the sleeve of her worn overcoat. And she felt her rough and thick hands, which her grandmother called "Green Hands," because they grew plump grains and fruits even from burnt or stony fields. Her neighbors also called her Green Hands. The herb man, who stayed overnight in her grandmother's house one time, was amazed by how well she could tell spots where medicinal herbs grew. He also called her Green Hands. She was called Green Hands on the farm where she worked through the recommendation of the herb man. But nobody in the city called her Green Hands. In the city she was called Miss O, in the style people use to call young women whose proper names they don't want to bother remembering. So, now nobody called her Green Hands any more.

She touched her bosom with both hands. They had begun to ache periodically. She thought she wanted to die before her breasts matured. She couldn't stand to think of becoming a woman in her circumstances. She had never been happy or gay ever since she left her hometown. Her flesh felt smooth and bouncy in the darkness. That surprised her. She wept a little thinking that her flesh would be torn and crushed under the automobile tires. She had an illusion that someone was calling her—"Green Hands!" Was it her grandmother? Or one of her neighbors? She brushed away her tears and listened. But it was only the low wind sweeping the earth in the distance.

She heard one more car approach. Lighting up the road with its high beam, the car dashed up. She raised herself a little and looked at the rather modest-looking car. For some reason, hot tears ran down her cheeks. Because she recalled how her grandmother looked on the day she left her hometown. Was she still alive? And what about my few neighbors in that high mountain village? Were they still there, or have they all left? On the morning she left her hometown, she saw her grandmother asleep, curled up like a shrimp. Grandmother didn't seem to have sensed that Green Hands had decided to leave. In their life together Grandmother made her draw water the first thing in the morning. Then they would work in the field and eat lunch together. When she got far away from her hometown and looked back to see that the mountains were not the familiar ones of her village anymore, she had flopped down on the road. When she opened her bag to take out the rice balls to eat, she found the rice cake and money that her grandmother had put in. Though she had hidden the cloth bag under the floor among rusted farm tools so her grandmother wouldn't suspect. . . .

From great fatigue and so many memories swirling in her head, she fell asleep momentarily. Though for a split second, she must have fallen into deep sleep. She dreamt that animals that looked like dinosaurs and other nameless reptiles were wrestling, tangled together. When she woke up with a cough, she saw the vehicle with the high beam running towards her slowly and a little unsteadily. It looked so funny that she forgot her dreadful dream.

"That's the one!" she murmured, rubbing her eyes. The vehicle, which looked one-eyed with only one of the headlights working, was coming toward the bend where she was hiding. It was a small truck. When she got up, closing her eyes tightly preparing to dash out, the car slowed down with a rumble and came to a halt. A man jumped out of the car with a flashlight. He circled the car once, checking its body carefully with the flashlight. He also tried the tires with a few light kicks. As the flashlight swept the car, she also looked at the car, which rather resembled a porcupine. Her heart, which had been beating wildly with the thought of death, calmed down a little. What should I do next? she thought. I was going to fling myself under that car. Why did it have to stop in front of me?

He was a small and thin man. She almost said to him, Excuse

me! The man's back, as he leaned forward a little with his legs spread apart to examine the car by the light of the flashlight, sent a tremor through her. It was unlike that of any man's she'd seen. She recalled the legend of the man who came to visit this world when winter mist rose from Mist Hill in her hometown, to collect all the worries in the world and take it with him. The man's back resembled the pillar of mist that rose from Mist Hill in her hometown when the winter wind hit it from all sides. She felt anxious lest the man should turn into a pillar of mist and disappear from her sight.

A few vehicles passed the parked truck. But she stayed where she was, not knowing what to do. At last she got up, picking up her travel bag that she had been sitting on. While the man was whistling, looking at a light in the distance, she climbed into the truck. Getting in the truck again, the man looked surprised to find a woman sitting beside him but didn't say anything. He merely noticed her soiled face, her tattered travel bag and her muddy feet. The truck started again with a rumble. He took her back to the city she had left behind.

Getting off the truck at dawn at the entrance of the capital, in the flower farm district, she waited for the city to come to life again. And she found work in one of the flower farms, which was in dire need of hands at the beginning of spring. She introduced herself as Green Hands, and the flower farmer agreed to give her room and board if she'd transfer the several hundred potted plants there into bigger pots. This time, she didn't cut off the wires from the baby pines and maples. And she didn't go to the highway again with the intention of jumping in front of a car.

She, too, suffered from insomnia. When she fell asleep in the evening tired out from the day's work, she dreamed she was a baby pine tree tied round and round with wires. She also dreamed of falling down a precipice. Her grandmother used to say that if you fell down a cliff in a dream that meant you're growing up. But she was already as tall as she'd ever be, so she didn't think the dream presaged her growing taller. One night, waking up again from a dream of falling down with all her hair standing on end, she recalled the one-eyed truck she met on the highway and the driver who looked from the back like the pillar of mist rising from her hometown hill. She remembered the flashlight revealing the phone number advertised with the name of his company on the side of the truck. The numbers were written in all different colors and were shiny like decorations. She dialed his number. At first she didn't talk but just listened to his voice from the other end of the line. Then, every evening, when the evening haze descended on the flower farms and her death wish rose again from the pit of her stomach and choked her, she dialed his number. Every day.

Birth of the Wind Chrysanthemum

On a clear and sunny day Bai first came to see Green Hands at the empty lot behind the flower farm. Mist was rising from the hills. The azaleas were in bud within a dozen feet of where they were standing, but Bai and Green Hands were too shy to admire the flowers.

Bai was the first to overcome his embarrassment and speak: "Please call me Bai. It's the nickname I gave myself. I am a mover by day and I dream of going to the North Pole at night. Bai means a man who walks the plains of the North Pole."

"And I'm Green Hands. I was born among the mountains and drifted here. I'll be seventeen come next September."

Even though they didn't know it the first time they saw each other in the truck, they realized today that both of them had been running towards each other steadily from long, long ago. However, each of them had been alone for such a long time that they didn't know what to say and so just stared at each other with wide-open eyes. The woman who made telephone calls to the North Pole every night was silent, just as she was on the phone. The man who had whistled on the highway that night and answered her call every night made her heart beat so wildly and her hands shake so violently that she wanted nothing better than to flee from him. But they both stood there transfixed, unable to utter a word, because they were on fire, as if they had caught a contagious, flammable disease.

The first emotion to hit them was sadness. Green Hands looked pitiful to Bai, and Bai looked pitiful to Green Hands. Each was sad because the other had such tender eyes. They were also sad because they didn't know what to do, and from the thought that meeting people brought such sadness. But their sadness was nothing compared to the fever that inflamed them immediately afterwards.

All night, both of them tossed in their sleep from the fever that seemed to set them on fire and made them delirious. Pulling the quilt up to his head, or squeezing her head with both hands, Bai and Green Hands wondered whether the disease they caught was typhoid fever, measles, or cholera. The next day, their fever subsided a little, but mirrors revealed the ravages wrought on their cheeks and eyes by the previous night's fever and sweating. There were dark rings around Bai's remarkably deep eyes, and Green Hands' cheeks were so deeply furrowed that she had dimples all day even though she wasn't smiling. Stunned by the sudden incomprehensible fever, she wasn't in the mood for smiling.

After that long and lonely night, strange things started happening to both of them. The next day, Bai started out early to move a gloomy-voiced pianist's piano from the southwest to the northeast of the city. He drove his truck along the road indicated on the map. But somehow or other his truck had veered off the road on the map and was running on a strange road at full speed. And he seemed to hear a military march booming from the piano in the back of the truck whenever the speedometer went over a certain point. After quite a while, the truck stopped in front of Green Hands's flower farm. Bai was astonished. At that moment Green Hands was walking towards the water faucet to fill the water can to water the orchids. But somehow, her legs moved of their own accord towards the gate of the vinyl house, and her hands were quickly pushing aside the tall gourd vine blocking the doorway. When she flung the door open, there stood Bai in the early morning light, looking as if his two big eyes had become two great cavities.

It went on like this for a whole week. As if tossed to each other by a tyrannical storm, they found themselves standing face to face with each other, wondering how it happened. Bai and Green Hands looked at each other as if their eyes had become magnets. Soon, they found that not only their eyes but also their hands, feet, legs, chest and head had become magnets pulling at their counterparts. Once, their lips became magnets and pulled each other so hard that Green Hands felt as if her front teeth had broken. Of all the magnetic activities of their body parts, they loved that of their lips best. And their lips had the strongest magnetic pull as well. When the magnetic power of their lips worked, they felt as if they had been sucked into a long tunnel lit up with innumerable crimson lamps and came out on top of a high peak that was surrounded with ineffably pure air. It reminded Green Hands of the hills of her hometown and Bai of the plains in the North Pole of his dreams.

"Why, what's the matter, Green Hands?"

"I just saw the hills of my hometown. I'd forgotten about them for a long time."

"And I . . . I was walking on the plains of the North Pole."

"What are there on the plains of the North Pole?"

"You, and snow."

"And you are on the hills of my hometown. And the hills are covered with snow."

While this went on, strange things were occurring here and there. A runaway girl's suitcase was delivered to a bachelor's bedroom, and the owner of the flower farm had to apologize to the customer who had to take an orange tree instead of the gardenia he'd ordered. But the strange occurrences did not always result in complaints. Sometimes customers were ecstatic to see a Benjamin tree that had twice as many leaves as when they had entrusted it to the farm, or the orchid that had no less than seven stalks covered with white petals. The small orchid, which had been drooping and hadn't bloomed for many years, suddenly had three flowers, so the farm owner had the greatest difficulty assessing Green Hands's usefulness. Seeing her escaping to the rear mound at every opportunity, he thought he'd throw her out as soon as he caught hold of her, but when she appeared in front of him, he forgot what he was going to say to her.

Bai and Green Hands's magnetic activities grew more and more intense, so much so that they couldn't bear to spend a minute apart from each other. They longed for each other so violently that they were gloomy when apart. When they were together, Bai felt dizzy and confused, as if he'd been running continuously on the dark roads of a country where it was night all the time. Green Hands felt dizzy, as if she'd become a small pebble a thirsty child threw into a bottomless well. They were even more confused and lost than when they had entertained lonely fantasies or contemplated suicide before they met each other. They wished, if possible, to crash into each other's bones and melt into each other's flesh. They would have swallowed each other whole if it had been possible. Too young to understand all these contradictory quirks of desire, they felt paralyzed.

Bai no longer had the peace of mind to move other people's household goods, and Green Hands couldn't stand to see the miniature trees being strangled by wires. She felt as if the trees would bleed and their flesh would burst.

One day in late summer they were sitting on the mound behind Green Hands's flower farm and looking up at the yellow cloud. Green Hands spoke first.

"How far can we go if you fill up your tank?"

"Far. Very far, Green Hands. We can go very far."

And so they agreed to leave for that far place where the truck would take them. Then, for the first time since they began seeing each other, they spent a whole day apart from each other. To prepare for their long journey.

"We're going to take only the basic necessities, just as if we're going to a desert island."

"Right. Only the basic necessities."

Green Hands, who had nothing more than a few clothes to take, finished packing in no time and waited listlessly. And she packed these old clothes only because their pockets were filled with seeds, seeds that had got in there sometime, somehow. She put the clothes into her bag making sure the seeds didn't spill out, and waited for Bai. Then she chuckled low. She had thought of a good way to while away the time that remained until Bai came to pick her up. She began to undo the wires strangling the baby trees lined up under an awning. On a few of the trees the wires had pushed into the flesh, so she had to cut them with a cutter. After taking the wires off all the several dozen bonsai pots, Green Hands filled the big watering can and watered them until the pots were soaked through. Then she looked up at the sky to see whether it wasn't too late in the day to water the plants the farm owner kept in the shade and neglected to look after. She saw that night was approaching.

Bai sorted through his uncle's trunk to discard rusted gadgets and put the maps and compasses on the truck. They made a sizeable load. Every time he put an item on the truck he asked himself if he would need that on a desert island. Then he went to say goodbye to the landlord's family, who had been very kind to him. It hadn't taken him long to put his things in order and pack, but it took almost a whole day to bid good-bye to his landlord's family. All the family members had ideas about what he would need to begin a new life. There were long debates, and then each of them put on his truck one item he or she thought would be essential to the new couple. So, his truck became loaded with the big bottle of spirits from his landlord who had been keeping it hidden deep in his closet, the cooking pot from his landlady, the quilt from the eldest daughter, the silk necktie from the eldest son, and a week-old puppy from the younger son.

So, it was midnight before Bai and Green Hands could finally go on their way. Bai took out the compass and drove south at first, then northwest after a week, and then northeast after a month. They just drove on, without worrying about lodging or eating. To shake off the nameless loneliness that assailed them, they drove day and night. Sometimes they drove all night until dawn broke over the dark mountain. At such times they stopped the truck and gazed at the breaking day with their arms around each other. Wherever they went was a desert island to them. Occasionally, they stopped to work for a few days at a restaurant or on construction sites or on farms and reached Green Hands's hometown after a few months.

After a long time, they gave birth to a rare flower that they named Wind Chrysanthemum. Bai was then twenty-two and Green Hands, nineteen.

The Secret of Wind Chrysanthemum

Who can tell precisely how Wind Chrysanthemum came into being? Who can describe its shape and fragrance accurately?

"Wind Chrysanthemum. Your nickname is the North Pole flower. The basis of your life is the frozen earth, so you have grown strong on the high mountain in the cold shade of the cloud and in the chilly north wind. Your pale purple blossom has fifty-five petals, which is eleven times five, the number symbolizing the will to survive. With them you strive to catch the sunlight filtering through the cloud. Your pure fragrance, which is the crystallization of the intense and varied passions of your small body, is a sad tribute to the world. To fight the dry climate your stature is short, your lonely leaves are evergreen, and your modest stalks are covered with down."

This is one of the rare descriptions of the Wind Chrysanthemum that have survived.

Not even Bai and Green Hands can tell exactly how they came to cultivate the first Wind Chrysanthemum patch in the world. Of course they remember only too vividly the day they first discovered the flower. When first discovered, the plant had only a few drooping flowers. It is hard to believe that the plant later created such a sensation. The north wind that Bai blew on it and the care that Green Hands poured over it day and night for a thousand days made the plant so special. After that everybody knew the name of Wind Chrysanthemum.

When Bai and Green Hands arrived in Green Hands's hometown, the place that had the shortest hours of daylight in the whole country, the village was almost completely deserted. It was the little puppy, tired out from the long travel, who looked the happiest to reach their destination at last. In Green Hands's old house standing high on the slope and looking out onto the ridge, her grandmother was waiting for her return to bid her last good-bye. So, the first thing Bai did on arrival was to close the old woman's eyes and dig a small grave for her shrivelled body.

"I've lived too long, so let me go. Please plant over my grave the seeds in the pouch under the floor." Those were her last and only words. Green Hands found the familiar pouch under the floor, and planted the seeds in it together with various other seeds from out of her dress pockets. As it was late autumn, Green Hands's heart tore even while she sowed them, because she knew they couldn't sprout.

After burying the grandmother and making preparations for the winter, Bai and Green Hands took their first good rest since they met. They forgot their loneliness, hunger, cold and anxiety and slept. Days are short on that steep, high mountain, so even though they woke up from time to time, it was always dark so they went right back to sleep. Sometimes they kept on sleeping because they dreaded waking up. In sleeping, they lost count of the days. When they woke up at last, they found five pale purple buds on a small modest plant that had sprouted on the hill to the rear of their house.

Green Hands was the first to see the flowers. It was in deep night, snow fell in huge flakes and her breath froze as soon as it escaped her mouth. She seemed to hear her grandmother's voice telling her that it was the coldest winter in eighty-seven years. With a flashlight in her hand, Green Hands went out in the icy wind to bid good-bye to the fragile buds she hadn't had time to bring indoors. There she emitted a cry. When a gust of wind whipped through the blinding blizzard in an angelic soprano, the five buds heaved themselves and opened their petals. Astonished, Green Hands lifted the clear plastic cover she had put over the fragile buds. In the merciless wind that seemed ready to rip off the leaves and tear out the roots, the flowers blossomed bigger and bigger and the fragile stalk stood erect, like an owl's ear straining to hear a ghostly sound. Green Hands gave the plant the name of Wind Chrysanthemum, because it bloomed miraculously in the wind. But Bai, who had rushed out at hearing Green Hands's cry, thought of another name. Standing beside Green Hands and watching the bud opening slowly and the petals unfolding, Bai thought that it might be the flower he once saw on a postcard, which said that it was the only flower that bloomed on the North Pole. Green Hands knew many flowers, having spent her child-hood on the mountain, but she had never seen that flower before.

The flowers, however, began to droop as soon as the wind died down and sunbeams began to spread on the mountaintop. The leaves drooped, the stalks shrivelled, and the flowers dropped their heads. Then, one sunny and warm day, the flowers wilted. It was no use giving them water and covering them with plastic to keep them warm, or taking them indoors in a pot. However, when one flower wilted another bud formed, and thus the flower eked out a precarious life, causing Green Hands infinite anxiety.

It took them a long, long time to create a small colony of Wind Chrysanthemums. Bai and Green Hands spent a lot of time and care into getting to know the flower's constitution and multiplying the five flowers into ten, and from there to create a patch of Wind Chrysanthemums below the ridge. It took almost all of the best part of their youth to learn that Wind Chrysanthemum takes root only in cool shades, that it dislikes unfiltered rain and dew, that its pale purple color grows deeper in the winter and that its fragrance grows stronger when cold wind blows. After long and careful observation, they discovered that the white down covering the stalks secretes sticky white fluid. Each individual flower had a slightly different fragrance, which was strongest during the night and at dawn. The fragrance was so strong that it sometimes kept them awake at night. On such nights they had waking dreams of flying over mountaintops on the back of a white pegasus and capturing a glimpse of the Elysian fields or diving into the deep seas and climbing gleaming underwater rocks.

To create the freezing cold air, heavy snow and strong gale necessary for the Wind Chrysanthemum to bloom, Bai poured his heart and soul into assembling a powerful propeller and vapor freezer from out of the auto parts left behind by his uncle. From experiment and experience they learned that the chrysanthemum that was exposed to thirty days' storm and heavy snow had the healthiest and longest-lasting flowers and the strongest fragrance. To make the fragrance stronger, Green Hands tried mixing the juice from gardenia stalk, a water pepper root and a piece of hemp into the water from the fountain. Or she collected the rainwater on the seventh of July by lunar calendar, let it stand for fifty-five days, and mixed it with a piece of chicory, bunting's feathers and new shoots of besom. Giving different water mixtures produced a subtle difference in the fragrance of the flowers. Bai and Green Hands completely forgot their loneliness, and time passed quickly.

Green Hands's inability to tell people how to cultivate Wind Chrysanthemums was not a falsification by omission, as some of her critics contended. It was simply that she had used so many dif-

ferent kinds of mixtures and solutions to water the flowers that she
often got it mixed up herself. Besides, as other people couldn't dis-
criminate between the subtle differences in the fragrance produced by each solution given, her laborious explanations were useless.

When Bai and Green Hands first took the flowers to the nearby
town on a market day and lined them up for sale in the shade at a
little distance from the market, nobody paid any attention to the
pale purple perennials less than a foot high. They stayed there for
a whole day, but they weren't able to sell a single one of the ten
healthiest and most vigorous-looking Wind Chrysanthemum plants
in the wooden pots specially carved out by Bai. A few children
strayed towards the plants, it is true, drawn by the peculiar fragrance, but their parents quickly dragged them away, while casting
suspicious glances at Bai and Green Hands. In dire need of fuel to
operate the propeller, Bai and Green Hands took the plants to sell
at the biggest flower shop in town, but the shopowner refused even
to look at them, taking them for some weed that grows out in the
fields and mountains. Green Hands held up one plant close to the
shopkeeper's nose, but its fragrance was unfortunately lost, mixed
with those of so many other flowers in the shop.

So, there was nothing for them to do but to reload the pots
onto the truck and drive back home along the darkening road.
They stopped briefly in a small village inhabited by about a dozen
families. It was the village that came into Green Hands's eyes when,
many years ago, leaving behind her home village to find a better
life in the nearby town, she sat down on the ridge and ate the rice
cakes her grandmother had packed in her bag. The village looked
peaceful, and the mountain snugly sunk in darkness soothed their
tired hearts. It was Bai who came up with the idea of leaving a pot
of Wind Chrysanthemum in front of each household of that village. It was his way of consoling Green Hands's loneliness and misgiving of that day long ago. So, the pots were left as presents at the
doors of the village people who were fast asleep after a hard day's
work.

At about the time the plant from heaven-knows-where had
given off its fragrance for a whole season and the flowers were
about to fade, several of the families of that village moved to Bai
and Green Hands's remote mountain village, after searching far
and wide for the source of the fragrance. Wind Chrysanthemums
thus spread from one village to the next, from village to town, and
from town to city.

As the plants' colony grew bigger, more and more propellers were needed. Having discovered that the force and direction of the wind made differences in the shade and fragrance of the flowers, Bai and Green Hands teased their brains out trying to find ways to combine the best color and fragrance. They succeeded in growing eight kinds of Wind Chrysanthemums, each with a distinct fragrance. One had the fragrance reminiscent of the calm, deep sea; another had the whiff of the wind sweeping over the vast plain; another seemed to transport one into a primordial paradise; still another led one to an immemorial past . . . Bai and Green Hands gave each fragrance a name from the scene that passed through their minds on smelling the flowers first.

People came to settle there from the nearby villages and the small city, to help with the cultivation or distribution of Wind Chrysanthemums. By the time the village head living beyond the mountain, astonished by the sudden influx of residents, arrived with a warning from the provincial governor, the Wind Chrysanthemum colony had spread over more than half the mountain ridge and several dozen households had settled nearby.

Wind Chrysanthemum Fever

People came from farther away. The first one to arrive from afar was a pale-faced man who breathed hard, as if he had run all the way to this remote corner of the world. "I'm a human Wind Chrysanthemum," he announced on arrival, much to the astonishment of everyone. "Please allow me to stay here and study the flowers. I promise I won't bother you."

The man introduced himself as a Mr. Ko, who suffered from the low-altitude disease. He said that he could preserve his health only in high mountain air and in strong wind, just like the Wind Chrysanthemum. The man, who was almost forty now, had been suffering from the disease since he reached adulthood, and had roamed all the high mountains in the country in search of a cure, but to no avail. Bai and Green Hands didn't understand his disease but allowed him to stay and promised to tell him anything he wanted to know about the flowers. Ko said that his body and soul were worn out, like the heels of a madman who roamed the deserts of the world for centuries. He said he had heard about the flower while staying on a snow-covered mountain in the neighboring country.

He built a hut beside the colony of Wind Chrysanthemums in
the direction of the wind from the propeller, and began to study
the flower. His small hut began to be filled with all kinds of laboratory equipment, and every weekend he took many small vials to his
friend's laboratory located six hours' distance from there.

"Aren't I lucky to find something worth devoting my whole life
to at last!" he was heard murmuring to himself.

By devoting himself exclusively to studying the flower, Mr. Ko
was able to produce after two years a tablet that he named "Bapa"
tablet. The name was a tribute to Bai and Green Hands, made up
of the first syllables of their names. But, since there weren't many
people afflicted with his disease, the tablets had no commercial viability and he often fell into gloom. He wasted his fortune advertis-
ing in the newspapers for patients of low-altitude disease, and
wrote numerous proposals to pharmaceutical companies for mass
production of the tablets. He didn't neglect to enclose a petal of
Wind Chrysanthemum in the envelope, so that his letters would
convey the fragrance. But the letters he received from the post-
man, who complained each time about having to climb the mountain in order to deliver one letter, always contained bad news.
Some companies didn't even bother to write back, so the letters
stopped coming after a while. Mr. Ko was beginning to think that
he might be the only one in the country suffering from this disease. Noting his distress, Green Hands pitied him so much that she
wished she would get the low-altitude disease just to console him.
For his forty-second birthday, Green Hands cut and dried forty-two
of the most beautiful and fragrant Wind Chrysanthemums, put
them in a basket woven from their stalks, and gave them to Mr. Ko
as a present. The ten fragrances of the flower blended divinely in
the basket, like a symphony of the most exquisite instruments, and
spread from his room to the whole village, from the village to the
mountaintop, and from the mountaintop to the Heavens.

At first the Wind Chrysanthemum fever spread slowly and quietly, like the wind of May, which the people of the area called
Marang. Or tenderly, like the fragrance of the flower. Some fragrances of the flower spread for miles on the wind. People could
get to this remote mountain village by following the fragrance.
Poets sang of the color and fragrance of the flowers, and two poets
offered to weave the saga of Bai and Green Hands into an epic.
Poet K's "North Pole Flower," which was printed in a daily newspaper around that time, didn't draw much attention at first, but it
began to be recited by more and more people and was soon made
into a song by a composer affiliated with the Nature Poetry
Association.

In a forgotten village high up on the mountain
A lonely couple grew a flower.
Wind Chrysanthemum, your tough fragility
Is a whiff of eternity.

In the pale purple twilight
Your dream is primal peace.
You are a lover's yearning for the North Pole
Turned into floral fragrance.

I offer you my love.
I offer you my purity.
Your fragrance lulls my grief
And your smile thaws my loneliness.

At about the time the song "North Pole Flower" became a popular tune, the Wind Chrysanthemum fever that began as a breeze turned into a raging storm. Crowd after crowd made their pilgrimage to the remote mountain village. Newspaper reporters came to interview Bai and Green Hands; a photo artist brought five cameras and two assistants to take shots of the flowers for a special exhibition and a calendar. They took pictures for two whole days, going up the trees for a bird's-eye shot, or prostrating on the ground for a worm's-eye shot, or with the lens almost touching the petals for close-up shots. They snapped pictures of Bai from the back, looking at the flowers with his hands folded on his back, and of Green Hands looking up at the mountain, with her head wrapped in a towel. Bai and Green Hands's skin was so tanned by the sun and the wind that it was as smooth as baked potatoes, and chapped here and there. They were smiling. They looked happy. When asked about the couple afterwards, one of the photo artist's two assistants reminisced, "Oh, they looked so happy, my heart ached to see them."

Green Hands always wore a towel wrapped around her head in the photographs.

Sometimes she looked at the crowd with frightened eyes. The sight of so many people sometimes awoke in her the memory of the loneliness she never understood. But Bai reassured her every time she was struck by fear: "No, we'll never be lonely again, as long as our magnetisms work in us. We earned it the hard way. We have found our North Pole."

Green Hands had a worry she didn't tell even Bai. It was her hair. It kept falling out. She didn't know when the trouble started, because at first she didn't pay much attention to the problem. She just assumed that old hair would be replaced by new ones. Just like dust particles. Or dandelion seeds. Or like the mist that brooded on the mountaintop in the morning, disappeared during the day, and descended again in the evening. But by and by she realized that her hair kept falling out without growing back. Once as profuse and abundant as heather on the steppe, her hair became sparse. At some point Green Hands realized that the loss of her hair was related to the endless birth of Wind Chrysanthemums. Her remaining hair was still lustrous as pebbles in a clear stream, but she shaved it all off and wrapped a towel around her head. Her hair was infinitely less precious to her than growing the transcendently beautiful Wind Chrysanthemums.

As the song "North Pole Flower" gained greater popularity, the beauty and fragrance of Wind Chrysanthemums became more widely known, and more and more people wanted to have a pot of the plant on their windowsills. And it became fashionable among young people to give Wind Chrysanthemums as a present to their sweethearts on the nineteenth of April, the anniversary of the 1960 Student Revolution. A young man is said to have worked at a gas station for five months to buy a pot of Wind Chrysanthemum for his beloved. As it became rumored that one of the fragrances of the flower had aphrodisiacal effect, managers of the so-called love hotels in the vicinity of Seoul bought up Wind Chrysanthemums in the black markets. This was one of the things that made Bai and Green Hands sad. They could not possibly grow as many Wind Chrysanthemums as people seemed to want. Wind Chrysanthemums had to have thirty days' icy north wind while they were in bud, and many of the more fastidious ones refused to bloom even after that. And Bai and Green Hands had neither the land nor manpower to expand the colony indefinitely.

Many fake Wind Chrysanthemums made their appearance in the flower markets and confused people. The fake Wind Chrysanthemums had no fragrance, nor fifty-five petals. Their petals had neither the indescribably delicate pale purple tint, nor the texture that was like the eyelids of sleeping babies seen in September twilight. The fake flowers wilted in a few days. Zang, the new puppy that Bai received as a present on the day he left Seoul and had in the meantime reached maturity as a dog, grew busy. Zang had to guard against the thieves who sneaked into the mountain during the day and stole the flowers at night. Some of the thieves, unable to steal the flowers, crushed them with their boots out of spite. These people didn't know that the roots made the flowers what they were. They didn't know that, once separated from their roots, the flowers lost their fragrance almost at once and wilted. And those who tried to dig up the whole plant with their long roots were sure to be found out by Zang, whose ears could catch the faintest rustle from far away. A big-scale florist offered to buy up the whole colony at an enormous price, and another wanted to purchase Bai and Green Hands's cultivation secrets with a bigger patch of land at a higher altitude.

Green Hands's home village, which had become the Wind Chrysanthemum colony now, was not a very scenic place. Since Wind Chrysanthemums began to spread on the mountain, however, its aspect had changed drastically, so that now many mountain climbers sought it out. Shops and eateries sprouted at the entrance of the mountain to cater to the endless stream of hikers. Cakes and pancakes decorated with Wind Chrysanthemum petals made the vendors rich. Manufacturers of souvenirs, such as clear plastic prayer beads with petals inside, canes with handles in the shape of the flower, back scratchers with scratching hands painted in what was supposed to be the flower's pale purple color, and towels with floral prints, raked in profits.

Summer was a difficult season for Bai and Green Hands. When spring came, Bai and Green Hands had to mark the areas for each variety of the flowers with white paint, and build coldhouses appropriate to each of the twelve different varieties of chrysanthemums having different fragrances, hardihood and color. When that was done Bai and Green Hands were exhausted, but the coldhouses looked like so many igloos that Bai felt like he was on the North Pole. Some of the tourists and flower shop owners were not content just looking at the fantastic coldhouses and tried to sneak into them, so Bai had to spend the whole day sitting under the shade of a tree with Zang to keep intruders out. Green Hands on her part had to spend the entire summer in the coldhouses, tending the flowers stricken with fever.

One sweltering summer's day, Bai and Green Hands had unexpected visitors who made them realize how far the Wind Chrysanthemum fever had spread. The two visitors had climbed up the mountain to the farm in spite of the boiling hot storm that kept spiraling up to the top. The two had traveled thither together, but weren't lovers, or even good friends. They had just happened to share the transportation, and were, in fact, rivals who were on very bad terms with each other. Bai and Green Hands were able to converse with these foreigners, for foreigners they were, with the help of Mr. Ko. Bai, thinking these foreigners might be people from the North Pole, excitedly spread his map before them. But the man pointed to the Netherlands and the woman to Italy.

The man emphasized that he was a descendant of Hamel, who was the first Westerner to write a book about Korea. Then the woman said that although her ancestor, Marco Polo, was prevented by unfortunate circumstances from reaching Korea, he was nevertheless the first Westerner to travel to the East and write a travelogue. Shaking her abundant dark hair, she contended, moreover, that Marco Polo's travelogue not only preceded Hamel's journal by four centuries but was greatly superior in literary and scholarly value. The argument between the two foreigners aggravated the heat and the mugginess of the day. So, to make peace between them, Green Hands fetched a Wind Chrysanthemum with a strong primitive fragrance that had a slightly mesmerizing effect.

Recovering calm, the two visitors broached their business. Both of them were in the dyeing and fragrance manufacturing business. Hearing about the incredible fragrance of Wind Chrysanthemums, they had come to this remote mountain in the Far East to see about the possibility of extracting a totally new kind of fragrance from the flowers. Bai and Green Hands led them into one of the coldhouses. As soon as they stepped into the house, the two hugged each other like lovers who had found each other after searching the whole world, and shrieked in glee. The coldhouse contained North Pole fragrance Wind Chrysanthemums, the fragrance Bai and Green Hands liked the best of all.

They wanted to visit all the twelve coldhouses. But their huggings and shouts of joy weren't repeated every time.

"Oh, this one resembles PJ07965," remarked Hamel's descendant as they entered the second coldhouse.

"Not at all! This is similar to NH8247, which also goes by the name Aegean," observed Polo's descendant.

"But how do you know about Aegean? That's the fragrance my company developed in the strictest secrecy and haven't commercialized yet."

In lieu of an answer, the woman tapped her high nose with her long and thin finger. "I can sniff anything that's going on in the world with my nose. Even what goes on in your mind," she said.

After that, neither of them tried to overawe the other with arcane trade designations of fragrances.

"Oh, how pale St. Gabriel's rose would seem beside these, and how tepid the fragrance of St. Philomene in comparison with this scent!"

"Oh, the Garden of Delight! the Garden of Ecstasy!"

"The River of Eden, Omphalos! Omphalos!"

They uttered many exclamations incomprehensible to Bai and Green Hands as they toured all the twelve coldhouses. Then they were silent. After that, they sat gazing at each other like ones in stupefaction, and then left, holding hands in silent sympathy. They never appeared again.

The most frequent visitors were botanists and horticulturists. Sometimes they came in groups, but most of them came singly to ask funny questions, to chew on the petals or to sprinkle some solutions on the stems. Some of them brought microscopes with which they studied crushed petals or stamens. They all mumbled about DNAs and genes, tilted their heads in doubt, and tried to peer into Bai and Green Hands's house like detectives looking for clues. One of them swept the dust on the terrace of the house into a plastic bag to take back, and many scooped handfuls of earth into bottles, and some of them took lingering sips of the water from the well. One researcher transcribed in his notebook the almost undecipherable serial number carved on the propeller that Bai had constructed out of his uncle's auto parts. They seemed desirous of taking back a strand of Green Hands's hair or, if possible, a piece of her flesh. They often got angry with the people of the village for not helping them with their research.

Many Wind Chrysanthemums became ill following these weekends. After so many visitors touched, rubbed and plucked at them, the number of petals decreased or the down dropped off from the stalks. Some of them wilted and died even if Green Hands wrapped their stalks with bandage. After each strong wave of Wind Chrysanthemum craze, many of them died, and that in turn only fanned the craze. That put Bai and Green Hands in a painful dilemma. They couldn't forbid visitors altogether, neither could they let the flowers go on suffering at the hands of the overinquisitive crowd. Mr. Ko and the neighbors were a great help and support to them. The villagers, who knew what the flowers meant to the young couple, abandoned their work on weekends to come and help guard the flowers from the crowd. But notwithstanding all the villagers' vigilance, some visitors still insisted they wouldn't leave unless they were given a few young plants.

Mr. Ko, after the failure of his plan to commercialize the low-altitude disease tablets, decided to devote the remainder of his life to recording everything related to the cultivation of Wind Chrysanthemums. It is he who wrote so many tributes to the flowers. Sometimes, while in his creative mood, he wrote one tribute a week. And he wrote them on the special notepaper he had made

using a secret method, with a special ink that gave off a delicate
fragrance. But because he kept them such a secret, no one except
Bai and Green Hands ever saw his notebook. In his rare good
mood Mr. Ko read to the villagers one or two of his tributes.
Unfortunately, all of them have been lost except for one, which
remains to bear witness to there having been such a flower.

Two hot air currents kept the mountain under siege for many
days, but Bai and Green Hands were oblivious to heat, engrossed as
they were in growing a chrysanthemum with the most incredible
fragrance. They watered the plants with the solution of collected
dew and eighteen other ingredients, including eggs of migratory
ducks, tails of glowworms, the pistils of bush clover blossoms, and
skins of mountain cicadas. They roamed the mountains to collect
enough dew and watched the plants all day long to see when they
seemed to need watering.

After the hot summer wind and the cool autumn wind and the
icy winter wind had swept over their place on the mountain far
removed from the busy world, Bai and Green Hands at last saw the
flowering of the Wind Chrysanthemum with an indescribably
enchanting fragrance. It had the purity of the cleanest North Pole
air, and had the farthest dispersal span of any floral fragrance that
had yet existed. They named this thirteenth fragrance Hoha.

Wind Chrysanthemum's Doom

"Silence! Silence! Please stop chatting and let's begin our conference. First, would you introduce the agenda?"

"Yes. As stated in the handout, the Ministry of Botany and
Forestry has to make decisions on five different agendas. We have
about forty minutes to deliberate on them."

"Why forty minutes?"

"Yes, why only forty minutes?"

"But what's that there?"

"That's the flower in question."

"Oh, is that the one?"

"Did you all take a good look? Isn't that just one of the domes-
ticated flowers originating from abroad? Didn't we discuss that last
time?"

"I think it looks different. Now, who wants to speak first? Why
don't you go first, on behalf of the pharmacologists?"

"Why me?"

"Well, somebody has to speak first."

"Okay. I'll try to sum up the situation. Three pharmaceutical companies have applied for patents involving this plant. One company has developed a cure for respiratory diseases such as asthma, from extracts of the plant's sap. Another company is currently developing a preventive medicine against Alzheimer's from the plant's petals and stamens. And I understand that there's a company that is already selling a drug for urological disorders using the unusually long roots of this plant. Of course, it is an unauthorized drug as yet. So, we have to examine the three drugs and approve one that has the best potential for contributing to the health of the nation. In my opinion, urological organs are more troublesome than respiratory organs, Alzheimer's disease is more serious than urological disorders, but at the same time respiration is more essential to survival than Alzheimer's . . . "

"Please come to the point."

"To be brief, the patent applications of the three companies involve only numbers two, seven and eleven of the thirteen different varieties of the plant, classified according to their different fragrance. That is, the respiratory cure makes use of the number two Wind Chrysanthemum, and the urological cure number seven, and so on."

"But why is that a problem?"

"Why can't we approve all three?"

"We can't, because there is a limit to the production of the plants, as we all know."

"I'm sure there's a way to mass produce the plant. We have just to find a way."

"Excuse me, but let me put in a word of explanation."

"Let *me*. In a word, all the companies concerned are convinced that it is inefficient and uneconomical to cultivate so many varieties in the small colony of the plant. That is to say, we have to approve only one of the drugs, and one that's most helpful to our nation's health, and give the company that produces it authorization to massively cultivate the variety needed for that drug."

"That's what I think, too. So, why don't we do that?"

"Please make your case brief."

"In my opinion, the urological cure is the most important. After all, everybody has to relieve himself."

"It's my understanding that a resident of that area has already developed a medicine from the plants a long time ago."

"You don't say! You mean somebody's already won a patent?"

"Oh, I think I'll have to explain, as it concerns my own district. That medicine is of no importance, because it is a kind of folk cure

developed by a man suffering from an extremely rare disease. It's a
strange disease called the 'low-altitude disease,' and instances of it
are so rare that only two cases have been reported in the country
in the past five decades. Let me add that many people have taken
up residence in the area for reasons such as that of the patient with
the strange disease, so we are running into administrative problems in our county. My purpose in coming to this conference is to
get the settlement grant for the new residents in that area
approved by this ministry. Please refer to the handouts for itemized
anticipated expenditures."

"Now, how can we decide on anything if all of you propose a
different agenda? Come to the point, please."

"May I be allowed to continue?"

"We've had many letters in our association in the past few
years. They were mostly complaints about violations of the ordinance for disclosure of cultivation methods of plants. Eighty percent of the complaints were about the cultivators of the plant, who
refused to comply with the ordinance."

"Now listen to this. As you all know, many cosmetic companies
have petitioned for permission to extract perfume from the plant,
as joint ventures with Western cosmetic companies. They have
gone so far as to settle on the perfumes' names, such as 'Blue
Wind,' 'Philomene,' 'Pôle Nord,' and 'Omphalos.' The varieties
they're interested in are numbers four, nine and eleven. Now, here
we seem to have a convergence of interest with one of the pharmaceutical companies. They, too, want only one variety to be grown in
the whole colony. The cosmetic companies also want it, for financial viability. I noted that one of the pharmaceutical companies is
interested in number eleven, which is also one of the varieties one
of the fragrance makers is interested in."

"Well, that's the one for the Alzheimer's."

"That's correct."

"I don't think any of the companies would give up without a
fight. They spent tons of money and more than a year in developing those cures or perfumes."

"Other matters are as complicated as well. That's why we're
here to discuss the problems."

"How about this? I suppose nobody can say that Alzheimer's
disease is less serious than urological disorders."

"That's right. I propose that we approve the exclusive cultivation of number eleven variety in the colony."

"If we pass that, can we be sure of the subsidy?"

"I move that we approve that. We're none of us all that far
from old age."

"If we approve that, we can enforce the horticultural ordinance on the cultivators to disclose the cultivation method of at least that variety. Then it might be possible to expand the colony and increase the production."

"Then what about the subsidy? That place is within the jurisdiction of my county. There's sure to be an additional influx of residents if we approve commercial cultivation."

"Now which is it you want? Subsidy? Or reduction of residents?"

"That's only of secondary importance. This is unofficial as yet, but a number of big industries have applied for permission to build a recreation and leisure complex there. If we can get that approved, then it will be a great addition to the revenue of our county. That area has the ideal climate and terrain for a summer and winter resort. My superiors have long been lamenting that such a golden piece of land is going to waste as a weed colony."

"Most of the residents are illegal, aren't they?"

"More or less. Some of them were original residents who had left the place and since returned."

"If there weren't these petitions from pharmaceutical and cosmetic companies, we could have cleared away the weed patch completely and turned it into a resort town."

"I heard that the number eleven fragrance is quite pungent. Am I right?"

"Oh, what does that matter?"

"Do you like skiing?"

"Before I leave this room I must bring up what we left off last time without having come to a decision. May I read this invitation from the International Flower Exhibition Association?"

"Please read only the pertinent passage."

"'Our association is particularly interested in that rare flower of your country, commonly designated Wind Chrysanthemum (botanical name undecided).' I'll skip the rest of the paragraph because it's too long."

"You mean the plant still has no botanical name?"

"Let me go on to the next point. 'We would like to invite you to display seven rare flowers of your country at the World Rare Flower Exhibition to be held later this year in this city. We are certain that that will further promote friendly relations between your country and ours. We would appreciate it if . . . '"

"But you read that letter the last time!"

"Did I? The problem is, there's a great deal of conflict between the various botanical and horticultural societies over this matter. The National Gardening Association wants to send three kinds of roses of Sharon, two kinds of pines and two kinds of bamboos to represent the spirit of our country. The southern and western associations insist on sending plants that thrive best in their regions, mostly orchids. So, that puts us in a dilemma."

"We can't waste our time discussing again what we've already gone through the last time. How can we represent our country in an international exhibition without the rose of Sharon?"

"But the rose of Sharon isn't a rare plant. We can't violate the conditions of the exhibition from our very first participation."

"But which is more important? 'Representative,' or 'Rare'? 'Representative,' surely."

"Other smaller associations have also come up with suggestions that are hard to disregard. The International Gardening Lovers' Association applied for participation with very rare plants they have developed such as improved roses, genetically crossed trifoliate orange and camellia and indigenous briar. What complicates our work even more is that the letter of invitation specifies Wind Chrysanthemum as the plant they're particularly interested in. No horticultural association even mentioned Wind Chrysanthemum in connection with the exhibition. So, what are we to do?"

"Does that bother you so much? Why don't you include a mutated Siberian Chrysanthemum, then?"

"How about the number eleven Wind Chrysanthemum?"

"That cures Alzheimer's disease!"

"Now look. How can such a humble flower represent our country? Maybe it existed in North Korea for a long time. Maybe the wind happened to blow it down south."

"Well, I can see you're pretty mad. You wouldn't be using your native accent if you weren't."

"Excuse me, but our forty minutes are already up. We'll make that our conclusion and close this conference."

"But what conclusion do you mean?"

"What we've just come up with."

"Bai, why are people leaving here every day?"

"I hear they got work on the new construction site beyond the ridge."

"And what made Zang die so suddenly?"

"I suppose someone fed him poison. But don't be too sad. Zang has gone to Heaven. His life on earth wasn't so easy, so he deserves a good rest."

"Bai, we can't cultivate only the Para Wind Chrysanthemum as the order says, can we?"

"Of course not."

"I won't give up even one kind of our flower, ever. What can we do?"

"We'll think of a way tomorrow."

"If all but the Para chrysanthemums have to go, Mr. Ko will get sick again. You know the Para doesn't yield the sap for the low-altitude disease tablet."

"I know. But at least Mr. Ko won't be lonely anymore."

"Yes, it's lucky there's another patient with his disease."

"But it's sad that such a young man should be stricken with such a disease."

"Do all low-altitude disease patients have such deep eyes?"

"I guess they do."

"Do you know why?"

"No. I was just wondering."

The War over the Botanical Name

Mr. K. had been devoting himself to the study of Wind Chrysanthemums but he felt he was up against the wall in the final stage. A rare breed of chrysanthemum that has never been found anywhere else! He had invested a great deal of time in proving that Wind Chrysanthemum resembles, in its biological character, *Chrysanthemum montuossum,* the alpine breed of chrysanthemum, and in appearance resembles *Erigeron Alpicolana Chrysanthemum lubellum,* but is made up of special tissue structure that bears no resemblance to any known variety of chrysanthemum. However, that was as far as he could go, as he could not establish a single fact concerning the formation and evolution of the flower's mutated genes. He could not accomplish the historic task of giving the rare flower a botanical name without giving information about what makes it the unique plant it is. He had visited the colony many times with his student assistants. He had even gone as far as to make his assistants hide in a hut in the rear of the ridge to note the plants' hours of exposure to the sun, the amount and method of watering them, and the moisture in the air. But he could make no progress. He interviewed the young couple who grew the plants, but their awkward explanations conveyed no decisive information. Moreover, he got the impression that they were lying about some things. So, he felt an urgent need to get the ordinance for disclosing the cultivation methods enforced and to ferret the secret out of them. His meeting with Mr. Ko, who, under the pretext of con-

valescing from his disease, was residing close to the plants' colony
and writing the whole history of the plant, was highly unpleasant as
well. The man said he had been living near the colony almost from
the first and recorded the birth of every single one of the plant's
varieties, but instead of feeling honored by the eminent botanist's
interest, tried to foil his research every step of the way. Mr. K.,
therefore, decided that there was no point in visiting the plant's
colony anymore.

Discovery of a rare plant was such an uncommon occurrence
these days! The fact that *Index Kewensis,* the publication of Kew
Gardens, the British Royal Botanical Garden, grew thinner and
thinner and came out at longer intervals was proof that discovery
of new plants has been pretty much exhausted by now. The
thought of *Index Kewensis* always made his heart leap, as if he was
once again the young scholar he was in his thirties. The most
ardent wish of his life was to have a paper published in *Index
Kewensis.*

Mr. K. first heard about Wind Chrysanthemums a few years
back from a flower shop owner in a provincial city he visited for a
lecture. The moment he smelled the poignant scent of the plant
only half a foot tall standing in a corner of the shop, he knew at
once that this was a rare plant that does not grow anywhere else in
the world. Trying to suppress his excitement, he had asked the
shopkeeper the name and origin of the flower.

"People living up the mountain brought them. If you buy all
three pots, I'll give you a real good deal," the merchant had said.

The professor purchased the three pots and came back home
directly, cancelling all his appointments. At home, he realized
more strongly with passing time that the flower had a very special
power of reviving forgotten memories and emotions in him. He
remembered the innocent youthful smile of his wife whom he had
lost a decade ago. He found himself tearing at his white hair and
sobbing, recalling one spring day in his youth when he and his
wife, then a new bride, took a walk together.

He had established himself as a scholar early on with his
research on rare plants and had served three consecutive terms as
the director of a major botanical garden in the country. His findings were utilized by many industries, so financial rewards for his
scholarly achievements have been considerable, too. It surprised
him, therefore, that such a small and insignificant-looking flower
could affect him so powerfully. Sometimes he found himself sitting
vacantly in the middle of his spacious garden, reviving poignantly
delicious memories of his childhood. His garden, filled with costly

rare orchids and other expensive plants, suddenly lost their glamour on account of the small weedlike plant.

Thus, Mr. K. took up the flower as the flower of destiny for his twilight years. "Yes, let this be my final achievement," he told himself.

His ardent desire to unravel the mystery of the plant and to give it his own name before he left this world to join his wife and ancestors kept him awake at nights. He also felt that success in this project would make up for the one great failure of his life, the memory of which still stung him. While he was still young, he had narrowly missed giving his name to a rare plant. It was a plant that was commonly called a "mountain sawteeth." He had spent several years studying it and had completed a definitive paper on it, but just as he was about to send it to a scholarly journal he found a paper on it written by a Japanese botanist. He vowed that he would never let that happen to him again.

Chrysanthemum montuossum KGB! That was the name he was going to give the plant. The initials, of course, stood for his name. He never for a moment doubted that even though he did not invent the plant, he was the first one to recognize its true value and therefore deserved to have the plant named after him. He did consider calling it *Chrysanthemum banti,* to imply that the plant grows best in the wind. But he crossed it out from the list of possible names, as that name would remind people of the young couple who insisted that they invented the plant. A botanical name could mean no more to the young couple than a dandelion fuzz blowing in the breeze. It was his conviction that a botanical name should be named after an authoritative scholar. Though there were a few points that still needed to be clarified, he concluded his research in a hurry and published it in the *Journal of Alpine Plants,* volume 45, number 2.

Mr. L. became interested in Wind Chrysanthemums after he heard that Mr. K. was working on it. The flower had become known quite widely by then, so he could gather a lot of information easily. Mr. L. regarded Mr. K. as a tumor eating him up from the inside. He simply couldn't stand Mr. K.'s solemn attitude and conviction that he is right about everything. It is true that, having been students of the same teacher several years apart from each other, at one time they were close friends and collaborators and had worked together on a number of projects. But, ever since the time Mr. L. raised questions about Mr. K.'s classification of the variant strains of tail fern growing over parts of Asia, their friendship changed to hostility. Mr. L., however, was too busy with important matters to elaborate on his objections. He despised the type of scholars like Mr. K. who wasted their time on pure research and wanted to have their names attached to the botanical names of plants. In his youth Mr. L. had aspired to be a career military man like his father and uncle, but he injured his arm playing football in school, so he had to give up a military career and settle for an academic one instead. However, his ambition was still with glory and valor instead of with laboratories and flowers. So, his approach to the flower in question was wholly different from Mr. K.'s.

As advisor to the Society for Promotion of Industrial Application of Botanical Research, The Cooperative for Globalization of National Flowering Plants, and The Committee for Fair Botanical Practices, Mr. L. was informed that the plant called Wind Chrysanthemum had given rise to a number of grave problems. The organizations not only informed him of the problems but offered him research grants to solve them, knowing full well his patriotic fervor and his enthusiasm for clearing away problems. Thereupon, Mr. L. formed a joint research team and tried to discover more quickly than Mr. K. all the important aspects of the plant—its characteristics and ideal environment for growth. It came to his attention that an amateur researcher whom he met on his visit to the plant colony had valuable information concerning the plant.

He suspected the man at once. He felt that the man's "disease" was only a pretext, and that his "having fallen in love with the flowers" was a nice little fiction. But, anyway, Mr. L. needed the man's day-to-day record of the plant's origin and the creation processes of all the varieties. Valuing speed more than the propriety of research procedures, Mr. L. sent his associates to the plant colony to worm as much information out of the man as possible, and dictated a series of letters addressed to him, making a number of offers that he was sure would interest him. He promised him help in getting the secret of the cure for the low-altitude disease patented, and to finance the publication of his book. He figured that if his team couldn't come up with satisfactory results by the end of the grant period, they would have to "borrow" the man's knowledge.

Mr. L. did not care much about what botanical name should be given to the plant, but getting wind of Mr. K.'s hope of having it designated *Chrysanthemum montuossum KGB,* he felt he simply couldn't let that happen. The name might cause a misunderstanding that the plant was invented in a dark cell in the old Soviet

Union. In Mr. L.'s opinion, *Chrysanthemum koreanum* would be a far more appropriate botanical name for the plant than *Chrysanthemum montuossum KGB*. Of course, it would be entirely possible to attach his own name to the plant if his research yielded the results he intended, but he was, if anything, selfless and patriotic where the honor of his country was concerned. Such selfless patriotism was a family tradition, and he rather enjoyed the sense of patriotic self-denial.

Acting under the assumption that the name he decided upon would be adopted, he recommended the inclusion of the plant in the Nationwide Rare Flower Competition and Special Exhibition of Alpine Plants, events for which he was serving as a referee, to make the plant better known. And before he could finish the research for the paper on the plant, he wrote to the organizers of the 78th International Plant Geography Convention that he would be participating with a rare plant.

Chrysanthemum montuossum KGB! Chrysanthemum koreanum! Mr. M. recited the names contemptuously to himself while shaving off his beard which he hadn't trimmed for three days. His beard cleared away, his smirk was visible. Mr. M. always shaved before making an important decision. As soon as he finished shaving, he called up his research lab, to see if they found out anything. But his assistants returned the usual answer that they found nothing worth noting. He knew it was unreasonable to expect the old machines in his laboratory to yield any miraculous revelations. But he just couldn't see why the analysis by his lab always produced the result that this rare plant was a common species of chrysanthemum. Then he made another call to a company that was interested in making an industrial use of the plant. Hearing that the patent he had been striving so hard to earn wasn't granted, he thought he had to choose one of the two courses open to him. Mr. M. wasn't a distinguished botanical scholar, nor did he aspire to become one. It didn't really interest him that Mr. L., who came from the same hometown as he, and Mr. K., who always regarded him as a phony, and other plant specialists such as Mr. N., Mr. O. and Mr. P. were engaged in the study of this flowering plant that seemed to be the craze of the decade.

It is true that Mr. L., who always behaved like a member of the royalty at the gatherings of fellow hometowners, got on his nerves, but his real reason for wanting to give the plant a botanical name of his choice was the advantage it would give him in winning various kinds of patents. And that meant money! He could have a completely modern new laboratory! That was why he had jumped into the race.

He was a man who could look far ahead. In his eyes, Mr. L. had too strong a streak of heroism, so he was vain and not too good at guarding his secrets. As for Mr. K., he was excessively proud, but Mr. M. knew instinctively that by flattering Mr. K.'s pride he could be maneuvered to fight Mr. L. on his behalf.

Being meticulous about his appearance, Mr. M. stood before the mirror, examining his denim trousers and blue cotton T-shirts. He was dressed casually because he didn't want to alienate the plant growers. He rehearsed in his mind a script he had carefully formulated. Could it have been his imagination that he thought the growers of the plant and their neighbors, who were notorious for their hostility towards outsiders, were friendly to him? He didn't think so. He had confidence in his engaging appearance and his diplomatic skills.

He was going to suggest a deal to the growers. If they would give him the information he needed, he would get the botanical name of their choice accepted, by writing and publishing his paper before anyone else. And he also had notes for a lucrative business deal detailing dividends and other complicated matters to propose to the simple couple. Moreover, the name he had in mind for the flower was an incomparably more beautiful one than those Mr. K. or Mr. L. had in mind—names that his informants wormed out of their heads for him, so to say. *Chrysanthemum bantipherum!* A wind-embracing chrysanthemum! What a poetic, alpine name! If the plants' growers had even a glimmering of the beauty of the plant world, the name would make them ecstatic! Or, if they were really attached to the flower's nickname of North Pole Flower, he'd be willing to give it the name of *Chrysanthemum arcticum*. He had also heard that the nickname of the young woman who created the flower and all its varieties was Green Hands. Well then, *Chrysanthemum azureum* was not a bad botanical name, either, he thought. He started his car.

"Bai, is the North Pole very far from here?"
"Yes. Very far."
"Could we get there if we filled up the tank?"
"Well, we may have to make a raft to get there."
"Then we'd have to learn to row the raft."
"Yes."
"Wouldn't the sea wash away our magnetism?"
"Not if we cross it on a stormy day. There's electricity in lightning, you know."

"Do you think flowers will bloom on the North Pole?"

"Of course. I saw pictures of the North Pole with flowers on it."

"Bai, when we get to the North Pole, let's don't call our flower Wind Chrysanthemum. Let's call it North Pole Flower."

"Yes, we'll call it that if you like."

Death of the Wind Chrysanthemum

If it hadn't been for the totally unexpected development, the competition surrounding the botanical name of Wind Chrysanthemums might have gone on for a long time, getting more and more complicated. But something occurred to put an end to the competition. The first to learn of the development was Mr. L. He received a letter of rejection from the organizers of the International Plant Geography Convention, to which he had written to propose reading a paper. The letter said in part:

> We regret to inform you that an official report concerning the rare plant you proposed to read a paper on, under the tentative botanical name of *Chrysanthemum koreanum*, has already been published in the *New Journal of Botany*, volume 37, number 2.

As soon as he read this letter, which didn't give the name of the author of the report, Mr. L. assumed at once that the author could be none other than Mr. K. and hated him with all the violence in his guts. But, not long afterwards, he found the said journal in his mailbox. It was mailed to him anonymously. Tearing the journal out of the envelope, he ran his eyes through the contents page. The author of "An Approach to the Biological Character of *Chrysanthemum multiodoratum bapa*" was not Mr. K. but a certain Mr. A., whose name he'd never heard of. The list of contributors gave no information about Mr. A. other than that he was affiliated with a certain provincial university in Korea. Like a rider galloping straight to his destination, Mr. L. skipped to the conclusion. The botanical name the author of the article proposed for the plant was *Chrysanthemum multiodoratum bapa,* which meant Bapa chrysanthemum with multiple fragrances. Mr. L. did not have the patience to read the author's reasons for proposing such a weird name, so he flung the journal on the floor. Then, picking it up again, he threw it in the wastebasket with all the force his well-exercised muscles could muster.

At about the same time, Mr. K. was amazed to find the article in the journal he subscribed to. His face turned the color of white paper lit by a yellow electric bulb. At that very moment, a spring

breeze stirred the Wind Chrysanthemum on his coffee table and its
pungent fragrance stung his nose. Strangely enough, on that day
the fragrance not only made his eyes water with a strange passion,
but it also made him nauseous. With tears gushing out of his eyes,
he skimmed the article with lightning speed. He didn't know
whether his tears on that day were inspired by a certain nameless
grief the chrysanthemum's fragrance often evoked in him or by
fury. The beginning of the article in question was quite similar to
the paper he'd already published in a domestic journal. Who could
this nonentity be? He knew every plant specialist in the country.
Overlooking the fact that the article answered the questions he was
unable to answer, he decided that this A. was a plagiarist. Taking a
tranquilizer that he had gotten into the habit of taking whenever
something happened to upset him, he surveyed his garden with
gloomy eyes. Should he admit this second failure? Or should he do
everything in his power to deny it?

Mr. M.'s reaction was different from the others'. First of all, he
was an optimist and was much less sensitive about it than the others. He didn't allow himself to be hurt by an unexpected paper.
Neither was he the kind of man to give up profitable projects he
had set his heart on. He began collecting information necessary
for nullifying the effect of the report. On it depended the future of
his laboratory and its more than a dozen staff. That day, too, he
had made about a dozen telephone calls in the morning. These
were social calls he made every morning to cement his friendly ties
with persons who could be of use to him in one way or another. He
never skipped this routine unless he was severely ill. He asked his
colleagues to find out about this Mr. A. He thought Mr. K. or Mr. L.
might know something about him, but his instinct warned against
contacting his rivals as yet. Shaving his beard with even greater
care than usual, Mr. M. drew up plans in his head.

Then, a sudden marvelous idea hit him. Mr. M. rushed to his
study with the shaver still in his hand. He took out a thick folder
from his file cabinet and carefully examined the data concerning
the plant. When he had gone through most of the data, he
received calls telling him about Mr. A. Hearing from them that Mr.
K. and Mr. L. had also asked for information concerning Mr. A.,
Mr. M. could vividly see their furious and despairing faces, but the
pains his rivals must have suffered didn't give him a perverse pleasure as they used to. Most of the information he received concerned Mr. A.'s personal history, and included very little about how
he gathered his data and reached his conclusions. However, one of
his colleagues had found out that Mr. A. did not submit the article

to the *New Journal of Biology* himself, and only sent a draft of it to a Dutch friend of his whom he knew from his days of study in Amsterdam, just to get a personal opinion. The friend had sent it to the journal. Each of his informants gave information that partly contradicted the others', so Mr. M. was rather confused, but one thing became very clear to him: that the way to survive lay in working together closely with Mr. K. and L.

Unlike his attitude in asking for the information, Mr. M. was now listening to the facts about Mr. A. quite calmly, taking notes. All his informants thought that Mr. A. was not a remarkable man in any way. Mr. M. had formed the following composite picture of Mr. A. from the information he had:

Mr. A. is five feet nine inches tall, and weighs one hundred and forty pounds. He is reputed to be an even-tempered and reliable man, and not given to self-display. Like most botanists he likes to travel. His parents raised pigs on a small scale, so his circumstances were by no means easy while he grew up. He studied for two years in Amsterdam on a scholarship, and since his return from abroad has been teaching in his alma mater in the C. province. He has a son and two daughters, and divides his time between his laboratory and his home. He is not affiliated with any academic association, and his only membership in a social organization is that in the Amateur *Go* Lovers' Society. His publications include *The History of Botanical Science, The Distribution of Double Seed-leaved Woody Plants in C. Province,* and about a dozen articles in journals, but none of them received much attention. His most recent article, printed in the *New Journal of Botany,* entitled "A Biological Approach to the *Chrysanthemum multiodoratum bapa,*" is his first article on flowering plants.

Mr. K. and Mr. L. also received information to the same effect concerning Mr. A. a little later.

As soon as he recovered a measure of calm, Mr. K. drafted a long letter of protest to Mr. A., in fact a solemn lecture on the need for strict honesty in academic writing. He told his younger colleague that he was extremely sorry to find almost half of his own findings, which he had already made public, in the younger scholar's paper, and that unless the latter made a formal apology and took corrective action, he would take the matter to court, for the benefit of posterity. He meant the letter to be the most solemn and moving letter he had ever written in his life. He polished the letter repeatedly, to make it all the more moving for those who'd discover it after his death. Before putting it in an envelope he read it

aloud from the beginning to the end. Right at the moment, he got
a whiff of the Wind Chrysanthemum fragrance, which reminded
him of a certain letter he had written about fifteen years ago and
did not mail, and made his voice tearful. But he didn't stop the
recitation.

Mr. L. turned up the volume of the military march to full blast.
With his jaw propped on his hand, he gave himself up to the thrill
of listening to the military march. The beauty of order and repetition! What? *Chrysanthemum multiodoratum bapa?* What a short-sight-
ed and unaesthetic name compared to *Chrysanthemum koreanum!*
The man must be the type of person who never listens to a military
march. The military march drummed on his heart, telling him he
should redouble his zeal to quell and punish all those who violated
order. But of course if asked exactly what order Mr. A. had violated, he wouldn't have been able to say. To figure that out he was
playing the record over and over again. Because he truly loved repetition.

The adverse wind against Wind Chrysanthemums was a verita-
ble tempest, as sudden as it was nonsensical. No one knew where
the tempest started. It was hard to pinpoint its origin, as it rose
from various and sundry sources and combined to create an irresistible tempest. Like all tempests, once it rose it generated energy
internally. The tempest swept the whole country and overturned
the souls of men, as a whirlwind sweeping a desert turns a caravan
into a sand mound in a minute. The flower that inspired so many
romantic reveries in those fortunate enough to possess one, began
to have dark associations attached to it.
    Its sea fragrance that inspired calm reflection; its cloud fra-
grance that soothed nervous spirits; its Hoha fragrance that
seemed to evoke the music of celestial dancers, all were now suspected of having dangerous effects on the body and soul. Some
contended that the flower was a variety of the poppy. Cited as
proof was the case of a teenage girl who stole money from her parents to purchase a plant. Its sap, petals, stamen and roots, which
were greatly sought after as possible cures for asthma, Alzheimer's
and urological disorders, were suspected of triggering or aggravat-
ing stomach spasm, nervousness and hard stool, and people began
to hate the plant itself. One magazine printed the "then" and
"now" pictures of its cultivator as proof that the mere sight or smell
of Wind Chrysanthemums could have a powerful depilatory effect.
It was rumored that the Department of Health would soon be con-

ducting a thorough investigation of the negative effects of the plant. The plants could soon be exterminated, depending on the findings of the investigation.

Shortly afterwards, a newspaper carried an article on the publication of *A Study of Wind Chrysanthemum,* coauthored by the three most prominent botanical scholars in the country, under the title "A Meaningful Reunion After Long Separations." The article praised in highest terms the public spirit that motivated the three scholars to overcome their long rivalry and collaborate on a research to put an end to the many false hopes and myths surrounding the plant. The article quoted Mr. L. as saying:

"We were brought together by the common concerns about the plant and our shared views on the delusions it produced. In other words, the problematic plant ironically served as a peacemaker and reconciler for the three of us. After all, Mr. M. comes from my hometown, and Mr. K. and I studied under the same teacher."

The article sketched the findings of the three scholars in the first half, and in the second half enumerated various cases that suggested the fantastic expectations people had of the plants. It didn't give any scientific proof that the expectations were baseless, but the book and the short article served to convince people that the plant was a sham and that they had all been deceived. Mr. A. published a reply to the three men's arguments, but it didn't draw much attention from the general public, and only made him suspected of complicity with a company that had invested quite a lot of money in making commercial use of the plant.

There was no need to ban the sale of various products made from the plant, products that used to enjoy phenomenal popularity. The once enthusiastic purchasers sued the manufacturers for compensation. A number of cases filed involved fake victims such as a chronic heart patient or a sufferer of hereditary depilatory problems, which had nothing to do with Wind Chrysanthemums. So, the suits didn't result in the cultivators going to jail or paying compensation. However, the residents of the county where the plant colony was located staged a violent demonstration in front of the county hall, demanding the extermination of the colony. The county governor could make them disperse only by promising to do what they wanted. The construction of a resort town on the site was a certainty now.

Exactly seven months after the rise of the adverse tempest, the plant colony was mowed down and the flowers disappeared from the earth. The only extant record concerning them consists of Mr.

A.'s article in the international journal, which was never reprinted in any of the domestic journals, and some tributes written by a certain Mr. Ko, a friend of the cultivators and a man suffering from the low-altitude disease. His notebook on the flower was meant to be a detailed chronicle of the most miraculous botanical event in history, written on the paper made from the dried leaves of the plant pressed together and with the purple ink extracted from the plant's petals. But it went up in smoke, after somebody stole it one day, because old people who still clung to the belief that the plant had preventive potency against Alzheimer's rolled up all its leaves into cigarettes and smoked them.

Journey to the North Pole

It was pitch dark that night. And stormy. Wagner's *Tristan and Isolde* was booming out from the open window of an unlit room in a seaside villa. A man was sitting on the sill of the open window, gazing at the silhouette of the bay illuminated now and then by lightning. He didn't seem afraid of the fierce storm. The mixed duet was ascending to a tragic climax, as if to lull the rough tempest. It was a love duet.

"O sink down upon us, night of love. Make me forget I live. Take me into your bosom. Free me from the world!"

On the shore, a small truck appeared staggeringly from the east and slid down the coastline, with its specterlike headlight trembling in the tempest. Then it stopped on the shore.

"Holy twilight's glorious presentiment obliterates the horror of delusion, setting us free from the world," the song continued.

Two shadows alighted from the truck, and approached the sea, whose waves' white crests flickered in the darkness. The man sitting on the windowsill caught a glimpse of two flitting shadows walking into the heaving sea, and took them for two passionate lovers immersing themselves in the waves to cool their inflamed bodies.

"Heart to heart, lip to lip, bound together in one breath, the world which dying day illuminates for us," the duet went on.

When another gust of wind hit the shore, the pale headlight of the truck died out, leaving the shore in complete darkness. The lovers' duet continued, as if in defiance of the tyrannical storm. Could the lovers hear this song? Have they come out of the ocean? The man in the villa couldn't be sure. Darkness had completely swallowed the shore.

"I myself am the world, supreme bliss of being. Life of holiest loving, never more to awaken, delusion free sweetly known desire."

Lightning struck from afar. The streak of light that cleaved the air momentarily illuminated the shabby truck lying abandoned before the white crest of the heaving waves. The man in the window went back to his room to change the disc.

The next day the truck stood on the shore in the clear sunshine after the storm. It stood there for many days afterwards, and children used it for play until the Coast Guard towed it away to the junkyard.

The Monument Intersection

୵୵

O Chŏng-hŭi

O Chŏng-hŭi, born in 1947, is one woman writer who can never be accused of romantic dreaminess or sentimentalism. Her works usually focus on the internal landscape of the individual. She finds that internal landscape bleak, with each individual living in his or her prison of meaningless routine and frustrated desires. It is not that her characters have clearly defined ambitions or aspirations that were foiled. It is rather that the dark forces and the limitations of life make them seethe with fury and weariness internally, and unable to express their unhappiness except through ineffectual gestures of rebellion. Most of O's central characters are women in their thirties and forties who suffer from the emptiness and futility of their lives and who in the end take an action that disrupts the daily order and is often self-destructive. Needless to say, they are unable to form meaningful relationships with other people. It is quite surprising that despite this common thread running through most of her women characters, each of them is clearly individualized. Reading her stories requires courage, because the despair and frustrations are so vivid and palpable that one can become quite depressed. O Chŏng-hŭi is an unrelenting and unflinching chronicler of the hollowness that is at the core of modern life.

"The Monument Intersection" (1983) departs from her usual stories. Even though it has her usual dense structure and sure touch, it deals with an era and a community rather than the inner landscape of one or two people. Set in North Korea immediately after the national liberation, it examines how history impinges on the lives and consciousness of people. Interpersonal and psychological conflicts, of course, exist prior to history. But history often determines the form conflicts take in a particular society at a given time. Each member of the illiterate shipowner's family battles his or her own demons and tries to do what is required. O cleverly chose as the central consciousness of the

story a nine-year-old boy who is too young to have an intellectual
understanding of his society or to analyze his own feelings but who
nevertheless has keenness of perception and strong emotions.

The ships that sailed out on the first of the month returned after a fortnight with full cargoes of fish.

Brought in by seven big ships, the fish were carried directly to the owner's low-fenced house located near the port. The hordes of yellow, dark and white fish, which seemed to have been frozen in the posture of desperately struggling to escape from the net, thrashed wildly when they were poured out onto the straw mats, as if to jump up into the air for freedom. They must have realized, in those moments of their death, that those were their last moments in which to assert their dignity as living beings, so they vainly strove to prolong the moment. Soon, their sleek and smooth bodies would be torn by hooks, and their gorgeous scales would lose their splendor. And then there would be a time of silence and disintegration. But as yet they emitted a faint gleam, even though their jaws had fallen open and their eyes were filmy.

Bonfires were lit and tents were erected in a corner of the yard. Pig intestines were steamed in the iron kettle brought out from the kitchen, and the owner's old wife kept scooping up ox blood to put into the boiling soup.

The fishermen sorted the fish by kind and again by size. The men's voices were husky as they rhythmically counted the number of fish they packed into crates. The piled crates reached the low eaves of the roof. The small and ruddy-faced ships' owner watched the crates piling up and recorded their numbers in his notebook. He was illiterate, but he had no difficulty reading and writing numbers. However, he stubbornly used only the special signs and figures of his own devising, which nobody else could decipher. It gave him indescribable satisfaction to record his property in hieroglyphs that only he could understand—the feeling was akin to having the only key to a locked full granary, and being sure nobody could steal the key. It also gave him a sense of pride of owning a world all his own. Yes, having a magic password that nobody could wrest out of him felt like owning a kingdom. Those who took a peek into his notebook only found unintelligible signs, as indecipherable as the hieroglyphs inscribed by ancient tribes on mud blocks. Even if anyone could guess, after brooding long over it, that the seemingly random and meaningless signs had some inner logic and represented numerical figures, they could not penetrate the signs' obstinate refusal to reveal themselves. Any attempt to discover their meanings was bound to be frustrated, because the signs constituted an order unto themselves and had meaning only through the secret pact between themselves and their creator.

The sea took on the color of India ink, and the bonfire burned brightly under the setting sun. The fishermen's wives sitting in the tent sliced open the fish's sides to take out their guts and rub salt inside, in order to make salted fish for baking and broiling.

The fish, having smelled the earth, lay on the ground with ashen pale complexion submitting to their indignity, but their scales shone everywhere. The long rubber boots of the men, the iron hooks that picked up the fish by the gills, people's clothes, hair, mouths, and ears were all covered with fish scales. So, people emitted a silvery sheen as if they had been baptized with liquid silver.

"Be careful. Marred fish are worthless," the owner shouted. Shouting was the only way he knew of expressing his elation. The owner's wife sliced the stuffed and steamed pig intestines and handed them out to the workers with bowls of rice in soup.

The biting wind of January blowing from the sea, the savage night wind from the sea, flapped the tent awnings and made the flames shrink and flutter.

"You've had bounteous catch for several years in a row now, haven't you? I think your daughter-in-law must have brought you luck," an old woman complimented the owner, as she munched on the stuffed pig intestines with her toothless gums. She was a neighbor who came to their house looking for scraps of fish each time the ships came in. Recalling that he bought his first motorized ship the year his oldest son got married, the owner thought she might be right, and looked at his daughter-in-law.

His daughter-in-law was busy baking pancakes on the greased lid of the iron kettle turned upside down, and her face was red from the heat. Seen from the back, her torso was thick and her shoulders and waist were round. Even though she had given birth to three sons in seven years, her body was still firm and solid, like a firmly packed Chinese cabbage. The daughter-in-law would go back with the children to their house in town in two or three days. That is, she would leave after the fishmongers carted away the fish in predawn hours, the wages and dividends were paid to the fishermen and ships' crew, and the mats and tents and food and utensils were cleared from the yard. That was also the time when the owner locked the carefully recorded notebook in his small safe and lay down to get a wink of sleep. After that, he would mend fishnets in his house with only his wife and the servant boy, or call in the blacksmith to repair the worn ships. Soon enough, fishermen would gather to join the next fishing trip. Sometimes the owner made a tour of the taverns and gambling joints to find cheap labor among men held hostage there for their gambling debts.

The owner had grown old on the sea, on the Yellow Sea whose water was muddy and grey and whose waves and storms were unpredictable. The sea, like an old whore, was affectionate, caustic and changeful. Maybe it was like a lover who never gave assurance of her love. Sometimes, sailing far out in search of fish, he would bend over the ship's side like an old farmer at seedling time to gaze into the thousands upon thousands of the furrows of the sea, which undulated, swallowing the traces of his past. In the past when he used to sail out on flatfish expeditions in the winter, he could catch a glimpse of the dark shores of China beyond the sea from Taech'ŏng-do Island, which he reached after a week's sailing on the clear and cold sea. He had heard that in the long-ago past a Chinese, fleeing his country in a salt vessel for some crime he had committed, landed in the port of Haeryŏng and settled there to become the ancestor of his, Chin, clan, but that belonged to the realm of legend. Moreover, he was not born in this area. He came here as a two-year-old on his widowed mother's back when she sought her husband's hometown to settle in after her soldier husband died in the military revolt of 1884.

If he sailed north past Sŏhan Bay, he could see the Yalu River flowing into the Yellow Sea. The color of the sea changes where the river and the sea merge. When it reaches the sea after flowing across the landscape, the river lingers and hesitates, and then, after awhile, it unwinds itself as if in resignation, and spreads out into the sea in light currents. All rivers merge into the sea. It was a wonder and a revelation to him in his youth that all rivers, which originate in the high peaks of mountains or steep valleys between rocky cliffs and flow through strange fields and villages, eroding land here and depositing soil there, at last lose themselves in the sea.

But from his sixtieth year the owner stopped going out in his ships. He purchased his seventh motor ship during the past year, and became known far and wide as the rich and stingy shipowner.

As a man who had spent his entire life being a fisherman and settled in the port as a shipowner in his later years, he had a clear and simple notion about life. Life was a small ship on a wide, wide ocean! He didn't buy even an inch of land. People, when they earn money, buy up paddies and fields as the safest and surest investment, but all fishermen know that it is a stupidity to catch fish during the spawning season. Fishermen must wait until the fish eggs, spawned when the females cannot hold the eggs in their bellies anymore, would grow up to fill the wide sea. The old shipowner knew of no surer way of sowing than moneylending. The pleasure he derived from entering in his book, in hieroglyphs only he could understand, the money he sowed in the field of his whole neighborhood, was exquisite, and all his own.

He knew that the business of operating fishing vessels would end with himself. His first son, who learned accounting and bookkeeping in a commercial high school, had set up an ironworks factory and was living in town with his own family. War was going on outside the Korean Peninsula, and ironworks was a timely enterprise.

The sea would always flow in and ebb out with its muddy water, and fishermen would always chase fish in boats and ships, but his son, who had never been out on the sea, would never understand him. Just as he himself never knew his father who died when he was a baby. Lives thus seep underground and at last merge into the invisible current of life force, their individuality lost. Can you pick out the stream of the Ch'ŏnji Lake of Mt. Paekdu in the Yellow Sea? The fierce winter wind that breaks off tree branches—from what tropical and flowering land did it originate, and how many lands and waters did it freeze and melt?

When the bonfire shrank, someone threw pieces of broken fish crates on it. The thin wooden boards of the crate, wet with rain and snow, hissed, emitting white smoke, and when that subsided red flames shot up, warming the air. The wind from the sea made the flame curl and flicker. The sea had lapped up almost to the base of the board fence. It must be the same sea that he first saw, tied to his tired and worn young mother's back when she first drifted into this area. Seeing the swollen sea at high tide and the full moon of mid-month soaring above it, and the wind lingering in his yard flirting with the flame, he suddenly seemed to see the principle of endless change, the endless cycle of birth and death and the permutation of earth, water, fire and wind into each other. "Pongmyŏng!" He suddenly called his servant boy. He would tell him to bring an armload of dried split logs.

If the fire is big enough, it should drive away the wind.

Hyŏndo woke up, hearing someone calling him loudly. It might have been a dream. He couldn't hear a voice calling him anymore but saw instead the light flickering outside the paper-panelled door, which looked as if it was heaving and fluttering along with the flame. Sometimes the flame soared and rushed towards the door, looking as if it might burst the lattice of the door and flood into the room.

"Oh, this is Grandmother's house. And those are Grand-

mother's clothes," he whispered to himself, taking his eyes off the
whitish apparel hanging from the beams. Then he saw the dark
pair of closet doors. He felt his groin tingle from the fear that the
closet doors might silently slide open and a ghost with long dishevelled hair would step out. He could hear low voices from beyond
the door, long boots thudding against the ground, water being
poured off, and a knife being sharpened on a whetstone. When the
flame outside soared high and bright, it illuminated the talisman
pasted on the closet door, which had a bird with two heads and
three legs painted on it. It looked as though the bird might fly out
of the picture and swoop down on him. "Mommy!" he cried to
himself and pulled the covers up to his head.

His grandmother went to her favorite shaman every winter to
get the prediction for the new year and buy talismen. Talismen
were everywhere in his grandparents' house. They were on the pillar of the gate, above all the doors, and on the wall of the main
room, like seals. When he asked his grandmother why she put them
up, she answered at once that they brought good luck—helping to
catch abundant fish, calming the fierce wind at launching times,
and preventing the three disasters and eight troubles. Sometimes it
seemed to him that what supported his grandparents' house was
not the beams and pillars but the talismen. They seemed to be desperately straining to stave off the sinister force that was creeping
into the house. Could all those disasters and troubles have been
sealed in by the talismen, like the genie trapped in the magic bottle
in a story? Or, could it, on the contrary, be that the scarlet unfading
talismen are giving sure intimation that the spirits in the nether
world are going to extinguish everything in the house?

It wasn't only the talismen that scared him. There was a
kitchen god in the kitchen, the toilet god in the outhouse, and
twelve baskets containing outfits for twelve kinds of shaman ceremonies along with a straw effigy in the barn. The straw effigy, held
together with straw ropes, was a nest for the weasels and had a clay
pot with rice in its belly.

Hyŏndo had heard that there were many weasels in his grandparents' house. He had heard that weasels scurried all over the
house at night, excited by the smell of fish, but he had never seen
one yet.

"You can't see Karma with your eyes. Karma leaves you first
when your house falls. It's a bad omen if you see Karma with your
own eyes. You must pretend not to have seen it, even if you happen
to see it, and you must never, on any account, do it harm."
Grandmother had said that she herself saw Karma only once in her

life, and that was twenty years ago when she moved into this house after buying it from the former owner who went bankrupt and left the town. Grandmother was always reverential and devotional towards Karma. It seemed as if she had unfailing faith in Karma because it wasn't visible. "Your grandmother's something of a shaman," Mother had once whispered to him. "She's so superstitious. Islanders are superstitious." Mother, who had gone to high school in town, complained about her illiterate mother-in-law behind her back.

"Have some more. You've been doing hard work," Grandmother was saying to the fishermen and villagers.

Hearing Grandmother's husky voice, Hyŏndo pulled down the cover and looked around. The bonfire in the yard had apparently died down, but he could see in the opaque darkness his two younger brothers and his aunt with the baby at her breast. The baby sucked at the breast from time to time in her sleep, and Aunt's eyelids, which were perpetually soggy from constant weeping, trembled every time the baby sucked. Aunt's face was gaunt and sallow, but her breasts were fair and plump. The baby sucked her mother's breast vigorously, with her black head buried deep in her mother's bosom. "Bad luck, six fingers," Hyŏndo muttered to himself, in imitation of Grandmother. And Grandmother wasn't the only one who regarded the baby as a harbinger of bad luck. The baby had six fingers. Aunt had married a lumber merchant from North Hamkyŏng Province—Hyŏndo's folks referred to him as Hoeryŏng Abai, a guy from Hoeryŏng—when she was nineteen, gave birth to the girl inside of a year, and was deserted by her husband. The baby had an unusually abundant black hair. Aunt, who spent half her days in her parents' house with tearful eyes, always carried the black-haired girl on her back. Grandmother gave the baby evil eyes, and grabbed and shook her hair, muttering "abundant hair, hard fortune." Hyŏndo crawled past his sleeping younger brothers over to the little girl and gazed at her. The baby sucked her mother's breast making squeaky sounds, and beside the thumb of her hand entwining her mother's nipple hung a soft and limp sixth finger. Hyŏndo lightly touched the superfluous finger.

Suddenly, he felt an aching sensation in the pit of his stomach. It was the same the night before. But the outhouse was in a dark corner of the backyard, so he suppressed the urge to relieve himself. After breaking wind several times and trying to contain his urge, he had to push open the door. A gust of cold wind rushed in. The work must have almost ended. The bonfires were reduced to mere red glows, and the tents were removed as well.

"What's that boy doing? Close the door, or the kids will catch cold. Do you want some snack?" Grandmother said, grinning at him.

"I need to go to the outhouse."

"What a bother the boy has to go to the outhouse every night," Mother muttered, coming out of the kitchen with a gourd full of hot water, without looking in his direction.

"Hey, Pongmyŏng, take Hyŏndo to the outhouse," Grandmother shouted. Grandfather was slicing flatfish to be spread and dried.

Pongmyŏng muttered something discontentedly and led Hyŏndo to the backyard. When passing the storage barn in which the symbols of the twelve household gods and the ferret image were hung, Hyŏndo held his breath. The full moon gleamed coldly in the sky, and the old pear tree that had become barren from having been incessantly beaten by the salty sea wind cast its jagged shadows on the frozen ground.

"Hurry up. I'm freezing." Pongmyŏng opened the door of the outhouse for Hyŏndo, wrapped his nose with an exaggerated gesture, and retreated a few steps. Hyŏndo squatted down on the plank with the door wide open, and looked up at the old pear tree. Don't trees ever get scared? Don't they ever feel cold? Could it be that like all old things this tree also has in it a divine spirit that grew in it with the years of wind and rain, like Grandmother said? Musing, he caught sight, in the moonlight, of something small and swift crossing the yard and disappearing into the shade with the speed of an arrow.

"Pongmyŏng!" he screamed in a fear-stricken voice.

"What's the matter? I'm here. Hurry up and come out if you're done," Pongmyŏng said, sticking his head through the door of the barn, where he had been picking out and eating the eyes of the dried corvina hanging in strings from the beams.

The monument crossing was exactly halfway between Hyŏndo's house and his school. As soon as school was over, Hyŏndo ran to the intersection in one dash. Then, for reasons he didn't understand, his feet stalled and he sighed. What was the secret expectation that made him ignore his mother's stern injunction not to loiter in the streets but to come straight home from school?

The intersection, with the train station, post office, agriculture cooperative and the police station occupying the four corners, was also the center of the district of Japanese shops and houses, so there were bound to be some incidents taking place every day. By just loitering for awhile, Hyŏndo could witness exciting happenings.

The intersection was said to have been a big fairground before the Japanese came and erected buildings. It was the junction where the roads to Haeryŏng, Kaesŏng, Shinŭiju and the train station met. A small abandoned monument stood beside the road leading to the train station. The monument, which had no surrounding fence or encasing pavilion, used to be dark gray at first, but eroded by time, it looked whitish from the inscriptions, which were illegible.

Once upon a time, long, long ago, war and a severe drought hit the country. At first, people peeled off barks of trees and dug up roots of grass to eat, but at last became so desperate that they ate their own children. The men turned rebels and robbers, and the women prostituted themselves to Chinese marauders. Prayers didn't bring rain, and offerings didn't soothe the savagery of the people who had turned into cannibals. At last they made a big offering and buried in the ground virgins' hair and men's topknots. In those days one's hair was deemed more precious than one's life. Then the war ended and rain came. So, people set up a monument on the spot where they had made the offering.

But perhaps it was only a legend, or a made-up story invented to teach a moral lesson. The inscription on the monument had long ago become illegible, and the minute letters covering the monument became so eroded that they didn't give the slightest clue as to what they purported to say.

Without knowing whether it was erected for expiation or celebration, people just called it "the monument" and called the intersection where it stood "the monument crossing." With the passage of more time the name lost its association with the abandoned and shabby piece of stone standing beside the road, and people called the intersection "the monument crossing" from habit. What could be the relationship between the lives of people passing the busy intersection day in and day out, and the modest stone occupying a small corner of it? Sometimes, when they saw a beggar frozen to death against the monument, or when they saw children scampering away to their homes after climbing and sitting astride the monument as if it were a hobbyhorse, they recalled that they, too, had spent a part of their childhood on it and would regard the monument, which looked much smaller and shabbier than it looked in their childhood, with momentary nostalgia. Perhaps the incomprehensible feeling they had, a feeling akin to acceptance of a higher order, was not merely a heartache for the lost childhood but a kind of recognition of the presence and symbolic significance the monument had come to assume standing there over the years.

The area around the monument was always sunny. And it was now springtime, too. That the beggar woman and her daughter, who had not been seen since late autumn, were sitting in front of the monument was proof enough that it was spring. The mother beggar was hunting for lice in her daughter's hair, which was rumpled like a magpie's nest. The mother and daughter must have survived the winter somehow. Beside them an old comb vendor was dozing in the sun, with her wares spread out on a piece of cardboard. The old Russian shoe repairman, who used to fix shoes near them, was not visible anymore. Until late last autumn the man who was always wearing a worn and thick Lubashka that was coming apart at the seams mended old shoes and drove nails into them. Did he go somewhere during the winter? Somewhere very, very far?

Hyŏndo first saw white Russians when he was very small and used to live at his grandparents'. One day he had followed his mother into town. It must have been somewhere around this intersection. The Russians, consisting of an old man, an old woman, a young woman and two small boys, looked like a family. Their faces were so white they looked powdered, and they were wearing strange clothes. The old man was playing a fiddle, and the young woman stopped before each one in the circle of onlookers and proffered her hands, in one of which were colorful clothes and in the other a basket of cosmetics. The spectators grinned sheepishly and took a step backward. The two boys stood immobile beside the old woman and gazed at the spectators. Hyŏndo's mother hesitantly reached into the basket and picked up a flat box. Then she hastily paid the woman and left the circle of onlookers, pulling Hyŏndo away by the arm. Who are they? Where do they live? Hyŏndo had asked his mother, thinking of the big box that had been beside them. "They have no house. They sleep in the inn," Mother had replied. "How come they don't have a house?" "Because they left their home. I guess they'll leave here soon, too. They came from very, very far. They left their country and drifted through Siberia and Manchuria and reached here. I suppose they'll be roaming until they die. Once you leave your home you can't stay for very long anywhere. Because you can't bear to think that's where you'll die."

How could he have understood his mother's words? Nonetheless, Hyŏndo, then five years old, had sobbed bitterly like when he woke up from a sad dream. Drift? How can people drift here and there, without a house, like a river?

Strangely enough, the image of the Russians was deeply engraved in his brain. He had never seen them again, even though he made occasional trips to town with his mother and had later moved to town. He never saw any Russians at all after that. White Russians, who could be seen occasionally in the town, had disappeared altogether, as if they had indeed been swept away by a river.

Taking hold of the monument, Hyŏndo jumped up and sat astride it. The monument was much taller than him, but it was not difficult to climb up on it. He shook his feet above the beggar mother and daughter, scattering earth on their heads, but the mother beggar, absorbed in hunting lice from her daughter's hair, didn't seem to notice.

Sitting atop the monument, Hyŏndo had a good view of the streets. A rickshawman was dashing through them, raising dust in the spring wind. A Chinese vendor, dangling glass cases on both ends of a pole slung on his shoulder, passed by, swinging his hips. Red bean cakes wrapped in hazel leaves would be in the glass cases. A few small urchins trailed the Chinese. They threw dust on the vendor's swinging hip under the long tunic and ran away, shouting, "You Chinese, that's to make your buttocks spin!"

The Chinese inhabitants of the area tilled vegetable patches outside the town gate and raised pigs. Their meals consisted of plain flour pancakes and raw scallions. They walked to this faraway port for trade, pushing vegetable carts. "The Chinese kill lice by clamping their teeth on them, and they never wash their clothes. When their clothes get soiled they sell them to someone poorer. Then that person wears them until he can't wear them anymore, and sells them to someone still poorer," Grandmother had said, pointing to the clothes the Chinese were wearing. Most of them were shiny with dirt. Well, the shiny tunic the pastry vendor was wearing may have been once worn by Magnate Wang, the rich man from Beijing who used to live in the house with the gilded gate.

Yesterday Hyŏndo saw an old Chinese being beaten and dragged away by a saber-rattling policeman. They said he was an opium addict caught stealing something from the store. He kept wiping his nosebleed with the back of his hand and bowing and supplicating to the policeman. The policeman, who hardly looked twenty, swore "You dirty dog!" and hit the old man's face with a whip. Children and grown-ups followed the two to the police station. Hyŏndo watched with bated breath the old opium addict struggling and straining, blocking the doorway of the police station with his body, but being hauled inside. Hyŏndo had heard that terrible things went on in the basement of the police station. The children whispered among themselves, breathlessly, that the police put pencils between a suspect's fingers and twisted them, or stuck a long rod into his anus and pulled it out through his mouth, or hung him by the ankles and poured water mixed with red pepper into his nostrils, or pulled out his fingernails and toenails. Hyŏndo had also heard that prisoners were driven to the train station at night, with their faces covered in hoods. He'd heard that it was because of such tortures that Ŭlmo's older brother, a genius who used to be a college student in Japan, went out of his mind and climbed the roof every night, like one calling on the spirit of the deceased. Mother always said, to stop the baby from crying, "Hush, a policeman is coming." She used to say the same thing to Hyŏndo when he was a baby. He was so scared of policemen that he stopped crying as soon as his mother mentioned a policeman.

His teacher had told them that Japan and Korea were one country and one nation, but he knew it was not true. The Japanese did not come up in any of Grandmother's stories.

When people muttered, in the tone of self-derision, that Koreans were a people without a country, the picture of burnt ash, or undulating waves, or figures in old legends, loomed up in his mind. Nobody in his family talked about things like nationality and independence. When he uttered such words, the grown-ups snubbed him, saying, "That's something you kids had better not think about," and told him to play outdoors. But, from time to time, the question, "Who am I?" flitted through him, a second grader in Haeryŏng Primary School, and it sometimes seemed to him that his present life was merely an interim period for something that was yet to come, and the question of his identity was an opaque shadow flitting over it.

Hyŏndo jumped down from the monument. It was partly because he recalled his teacher's order to see how Shinzang was doing, but also because it didn't seem likely that anything exciting was going to happen at the intersection, and he had begun to feel bored.

Shinzang's house was located toward the rear of the intersection, in the district of one-story Japanese wooden houses. Wending his way through the alley lined by windows decorated with geranium and begonia pots, Hyŏndo reached Shinzang's house at the end of the alley and rang the bell. Shinzang, who sat next to him in school, had been absent from school for three days.

Shinzang's mother came to open the gate, wiping her wet hands on the apron worn over Japanese women's long bloomers, and recognized Hyŏndo at once.

"Oh, it's Chinsang!"

"Teacher said to look in on Shinzang," Hyŏndo said, making a bow.

"Oh, come in, come in. Shinzang's very ill."

The porch was right inside the gate. Shinzang's mother opened the sliding door of a room in the middle of a narrow and dark corridor.

Shinzang was asleep, covered with a blanket.

"He took his medicine just now and fell asleep. But he'll wake up soon," the woman said, moving her thin and bluish lips and blocking the doorway as if to cut off Hyŏndo's retreat. With her hair pinned up into a bundle and her face dry and sallow, she didn't give any feeling of beauty or youth. "Look at those dirty sluts, who wear unlined skirts and use no toilet paper. But they pretend to be civilized and think us dirty," was what Hyŏndo's mother said when she saw Japanese women hurrying past the streets of Korean houses covering their noses with their hands.

Coming in from outside, Hyŏndo felt hot and sweaty, but a stove was burning in Shinzang's room and a kettle was boiling on top of it, emitting steam. The air was hot and humid.

"Shinzang always says Chinsang is his only friend. Please take good care of my son," Shinzang's mother said, peeling a pear. Hyŏndo felt embarrassed and stiff in the neck, and kept rubbing the tatami mat with his finger without responding to his friend's mother.

"Shinzang can't sleep long. He'll wake up soon. So, please stay. Oh, he'll be so glad to see you. He's been feeling so bored," the sick boy's mother said, and left the room.

Relieved, Hyŏndo stretched his legs and looked at Shinzang. His head looked big and heavy on his pillow, but his body looked tiny under the blanket. He was a hunchback. Walking with his head tilted to one side as if it was too heavy for him, he often reminded Hyŏndo of a young and skinny camel.

Was Shinzang really asleep? His face was pale, and blue veins crisscrossed his sunken eyelids as he lay there so still that he seemed hardly to be breathing. It was true that Hyŏndo was his only friend. The Japanese boys in his classroom excluded Shinzang from their circle. It was not just because he was a hunchback. It was because of his elderly father, who got paid for performing the ritual for the dead when a Japanese died. It seemed like his old father hovered behind his hump, flapping his black garments like a bat. The Korean children called Shinzang the Japanese shaman's brat.

Shinzang was as quiet and docile as a girl. He always did what Hyŏndo wanted and tried not to displease him. Hyŏndo's feelings

toward Shinzang were more like a triumph than a friendship. At
first drawn to him from masculine curiosity for the alien and the
exotic, Hyŏndo soon regarded Shinzang as an object of his desire
to dominate and command as well as of his tenderness. Or was it
rather an attraction to the complete yielding and submission of the
weak boy and the comfort such docility and pliancy seemed to
offer?

Shinzang seemed to regard Hyŏndo as his safe and sure haven.
When Hyŏndo first came to his house, Shinzang had whispered to
him, "They say I was born to die young. So, they put a doll with my
name written on it in the shrine and prayed for an extension of my
life."

Shinzang slept long, contrary to what his mother had predicted. He didn't wake up even after Hyŏndo ate the whole plate of
peeled pear. Thinking of awakening him, Hyŏndo went up to him
and took hold of his fragile hand that lay upon the blanket. It was
warm and moist. Hyŏndo put his lips to that hand. The slightly
acrid taste of the old pear that lingered in his mouth vanished in
the fragrance of the feverish hand. Forgetting about waking him,
Hyŏndo gave himself up to the infinite softness and snugness of
the hand's warmth. Or maybe the snugness was coming from the
profound and innocent sleep of his friend.

The room was quite still, except for the noise of steam from
the kettle. The clatter in the kitchen had ceased, too. Startled by
the stillness, Hyŏndo let go of Shinzang's hand and looked around,
putting some distance between himself and his sick friend. All the
doors were closed, and there was an eeriness, as if the house was
deserted.

Looking at his sleeping friend, Hyŏndo silently pushed open
the sliding door leading to the next room. The spacious room,
which had white plaster walls and tatami mats so new that they
looked green and smelled of grass, was empty save for a few cushions piled in a corner.

Without any definite idea of what he would do, Hyŏndo peered
around the room, trembling at the thought of eyes watching him.
Calming his beating heart, he slid open the door of the dark closet
and softly closed it again. Then, crossing the room, he opened the
door to the corridor. He caught a smell of mothballs coming from
the end of the dark corridor. He knew that the shrine closet was at
the end of the corridor, opposite the toilet. When he first came to
visit, Shinzang showed him around the house, but at the end of the
corridor Shinzang had stopped him, saying, "No, you mustn't look
there. That's where we have the spirit tablet." Although Hyŏndo

felt quite sure there was no one in the house except the sleeping Shinzang, he crept towards the shrine closet as quietly as he could. The sliding door opened noiselessly. He peered inside. Right in front of him lay the wooden box containing the spirit tablet, and inside it was a vase with red flowers, a small black box and a wooden doll. The doll was clad in the indigo, red and white patterned clothes commonly worn by Japanese men, and its face painted white had long dark eyes and scarlet mouth. It looked like a laughing mask. Was that Shinzang's doll? Wondering, Hyŏndo set one foot into the closet to look more closely but stepped back startled. He saw a man sitting against the wall beside the door. The old man was sitting upright, in the lotus posture of a seated Buddha. His beard and hair were completely white, and his upper garment was raven black. He was as neat and still as a painting on the wall. He seemed to be totally unconscious of Hyŏndo's movements and presence.

Running along the corridor, Hyŏndo heard repeated urgent sirens. He was quite accustomed to air raid sirens by then, but he murmured to himself, as if in sleep, "What's this noise?" The tension and tremor that threatened to burst his veins only a moment ago had completely died down. He lurched on to the other end of the corridor, past Shinzang's room, like one completely drained of strength. When he pushed open the glass door, a flowerbed filled with spring flowers met him like a sudden view in a mirror.

Leaning against the glass door, he looked down at the flowerbed and then looked up. An airplane far up in the sky glittered like a piece of metal. It flew in a peaceful, leisurely flight, and seemed to have nothing to do with the emergency heralded by urgent sirens. Where was Shinzang's mother? Is this really Shinzang's house? he thought vaguely. The B-29 plane flew away out of sight while he was gazing up at the blue sky, and a long siren signalled the end of the air raid.

Shinzang's voice called for his mother from inside the door, but Hyŏndo just left the house noiselessly.

In the street, which was disorderly from the air raid evacuation, a group of young men with white bands of cloth tied around their foreheads were marching toward the train station, waving Japanese flags. Old people in white clothes and weeping women followed the procession of ashen faces singing victory songs, and the red flags created a ripple of red circles in the air.

They were young men leaving by trains and ships for the southern Pacific islands to fight. Young women sang lines from a dolorous song, "My beloved lying under the palm trees, my heart glows warm thinking of him." Korean housewives buried bronze and steel utensils underground to hide them from the Japanese police-men and town clerks, but to the children, news of victory in the tropical islands seemed to promise unlimited amounts of rubber and lumber and mountainous heaps of white sugar.

Numerous women came to Hyŏndo's house every day to ask his mother to sew a stitch on a cloth. Women asking passers-by in the monument crossing for a stitch was a common sight nowadays. It was because of the belief that a cloth of a thousand stitches from a thousand people could protect one from death. However, the grain chandler's son, who left with one such "thousand stitch cloth" died in the war.

Hyŏndo's uncle, who was said to be laboring in a military sup-ply factory in Japan, had also left by train. He had left three years ago, but Hyŏndo remembered him best as a face he saw in a pic-ture in the album taken many years ago. His uncle had thick eye-brows and a round face. Once, his maternal uncle commented, while visiting Hyŏndo's family, that Hyŏndo's younger brother, Myŏngdo, looked exactly like Chuhwan, the children's paternal uncle. His mother got angry at that and retorted, "Oh, no. He's the splitting image of his father." Hyŏndo had heard that his uncle was conscripted as soon as he came out of the hospital. As he was very young at the time, Hyŏndo didn't know what his uncle's illness was. But his uncle must have been gravely ill to have been hospitalized for such a long time. His grandmother suffered from heartburn, and drank a glass of liquor with every meal to soothe the pain. People whispered that she got her heartburn on account of her youngest son. It must be true, since on last New Year's Day, when Hyŏndo's family went to the grandparents for the feast, Grandmother cried and muttered, drunk with the wine that had been offered to the ancestors, "Oh, children are one's Karma. But I must count myself lucky that he didn't go to the coal mines in Hokkaido." People in the family refrained from talking about his uncle. Therefore, for Hyŏndo the image of his uncle was a vague composite gleaned from bits of overheard whispers of relatives. But he had a feeling that the silence about his uncle was a kind of tacit conspiracy of grown-ups and had something sinister and dark in it. When recalling his uncle and the mystery surrounding him, Hyŏndo felt both curiosity and affection, but at the same time a vague misgiving. It must have something to do with his instinctive idea that something momentous and strange was going on in the outside world, something he could not comprehend or explain but which he nevertheless felt distinctly. It was a feeling that a big wave that nobody could resist was coming to overwhelm them, or a premonition of an epochal change such as nobody had ever seen in their lives.

Those being drafted into the army were sent to battlefields day after day, waving the Japanese flag. And every morning at school they offered silent prayers for "those that died for the holy cause." B-29 planes appeared in the sky frequently and circled over their heads like vultures looking for prey, and immediately warning sirens tore his eardrums. However, his father's plants continued to cut metal and churn out battleship accessories and cannonballs.

The short spring sun began to decline. Hyŏndo started running home, feeling hungry and wanting to use the toilet, but realized that something was missing. He realized that he had left his schoolbag in Shinzang's room. But Shinzang's house was already a scene in distant memory, standing by itself in a faraway place.

Summer vacation began early that year. The airplanes came more and more frequently. Previously, the airplanes had made brief appearances and disappeared, like a warning signal, but now they circled low overhead and flew away at their leisure. Hyŏndo sometimes found a folded sheet of paper in the yard in the early morning. It was a mimeographed handbill, urging the Koreans to bear the hardships firmly, as the Japanese were losing the war and would soon surrender.

Father put those bills in the kitchen stove, muttering to himself, "Japan isn't likely to fall so easily."

As the air raids became more frequent in town, Hyŏndo and the five-year-old Sŭngdo were sent to their grandparents' home near the port. The world was in a turmoil with the danger from bombing and scarcity of goods, but the ships always brought in full cargoes of fish.

Even after the fish were carried away in ice-filled crates, flies swarmed over his grandparents' yard and laid eggs all over it.

Hyŏndo fell asleep in the wooden-floored living room after lunch and woke up when it was almost evening. Sŭngdo was still playing naked in the wash basin, splashing water. The sky and the sea were aflame with the sunset, and the sun falling into the sea was like a huge ball of fire. Having perspired while napping, Hyŏndo felt as if the fishy smell that always lingered in his grandparents' house clung to him. The sun went down and whiffs of breeze blew from the sea, but the heat did not abate. Is it morning, or evening now? he wondered, sitting up on the wooden floor and gazing vaguely at the red sea. In the rear of the house Pongmyŏng, the servant boy, was singing a popular tune in a voice rife with emotion. He must be lying on the floor with eyes closed and shaking his feet to the rhythm of the beat. Hyŏndo knew that on the days Grandfather was not home sixteen-year-old Pongmyŏng spent his days cooped up in his room listening to the gramophone, or peering into his hand mirror to squeeze out the pimples on his face. Pongmyŏng would play the gramophone all night, if Grandmother didn't yell at him. Hyŏndo came outside with the cards he had put in a corner of the veranda, even though dusk was falling. He had made the cards in the morning out of cardboard paper, and he was going to give a king card and an ace card to Sunjae. Sunjae was his friend of the same age whom he played with when he stayed in his grandparents' house. Sunjae's father was an old fisherman who sometimes sailed out on Grandfather's ships, but Grandmother didn't like him joining the expedition on account of his being a Christian.

The single-panel gate of Sunjae's house was locked from the inside. Hyŏndo could see light seeping out of the inner room, but nobody answered his repeated call. He went round the yard to the kitchen garden, located just outside the back fence of the house. He could see many pairs of shoes lying on the dirt floor just outside the inner room. But only one voice was speaking in the room. He could discern words like liberation, nation, sovereignty and so on spoken in a low but excited voice. He began walking away but turned back and called out Sunjae's name. He lowered his voice from fear, as he thought he was an intruder in a forbidden place.

The door of the inner room opened and light poured out onto the yard. "Who is it?" an unfamiliar voice asked. "I'm a friend of Sunjae's," Hyŏndo answered hesitantly, feeling naked in the flood of light. "It's my friend Hyŏndo," Sunjae said, sticking his head out. "He's the grandson of the shipowner," Sunjae's father also chimed in. "How long have you been standing there?" the first voice asked after a little pause. "A little while," Hyŏndo answered. "Is there anyone else?" the voice asked. "No, I'm all by myself," Hyŏndo replied. "Come in," the voice commanded. When Hyŏndo stepped up to the dirt floor, the owner of the voice looked out. It was an extremely youthful face, but one with piercing eyes. His black hairs, cropped short, were all standing upright. "Can you answer my questions?" the young man asked, looking directly into Hyŏndo's eyes. Feeling impaled by the glance, Hyŏndo could not utter a word, and only nodded in response.

"How old are you?" the young man asked, not relaxing the sharpness of his glance at all.

"I'm nine."

"Are you a Korean?"

"Yes."

"Are you truly a Korean?" the young man asked after a short silence.

Hyŏndo felt a hot lump pushing up from his chest into his throat. He answered, suppressing a sob, "Yes."

"Whatever may befall us, the important thing is the consciousness of our national identity. Do you understand?"

"Yes."

"Good. Come in. Children should learn, too."

Hyŏndo went up to the room and squatted beside Sunjae. Among the dozen or so people filling the small room, he knew only Sunjae and his parents. Most of the visitors were young men, and there were a couple of young women as well. A Bible and a hymnal lay in front of every one of them, but they were not open. The talk that had been suspended by Hyŏndo's appearance resumed. " . . . and it was destroyed, just like Sodom and Gomorrah of old. The terrible beam was no other than the vision of Jehovah clad in silver armor and helmet, come to judge the world. They, too, must have known that it was God's punishment that turned the huge city into one big furnace. They wouldn't dare believe that it was done by human agency. Japan is destroyed now, punished for its sins. They are transporting the Japanese in Manchuria into Korea by trains, preparatory to shipping them back to Japan." The people were listening to the young man with intense absorption. Hyŏndo could hardly breathe, feeling a surge of pain in his chest which threatened to burst open his rib cage. But he could not clearly understand that pain, implanted in his chest by the young man's piercing glance and intensified by the question about his national identity.

After a spell of showers the sun beat down more mercilessly. There wasn't an inch of shade in the yard, so the earthworm that came out during the shower got grilled by the sun. Grandfather was preparing to shave his head beside the water pump in the center of the yard. Testing the razor he had sharpened on the whetting stone on his palm, he looked satisfied. Then, pressing his scalp with his left hand, he shaved his head with his right hand, starting from the forehead and moving towards the crown. Where the blade had passed appeared a shining stripe, and short grey stubble scattered around him.

Hyŏndo had heard that Grandfather shaved his hair first when the ordinance against topknot was decreed towards the end of

Chosŏn Dynasty, and had lived all his life with a shaven head, just like a Buddhist monk.

"Hyŏndo, bring the mirror," Grandfather called out to him. Hyŏndo took down the mirror from the post and held it up in front of Grandfather's face. Grandfather twisted his head in an effort to look at the back of his head in the mirror and gingerly ran the razor down the back and sides of his head, muttering, "The stupid hag!" Shaving the back and sides of Grandfather's head was Grandmother's job, but she wasn't at home. Maybe it was not his wife the grandfather was blaming so much as his daughter. Grandmother had gone to her daughter, because her son-in-law, who had been gone from home without a word for more than three months, suddenly appeared and beat her daughter half to death. He was rumored to be working as a lumber cutter in Mount Paekdu and living with a prostitute. Grandmother left for her daughter's house early in the morning with her five-year-old grandson.

When Grandfather finished shaving his head, Pongmyŏng drew water from the pump. Grandfather didn't put his head into the basin at once, but looked into the water with downturned face. "Is he waiting for the foam to subside?" Hyŏndo thought absently. But the old man remained immobile in the stooping posture, pressing the rim of the basin with both hands. Was there some stray object in the water?

"Grandfather, shall I draw up water again?" Pongmyŏng asked in frustration, grabbing the pump handle.

"No. Never mind," Grandfather replied, waving his hand, still looking into the basin in which streaks of light floated like pieces of broken mirror. Oh, I know, Hyŏndo thought, Grandpa is looking at the reflection of his face and the sky and clouds in the basin. Hyŏndo also liked to look at the images in the basin, and often got yelled at by Mother for dawdling in the morning. How strange his face looked in the water! And how queer and still the sky and the house, the tree and the world in the basin of water looked to the giant standing upside down!

"Pongmyŏng, bring me the fishing pole," Grandfather said, mopping his head with a towel.

"To go fishing? It's too hot, sir," the servant boy observed, but handed his old master the fishing pole and packed a kettle of rice wine and some green peppers and red bean paste into a bucket.

"Would you like to come along?" Grandfather said, looking at Hyŏndo. Hyŏndo shook his head. Pongmyŏng had promised to catch him cicadae from the pear tree. Besides, he had always been scared of the sea.

"I won't be long," Grandfather said.

The pier was right outside their gate. Hyŏndo caught sight of his grandfather clad in yellow hemp shirt and vest, walking towards the shore with his fishing pole and wine kettle. The next minute, Grandfather's motorboat shot across the water, leaving a distinct trail.

After the rain the sea was clear blue, but the sun shone mercilessly, as if to dry up the sea and leave a pillar of salt. When the boat disappeared behind the island, Pongmyŏng, who had been watching the old man's departure, murmured, "I wish I'd given him his straw hat."

The boat disappeared from sight, as if it had dived into the water. The long strip of furrow gradually became blurred and at last disappeared altogether.

It was quite past lunchtime when the boat was towed in by a ferryboat operating between the port and Ox Island some ten miles away.

"I saw this boat in front of So'i Island on my way out. I saw an old man in it. After letting my passengers off in Ox Island, I had lunch and even took a nap before starting on my return trip, as there were no returning passengers. On the way back I saw the boat in the same place, with the old man resting his forehead on the rim of the vessel. I was going to pass by, thinking he must be dozing, but a strange feeling hit me. So, I called out to him a few times. He didn't answer. So I approached . . . " the ferryman explained.

The kettle was half empty, and the fishing pole hadn't been used. The custom of the area forbade people who died outdoors, especially people who died on the sea, from being carried into the house, so the old man was laid on the shore. He wasn't wet, and there was no injury on him, either, but his face had blue spots and his lower lip was swollen and bruised, from having been bitten hard.

Pongmyŏng took out his bicycle, and after kicking the air a few times in his confusion, started for the town at top speed. The whole village poured out of their houses and surrounded the old man's body. Hyŏndo left the throng silently and came into the house. He looked around the yard, which was still bright with hot spikes of the sun even though the heat was abating. The yard seemed to reverberate with the swishing sound of Grandfather's razor blade and filled with the image of Grandfather as he looked absently into the basin of water.

Hyŏndo looked into the mirror hanging from the post, just as his grandfather used to do. He could see a fear-strained boy's face,

and behind it, the sea rushing towards him, foaming at the crest.
He left the mirror and looked into the kitchen, the main room,
the second room, and the outer quarters. He even looked into the
dark and humid barn, opening the door oblivious to his fear of
seeing ferrets. He could sense evening was approaching, as the
cicadae had ceased their incessant screeching from the pear tree.
He climbed up the tree. The old pear tree could not bear fruit anymore, but its abundant foliage hid his small body snugly. Sitting
where the main trunk divided into two big boughs, he gazed at the
golden sunbeams of the evening filtering through the leaves. He
also gazed at the old house, the worn baked-tile roof and the sea
taking on the deadly hue of lead. Pressing his cheek against the
bough, he entrusted his whole weight to it. The rough bark of the
pear tree tasted salty, having been beaten by the sea wind for so
many years. Sticking out his tongue and licking the bark, he felt
comforted by the salty taste, for some reason. He was looking for a
smoother place to lean on when he saw a big cicada right above his
head. He carefully stretched his hand. The cicada, which was taking a rest after a hard day's screeching, was caught without any
resistance. He folded it firmly inside his palm, and scratched its
chest with his finger. The cicada began to screech at the top of its
lungs, shaking its pleated belly. The leaves shook, scattering the
scraps of sunlight. He kept scratching the cicada, and the cicada
kept screeching, until the sun went down. He felt as if the huge
tree and his own body with all his inner organs became a huge
vibration box, shaking to the cicada's screech. More and more people gathered on the beach. He saw a taxi that had run through the
new highway stopping at the pier and letting off his father and
mother. His baby brother Myŏngdo was strapped to his mother's
back. The crowd parted to make way for his parents. Father knelt
beside Grandfather's body and Mother walked into the house, crying bitterly. She went into the kitchen but soon came out into the
yard. She looked into every room and then ran towards the pier.
"Mom, I'm here!" Hyŏndo cried, but Mother didn't seem to hear.
"Bother the cicada," an old female neighbor who came into the
house with his mother muttered and threw a stone in the direction
of its sound, but the stone hit a branch and fell to the ground.
When Mother's figure became invisible, mixed with the crowd on
the shore, Hyŏndo shouted "Mother!" and clenched his fists.
Something crumbled in his fist with the sound like a sigh, and his
palm felt sticky with a thick resinlike fluid. The screech that shook
the earth had ceased, and dusk began to fill the void left by the
sound. He began to cry from fear and loneliness. Flying insects
flew into the tree, looking for a haven for the night.

The corpse was buried two days later, without having been brought into the house. The weather continued to be broiling hot throughout. The cause of the old man's death was diagnosed as sunstroke, but his old wife was firmly persuaded that her husband died smitten by a retributive bolt from heaven. Throughout the period Grandmother cooked white rice and threw it on the sea to conciliate the fish, whose wrath towards the old man for having caught so many of them in his life was responsible, she believed, for his sudden death.

The unexpected death of the old man gave rise to many questions and guesses, but the old man seemed to have taken care of his life in his own way. After the first offering at his grave, the bereaved family—including children—gathered in the main room. Grandmother took down from the closet the safety box and the small wooden box with drawers. They were things that, in Grandfather's lifetime, nobody else could touch. Like a priest performing a prescribed ritual, Father took them from Grandmother and opened them. In the safe was a heap of nickel coins and a few ten-*won* and one-*won* notes. Showing no sign of surprise, Father pushed the safety box aside. The wooden box contained five well-thumbed notebooks.

"God, what's this?" Father muttered in astonishment. He flipped over the leaves of a notebook quickly, dropped it, picked up another and leafed through it quickly, making the pages spring over with a flicker of his thumb and forefinger. Grandmother, Mother and Aunt, who had been sitting with feigned indifference, each picked up a notebook and looked through. Bewilderment and consternation spread over their faces. The notebooks of the old man known far and wide as a moneylender were filled with strange signs that nobody could even faintly guess the meaning of.

"Crazy old man! How can we get money out of anyone with this!" Grandmother hurled the notebook down on the floor, and Father smacked his lips with a bitterly disappointed look. Just then, Pongmyŏng shot into the house crying at the top of his lungs: "Quick. Turn on the radio. They say we're liberated!"

The Japanese shops and hospitals and most of the small stores near the main street were closed. People thronged to the monument intersection day after day, even though they had no definite business there. Those careful people who stayed cooped up in their houses, fearing that the news of liberation from the Japanese rule might be a trap of some kind, came out to the intersection after a couple of days. It was the habit of the people of this town to throng to the intersection whenever there was uncertainty or a sign of change. Because they knew that what they saw, heard and over-heard in the intersection would soon affect their lives.

"Stay in the house, for Heaven's sake," his mother told him every day, but every morning, as soon as he'd eaten breakfast, Hyŏndo rushed to the intersection.

Volunteer security men armed with weapons of the Japanese army patrolled the street in threes and fives. They all wore red arm-bands. The Japanese could not be seen anywhere. It was as if some-one had swept them all away with a broom. Many Japanese had gone into hiding, and it was said that not a few of them committed suicide. The flame from Shinto shrines and police stations set on fire by an angry mob dyed the night sky red. People rushed into empty Japanese houses and came out with furniture, kitchen wares and fabrics. They claimed that trampling clean wooden floors with muddy shoes, smashing windows and destroying household goods were acts of just retribution and vengeance, not of cruelty and bru-tality. They regarded it as dutiful and meritorious to punish their enemy who had oppressed and exploited them.

Summer was passing, but the school showed no sign of reopen-ing. All the grown-ups were so excited at the prospect of establish-ing an ideal new country based on a brand new ideology and new institutions that they simply could not attend to the educational needs of the children who had spent the summer in confusion and uneasiness.

Hyŏndo's school had become the military training ground for the volunteer security guards, even though "The First Primary School of Haeryŏng" nameplate was still hanging on the gatepost.

After hanging onto the wall for awhile with his friends to peek at the men training on the playground, Hyŏndo sauntered over to the monument intersection. There he saw a group of men shout-ing and waving arms. The Japanese police chief clad in his pajamas was being led away, with his hands tied together. The men did not disperse even after the Japanese was led into the police station and the door closed after him. They kept shouting that he should be beaten to death in the intersection.

"I wonder what happened to Shinzang and his mother? Are they hiding under the floor like the other Japanese? Have they been arrested and sent somewhere? Have they, perhaps, killed themselves?" Hyŏndo wondered. But he shook his head. "They're sure to be living in the silence of a late spring afternoon," he thought. "Come to my house. Mother said she'd make sweet red bean porridge for us," Shinzang had said to Hyŏndo on the last day before the vacation, pulling at his sleeve. But Hyŏndo had refused gruffly. Noting with sadness Hyŏndo's distant attitude, Shinzang confided to him, in an effort to win back his friendship, "I'm going to Japan this summer. I'm going to have an operation in a big hospital. But don't tell this to anyone else."

But Hyŏndo didn't go to Shinzang's house. Shinzang's hump repelled and embarrassed him. Or perhaps it was that the feeling of that spring afternoon he'd spent at his fragile friend's house, that feeling akin to having touched a deep well of some essence, had left a faint gleam, a mysterious mood in his heart, and made him afraid of contact with the reality of its basis. Or perhaps it was that the hot feeling that surged in his breast one summer night in his other friend's house when he confirmed his Korean nationality in response to the invisible voice contained a negation of his brief embrace of that mysterious silence of that spring afternoon.

Hyŏndo walked into the alley of Japanese houses behind the intersection and stood before Shinzang's house. The alley was strewn with broken flowerpots and glass. Almost all the houses had broken gates and smashed windows, and they were eerily silent, like empty houses. Hyŏndo could see that the gate of Shinzang's house must have also fallen down but was standing only because it was supported with crates from the inside. The gate opened easily when he pushed it with one hand. "Shinzang," Hyŏndo called out in a low voice, when there was no response at the opening of the gate. In the porch there were Shinzang's shoes and wooden clogs that Hyŏndo knew well, but the house was quiet. Was there a force in him stronger than fear? Hyŏndo stepped onto the wooden floor with his shoes on. The floor was already strewn with muddy footprints. The glass of the kitchen door was broken, so he could see the smashed cupboard and broken dishes scattered on the kitchen floor.

Hyŏndo opened the door to Shinzang's room. There was nobody in it, and the door of the wardrobe was knocked off, the chest of drawers was hacked, and garments were strewn on the floor. He walked across the room and opened the sliding door at the other end. Shinzang's mother, who was sitting right on the other side of the sliding door, looked up slowly, without a sign of surprise. There was a dish with lumps of seasoned rice on the floor. Shinzang whispered, "Hyŏndo," and put down his chopsticks.

"Oh, it's Chinsang," Shinzang's mother's tense face brightened. "Come. Come sit here."

Hyŏndo just stood there leaning on the doorpost, as if he hadn't heard her invitation.

"We were just going to have lunch. This is no food to offer a guest, but come eat with us," she said. Her face grew a little stiff as Hyŏndo still didn't budge, but she kept her conciliatory smile.

When Shinzang's eyes alighted on Hyŏndo's shoes on the door-sill, he whispered "Oh, I'm scared," and curled up his body.

"It's because Shinzang had terrible experiences lately. He's not scared of you. You're his only friend. We're going back to our country soon. I'd like to give you a souvenir," Shinzang's mother said, looking around the room.

As if pulled by an invisible force, Hyŏndo walked out of the room and stepped into the dark corridor. When he opened the door of the shrine closet, the hot and musty smell of a long-sealed-up tatami room rushed out at him. He blinked at the unfamiliarity of the room. It was not the same room that was so clearly imprint-ed in his memory.

The white-haired old man sitting there like a picture on the wall was not there. Could it be that the room disappeared the moment it was photographed in his brain? There were only a cou-ple of colorful dolls in the shrine tablet box which, with its curtains ripped off, was no more than two shelves now.

"Shinzang's father passed away," Shinzang's mother, who had followed him, whispered in his ear. "We have nothing worth giving out anymore. We gave away everything," she added.

Hyŏndo picked up a doll from the shelves and left the shrine closet, pushing away his friend's mother who blocked his way.

"Give it back. It's only a wooden doll," the woman pleaded.

In the backyard summer flowers were ablaze in full colors.

"I see you like dolls. I'll give you another. A much prettier one."

Shinzang's mother opened the closet of her room and hastily pulled out this and that.

"You mustn't take that. It's a spirit image," Shinzang wailed.

"No, take it if you want to. We don't need that anymore," Shinzang's mother said, and waved Hyŏndo away. As Hyŏndo was passing through the gate, Shinzang's tearful voice cried, "Thief!"

Hyŏndo stuck the wooden doll in his pocket and walked to the intersection. A young man was standing on top of the monument and making a speech to the people gathered there. "The days of darkness and oppression are over, and we're freed at last from slav-ery. Rise, people of the Republic! We should never be satisfied with only half of our country."

Ulmo's older brother, who had been famous for being a genius but had gone insane after being arrested and tortured by the Japanese for resistance activities, urinated on the monument-turned-podium, exposing himself. When he caught Hyŏndo's eyes, he grinned.

The young man's speech continued, but bowed down with the weight of deepening sorrow and loneliness, Hyŏndo did not stay to listen to him and headed for home in the heat of the late summer afternoon and the air of incomprehensible madness.

They marched in before autumn came. A banner was draped in front of the small brick train station and a platform was erected. Townspeople poured out into the monument intersection soon after breakfast. The inhabitants of the seaport and the nearby inland hamlet had walked several miles to this town, to welcome the liberators. People knew well already that the Russian soldiers, who crossed the Tumen River by train, were stationed in such hillside cities as Hoeryŏng, Najin and Unggi. It was whispered that the Russian soldiers were as tall as electric poles, had eyes like torchlights, and faces red as the masks of drunken monks in the mask dance dramas.

The train was late in arriving. The crowd, mobilized from early morning, sprawled out on the ground and shook the flags to fan themselves. The train arrived rather late in the afternoon, and Russian soldiers poured out.

The foreign soldiers, who had red insignia on yellow uniforms, marched out in an endless procession. It was the first time since the station opened that so many people got off the train at once. Whispers of surprise and curiosity swelled in the crowd as they waved the flags and shouted "Hurrah." It was true that the soldiers were tall and red-complexioned. But what was more surprising was that hunger and indifference were clearly written on their strange faces.

"Thanks to the righteous Red Army the Japanese are defeated and Korea is liberated from colonial occupation. The Red Army is our comrades and liberators who took away the yoke of slavery from our shoulders. Let us fervently welcome our liberators who have come all the way to our town of Haeryŏng, past Shinŭiju and Pyongyang."

All through the ceremony, the "liberators" looked at the cheering and applauding crowd with indifference or grinned stupidly.

They remained in the station plaza after the ceremony. The volunteer security men brought pails of water to the soldiers sweating under the broiling sun. The soldiers scooped out water to rub on their steaming heads or put it in their mouths to spray on women and children standing by watching them. The women

screamed and ran away, covering their faces. The townspeople dispersed, shaking their heads in doubt. Some people carefully rolled
up the hammer-and-sickle flags that had been handed out to them,
to show to their family. Maybe people had expected to see magnan-
imous faces of benefactors wearing laurel crowns and war-torn and
bloodstained uniforms. Or it may have been firmness and intelli-
gence they wanted to see on the faces of their liberators, so that
order would be restored in place of the chaos and disorder. But
the Russian soldiers only looked rough and shabby.

It seemed that their lodging had not been prepared. They sat
hunched like animals in the dusk in front of the train station and
tore out the dark and rough oat bread to eat, or lay down on the
ground using the bread as pillows. Now only beggars and children
still hovered around the monument intersection, which was lit-
tered with torn flags.

The soldiers left for their lodging at night. Shimsang Primary
School became their headquarters, and beddings and food were
collected from every household. The women who carried rice and
soup to them shuddered at how much they ate. The next morning,
the "Shimsang Primary School" nameplate was taken down and in
its place was hung the plaque "Haeryŏng Headquarters of the
Russian Army."

Hyŏndo woke up startled by a voice calling his name softly.
Mother was standing outside the door and was shaking his feet,
calling his name.

"Come out for a minute."

Hyŏndo rubbed his sleepy eyes and put on his trousers.

"I heard some noise from the plant," Mother said, and walked
ahead of him towards the tin-roofed building that housed Father's
plant.

Father's room was dark and quiet. He had gone to the port to
buy medicine for Grandmother, whose heart trouble had aggravated since Grandfather's death.

The plant was a long and narrow building constructed along
the wall, so its machine noise disturbed the house all day long.

Waiting for Hyŏndo to arrive, Mother unlocked the gate of the
plant and opened it. She moved quietly and carefully. They
stepped into the plant but could see nothing in the dense darkness. "What's the matter?" Hyŏndo whispered, but Mother just fumbled for the light switch. After groping for awhile, she whispered to
him, "I can't find it. You'll have to bring me the flashlight."

Mother was standing rooted to the spot when Hyŏndo arrived

with the flashlight from the house. Taking the flashlight from her
son, she waved it around the room. Iron pipes, power lathes and
sawteethed wheels sprang out of the darkness for a second and disappeared again.

"Who is it?" Mother shouted, even though Hyŏndo could hear
nothing. He only smelt the acrid smell of iron and heard Mother's
voice ringing out hollowly in the eerie silence.

Gripped by fear, Hyŏndo grabbed Mother's skirt, but she shouted again, as if that was the only way she could control her terror.

"Come out. Come forward."

Steps were heard from deep inside the plant, in the pitch darkness. Mother quickly flashed the light. When a face revealed itself,
she uttered a low scream. Hyŏndo clung tightly to her skirt.

"It's me, ma'am," the man said. His voice was confident, perhaps taking heart from the obvious terror of the mother and son.
Hyŏndo knew him, too. He was a factory employee, who had lost
his hand in a lathe accident the previous summer. People used to
call him a dimwit because he was still a bachelor in his late thirties
and was generally stupid and slow, but after the accident he was
called "hooked hand," because he had a hook installed on his cut-
off wrist. After he quit the factory on account of the accident, he
came to see Father a few times. He was drunk at those times, and
he wailed to his former employer, "Give me my hand. Give me my
hand." Father had scolded him away, saying: "Don't be silly. I
did all that the law requires of me. It happened because you
were inattentive. And it was your bad luck. How can I give you back
your hand? I'll turn you over to the police if you come to talk
such nonsense again." After that the man didn't come to Father
again, but Hyŏndo saw him hovering around the house quite frequently.

"What brought you here?" Mother asked in a tremulous voice,
aiming the flashlight at him. The light shook violently.

"Do you think I came to steal? Not on your life." The man held
up his right arm, making the iron hook glitter in the flashlight. "I
won't demand my hand back anymore. I'll just set this damn place
on fire. No one can take me to the police even if I set fire on this
and everything else. It's a new world. The wheel has turned, d'you
know? All those who fawned on the Japanese and lived like lords
are going to be beaten to death."

"Go away. Go away at once."

"Well, if you tell me to go, what can a cripple like me do except
go away?"

The man began to move, with a smirk on his face. He walked

towards the wall, as if pushed out by the flashlight, like an actor disappearing from the stage. Then he lifted his hooked arm and brought it down hard, once, twice, and thrice. Glass broke with an explosive clatter. The man disappeared through the paneless window. Mother searched the plant with the flashlight. The window next to it also had its pane knocked out. It must have been the noise of the windowpane breaking that Mother had heard from the house. Mother told Hyǒndo to hold up the flashlight, dragged out a large tin sheet, and covered the broken windows with it. Mother's face, lit by the flashlight, was blanched with fear as she struggled with the metal sheet.

Stepping down to the yard after locking the plant door, Mother murmured with a tired voice, "Oh, it's a scary world."

Hyǒndo thought of the Chinese boy he'd read about in his textbook. Once upon a time a rich Chinese silk merchant's house was broken into by thieves. The thieves tied the members of the family with rope and ordered the small shop assistant boy to lead them to the barn. The boy led the thieves as bidden, and while the thieves were bundling up bolts of silk and bagging gems, quietly stole out of the barn, locked the barn door from outside, and untied the master's family. Of course, the thieves were caught and the brave and clever boy received a huge award.

Why don't I have the courage and cleverness to protect my mother and my house? But Hyǒndo shook his head. The man was not a thief who came to steal. What shone at the end of his hooked arm was thirst for revenge and murderous hatred that could perhaps be assuaged only by setting on fire all those who had wounded and humiliated him. Hatred and vengeance were what filled the air of the whole town that summer.

On reaching their room, Mother whispered, "Don't tell Father what happened tonight. I guess there's nothing more dreadful than simmering resentments."

The school opened again in mid-September. It felt like a new school, as new mimeographed Korean and history textbooks were distributed instead of the Japanese reader, and most of the teachers were new as well. Every day the children did physical exercise and sang the Korean anthem to the tune of "Auld Lang Syne" on the playground. Singing the Korean anthem at the top of his lungs with the other children, Hyǒndo felt his heart swell with a love for his country and the resolution to do great deeds for it, especially at the passage "Let's keep this country as our own forever."

Like all other Japanese children, Shinzang was not seen anymore. But Hyǒndo knew that Shinzang and his mother were still in

Haeryŏng. The warehouse of the irrigation cooperative building had been turned into a temporary internment camp for the Japanese. The empty lot behind the cooperative was hung with colorful laundry every day. It had been said that all the Japanese would be sent back to Japan promptly, but they remained there until the end of that fall. Passing the lot on his way home from school, Hyŏndo caught sight of Japanese women washing laundry with red, frozen hands beside the water pump, their shaven heads covered with towels. People said that all the Japanese women had shaved their heads to deceive the Russian soldiers. Sometimes, a few Japanese children came to sit in the sun in the front yard of the cooperative, but they were soon dragged inside by their mothers. It was rumored that inside the camp children died of dysentery every day, leaking feces mixed with blood. People said that all the Japanese died once they caught dysentery. It's because they don't eat garlic, grown-ups said.

Was Shinzang, too, in there? Hyŏndo wondered, looking at the child gazing out of the warehouse clinging to the iron-barred window. Hyŏndo had seen Shinzang's mother yesterday morning. Nowadays Japanese women went round the village in groups of three or four, begging for food. The Japanese were excluded from food rationing.

As Hyŏndo was sitting down to breakfast with his family, someone knocked on the gate. When Mother opened the gate, three women with shaven heads stepped in with food boxes.

"Please have charity," they said politely, bowing deep. They were clad in male garments, but one could easily see they were women. Hyŏndo and Sŭngdo rushed out to the living room to look at the beggars. Mother picked up her untouched bowl of rice and stepped down to the yard. The tallest of the three women lifted her head for a moment before taking the rice in her receptacle. Hyŏndo thought the face looked familiar, and the next moment realized that it was Shinzang's mother.

Their gazes met for a brief second. Hyŏndo's heart beat wildly. In that split second, Shinzang, their house enveloped in indescribable silence, and the shrine closet with the prayer shelf flashed through his mind. Could she have come to his house disguised as a beggar to find the wooden doll, so she could prolong Shinzang's life? The day he brought the doll home, he had buried it deep in the closet among disused odds and ends, for fear of any of his family seeing it, and never took it out again.

The woman soon averted her gaze. Their eyes met so briefly that he couldn't be sure she recognized him. The women bowed repeatedly and disappeared through the gate.

The irrigation cooperative used as the Japanese internment camp, the Shimsang Primary School used as the Russian troop headquarters, and the daily public assembly held in the monument intersection were new sights and rituals in Haeryŏng now. Not comprehending their parents' anxiety, the children didn't want to go home directly from school. Their greatest attraction was the Russian troops. If you climbed up the rather low walls of the Shimsang Primary School, you could see Russian soldiers running in the playground with the upper half of their bodies stripped naked, in spite of the cold weather. The children exclaimed with wonder and fear, looking at their hairy chests and their arms strapped with two or three wristwatches, which they proudly held up for the children to see.

And they were eating all the time. They ate dark bread, and they cut pork with thick layers of fat, using old automobile tires as chopping blocks, and ate it raw. They cut and chewed stalks of ripening millet and gnawed raw corn. So, they left their trail everywhere. People called them animals, beggars and barbarians from the North.

People whispered that goblins nine feet tall with torchlike eyes haunted millet fields. And farmers going to their fields early in the morning saw women rising out of the dew-covered furrows of the millet field, trying to wrap themselves up in their torn clothes as best they could.

Women hardly dared to go out even in the daytime, and all the gates closed as soon as the sun set. The darkened streets rang with the trampling of the Russian soldiers' boots. They demanded women and watches endlessly and coveted the gold fillings on people's teeth.

The red-light district was the only place that came alive at night. When people heard the sad and melancholy songs of the men drunk on hard liquor coming out of the brightly lit brothel, they realized for the first time that the Russians, too, were human beings who missed their faraway homes and mothers and sweethearts. And people thought of the mercilessly cold continent, a country of incessant snow, the land of dark soil and dark fir trees and the barking of the wolves that rang through the frozen plains—images that excited longings in their breasts when they were young.

People were returning from faraway lands. The fathers and older brothers who had disappeared one dark night while the children were asleep came back as victors and heroes, and Hyŏndo's uncle also came back one day. On arriving, Uncle stood long at the gate, leaning against the doorpost and wrinkling his forehead, which had a burnt scar on it, like someone who was at a loss.

The ships didn't sail out, even though it was ebb tide. "Grandma, it isn't right that some people should have seven ships when so many haven't got even one small boat. Now, it's a blessed world in which everybody eats equally. Those who have been fattening on the tears of the people are no better than the Japanese."

Grandmother beat the floor with her palm, relating the words of the secretary of the newly organized fishermen's cooperative.

"It's all because the old man died. They think they can trample on an old widow. What a lawless world this has become!" And Grandmother couldn't stand the sight of Pongmyŏng, her former servant boy, stalking around with a red armband, having joined the volunteer security force, so she had moved to her son's house in town. "I don't want to lay eyes on a ship again, ever," Grandmother said.

"This is no time to grieve over insults. It's a different world now. We'd better sell the ships to whoever would buy them, before there is talk of confiscating them," Father said gloomily.

The machine noise had ceased at the plant for more than a month now. The workers quit, saying that now they could eat anywhere if they only carried their spoons around. Mother shuddered, saying, "Did anyone starve before for lack of a spoon to carry around? I'm sick of hearing 'people,' 'people'."

But Grandmother may have had other reasons for staying in town. Her gaze always turned towards the back room in which her younger son lived. It was towards that room her eyes turned every time she stepped into the house, and she halted her movements to listen for sounds from that room in the middle of sweeping the yard or scooping up preserves from the storage place. And she wasn't the only one, either. Mother and Father also watched Uncle with watchful and anxious eyes. Sometimes Grandmother would ask her daughter-in-law in whispers, "Did anything happen?"

"Oh, don't worry. He couldn't do that again. He must have stayed clean while in Japan. It's been three years," Mother would answer, trying to sound reassuring.

"I saw Samyong in the intersection yesterday. How my heart fell!"

"Oh, you mean that hospital assistant who gave him morphine? What shall I do if he comes looking for the children's uncle?" Mother asked, like one who received a hard blow.

Uncle stayed cooped in his room, and came over to the main

room only at mealtimes. Even though he was the center of the family's anxious surveillance, Uncle acted as if he lived all alone and didn't mix with the family even at mealtimes. It may have been from a consciousness that even his slightest move was carefully watched, as if he had been an insect in a flask, or because he knew that the concern of his family was no more than surveillance. But to the children their uncle was a novelty and an object of consuming interest.

Uncle spent his days lying on his back. He said that his head ached and felt clouded all the time, and that all the bones in his body ached. The medicine Grandmother brewed every morning didn't seem to do him any good. His room stayed closed most of the time, but Uncle sometimes opened the door to gaze at the bright sunlight or to clean the sores. He got the sores from being burned by the fire that erupted when the war supply factory he was working for got hit by a bomb. When the factory burst into flames, Uncle escaped with only a slight burn on his forehead. Blisters formed on his arms and legs touched by the heat, but he didn't think they would be serious. However, the blisters didn't heal and kept festering. "It was like a dream. There was complete silence, and the world became indescribably bright. And then terrible black clouds soared up, and the whole city was a burning sea," Uncle had said.

Hyŏndo recalled the words of the young man he had heard in Sunjae's house in the port. That blazing light was the figure of Jehovah in silver armor and helmet, come to judge the world, he had said.

He must have been referring to the bombing of that day. What did I do on that day? Hyŏndo screwed up his face, trying to recall the summer days, the hot and boring days spent in the port.

Uncle sometimes told him about his journey across the Korea-Japan strait, and the train ride through the south and crossing the 38th parallel over mountain paths.

Father brought medicine he'd bought from a vendor doing business across the North and South Korean border. The vendor had said that it was medicine used by American soldiers and a hundred percent cure for burn sores. But it didn't work on Uncle.

Each morning, there was a sheaf of hair that had fallen out during the night on Uncle's pillow. "See how I'm rotting away," Uncle muttered gloomily, as he threw out the balled hair into the yard.

"That's because you've grown weak. You need a good rest.

Young men are going insane all over the country. It's best to stay in the house in crazy times like this," Grandmother said to Uncle over and over again, grateful that her younger son stayed at home.

Snow, which began at dawn, ceased around lunchtime. But the sky was still lowering with dark clouds. Sparrows flew into the yard, which had grown more quiet because of the snow piled on the ground and the roof. Staying in the room eating potatoes baked on the brazier, Hyŏndo was listening to the flutter of sparrows outside. Father had gone to Yŏnbaek two days before to buy rice, and Grandmother had left for the port with five pounds of rice, saying that she'd go to consult the shaman after taking a look at the house and the ships. Mother had gone to the public plaza. Nowadays, there was a meeting in the plaza every day, and after the meeting people always marched round the town shouting slogans before dispersing.

Mother, who had to attend the meeting in place of Father for the third day in a row, came back home late in the afternoon frozen stiff. "Until yesterday they were saying we're dead against trusteeship, but today they said we must have trusteeship by all means. Today young men beat up an old man who went up to the podium and shouted that we'll lose our country again if we accepted trusteeship. I think he was beaten to death. There's no knowing to which tune we should be dancing to. If you so much as uttered a wrong word, you get dragged to the police and beaten to death. It scares the wits out of me," Mother sighed, telling Grandmother about the meeting of that day.

"What do the plain folks like us know about independence and sovereignty and things of that sort? I lived my whole life worrying only about ships and catching fish. So, though I have a son who's my Karma, I thought the world would be a paradise if only we got our country back. I thought if only we got rid of the Japanese the ships would bring in more fish, and we Koreans would live in peace and plenty ever after. But people have been accusing and fighting each other every day since liberation, so I only wish somebody'd get hold of this land, restore order, and let people live their lives. I don't care if it's Russians or Chinese," Grandmother said plaintively.

"You shouldn't say such things, Grandma. Why should foreigners rule this country? This country is ours," Hyŏndo protested sharply.

Grandmother smiled sadly. "You're right. Old people should learn from children," she said weakly.

Sparrows were still fluttering in the yard. What were they looking for in the snow?

Hyŏndo went out to the yard to see. Frightened birds flew away
at once. He found a basket, and tied a long string to its rim.

"What's that for?" Sŭngdo, who had followed him outside,
asked.

"Come. I'll catch you sparrows," Hyŏndo said to his younger
brother.

Hyŏndo balanced the basket upside down on a long thin rod,
and swept the snow around the spot. Then, going into the kitchen,
he took out a handful of rice from the rice jar hidden under the
kitchen floor. If Mother were to catch him stealing rice from the
jar, he'd surely get a sound beating. As rice had become scarce,
Mother had hidden rice under the kitchen floor and cooked meals
with rationed flour.

Scattering rice on the ground under the basket, Hyŏndo took
the end of the string and walked behind the gate to wait for the
sparrows to come back. Soon, sparrows began to descend on the
yard again. They alighted under the basket to peck on the rice. He
held his breath and snatched at the string. The basket fell on the
ground, and sparrows fluttered up wildly. Then, he heard a chuckle from behind. He jerked his head to see who it was. There was a
man behind him, though Hyŏndo had heard no footsteps. Perhaps
the snow had muffled the sound.

The man, who was wearing a cap pressed low, a worn suit jacket
and woolen mufflers, stroked Hyŏndo's head and smiled affection-
ately. Shuddering at the icy-cold touch of the stranger's fingers,
Hyŏndo shrank back and looked up at him.

Although he was obviously a young man, his complexion was
sickly and his skin dry, so that one could easily have mistaken him
for an old man.

"Your uncle's in, isn't he? Which is his room?"

When Hyŏndo pointed to the rear part of the house, the man
walked straight towards that quarter. His gait was shuffling, and he
looked emaciated, so Hyŏndo thought he must be an invalid.

Setting the basket on top of the rod again, Hyŏndo resumed
sparrow catching but he couldn't catch even one. Although he
pulled the strings after he saw sparrows right under the basket, the
basket was always empty when he felt inside. "What a waste of precious rice," he muttered, resentfully eyeing the sparrows.
Pongmyŏng, his grandparents' servant, had told him that sparrows
spend the night in empty wells. "If you cover the mouth of a well
with a net at night, you find sparrows stuck dead in the net with

wide-open eyes. Sparrows are early risers, so they fly out of the well early in the morning. When they get caught by the neck in the net, they struggle to get free, and end up tangled all the more tightly in the net. So all you have to do is to pick them off the net." Pongmyŏng had grinned spiritedly as he told this to Hyŏndo, as if he was actually taking sparrows off the net. But that carbuncular adolescent was now a volunteer security guard wearing a red armband and strode through the streets carrying a gun. Hyŏndo had never been to his grandparents' house since the day of his grandfather's funeral. Are the numerous talismens, the old pear tree that cast an eerie shadow on the paper panels of the door, and the ferrets that are said to crawl out at pitch black nights and brought in money and luck, keeping watch over the empty house? What big changes have taken place since then! The low talk ceased in the back room and the stranger left. Shortly after the man left, Grandmother returned. Seeing the footprints on the snow, Grandmother at once became tense and questioned Hyŏndo.

"Who was here?"

"A man came to see Uncle."

"Oh, you idiot! Why didn't you say Uncle wasn't home?"

Because Grandmother's tone was so fierce, Hyŏndo started to cry. Grandmother rushed to Uncle's room and opened the door ferociously.

"That bastard came, didn't he? What did he want? Why doesn't he leave you alone?"

"He said he came because he was glad to hear I came back alive," Uncle's tone, unlike Grandmother's, was tranquil.

"That bastard is a devil. He'll drag you to your death. Oh, why is he still alive!"

Grandmother took up the bush clover broom and swept away the man's footprints on the snow. She swept the yard so hard that the ground was hollowed out. She seemed to have forgotten her own habitual warning to others that to use the broom after dark is to sweep away luck.

Uncle didn't come over for dinner. Mother prepared a meal tray and went over to Uncle's room, but Uncle just told her he wasn't hungry and didn't open the door.

"I knew this'd happen. I knew it," Grandmother kept muttering. She, too, didn't eat any dinner, and just drank rice wine.

That night, Hyŏndo dreamed of the stranger all night long. In the dream, too, he touched Hyŏndo's neck with his icy hand and grinned familiarly, exposing his teeth and wrinkling his yellow face. "Catching birds, eh?" he asked, and walked towards the back

quarters with shuffling gait without waiting for Hyŏndo's answer.
The sound of his footsteps on the snow continued to be heard long
after he disappeared from view. The footsteps hovered all over the
house all night long, hesitantly, fearfully, longingly, shudderingly.
"Is there someone in the yard?" Hyŏndo murmured in sleep.

At dawn, Hyŏndo heard Father's low voice. "There's a rumor of
a land reform. Buying rice is getting to be harder than catching
stars. And the red currencies are worthless. Landowners are
preparing to cross the 38th parallel before their lands are confis-
cated and they're sent to Siberia or a coal mine." Oh, then the
footsteps were Father's, Hyŏndo thought and dropped off to easy
slumber.

It was late the following morning that they discovered Uncle
had left the house. Mother prepared a late breakfast so her husband, who had come back at dawn exhausted from the trip, could
get a few hours' sleep. Then she called Uncle but Uncle's room
was empty. Uncle hadn't even left footprints, as snow had fallen
throughout the night and into the morning and covered all traces
on the ground.

"He's gone to the opium den again. He couldn't stay away, not
with that fiend coming after him."

"I don't believe it. He swore he'd stay clean the last time he
came out of the hospital. He said he'd cut off his hand first,"
Father said reassuringly, but his face was dark.

"This is the third time. We work so hard to get him rehabilitat-
ed, and then those addicts lure him away again. I suppose there'd
be no saving him this time. We sent him away to that hell factory to
keep him away from opium. I wished he wouldn't come back. Just
think. How much heartache and disgrace we had to endure on
account of him!" Tears were streaming down Grandmother's face.

Was Uncle really an opium addict? Would Uncle, too, one day
be dragged away like other opium addicts, amid the abuse and fin-
ger-pointing of townspeople?

Leaving Grandmother's tears behind, Hyŏndo came out to the
living room floor and turned his gaze on the snow-covered yard—
as if to find beneath the snow traces of Uncle's desperate inner
struggle of the night before and his agonized footsteps.

The winter was long and cold. For growing children, it was also
a hungry season. Rice was taken away to feed the occupying forces,
and wheat flour was distributed. Mother, who was pregnant,
cooked the flour, covering her nose to keep out the loathsome
smell. Aunt came to their house with her baby daughter strapped
to her back at breakfast time and left after supper.

"How unfortunate for someone to be born at a time like this," Mother complained about her forthcoming baby, but Grandmother giggled merrily.

"No, the harder the times are the more children you must bear. Children bring their own keep into the world. Let's just hope it's another boy," Grandmother said. Grandmother, who was tall and stout for an old woman, had grown gaunt and weak from the time her younger son began to frequent the opium den. Not only on account of her heartache, but her aggravated heartburn caused indigestion. By now even the small children knew that Uncle was an opium addict. Uncle came back to the house once every few days, or sometimes he stayed away for ten days at a time and came back in garments soiled black and with gummy eyes. Mother had said that there was an opium den outside the town. Sometimes Uncle brought home candy bars or candy balls, but the children didn't want to take the treats proffered with soiled hands.

Uncle always left a mark of his visit in his wake. The phonograph, radio and wall clock disappeared. "You wait and see. This is only the beginning. He snitched even the bronze washbasin and bronze spoons. Once he stole a ring from the wife of your father's friend, so I was too ashamed to hold up my face before that couple," Mother said. Mother didn't refrain from complaining about her brother-in-law in front of the children now. "That hospital assistant Samyong was an opium addict. I hope he rots in hell!"

Now, disappearance of valuables was as commonplace an occurrence as rats carrying away soap bars. Uncle had been hospitalized for appendicitis when he was nineteen, and the hospital assistant gave him morphine shots for killing pain, which started him on opium addiction.

"Hyŏndo, carry this tray to Uncle," Mother called from the kitchen. It was Grandmother who carried food trays to Uncle, but when Grandmother was away, the chore fell on Hyŏndo. When staying home, Uncle spent most of his time lying on his back. He hardly ate now. The food tray was often left untouched.

When Hyŏndo brought the meal tray, Uncle, who had been cleaning his sores, grinned at him.

"Oh, my eldest nephew and family heir, welcome!"

Uncle was in his rare good mood. He looked much stronger than usual, too. "I'm detestable, aren't I?" Uncle asked, as Hyŏndo was coming away after putting the food tray in front of him. Nonplussed, Hyŏndo nodded, smiling in embarrassment.

"What do people say about me?"

"That you're an opium addict."

"That's right. That's what I am," Uncle said and chuckled.

Uncle, whose face had shrivelled yellow and most of whose hair had fallen out, looked like an old man. A strange yucky smell hung in Uncle's room. Was it the smell of opium? Or of rotting flesh? Of the two mixed together? Or did the two have the same smell? A sickly fragrance that intoxicates and then rots one.

Summoning courage, Hyŏndo asked, "Why do you take opium?"

"Because I can't bear this world. Once you take opium, you forget all your afflictions, both of the body and the mind. Opium frees you from worldly troubles and carries you to another world where everything's as you want it. You look down on the world from there, and it's an ugly, loathsome, disgusting place. Like to see how disgusting it is?" Uncle said and held out his festering arm. The sore the size of two coins. Rotting flesh. "These are erupting all over my body. Soon, they'll be infested with worms. This is what our bodies are like. Is this because of our original sin?" Uncle's voice grew lax and low. His eyes also became unfocused and vague, like a sleepy person's. He lit a cigarette with a mechanical movement, puffed at it once, then lay back again. "Oh, this feels good. It's just as if I'd died. No, it's just like before I was born. But this will be the last time. I'll be clean from tomorrow." The last sentence, however, was a hardly audible murmur. His eyes were half open, but he wasn't even conscious of his mattress catching fire from his cigarette. Hyŏndo took the cigarette away from Uncle's oily and humid hand, rubbed it out against the ashtray, and covered him with bedclothes. Coming away, Hyŏndo reopened the door and took a long look at Uncle's room. It seemed like he was leaving behind a ragged body, from which the spirit had fled, and whose flesh would dissolve into air with a fragrant and musty smell.

The doctor Father had called in to treat Uncle's sores shook his head. "This is a brand new disease. You said he was in Hiroshima, didn't you? This is a disease that people who were exposed to the atom bomb explosion got. And to shoot opium into such a body is like pouring gasoline over fire."

Some thirty Japanese were walking in a group towards the train station. Most of them were shabby old people and children, and they each carried a small bundle. All the women in the group had shaved their heads and were walking with their eyes fixed on the ground in silent despair, like convicts. They had endured the hunger and the cold in the hope of returning to their country, and they were leaving Haeryŏng in groups of twenty to thirty. They were put on the train under the surveillance of armed security guards, but no one knew where they would be sent to.

Hyŏndo, who had been looking at the goings-on around the intersection sitting atop the monument, jumped down upon spotting Shinzang's mother in the group. She was carrying Shinzang on her back. "Shinzang!" he called out in a loud voice and approached them, without thinking what he'd say or do to them. A few people in the group looked back, but Shinzang's mother kept on walking, as if she hadn't heard.

"Shinzang!" Hyŏndo called out again and waved his hand, but this time nobody looked back.

Shinzang seemed to have shrivelled even more, and only his hump rose above his mother's shoulders. He was leaning his yellow face against his mother's back and looked as if he only wanted to take in a little more of the pale sunshine of early spring. His face seemed to bespeak a resolution never to answer anybody's call again.

Hyŏndo stopped following them. It was no use. In the dusty spring breeze that chilled you to the marrow their backs receded, disappearing into minor history. Feeling lonely and achy as if he'd been left all alone in the wide world, Hyŏndo whispered Shinzang's name several times to himself.

In his house a big scene was taking place. Uncle, who had been away for nearly ten days, had come home and was going out with the sewing machine head but ran into Father at the gate. Father picked up the long broom that stood beside the gate and hit Uncle hard. Uncle fell down on the ground like a scarecrow. "Why don't you just drop dead!" Grandmother screamed, tearing her blouse lapels. In the twinkling of an eye, villagers thickly surrounded the house. Hyŏndo's house was now called the drug addict's house instead of the factory house as in former times. Father dragged Uncle inside by the scruff of his neck. Uncle suddenly took out a sharp kitchen knife from his bosom and, striking it into the floor, glared at his older brother. "All right. Let's get this straight this time. I know that my mother and my own brother and sister loathe me and even my young nephews regard me as a filthy insect. But do you think I don't know that you sent me off to the Japanese war supply factory in your place? I know you hoped I'd die there. The draft was in your name, but you bribed the town hall clerk to put in my name instead of yours. What idiot would draft a drug addict to hard labor? Do you think I braved death and crossed the 38th parallel because I missed you all? No way. I came to get this straight with you. But what's the use? My youth won't return, nor will my health be restored. So, let's forget about that. Just give me my portion of Father's legacy. He was a rich man, so there must be my portion. Just give me that and I'll make myself scarce once and for all."

"You misunderstand. It was to cure you of your habit that I sent you to the war factory. If you'd stayed here you'd have died in an asylum. You know what the Japanese do to opium addicts. And as for Father's legacy, only the dead man knows where all his money went."

Father threw down Grandfather's notebooks on the floor in front of Uncle.

Uncle began to sob bitterly. "Look, brother. I'm hurting so bad I can't stand it. My whole body's rotting. I must have a shot or I'll die howling mad with pain. I know I hurt my family, being a dope fiend, but do take some pity on me. Just let me have one shot today and I'll stay clean. I promise. You can tie me down to the posts in this house. Honest, I'll stay clean." Uncle implored Father, crawling up to him on his knees.

Grandmother picked out her silver hair barrette and threw it to Uncle. "Here. Take this. Take this and stay in that cursed den as long as they'll let you for it. You pitiful scum!"

After Uncle left, Grandmother looked for her nickel barrette and fixed her hair with it. Then she bundled up Grandfather's notebooks in a cloth. Father tried to dissuade her, saying, "It's no use. Who'd repay their debts to a dead man?" But Grandmother left, saying, "I know there's not one man on the port who isn't in debt to your father. I'll make them pay back."

But Grandmother never returned home. After a squabble with a debtor she drank heavily and had fallen down on the night road. Uncle, who had left with her silver hair barrette, didn't come home for her funeral.

The day after Grandmother's funeral Father was summoned to the people's committee office in the town hall. On returning home, he whispered to Mother in a low voice: "We'll have to sell the house in the port and the ships. I think we can sell them if we lower the price. Things are looking awfully bad. I heard that the brewery owner was sent to a coal mine, and the dentist fled to the South with his family. They say the patrol around the 38th parallel line is tightening, but . . . Now that Mother has passed away there's nothing to tie us down here, is there?"

Houses became empty overnight. Every day the number of empty seats in the classroom increased. Boys who went home with the other boys the day before stopped coming to school one day. Hyŏndo felt betrayed and left behind when, calling his friend's name at his house on the way to school, only silence and desolation came from the empty house, or when friendly neighbors disappeared overnight without a word of good-bye.

Everybody whispered that Ŭlmo's family, who had left for the South leaving behind the insane oldest son and the faithful dog, saying that they would go South even if they'd have to pave the roads with money, were all shot to death, and the deserted son went around crying through the streets begging for food. Still, despite such danger, people fled to the South, leaving behind their houses and land.

"We have to hire a boat," Father said and went out with the sheaf of money they had hid deep inside their cabinet. It was the money they got for the ships they sold in a hurry, after Grandmother's death. Father could not make up his mind even after he was told that he was on the list of "exploiters" and "national traitors." He said, "I made my living working hard, that's all, so I've nothing to fear." Like most people he regarded the 38th parallel as a temporary dividing line drawn for disarming the Japanese army.

Mother also couldn't make up her mind about leaving her hometown. She was born and grew up in Haeryŏng. Immigrating to the South sounded to her like going to a foreign country. To begin life again in a strange place among people with strange accents and different customs was not an exciting adventure to her, who had three children, was pregnant with a fourth, and had to take care of a helpless and unhappy sister-in-law and an opium addict of a brother-in-law who was an atom bomb victim into the bargain. The prospect struck terror into her. But anyplace would be a strange land once you left your hometown.

Father returned at night.

"We're leaving at night on the last day of this month. That's a week from today. There are sentries all along the shore of the port, so we have to go to the Dragon Bay in Pyŏksŏng by eleven o'clock at night. They're going to get the boat out to the big sea tomorrow," he said. People called the distant sea outside the range of the ebb and tide the big sea. Mother pointed to the back room with her eyes. Father shook his head. "It can't be helped. Even if he could be cured of his addiction, atom bomb disease is incurable. And we don't know how we'll manage in the South. So, we must go and settle down first, and then come for him or send for him. There's sure to be a way."

Pyŏksŏng was a fishing village that lay across the bay from
Haeryŏng. Father said that he would have a barge carry their things
and load them on the boat. Then they would wait for the moonless
night. The day after they had a few essential clothes, foodstuffs and
household utensils taken out by a handcart in the depth of the
night, the family climbed the Hyŏngsŏng Mountain. It was the only
place in town from which they had a view of the sea. The weather
was cold, but the children were excited, thinking the expedition
with a food-filled rucksack a picnic.

The chilly spring wind seeped into their clothes. They could
see the sea in the distance, and the curving Haeryŏng bay. Father
raised his hand to point to the sea beyond Kŏido Island. They
could barely discern a boat with a furled sail on the horizon. It was
the boat in which eight rowers would take them to a strange land.
Their things were already loaded on it. They looked at the boat for
a long time, squinting their eyes.

"Who is it?" Mother shouted, her heart sinking at the sound of
footsteps in the yard. "It's me, sister," Aunt's voice said. "Come in."
When Mother opened the door, Aunt, carrying her baby daughter
on her back as usual, stepped in quickly. She untied the sash of the
baby wrapper and laid her baby down on the warmer part of the
floor. The girl with the abundant and lustrous black hair was
asleep. Mother caressed the baby's hair, exclaiming "how gorgeous!" Aunt smiled desolately. "Mother always blamed my poor
luck on the baby's hair and used to grab it and shake it," she said
with a sigh. Then, catching sight of the clothes lying on the floor,
she asked, "Are you going South?"

"Who said such a thing?" Father asked back, frowning. They
had never even hinted it to anyone.

"You're not going to desert us, are you?"

"Who do you mean, us?"

"Second brother and me. Take me along with you. After your
parents die, your oldest brother is a father to you. When do you
leave?"

"We haven't decided yet. We're thinking of leaving, it's true,
but we don't know anyone in the South. So, how can we make up
our minds easily?" Father said, avoiding his sister's eyes.

"Just take me along. I won't be a burden to you, I promise. I'll
earn my keep."

"We'll go first and we'll come back for you. Even though the
patrol is tight, lots of people come and go."

Aunt's body shook, and blood rose to her face. "No, you
mustn't leave us behind. Second brother will die. I hear they're

arresting drug addicts. They say they starve them to death or send them to coal mines. We're your only blood kin, aren't we?"

"What about your husband?"

"I hear he joined the Red Guard. He's not my husband anymore. We must have been deadly enemies in our former lives. I'm scared to death of him. The only people I miss are my dead parents," Aunt said and began to cry, her lips twitching violently.

"The ship is leaving from Dragon Bay the day after tomorrow. Come straight to there."

Mother looked at Father, uncomprehending. The last day of the lunar month was tomorrow.

Aunt's narrow freckled face brightened up at once. She wetted her dry lips and said, "Oh, thank you. Thank you." She picked up her sleeping baby and strapped her to her back. "Well, I think I'd better go and start getting ready. I'll be there the day after tomorrow," she said and rose to leave. Then, at the gate, she gazed at the house and said, "Well, I guess I'd have to bid this house good-bye today." The pale green baby wrapper with the red trimming looked gorgeous, even in the chilly spring wind.

"It's awfully cold. Sugi might catch cold in this wind. Here. Wrap her head with this," Mother said, placing her youngest son's fur-lined jacket on the baby's back. The baby's head of lustrous black hair smote her heart, so Hyŏndo's mother felt she couldn't part with her without giving her something.

"Oh, but Myŏngdo needs it, too," Aunt said guiltily, but wrapped it around her daughter with a happy smile.

Mother had told him not to go to school but to help her around the house that day. It was exciting to cut school. Mother began house cleaning as soon as she washed the dishes after breakfast, with a towel wrapped around her head. Father started for the grandparents' graves, with bundled-up offerings of dried fish, fruits and a bottle of spirits.

Mother first took down the box house containing Grandmother's memorial tablet, to which they had been making offerings of meals morning and evening. Hyŏndo asked her, "Isn't Grandmother going to be with us anymore?" Mother had told him that the memorial tablet house was where Grandmother's spirit dwelt, and that while her spirit dwelt with them she watched over the house and family just like when she was alive. "No. Why would she stay in this house when we aren't here any longer?" Mother answered, taking the incense holder and other utensils out of the box house with deft movements. Hyŏndo guessed that something very serious was taking place. His parents had said nothing unusual and they went on just like on other days, but he was aware of a silent current, a furtive haste in the house during the past few days.

After sweeping the yard as Mother had bidden him, Hyŏndo stole out of the house.

"You mustn't stay out long," Mother shouted at his back.

Hyŏndo ran towards the monument intersection. Because that day a big celebrity was expected in Haeryŏng. The celebrity had dedicated his whole life to fighting for the country's independence, and the patriotism and valor of the independence fighters under his command was famous not only throughout Manchuria but all over Russia as well. Of course, he had played an important role in driving out the Japanese from their fatherland. He had longed to step on the soil of his liberated fatherland for a long, long time. Hyŏndo's teacher had said that he was a man who would light up our dark history like the sun. A figure who would light up our dark history like the sun! Oh, what mark would he be carrying, and what halo would he be surrounded with as he steps into Haeryŏng? Would he be carrying the sun on his forehead? The brilliant rhetoric of his teacher had set Hyŏndo's heart all in a flutter and dazzled his vision.

It was already broad daylight. People were arriving in the intersection, carrying flags. Hyŏndo thought: If I stood on the monument I'd have a good view and wouldn't be pushed and shoved by the crowd. I'll stand tall on the monument and take a good look at the man who made the dark history and the landscape tremble, dashing through the frozen continent on horseback. Luckily, there was no one on top of the monument yet. Only a few children were standing around it. Hyŏndo tried to cut through the circle of children but halted and took a backward step. His uncle was sitting, leaning against the monument. There was no mistaking it was Uncle, though his hair and beard had grown bushy and his face had shrivelled like an old corpse's. The children whispered to each other, "Is he a madman?" "Is he dead?" and poked him with a rod. Uncle did not react, but dribbling at the mouth, he kept gazing with his vague eyes at the bright blue sky beyond the children's heads. Hyŏndo knew that his uncle was neither mad nor dead. He was only intoxicated with opium and was floating in a world of his own, far away from the strife and tension of this world. His wrist, jutting out of his jacket sleeve, was as thin as a twig. An ant was crawling up his wrist covered with sticky fluid. Mother had said that opium addicts die when their heads drop like a cut stalk while dozing in the sun like sick hens, after they grow so thin that they have no flesh to stick needles in.

Hyŏndo hadn't seen Uncle since the day Grandmother died. Uncle hadn't returned home from the day he left with Grandmother's silver barrette.

Looking at his uncle, Hyŏndo's burning desire to behold the halo that had taken hold of his imagination so strongly suddenly wilted. Don't we all have halos of one sort or another? Doesn't the sun shine on all of us equally?

More and more people were gathering in the intersection but Hyŏndo left the place. Feeling Uncle's eyes holding him back, and blushing at himself for not daring to look back at Uncle, he walked away as quickly as his feet would carry him.

At home, Mother was cooking rice for dinner, even though it was broad daylight. The house had been thoroughly cleaned already. "Where have you been for so long? Why don't you stay home on a day like this?" Father, who was back from the mountain, scolded him, frowning.

The attic closet door was wide open. The closet, which used to be a mess with heaps of rarely used appliances, broken-down machines, old clothes and so forth, was completely tidied.

Hyŏndo climbed the attic closet. He looked for the child doll among the things sorted from the heap, but it was not there. His mother must have thrown it away. Hyŏndo came down from the attic and lifted the piles of old books, newspapers, and other rubbish.

"What're you looking for?" Father asked him.

"My thing," Hyŏndo answered gruffly.

He found the doll from among the rubbish. "What's that?" Father asked Hyŏndo as he was looking at the wooden doll. "It belongs to a friend of mine. I'll return it to him tomorrow," he replied, thinking "Oh, but Shinzang's already left." When he blew away the dirt on it and rubbed it with his palm, its fair face, long and dark eyes, and red smiling mouth came alive. "Oh, it's a Japanese thing. Throw it away. You can't return it," Father said sternly, but Hyŏndo stuck it in his pocket. Didn't Shinzang's mother say, "It's no use to us now. You can take it if you want," as he was leaving their house with it?

After eating an early supper, Mother made balled rice. She put five of them in a tray, covered it with a cloth, and told Hyŏndo to put it in Uncle's room.

"But Uncle's not home," Hyŏndo said. He thought of telling his mother that he saw his uncle that day beside the monument, but decided not to.

"Well, he'll have to eat if he comes home," Mother said.

There was a small kettle of water on the tray as well.

Mother took out from the chest of drawers a cotton-wool-padded outfit and cotton outfit and called Hyŏndo again.

"Here. Put these in Uncle's room as well."

Uncle's room was tidied and swept clean, too. There was a set of clean new bedding folded up on a corner of the floor, but the floor was cold, as the room hadn't been heated since Uncle left with the barrette.

Dusk began to fall. "What time is it?" Mother asked Father, waking out of a reverie. "It's still only five o'clock," Father said, consulting his wrist watch. "Oh, the floor is growing cold," Mother exclaimed and jumped up. "What's the use of adding fuel now?" Father snubbed her. "Oh, but Sister will put the baby on the floor the first thing when she comes tomorrow," Mother said. Father said nothing and just cast his eyes on the darkening window.

"Hyŏndo, bring some paper to kindle the fire," Mother told him. After feeding the heating stove of the inner room with a whole bundle of firewood, Mother went to the back room. Hyŏndo brought his mother an armful of old books and newspapers from the rubbish heap in the corner of the yard.

When he stuck a lighted newspaper into the stove, the crickets that had been nesting in the dark and humid stove jumped up in fright like springing dolls. Mother pushed lighted wood deep into the stove.

"Why do you warm up an empty room?" Hyŏndo asked, swallowing his words about having seen Uncle.

"Your uncle will be cold when he comes home," Mother said. Then, untying a new bundle of firewood and lighting up the sticks one by one, she murmured, more to herself than to her son, "How long will the warmth last? Till tomorrow afternoon? Tomorrow evening?"

Mist was gathering thickly. The light from the port glowed dimly across the bay. They walked towards the Dragon Bay, trying to muffle their footsteps. A small barge would be waiting for them hidden behind a rock. Two-year-old Myŏngdo was asleep on Mother's back, and five-year-old Sŭngdo was asleep on Father's back. Only ten-year-old Hyŏndo had been walking the night road for three miles, carrying a small rucksack on his back.

When they rounded the rock, the boatman in the barge stood up to greet them.

"Step right in," he said.

Although the boatman was holding the side of the barge firmly, the vessel shook dangerously each time one of them stepped into it. It was quite full when the family took their seats.

When the boatman forcibly pushed the barge out towards the sea, the rope loosened itself and the barge was launched.

The moonless night was dark. They could see nothing and only heard the sound of the water lapping against the sides of the barge.

When the barge got a few hundred meters away from the shore, they heard urgent steps on the shore. They were the footsteps of two or three people. The bargeman halted rowing for a second and listened, but soon resumed rowing.

Two figures loomed up on the black rock the family had just left. "Sister! Brother!" It was Aunt's voice.

"Can we go back and get them on board?" Father asked the boatman urgently. The boatman shook his head. "No. They're going to patrol the shore soon." The barge was already far out on the sea. "I've brought Second Brother, too. How can you leave us behind? How can you?"

Mother stopped her ears and leaned against the side of the barge. "Don't look back," Father told her angrily. The boatman rowed more vigorously.

"What would Mother think about your leaving us like this!" Aunt shouted, but her voice was soon swallowed up by the roar of the waves. Mist was growing thicker and thicker. Hyŏndo and Sŭngdo had their eyes riveted on the shore, even though they were already too far away from the shore to see anything on it even if it hadn't been pitch dark.

"Mother, what's going to become . . . " Hyŏndo began in a low voice, but Mother slapped his shoulder hard. "Be quiet," she said. She was afraid of the thoughts that might be crossing the children's minds.

"It's lucky we have this thick mist," the boatman's heavy voice said.

"How far do we have to go?" Father asked the boatman.

"Oh, we'll reach the boat in just half an hour. We have to be quiet. On the Ox Island there are Russian soldiers and the watchpost of the security guards. We're safe once we get past that island," the boatman said.

Two-year-old Myŏngdo, who had fallen asleep, woke up and began to cry.

"Stop the crying, ma'am," the boatman told Mother in a low voice. "It's dangerous from here."

The baby might have wet his pants. Mother unstrapped him

and dandled him but he didn't stop crying. She opened her blouse and gave him her breast, which didn't produce milk anymore, but he pushed the tit out with his tongue and screamed even more loudly.

"Ma'am, you've got to stop him, or we'll all die," the boatman said urgently.

Someone seemed to be shouting from a distance. And a muffled gunshot rang through the mist. Father made the children prostrate themselves on the floor of the barge and lowered his own torso as well. "Stop his mouth," he ordered Mother. Mother pressed the baby's mouth with her palm. The baby's breath was hot like a fever. And he struggled, straining his arms and legs. "Oh, Myŏngdo, my baby!" Mother pleaded. The baby's struggle was so fierce it terrified her. Almost beside herself with terror, she pressed the baby's face with her hand. In her panic she could think of no other way to stop the baby from crying.

"It's all right now. We're past danger. You can breathe easy," the boatman said and rowed vigorously. Because of the thick mist they couldn't even see the boatman in the same barge. Myŏngdo wasn't crying anymore, and was limp in his mother's arms.

"Boy, did that child scare me! He must have sensed danger, too, young as he is," Father chuckled low, in relief.

"I'm doing this for the fourth time this month, and the watch is getting tighter and tighter. Well, come back when times are easier. What place on earth could be as good as home?"

It was the time of the year all the ships in the port would be going out to catch yellow corvina, the fishermen singing, "Let's go to fish up money. Let's go to Yŏnp'yŏng Sea to fish up money."

But the children's mother knew instinctively that they wouldn't be coming back. The sea, which was growing rougher as they went farther and farther out, was pushing them away from their hometown. It felt like a gesture of exclusion. The darkness and the thick mist hid from her view even her baby now lying peacefully on her lap. When she turned her wistful eyes towards where they had boarded the barge, she thought she caught a glimpse of her sister-in-law still calling to them from the top of the Black Rock. Or rather, she had a dazzling vision of the lustrous black hair of the baby strapped to her mother's back. The baby's hair was more lustrous than the needles of a blue pine.

That moment, she emitted a low groan, pressing her side. The baby in her womb had kicked her. It was the baby that would be born in a strange place early that summer.

The Rainy Spell

~~

Yoon Heung-gil

Yoon Heung-gil, born in 1942, is an author who eludes classification. It is not because he has intentionally rejected the dominant literary trends. In fact, he has treated many of the themes other contemporary authors favored—the problems of social injustice, economic inequality, abuse of human rights, and the aftermaths of national division. But there is always more to savor in his stories than in the average writer's, even when he treats the same subject. While indignation predominates in the works of other writers, pity runs stronger in his stories. And his characters are always fuller. Having experienced excruciating emotional and psychological conflicts all through his penurious childhood and adolescence, Yoon has an acute understanding of the worms that gnaw at the root of the human psyche and man's innumerable compensatory mechanisms. Thus, even his villains have some redeeming qualities, and his heroes, human weaknesses. This, together with his verbal wit, irony and inimitable handling of his native Cholla-do dialect, constitute his charm. After taking us through numerous pitfalls and trials that lie in ambush for humanity, Yoon offers a possibility of meaningful survival.

"The Rainy Spell," first published in 1978, is still rated as one of the finest short stories to deal with the Korean War experience. Because it was a war in which a homogeneous race slaughtered each other, the Korean War left a wound in the Korean psyche that is still not completely healed after half a century. The momentous encounter between the two grandmothers with sons in the opposing war camps is inno-

Reprinted with permission from M. E. Sharpe from *The Rainy Spell and Other Korean Stories*, revised and enlarged edition, 1997, M. E. Sharpe.

cently reported by a child who gets caught up in the grown-ups' games
of hate. The final reconciliation between the women holds out a hope
for healing and transcendence.

1

The rain that had started to pour from the day after we reaped the last pea-pods showed no sign of letting up, even after many days. The rain came sometimes in fine powdery drops, or in hard, fierce balls, threatening to pierce the roof. Tonight, rain enveloped the pitch darkness like a dripping-wet mop.

It must have been somewhere right outside the village. My guess is that it came from somewhere around the empty house beside the riverbank that was used for storing funeral palanquins. The house always struck me as an eerie place, and even dogs would bark in long, dismal, foxlike howls when going near it. But it might have come in reality from a place much farther than the empty house. The distant howling of dogs filled the silence following the thinning rain. As if that far-off wail had been a military signal, all the village dogs that had managed to survive the war began to bark in turn. Their barking was unusually fierce that night.

That evening we were all gathered in the guest room occupied by my maternal grandmother, because she was greatly disturbed by something and we had to comfort and reassure her. But Mother and Maternal Aunt's efforts to say something comforting ceased after the dogs began to bark outside. Stealing glances at Grandmother, they repeatedly turned their eyes towards the darkness beyond, separated from the room only by the door panelled with gauze mosquito netting. An obscure moth with tremulous wings had been crawling up and down the doorpost for a long time now.

"Just wait and see. It won't be long before we'll know for sure. Just wait and see if I'm ever wrong," Grandmother murmured in a sunken voice. She was shelling peas from the pods. The peas would be cooked with the rice for breakfast the next morning. Sitting with her lap full of damp pea-pods, she shelled the peas with sure, experienced hands—first breaking off the tip and slitting open the pod, then running her finger through it. When the bright green peas slid out to one side, Grandmother cupped them in her palm and poured them into the bamboo basket at her knee, and dropped the empty pod into her lap.

Mother and Aunt, who lost the chance to make a rejoinder, exchanged awkward glances. Outside, the rain grew noisy again, and the dogs barked more fiercely, as if in competition. The night grew still stormier, and from the direction of the storage platform came the clatter of metal hitting the cement floor. The tin pail hung on the wall must have fallen down. A sudden gust of wind and rain rushed into the room, rattling the door and blowing out the kerosene lamp that had been flickering precariously. The room sank under the sudden flood of darkness and sticky humidity. The moth's wings also stopped quivering. A dog began to bark three or four houses beyond ours in the alley. Our dog Wŏlly, who had kept silent till then, growled. The wild commotion of the dogs, which had begun at the entrance of the village, was coming nearer and nearer our house.

"Light that lamp," Grandmother said. "Light the lamp, I said. Didn't you hear me?" Feeling about the room in the dark, Grandmother made a rustling noise. "What evil weather!"

I groped about the room, found a match and lit the kerosene lamp. Mother trimmed the wick. A strip of sooty smoke curled upward and drew a round shadow on the ceiling.

"It's always wet like this around this time of the year." Mother spoke in an effort to lessen the uneasiness created by the weather.

"It's all because of the weather. It's because of this weather that you're worrying yourself sick for no reason," Aunt also put in. Aunt had graduated from a high school in Seoul before the war broke out, when my mother's family lived in Seoul.

"No. It isn't for no reason. You don't know. When has my dream ever predicted wrong?" Grandmother shook her head left and right. But even as her head shook, her hands worked surely and steadily.

"I don't believe in dreams. Only the day before yesterday we received Kiljun's letter saying he's well and strong."

"That's right. You read yourself where Kiljun said he's bored these days because there aren't any battles."

"All that's of no use. I knew three or four days beforehand when your father died. Only, that time, it was a thumb instead of a tooth. That time I'd dreamed my thumb just came loose and disappeared."

Oh, the hateful account of that dream again! Doesn't Grandmother ever get tired of talking about that dream? Ever since she woke up at dawn, Grandmother had kept murmuring about her dream, her eyes vague and clouded. Continually moving her sunken, almost toothless mouth, she kept hinting that there was an inauspicious force rushing towards her. She had only seven teeth left in all; she had dreamed that a large iron pincer from out of nowhere forced itself into her mouth, yanked the strongest of the

seven, and fled. The first thing Grandmother did as soon as she
woke up from her dream was to feel in her mouth and check the
number of her teeth. Then she ordered Aunt to bring a mirror
and checked the number again with her eyes. Still not content, she
made me come right up to her face and demanded repeated assur-
ances from me. No matter how often anybody looked in, there
were seven teeth in her mouth, just as before. Moreover, the lower
canine tooth that she treasured as a substitute for a grinder was as
soundly in its place as ever.

But Grandmother wouldn't give credence to anybody's testi-
mony. It seemed that to her it was out of the question that the
canine tooth could remain there as if nothing had happened. Her
thoughts strayed from reality and dwelled only in her dream. She
refused to believe that her daughters and son-in-law were telling
the truth, and she even doubted the eyesight of her grandson,
whom she always praised highly for being good at threading needles. Not only did she distrust the mirror, but she even disbelieved
her own fingers, which had made a tactile survey of the teeth
inside her mouth.

Grandmother had spent the whole long summer's day muttering about her dream. It taxed all of our nerves to distraction. The
first one to break down and mention my maternal uncle's name
was my mother. When Mother incautiously mentioned the name of
her brother, who was serving at the front as a major and comman-
der of a platoon in the Republic's army, Grandmother's flabby
cheeks convulsed in a spasm. Aunt cast a reproachful look at her
elder sister. Grandmother, however, ignored Mother's words.
Having judged that there was no other way of setting the old
woman's mind at ease, Aunt also began talking about Uncle before
long. But Grandmother never uttered her only son's name even
once. She just kept on talking about that hateful dream.

As darkness began to set in, it became difficult to tell who was
being comforted and who was giving comfort. As the night deepened, Grandmother's words became more and more darkly sugges-
tive, as if she were under a spell, and her face even took on an
expression of triumphant self-confidence. Mother and Aunt, on
the other hand, fidgeted uneasily and gazed vacantly at the pea-
pods they had brought in to shell. In the end, all work was handed
over to Grandmother, and Mother and Aunt could do nothing but
listen to the endless incantatory muttering of the old woman.

Rain was pouring down like a wet mop over the whole surface
of the village. The three or four dogs that were lucky enough to
survive the war mercilessly tore the shroud of darkness, filling
every space with their shrill howling. Grandmother kept on

shelling with expert hands, putting the bright green peas into the bamboo basket and the empty pods back into her lap. Our dog Wŏlly, who received no kindly attention from anyone these difficult, gloomy days, began barking in surprisingly furious and ringing tones. Just then we could hear footsteps rounding the walls of the house next door. These were not the footsteps of just one person. There seemed to be three, or at least two. Someone must have stepped on a puddle; there was a splashing sound, and hard upon it came a grumbling about the terrible weather.

Who could those people be? Who would dare trudge through the village in this pouring rain in the depth of the night? Even though the war front had receded to the north, it was still a dangerous time. Communist guerrillas still occasionally invaded and set fire to the town police station. No one with any sense of propriety ever visited other people's houses after dark, unless on some emergency. To which house, then, could those people be going at this time of the night? What mischief might they be brewing, tramping the night streets in a group?

Mother grabbed hold of Aunt's hand. With her hand in her sister's keeping, Aunt stared into the darkness beyond, which was visible through the gauze panels of the door. Underneath the wooden porch adjoining the inner room, Wŏlly was barking desperately. Even Grandmother, whose hearing was not very good, had already realized that the band of men had stopped in front of the twig gate of our house and was hesitating there.

"Here they are at last. Here they are," Grandmother murmured in a parched voice.

"Sunku!" Someone called Father's name from beyond the twig gate. "Sunku, are you in?"

In the inner room Paternal Grandmother let out short, raspy coughs. We could hear Father stirring to go out. Hearing that, Mother whispered in a frightened voice towards the inner room. "I'll slip out and see what's going on. You stay where you are and pretend you're dead."

But Father was already in the hall. Putting on his shoes, Father bade us to heed Mother's words. Wŏlly, who had been yelping frantically, suddenly ceased barking with a sharp groan. Father must have done something to him. Crossing the yard, Father spoke cautiously, "Who is it?"

"It's me, the village head."

"Why, what brings you here in the middle of the night?"

The bell attached to the twig gate tinkled. We could hear the men exchanging a few words. Then there was silence again outside, and only the vigorous dripping of rain filled our ears. Mother,

who had been standing irresolutely in the room, could bear it no
longer and threw open the door. She rushed outside, and Aunt followed her quickly. In the inner room Paternal Grandmother emitted a few hoarse coughs. Right beside me Maternal Grandmother
was shelling peas steadily, completely absorbed in the work.
Running her finger through the pod, she murmured, "It won't
shake me a bit. I knew we were going to have some tidings today or
tomorrow. I knew it for a long time. I'm all prepared."

I couldn't sit still. After some inner struggle, I left Maternal
Grandmother alone and stole out of the room. Even on the dirt
veranda I could hear her parched voice saying, "I'm not shaken,
not I."

It was much darker outside than I had thought. Each time I
moved my legs, Wŏlly's wet, furry, smelly body hit my inner thighs.
The dog kept groaning and licking my hand. The rain was heavier
than I had expected. It bathed my face and soaked my hemp shirt,
and made me drenched as a rat that has fallen into a water-jar.
Wŏlly gave up following me and retreated, growling fearfully. The
grown-ups' contours were visible only when I drew quite close to
the twig gate. It looked as if whatever information they had
brought was passed on. In spite of the pouring rain, the grown-ups
just stood still. I could dimly see the heads of two men covered with
military waterproof cloth and the familiar face of the village head
who stood facing us. Father and Aunt were supporting Mother's
trembling, sinking body. After a long silence the village head
spoke.

"Please give your mother-in-law my sincere condolences."

Then one of the two men wrapped in waterproof cloth spoke.
He hesitated a great deal, as if extremely reluctant to speak. His
voice, therefore, sounded very shy.

"I really don't know what to say. We're just as grieved as any of
his family. It was an errand we'd have been glad to be spared.
Goodbye, then, sir. We have to go back now."

"Thank you. Be careful in the dark," Father said.

They slipped through the twig gate, picking their way with
their flashlights. A sob escaped from Mother. Aunt reproached her.
Then Mother began to cry a little louder. Without saying a word,
Father walked ahead towards the house. Aunt followed, supporting
Mother, whispering to her, "Please take hold of yourself. What will
Mother do if you cry like this? Try to think of Mother, Mother!"

My mother covered her mouth with her hand. In this way, she
managed to control her sobs when she stepped into the room.

Father, who had reached the room before any of us, was kneeling awkwardly before Maternal Grandmother, like one guilty, and

was turning something over in his hand. It was the wet piece of paper that the village head must have handed over to him. Father was dripping water like just-hung laundry. But it was not only Father. All of us who had been outside, including myself, were making puddles on the floor with water dripping from our clothes. The thin summer clothes of Mother and Aunt were clinging to their skin, and revealed their bodies inside as if they were naked.

"I told you," Maternal Grandmother murmured again, as if to herself. "See?"

For some time now I had been watching Grandmother's moves with great uneasiness. I was paying more attention now to her working hands than to her incessantly moving sunken mouth. I had noticed a change in the movement of her hands. It seemed that no one except me noticed the change. As before, she was working with lowered eyes, but when we returned to the room from outside, Grandmother's two gaunt arms were trembling slightly. Moreover, she was unconsciously dropping the freshly shelled peas into her skirt that was filled with empty pods. I was afraid she would keep on making the mistake, and repeatedly looked out for a chance to give her a hint. But each time I tried, I found I could not open my mouth, so oppressive was the silence in the room. I could do nothing but watch her shaking, wrinkled fingertips even though I knew she would be dropping the empty pods, good only for fuel, into the bamboo basket that ought to hold shelled peas.

"Haven't I been telling you all along we'd have some tidings today, for sure?" Grandmother, whose hitherto pale face was momentarily flushed and looked ten years younger, murmured again. But as she broke the tip of another pod and ran her finger through it, she instantly turned ashen pale, like a corpse, and aged ten years more in the selfsame posture. Grandmother was in a strange state of excitement. We could feel it from the way she swallowed till her entire throat trembled.

"I knew several days beforehand when your father died. I suppose you resented me, thinking this old woman mutters ill-omened words as a pastime, having nothing to do besides eating. But what do you say now? I'd like to know what you think of my premonitions. Do they still sound to you like the prattle of an old woman? You mustn't think that of me, you mustn't. Even though I can't see and hear as well as you, I don't go around jabbering empty words. You're greatly mistaken if you think old women have nothing better to do than wasting precious food and babbling. To this day my dreams have never been wrong. Whenever we had a calamity coming, my dreams have always predicted it."

Sitting fully erect, with her head held upright, she reproached her daughters for not having acknowledged her prescience. Her face was again flushed red. As she looked at her daughters, her bloodshot eyes seemed to glow with triumph. She seemed overcome by an irresistible desire to brag about the accuracy of her prophecy. As I gazed at her ridiculously triumphant expression, something like a spell hit me: my maternal grandmother suddenly looked to me like a weird, dreadful being. I could not help giving credence to her assertion that she had always, like an inspired prophet, unerringly predicted the approach of tragedy. Grandmother had gained her victory in the battle declared by herself, and she seemed still to have abundant energy left over after the battle to upbraid us for any imagined slight to her authority. This aspect of Grandmother left a deep, ineradicable impression on me, as if she had been a being of inscrutable, unapproachable power.

Mother's sobbing was rising by imperceptible degrees. It began as thin as a thread, so that the other people in the room hardly perceived it at first. But as no one tried to stop her, even when her sobbing rose considerably, she began at last to cry with full force. A mosquito had alighted on the nape of Aunt's bloodlessly pale neck and was sucking blood. But Aunt did not stir. She sat there like one out of her wits, even though the mosquito sucked until its belly was round and pink as a cherry. The door of the room stood open. Even though mosquitoes swarmed in through the open door, nobody bothered to close it.

One could clearly guess at the progress of the people covered with military waterproof cloth by the shifting direction of the dogs' barking. Receding from the moment the men left, the barking moved further and further to the end of the village, and at last died down entirely. A black flying insect that had come in without my noticing was disturbing the air of the room, flying around unchecked. At last, after it zipped through the room several times and almost put out the lamp, it was caught in my hand. It was a mole-cricket. It writhed between my thumb and forefinger and tried to get loose. Straining its strong forelegs which it used to dig up earth, it tried to break my grip. But of what use were all its desperate struggles? Its life and death were completely at my mercy. I could kill it or let it live just as I liked. I began to put more and more pressure on the two fingers holding the insect. Just then I heard Grandmother murmur again.

"I'm not shaken. I knew all along this would happen. I'm all right."

Then, Mother's sobs reached their peak, and the whole room

was filled with the painful, drawn-out lament that seemed to gnaw into our very bones.

"Poor Jun, poor, poor Jun, what a fool you were to volunteer when others went into hiding to dodge conscription! Poor Jun, poor Jun, why didn't you listen to me when I told you not to become an officer? Now, what are we to do? What are we to do?" Her voice prolonged the words and trailed off into moans whenever she uttered the name of the dead man.

The heart-rending sobs of Mother, which filled the room in no time, soon spread into the yard steeped in darkness, and on the film of her sobs piled, layer upon layer, the shrieking rain of the long rainy season.

2

Gŏnji-san always looked dignified, standing tall surrounded by a host of lesser mountains and hills and piercing the sky with the tip of its peak. There was a time, however, when this stately mountain took on a ridiculous aspect. For a time Gŏnji-san became a place where grown-ups gathered at night to play with fire. Sometimes we could see mist rising from the top of the mountain even in broad daylight. What an enormous amount of water must have been made there by the grown-ups at night! Having experienced the bitter humiliation of making the round of the village wearing a rice winnowing basket over my head as punishment for bed-wetting, I could not help looking with suspicion at the running brook in the village that started from the mountain. The rustic, taciturn and dignified mountain looked absurd, suddenly sending up smoke and fire. For grown-ups' play, it was childish and silly, but peaceful and tranquil. I had not then realized the relationship between the signal fire and the massacres. I could not have understood why, time after time, immediately after flames rose up from the mountain, there was a street battle in town and one of the villages was laid to waste. But even had I understood the implications, the result would have been the same. In spite of my ridiculous thoughts on beholding the signal fire for the first time, Gŏnji-san shortly regained its dignified repose in my eyes and became even dearer to me.

One day, I found upon arising that thick black clouds had coiled around the mountain from its waist up. The rain had halted, but anyone could tell from the dark cloud completely covering the eastern sky around Gŏnji-san that an even bigger batch of rain than any we'd had was making preparations for an assault. From time to

time, lightning darted out from the dark corner of the sky and
pierced Gŏnji-san as sharply as the bamboo lance that I once saw a
man thrusting into another man's chest on the village road beside
the dike. And each time thunder shook heaven and earth, like a
wail sent out by the pierced mountain, I could very well imagine
what the pain of being impaled by darting lightning must be like,
and did not at all think the mountain cowardly for sending out
such a miserable scream. It was clear that Gŏnji-san was being tortured by the sky from early morning.

I could tell Maternal Grandmother's approach even with my
eyes closed. When she walked, her footsteps made no sound but
only her skirt rustled. Like a weightless person's, her walk was light
and careful. Having approached so carefully, she emitted a strange
smell. It was a very strange smell, such as one can sniff in the corners of an old, old chest, or an antique, or a deep pond of stagnant
water. I could feel the careful approach of my grandmother, from a
smell like that of ancient dust and the rustle of her skirt.

I was lying in the adjacent room, pretending to be asleep.
From the time I began to regard my grandmother as an awesome
being, I had got into the habit of pretending to be asleep when she
came near. Grandmother seemed to be taking twice her usual care
so as not to awaken her grandson from his nap. But I had already
inhaled a distasteful fill of her peculiar smell, and had guessed
what she was going to do. And I was not wrong, either. Her gaunt
hand fumbled into my underpants.* "Now let me feel my jewel,"
she would have said at other times. She would also have said, "This
one's round as an apple, just like his maternal uncle's." But today,
she did not say a word. She only silently moved her fingers, and felt
my groin. This nameless act, which began from the time Mother's
family came to live with us as refugees, was a big trial to me, and a
very insulting experience. I'd dare anybody to claim I'm not telling
the truth when I say I have never admitted my maternal grandmother's encroaching hand into my underpants without great displeasure. I don't know if there would be any seven-year-old who

---

*This and what follows should not be taken as sexual play. Because in
Korea only males could carry on the family line, it was not unusual for
grandmothers to feel their infant grandsons' sexual organs, to assure
themselves that the lineage was secure, and feel great pride if the grandsons had strong and healthy reproductive organs. It was unusual, however,
for grandmothers to feel the organs of grandsons as old as age seven, so
the grandmother's act here would indicate how critical is her sense of her
family line ending. The fact that the grandson is her heir only on the
distaff side also adds to the pathos of the whole act.—*Translator*

would willingly consent to be treated like a baby; for my part, I had prided myself for being a big boy with a sound judgment equal to any grown-up's, and such an act of Grandmother's was a severe blow to my self-esteem. But there was no shaking her off, as I knew such a refusal would grieve her deeply, so I could not but endure the insult.

Taking her hand off my groin, Grandmother sighed deeply. I could feel her gaze lingering on my face for a long time after her hand left my body.

"Poor thing!"

Leaving the two muttered words behind, she moved away. I opened my eyes a slit and peeped at Grandmother's back as she receded noiselessly, her wrinkled cotton skirt trailing behind her. I don't know whom she may have meant in her lamentation just now. There were too many poor things around me. There was, of course, my maternal uncle who had just been killed in a battle at the front. And to tell the truth, I myself was also very much of a poor thing. Since the incident of having accepted a Western sweet as a bribe from a police detective, I had been cooped up in the house for over a month now in penance, anxiously watching the moods of my father, who held command of housebound penance, and of Paternal Grandmother, in whose hands alone rested the power of forgiveness. But maybe the poorest thing of all was Maternal Grandmother herself. She looked completely worn out as she sat on the edge of the living-room floor. There was not a trace of the stubborn, awesome being we glimpsed on the night the notification came from the front. Today she was simply a shabby, withered old woman gazing vacantly at the distant mountain. My joy at being freed from her unwelcome hand turned to gloom at the sight of her pitiful figure.

For a few days after we learned of the death of my maternal uncle, the house was in chaos. Everyone was grieving, but my mother's grief was most out of control. Mother had tied her forehead with a white strip of cloth, as we children did on school sports days, and was bedridden with grief. She sat up from time to time to cry for awhile, striking the floor with her palm uttering loud lamentations, and then collapsed back on the bedding. At mealtimes, however, she sat up to eat hurriedly the bowl of barley Aunt brought in to her. As soon as she finished eating, she thrust away the meal tray and cried out with loud lamentations and sank back on her bedding. Lying on her back, she would repeatedly mutter that her family ought to adopt a son to continue the line.

Aunt's behavior was in sharp contrast to Mother's. From first to last, she did not shed a drop of tear, nor did she exchange a word

with anybody. She didn't eat a thing, either. Moreover, she silently
took over all of Mother's work, and cooked, washed dishes and did
the laundry. Until I saw her flop backwards on the third day while
trying to lift up a water pail beside the well in the backyard, I had
been thinking that Aunt must surely be eating something secretly in
the bamboo grove behind the house or in the dark kitchen. I had
set my heart at rest thinking that Aunt, who had unbelievably strong
will-power and sometimes completely confounded our expectations, would surely not go three days without eating a morsel.

But Mother and Aunt were not our greatest worry. What made
us most uneasy was the discord between my paternal and maternal
grandmothers. When my mother's family, which had moved to
Seoul to give my uncle and aunt the benefit of education in the
capital, suddenly appeared before us one day as refugees carrying
bundles, it was my paternal grandmother who welcomed the family
warmly and made the guest room available for them to move in.
We often heard my paternal grandmother express her wish that
the two old women could be a companion and support for each
other in these harsh times; and, in fact, the two old ladies got
along perfectly well, without even a single discord, until that unfortunate day. They got along well even after the Republic's army
recovered dominion over the South and my paternal uncle, who
had till then been going around flourishing his armband as an officer of the People's Army, fled with the retreating communist
forces, and my maternal uncle, who had till then been hiding in a
dug-out cave in the bamboo grove, joined the Republic's army.
Each victory or defeat in the war thus became a matter of conflicting emotions for the two old ladies.

The discord between the two old ladies began with that incident of my accepting the gift of a Western sweet from a stranger,
which incurred the fury of Paternal Grandmother, who branded
me a butcher of men who had sold his uncle for a sweet and, therefore, one not worthy to be treated as a human being. Maternal
Grandmother earned the displeasure of her counterpart by pro-
tecting and defending me. The decisive rupture between the two
grandmothers came on the day after we received the death notice
of my maternal uncle. It was my maternal grandmother who started the provocation. On that afternoon, too, the weather was sinister. Forked lightning darted out of the clouds, repeatedly impaling
the crown of Gŏnji-san. Maternal Grandmother, who had been
watching the sky standing at the edge of the living-room floor, suddenly began to utter dreadful curses.

"Pour on! Pour on! Pour on and sweep away all the reds hiding between the rocks! Strike on, and burn to soot all the reds

clinging to the trees! Pour on, strike on! That's right! Thank you, God!"

All the family rushed into the living room, but everyone was so stupefied that no one could say a word to check Grandmother's torrential curses. She continued to pour out vehement curses towards Gŏnji-san, which was said to be teeming with communist partisans, as if she could distinctly visualize red partisans being struck dead one after another by lightning.

"Has that old hag gone stark mad, or turned into a devil?"

The door of the inner room opened with a clatter and out came Paternal Grandmother, her face distorted with fury. I realized belatedly that there was one person in the house who could be Maternal Grandmother's match, and became tense.

"Whose house does she think this is, that she dares put on such horseplay?"

Maternal Grandmother looked around with vague eyes, like one violently shaken awake from sleepwalking.

"This is too good a spectacle for only a family audience, isn't it? I've heard of good deeds being repaid with poison, but I can't believe what I'm witnessing today. A fine display of gratitude this is, to one who gave you shelter from bombs! If you mean to go crazy, do so at least with a clean conscience. If you harbor such base ingratitude, lightning will strike you!"

After thus subduing the other with imperious reproof, Paternal Grandmother continued her upbraiding:

"Do you think your curses will bring your dead son back and kill living people? Don't you imagine such a thing! Life and death are meted out by Heaven, and Heaven only. One lives as long as one's allotted to live by Heaven. And it's because of one's own sins that a child dies before oneself. It's because of sins in an earlier life that a parent has to see a child die and endure the sorrow. It's your own fate that your son died. There's nobody to blame for it. You ought to know shame by now. Aren't you in your sixties?"

"All right. Granted it's because of my sins* that I've lost my

---

*This is not to be taken as the maternal grandmother's admission of having committed sins needing expiation. It is rather an announcement of her resolution to accept her suffering and sorrow in resignation. According to Buddhist theory of metempsychosis, one pays for one's sins in an afterlife, and thus there is no escaping the consequences of one's acts. This theory is often used by Koreans to "justify" and to reconcile themselves to their unmerited sufferings for which there can be no explanation in terms of universal justice of reward and punishment.
—*Translator*

son. Is it because you're a blessed woman that you reared a son like that?"

"Listen to that! Hasn't she really gone raving mad? What do you mean, 'a son like that'? What's wrong with my son?"

"Think. You'll know if you're not a fool."

"Because you have no son left to offer you sacrifice after your death, you wish the same for everyone!"

"Stop it, both of you!" Father shouted.

"Wait and see. My Sunchŏl isn't such a fool! You might not rest content until something happens to him, but Sunchŏl can slip through showers without getting wet!"

"Stop it, please!" Father shouted again.

Mother had been pinching Maternal Grandmother's thigh all along.

"Did you hear what your mother-in-law said? She, who's an in-law after all, calls me a woman without a son to offer me sacrifices after my death. Isn't it misfortune enough to have given up an only son for the country, without being despised by an in-law? What mad words can a woman not utter, a woman who's just lost a son? Does she have to reproach me thus for foolish words uttered in madness of grief, and flaunt before me her possession of many sons? Answer me, if you have a mouth to speak!"

Maternal Grandmother appealed to Mother, and Mother, with a tearful face, kept winking a pleading eye at Maternal Grandmother and pinching her leg. Paternal Grandmother, for her part, appealed to Father:

"Be careful how you judge, son! Is it wrong of me to rebuke an old woman who's praying for your brother's death? Must you, too, blame me? She may be your mother-in-law, but she's an enemy to me, and I can't live with her under the same roof! If you don't throw her out at once, I'm going to leave this house!"

"All right! I'm leaving! I would hate to live in this house any longer! I'd rather die out in the streets than stay a minute longer in a communist's hou—"

Maternal Grandmother's hoarse voice stopped dead. She slowly turned her head and vacantly gazed at my father. Finishing the word "house" weakly and at length, she looked at Mother this time. Lastly, she gazed at me intently for quite awhile, and shook her head left and right. Then she suddenly dropped her head. Her downward-bent gaze sank heavily on a bamboo basket. Silently pulling the bamboo basket toward her knee, she picked up a pea-pod with a motion as silent as if she had been a shadow. Her face was as grey as a corpse's, and remained so from then on.

The turmoil created by Maternal Grandmother's words shook up the whole house. When the word "communist" came out of Maternal Grandmother's mouth, all the family members doubted their ears, and stood still in stupefaction. They could hardly breathe, and could only watch her slowly moving hands. "Communist" was a forbidden word among us, ever since we became a marked house in the village, watched by the police on account of my paternal uncle. This taboo was as strictly observed as the taboo against eating salty shrimp pickles during scrofula. Oh, to trespass such a solemn taboo! Maternal Grandmother's mistake was a fatal one, which no amount of apology would render forgivable. The amazement of the family members was beyond description, but the one most shocked by the utterance was none other than she who said it. Maternal Grandmother did not offer any apologies. It was partly because all apologies were useless, but more likely because she tried to expiate her transgression by silently enduring all the censure of her in-law counterpart. No words can describe the fury of my paternal grandmother. She jumped up and down madly, foamed at the mouth, and almost fainted away. Then she tried to wrest an assurance from Father that he would expel Maternal Grandmother and Aunt from the house, and even Mother if she seemed sympathetic to them.

"You must drive them out this very day. And be sure to open all their bags before they step out of the gate. My silver hair-slide is missing, and it's not hard to guess who took it."

Aunt silently walked away to the guest room. After pouring out her fill of abuses, Paternal Grandmother lay down from exhaustion. The silence that ensued was soon shattered by the outburst of Mother's weeping. Instantly, Father's command fell like thunder.

"Shut up!"

Silence was a more unbearable torture than noisy unrest. Father strode out of the house. Maternal Grandmother remained on the living-room floor deep into the night, shelling peas with her gaunt, shaky hands. Father came back home only at dawn, dead drunk and reeking of sour alcohol.

Incandescent sparks of lightning kept piercing the crown of Gŏnji-san, thickly enfolded in black clouds. The signal fire that rose up almost every night from the mountain could not be seen anymore since the rainy season began. Maternal Grandmother, who turned her eyes from time to time towards the mountain, looked pitifully lonely as she sat on the edge of the living-room floor. She did not say a word today, even though lightning struck today just as on that other day. Ever since that unhappy quarrel with her in-law, she hardly opened her mouth. She kept moving her hands incessantly, the bamboo basket at her knee, as if shelling peas were the one and only task left for her in the world till her dying day.

3

A boy, who had recently come to live in our village as a refugee from the North, came over to where we were playing, accompanied by a man wearing a straw hat. The boy's face was all scabby. Pointing at me with his hand that had been scratching his bare, dirt-stained belly, he said a few words to the man. The man gave me an attentive stare from beneath the wide-brimmed straw hat that concealed a good part of his face. The boy from the North took what the strange man gave him from out of his pocket and sprinted away like a fleeing hare. The tall man with the straw hat walked up to me directly. His dark, tanned skin, his sharp, penetrating eyes, and his unhesitating stride somehow overpowered me.

"What a fine boy!"

The stranger's eyes seemed to narrow and, surprisingly, contrary to what I had expected from my first impression, a friendly smile filled his face. The man stroked my head a few times.

"You'd be a really good boy if you give straight answers to my questions."

The man's attitude made me extremely uneasy. I could not look into his eyes, so I opened and closed my hands for no reason and stood there with my head lowered. In my palm was my paternal grandmother's silver hair-slide, which I had rubbed against a stone mortar into a giant nail, and which earned me victory over all the neighborhood boys in nail fights.

"Your father's name is Kim Sunku, isn't it?"

The man unbuttoned his white tieless shirt.

"Then Kim Sunchŏl must be your uncle, isn't he?"

The man took off his straw hat. I had not said a word till then. But the man went on ingratiatingly. "That's right. Answer my questions like the clever boy you are!"

The man waved his straw hat as if it were a fan, holding open his tieless shirt to ventilate his body.

"I'm your uncle's friend. We're very close friends, but it's been a long time since we met last. I have something very important to discuss with your uncle. Will you tell me where he is?"

The man, whom I had just met for the first time in my life, used the standard Seoul dialect meticulously, like Aunt.

"Oh, isn't it hot! It's very hot here. Shall we go over there where it's breezy and have a little chat?"

He forbade the other children to follow. When we reached the shade of a tree on the hill behind the village, where other children couldn't see us, the man halted and fumbled in his pocket.

"I've got a very important message to convey to your uncle. If you tell me where he is, I'll give you these," the man said holding out in his palm five flat pieces of something wrapped in silver paper. He unwrapped one of them and stuck it in front of my nose.

"Have you ever tasted anything like this?" The dark brown-colored thing gave off a delicious aroma.

"These are chocolates. I'll give them to you if you just answer my questions straight."

I took a great deal of care not to let my eyes rest on the strange treat. But I could not stop my mouth from watering.

"There's nothing to be shy about. It's natural for good boys to get rewards. Now, won't you tell me? If only you tell me what I've asked, I'll be happy to let you have these delicious chocolates."

I don't know what it was that made me hesitate. Was it because I was undecided about the ethical propriety of accepting such a gift? Or was it the shyness of a country boy in front of a stranger, a shyness common to most country boys my age? I don't remember distinctly. But I think I remained standing there mute for quite awhile.

"Don't you want them?" the man pressed me. "You're sure you don't want them?" The man showed an expression of regret. "Well then, there's no helping it. I did very much want to see you acting like a good boy and give you these delicious things. I myself don't need these sweets. Here, look. I'll just have to throw them away, even though that's not what I want to do with them."

Unbelievably, the man really threw one of them onto the ground carelessly. He not only threw it down but stepped on it and crushed it. Casting a glance at me, he threw one more on the ground.

"I thought you were a bright boy. I'm really sorry."

He crushed the third one under his foot. Only two pieces of the sweet remained on his palm. It was evident that he was quite capable of crushing the remaining two into the ground. The man suddenly chuckled loudly.

"You're crying? Poor boy! Hey, lad, it's not too late yet. You just think carefully. Hasn't your uncle been to the house? When was it?"

It was at that moment that I felt I was powerless to fend off the sophisticated tactics of a grown-up. Then, as I thought that this man might really be a friend of my uncle, my heart felt a good deal lighter.

The first few words were the most difficult to utter. Once I began, however, I related what had happened as smoothly as reeling yarn off a spool.

My paternal aunt who lived some eight miles off came to visit us, walking the entire distance under the broiling July sun. There was no reason for me to attach any special meaning to Aunt's visit, as she had come several times to our house without prior announcement to stay for a day or two even in those days of unrest. But things began to look very different when Mother, who had gone into the inner room with Aunt, sprang out of the room with a pale complexion. Instead of sending me, as was usual, she ran out herself to fetch Father. Father, who had been weeding in the rice paddies, ran directly into the inner room with his muddy clothes and feet, without stopping to wash himself at the well. Mother, who returned hard upon his heels, fastened the twig gate shut even though it was broad daylight. Everybody seemed slightly out of their right senses. The whole family, except Maternal Grandmother, Maternal Aunt and me, was gathered in the inner room and seemed to be discussing something momentous. Around sunset, the three of us who had been left out were given a bowl of cold rice each. As I finished my meal, I saw that Father had changed into clean clothes. I looked suspiciously at Father's back as he stepped out of the twig gate into the alley paved with darkness.

"You go to sleep early," Mother told me, as she spread my mattress right beside where Paternal Grandmother was sitting. It seemed that everyone was bent on pushing me to go to sleep, even though it was still early in the night.

"Wouldn't it be better to have him sleep in the other room?" Paternal Aunt asked Mother, pointing her chin at me.

"I think it'll be all right," Paternal Grandmother said, "he sleeps soundly once he falls asleep."

"You must be dead tired from playing all day long. You must sleep like a log until tomorrow morning, and not open your eyes a bit all through the night. You understand?" Mother instructed me.

I knew that Father had not gone out for a friendly visit. It was obvious that he went out on important business. I wanted to stay wide awake until Father returned. I was determined to find out the important business of grown-ups from which I was being excluded. To that end, it was necessary to pretend to obey the grown-ups' orders to go to sleep at once. I listened attentively for the least sound in the room, fighting back the sleep that overwhelmed me as soon as I lay down and closed my eyes. But no one said anything of any significance. And, before the important event of Father's arrival, I had fallen fast asleep.

I was awakened by a dull thud on the floor of the room.

"My God! Isn't that a bomb?"

I heard Paternal Grandmother's frightened voice. The two bulks that were blocking my sight were the seated figures of Father and Mother. Dull lamplight seeped dimly through the opening between them.

"Undo your waistband, too," Father said to someone imperiously. The person seemed to hesitate a little, but there came a rustle from beyond.

"*Two* pistols!"

"My God!" Mother and Grandmother softly exclaimed simultaneously. Sleep had completely left me, and a chill slid down my spine like a snake. Even though I knew nobody was paying any attention to me, I realized it was unsafe to let the grown-ups know I was awake; so I had to take painstaking care in moving my glance inch by inch. I concentrated all my efforts on finding out what was happening in the small space visible to me.

"Has Tongman gone to sleep without knowing I was coming?"

As it seemed that Father was about to turn to me, I closed my eyes quickly. The shadow that had been shielding my face moved aside quickly, and lamplight pricked my eyelids.

"We kept him in the dark," Mother said proudly, as if that had been some meritorious deed.

"Don't worry. Once he falls asleep, a team of horses couldn't kick him awake," Grandmother insisted.

There was a short silence in the room. It seemed that nobody dared open his mouth. But my ears were brimming with the thick voice of the man who had sneaked into the house in the dark, carrying pistols and hand grenades. If that man is really my uncle, whose whereabouts the whole family had been fretting to know, his voice had, regrettably, become so rough as to be unrecognizable to me at first. His voice didn't used to be as rough as a clay pot that has been carelessly handled on pebbles, or so gloomy that nothing seemed capable of cheering it up. As far back as I could remember, my uncle chuckled heartily at the slightest joke, even though his elders might frown on such manners, and rarely remained aloof from disputes but always tried to involve others in them. He was easily excited or moved. But, no matter how I reckoned, there was no one but my uncle who could be the owner of that voice I had just heard. I imagined my uncle's face and form, which must have become as rough as the voice. Then, suddenly, I felt an uncontrol-lable itch in the hollows of my knees. The itch spread instantly to my entire body, as if I had been lying on ant-infested grass: I had an irresistible urge to scratch the middle of my back or my armpits or between my toes, places where my hands could not reach while I lay flat on my back. On top of it all, my throat tickled with an immi-nent cough, and my mouth filled with water.

Grandmother seemed most anxious to know what Uncle's life on the mountain was like. She heaped question after question on how he fared on the mountain. To all her questions Uncle answered barely a word or two, and seemed irked by the necessity of saying even that much. But Grandmother seemed not to notice Uncle's mood, and asked endless questions.

"You say there are many others besides you, but they must all be men. Who cooks rice and soup at each mealtime?"

"We do."

"You make preserves and season vegetables, too?"

"Yes."

"How on earth! If only I could be there with you I'd prepare your food with proper seasoning!"

No response.

"Do they taste all right?"

"Yes."

"I know they couldn't, but I can't help asking all the same."

"They're all right."

"Do you skip meals often, because you move around here and there?"

"No."

"Promise me you won't eat raw rice, however hungry you may get. You'd get diarrhea. If you do, what could you do in the depths of the mountain? You can't call a doctor or get medicine. Do pay attention, won't you?"

"Don't worry."

"And since it's in the depths of the mountain, it must be cold as January at night, even in summer like this. Do each of you have a quilt to cover your middle at night?"

"Of course."

"Padded with cotton wool?"

No response.

"Don't stay in the cold too long. And, for frostbite, eggplant stems are the best remedy. You boil the stems and soak your hands and feet in the fluid. That takes out the frostbite at once. If I were beside you . . . "

"Please don't worry!"

"How can I help it? It tears my heart to see your frostbitten hands and feet. The times are rough, but for you, my darling last-born, to get so frostbitten like that!"

"Please, Mother, stop!" Uncle sighed with impatience.

"Do, Mother, that's enough," Father chimed in cautiously.

"Do you mean I shouldn't worry, even though my son's hands are frostbitten?" Grandmother raised her voice angrily. Such things were of the utmost importance to her. But Father also raised his voice.

"It's going to be daybreak soon, and you keep wasting time with your useless questions! How can you worry about preserves and quilts when his life's at stake?"

Grandmother was silenced. Of course she had many more questions, but a certain tone in Father's rebuke silenced her, stubborn as she was.

"What are you going to do now?" Father asked, after a pregnant silence. It was directed at Uncle.

"About what?"

"Are you going back to the mountain and stay there?"

When Uncle was silent, Father asked him if he would consider giving himself up to the police. Father slowly began his persuasion, as if it were something he had carefully considered for a long time. Father emphasized again and again the misery of a hunted existence. Citing as an example a certain young man who had delivered himself up to the police and was now living quietly on his own farm, Father recommended urgently that Uncle do the same. He repeated again and again that otherwise Uncle would die a dog's death. A dog's death, a dog's death, a dog's death, a dog's death.

"Why do you keep saying it's a dog's death?" Uncle retorted sullenly. Uncle swore that before long the People's Army would win back the South. Vowing that he had only to remain alive until that day, he even recommended that Father should so conduct himself as not to get hurt when the government changed. Listening to his talk, I was struck once again by the great change in my uncle. His speech was fluent. In the old days, Uncle was never able to talk so logically. Because he had difficulty getting his points across by logical arguments, he often used to resort to the aid of his fists in his sanguine impatience.

Uncle began to collect things, saying that he must go up the mountain before sunrise. It must have been the pistols and hand grenades that he gathered up. Everybody moved at once.

"I won't let you go, never, now that you're in my house!"

I opened my eyes at last. In that sudden turmoil, nobody paid any attention to me, so I slowly sat up. Uncle's face was covered all over with a bushy beard. Father and Aunt were on either side almost hugging Uncle, who sat leaning against the wall on the warmer part of the floor. Grandmother snatched Uncle's arm from Aunt and, shaking it to and fro, entreated, "Because your brother told me lies, I thought you were staying comfortably somewhere. I thought you spent your days sitting on a chair in a town office somewhere doing things like giving hell to harsh cops. But now that I know the truth I won't let you go back to such a dreadful place! I'd die first rather than let you go!"

Grandmother wept, stroking Uncle's cheek with her palm.

"I'd let you go if I could go with you and look after you day and night, but since it seems I can't, I'll tie you down in this room and not let you out of my sight day or night. Why can't you stay at home, farm the land, get married and let me hold your children before I die?"

Aunt spoke for the first time in my hearing that night and talked to Uncle about the joys of married life, and Mother assented in support of her sister-in-law. Father talked again. He explained in minute detail the drift of the war, and tried to make Uncle realize that he was being deceived by the empty promises of the communists. Father said further that as he knew a couple of people in the police there would be ways to get Uncle released without suffering bodily harm. But Uncle at long last opened his mouth only to say, "Are you, too, trying to trick me into it?" and shook off Father's hand.

"What do you mean, trick you?"

"I've heard all about it." Uncle said that the police slaughtered all the people who, after being decoyed by promises of pardon in printed handbills, went down the mountain to surrender. Uncle said that promises of unconditional pardon and freedom were screaming lies and tricks.

"And you, too, are trying to push me into the trap?"

"What?" Father's arm shot up in the air. The next moment there was the sound of a sharp slap on Uncle's cheek. Father panted furiously and glared at Uncle, as if he would have liked to tear him apart.

"How dare you strike my poor boy!" Grandmother wept aloud, shielding Uncle with her body. Father pulled the tobacco box towards him. His hands shook as he rolled up the green tobacco. Uncle dropped his head.

A cock crowed. At the sound Uncle lifted his head in fright

and looked around at the members of the family. The short summer's night was about to end.

"I've killed people," he murmured huskily, like one who had just set down a heavy load he had carried a long, long way. "Many, many people."

Thus began Uncle's wavering toward self-surrender. It was a long persuasion that Father carried out that night, and his patience in delivering it was truly remarkable. At last everything was settled as Father had planned, and it was agreed that Uncle was to remain in hiding for a couple of days until Father obtained assurance from the police for Uncle's safety. Uncle was to go into the dug-out cave in the bamboo grove that Maternal Uncle had used for hiding during the communist occupation.

Everything was settled, and all that remained to be done was for everybody to snatch a wink of sleep before it was broad daylight. But that instant Uncle, who was about to pull off his shirt, suddenly bent forward and pressed his ear to the floor. Grandmother almost jumped from fright.

"What is it?"

"Ssh!"

Uncle put his forefinger on his lips and eyed the door of the room. Everybody's face stiffened, and all listened attentively for noise from outside.

"Someone's there."

My ears caught no sound. There was the distant chirping of grass insects, but I could hear nothing like a human sound. But Uncle had his ear still glued to the floor and didn't seem likely to get up. For awhile I heard only the loud pounding of my heart in that suffocating tension, but I caught the sound, the one Uncle must have heard. The sound, which was definitely not that of a pounding heart, was footsteps treading the ground with long intervals in between. The steps were so soft and careful that it was hard to tell if they were coming toward us or receding.

"Who's that outside?"

Father's voice was low, but the reprimand was severe. Then the sound of the movement stopped altogether. Suddenly it occurred to me that it was a familiar tread, of someone I knew very well. I quickly ransacked my brain, trying to figure out who it might be. The footsteps began again. They seemed to be moving a little faster this time. Uncle's body shot up erect. Within the blink of an eye the dark shape jumped over my seated form. The back door fell to the ground with a shattering sound, and Uncle's big bulk rushed away in the dark. He had already crossed the bamboo

grove. His movement was so swift that nobody had time to say a
word.

I came out through the frame of the back door that Uncle had
knocked down to the ground. I ran past the kitchen into the inner
yard. I wasn't at all afraid, even though I was alone. I surveyed
everything within the twig fence, from the yard and kitchen garden
down to the gates, but I could see nothing. When my eyes fell on
the unlighted guest room, however, I caught the half-opened door
of that room closing noiselessly, shutting out the dim, whitish glare
of the morning. I savored the discovery with rapture. It was indeed
a familiar tread, of one I knew very well.

"I'd have packed things for him to take if I'd known it would
come to this! I didn't feed him a morsel, nor give him one clean
garment! If only I'd known! How could I have not fed him one
bowl of warm rice! If only I'd known!" Paternal Grandmother
wailed, beating her chest. Paternal Aunt grasped my hand tightly
and pulled me to one corner. Then she whispered into my ear.

"You mustn't tell anyone your uncle's been home. Do you
understand? If you talk about such things to anybody all of us must
go to jail. Do you hear?"

Village people were surrounding my house, standing in multiple ranks in front of the gate. They were whispering things to each
other and trying to look over the gate into the house. The wailing
of women that I could hear from as far as the hill behind the village was coming from my house. As I approached, all eyes turned
on me. Villagers exchanged meaningful glances among themselves, pointing their chins at me, and whispered again. The palisade of people suddenly parted in two, as if to make way. A strange
man walked out ahead, and my father followed. One step behind
him I could see the man with the straw hat. He was holding, coiled
around his hand, the rope that bound both my father's hands
behind his back. On seeing me, he grinned and winked. Father
halted in front of me. His eyes seemed yearning to say something
to me, but he silently resumed walking. At the gate Mother,
Paternal Aunt and Paternal Grandmother were wailing and crying,
repeatedly collapsing and sinking to the ground. Only then did
pain begin to rise in me. During the entire day while I was ransack-
ing the village to find the boy from the North who had conducted
the man with the straw hat to me, the pain assailed me sometimes
with a sense of betrayal, or a terrible fury, or an unbearable sorrow
that stung my eyes and stabbed my heart. The man with the straw
hat had sworn to me that he would never tell anybody what I would

tell him. It was the first mortal treachery I had experienced at the hands of a grown-up.

From that night Maternal Grandmother became my sole protectress and friend. Between us there was the shared secret of sinners. It could have been that secret which gave the two of us the strength to support each other through many persecutions. Paternal Grandmother was a woman of very strong temper. If she so much as caught sight of me, she started back as if she had stepped on a snake, and she refused not only to talk to me but even to let me have my meals in the inner room with the family.

Father returned home after spending seven full days at the police station. My mother, who made frequent trips to town to take Father his food, sniffed and sobbed and sprinkled salt again and again on his head when he stepped into the gate. Father's good-looking face had changed a great deal in those seven days. His eyes were sunken, his cheekbones stood out, and his face, which had become pale blue like newly bleached cotton, looked indescribably shabby. But what hurt me most of all was the look of pain that appeared on Father's face whenever he moved his right leg with a limping lurch. On the night he returned, he ate no less than three cakes of raw bean curd which, along with the sprinkling of salt, was believed to be a good preventive against a second trip to the police station. Father had always been taciturn, but he uttered not a single word that day. From time to time he gazed vacantly at my face and seemed about to say something, but each time he withdrew his gaze silently. I was fully resolved never to run away should Father decide to give me a flogging, even if I were to die under his switch. And there, within his easy reach, were the wooden pillow and the lamp pole. I felt I could not withdraw from Father's sight without receiving my due punishment. I waited, solemnly kneeling before him. But Father did not utter a word about what had passed. He only issued this command before lying down to sleep.

"Tongman, if you ever so much as step an inch out of the gate from tomorrow, I'll break your legs."

Ah, how happily I'd have closed my eyes for good, if Father had wielded his switch like mad that night, leaving these as my last words, "Father, I deserve to die."

4

The rainy front stayed on. The sky sometimes feigned benevolence by suspending the rain in the morning or afternoon, but its frown did not relax at all; rather, the pressure of the iron grey clouds increased, and malicious showers poured down fitfully, as if suddenly remembering. Everything between the sky and the earth was so saturated with water that if you pressed a fingertip on any wall or floor, water seeped out in response. All the world was a puddle and a slough. Because of the rain-soaked earth, the well water was no better than slops, and you could not drink a single drop of it without boiling it for a long time.

Even amid such persistent rain there was an attack by communist partisans under cover of night. Though there was a good five miles' distance between our village and the town, we could distinctly hear the noise of bullets like corn popping. Father, who had been up on the hill behind the village in spite of the rain, said that he could see a scarlet flame shooting up in the night sky even from that distance. The detailed news of the surprise attack spread through the village in less than a day.

One villager, who had been to town to ascertain the safety of his brother's family, came by with our neighbor, Chinku's father, to give important advice to Father. As soon as he sat down on the edge of the living-room floor, he gave a vociferous report of his survey in the town, not knowing that Paternal Grandmother was listening in the inner room beyond a paper-panelled door. He said that houses in the vicinity of the police station had suffered much damage, and that the red partisans who made the attack had been severely beaten. According to him, only a handful of partisans made the retreat to the mountains alive. What was most shocking in his report was his description of the corpses of partisans that he said lay scattered throughout the town. He described in vivid detail the hideous shapes of the corpses covered by straw mats. For example, there was one corpse whose limbs were all torn off. He said another had sixteen or seventeen bullet holes. The description that attracted my interest was of a corpse that was thrown in the ditch folded almost in half, the backside inward. I was surprised to learn that a man's body could be folded over, like a pocketknife, with the back inside. I couldn't believe that was possible. Lastly, he transmitted the news that the corpses were on display in the backyard of the police station, ready to be given to relatives or friends upon request. That was the point of his visit to Father. He recommended by hints that Father had better pay a prompt visit to the town police station. Chinku's father, who came with him, urged the same. Throughout their visit, Father had a look of despair, and he showed great reluctance in following the recommendation of the two men. But when the village head, who was Father's childhood friend, came by later and offered to accompany him to town, he resolved at last to do so.

Paternal Grandmother did not try at all to hide her contempt for Father who left for town in the rain, donning an oil-paper hat cover over his bamboo rain hat. Paternal Grandmother had from the first opposed Father's trip to town. It was her conviction that the trip was entirely unnecessary. She even got furiously angry at her son, who still would not give credence to the decree of Heaven. What Grandmother maintained was simply this: whatever had happened in the town had nothing to do with Uncle; it was the providence of Heaven that Uncle would escape unharmed, no matter what danger he may have run into; Heaven had already appointed the date and even the hour that Uncle was to appear before Grandmother alive and entirely sound. Thus, it was utter nonsense that Father should make the long trip to town to wade through corpses in search of his brother. Grandmother, if no one else, had complete faith in this. Well, she not only had complete faith, but she had made detailed preparations for the happy event, and was waiting with outstretched neck. There was a reason for Grandmother's conviction. Since the unfortunate flight of her younger son, Grandmother's days had been a time of unbearable agony. She couldn't sleep, she couldn't eat, and she fretted all day long, waiting for news of her son. Then one day my paternal aunt, who had come to pay a visit, suggested that she consult a fortune-teller in the village next to hers. Carrying a heavy bundle of rice on her head as fee, Grandmother made the trip to the fortune-teller, reputed to have divine prescience. Late in the evening, Grandmother returned home with a beaming face and summoned all the family to give highest praise to the blind man's foresight and to relate his oracle. Well, the ardently awaited day, the day that was fated to bring our uncle home at a certain hour, was only a few days ahead of us now.

Father and the head of the village came back from town empty-handed. That Father's trip had been in vain as good as meant to us that Uncle would be returning home alive. But it was strange that Father remained as taciturn as ever. Father's face showed two very different strands of emotion woven together. His face wore in rapid and irregular succession a look of relief, or a look of bleak despair. It seemed that Father, even if he could regard the absence of Uncle's corpse in the police station yard as an indication that Uncle was still alive, could not rest easy when he thought of the hardships and danger Uncle would have to endure in the future. But Grandmother was not bothered by such considerations. She became triumphant at once, and nearly shouting, declared that it was just as she had told us from the first, that her son Sunchŏl was not an ordinary human being. Then she fell to weeping aloud and, rubbing her palms together heatedly in fervent prayer, with her old worn-out face all muddled by continuously gushing tears, she made full, deep bows in all directions, in token of her gratitude to Heaven and Earth, to Buddha and the mountain spirits, ancestors and household gods. She looked like one gone mad, but her innocent faith and boundless maternal love moved all of our hearts. We all decided to believe. How could we have calmed her down without believing in what she believed? Every member of the family repeatedly recited, solemnly and religiously, the date and the hour that my immortal uncle was destined to return to us. It was only after we realized that daybreak had stolen almost up to the room that we went to bed, to have a preview of our happiness of that day in dreams. It was a long, long day that we lived that day.

Lying on my back in the guest room occupied by my maternal grandmother, I was dimly measuring the density of the rain outside by its dripping sound. The noise, which lifted and resumed and thickened and thinned, tickled my eardrums like the soft tip of a cotton swab. As I was still struggling with a heavy drowsiness on account of the fatigue from the night before, the noise of the rain sounded like a distant whisper in a land of dreams. Still under order of confinement at home, I regarded the long, tedious rain at times as a blessing. Had there been clear sunshine outside to make the fields and hills ablaze with light, wind that shook the trees on the hills, and the cool chirping of cicadas, all the light and sounds of the world might have seemed like a curse to one who had to stay confined indoors without any amusement or distraction. On those occasional afternoons when the rain lifted a bit, I could hear very clearly, while sitting in the room, packs of children noisily galloping through the village streets. Whenever I pictured the children gleefully drawing willow fish traps in the weedy pools around the river or in the forks of the irrigation ditches, and the silvery-scaled, plump carp they would scoop up, I couldn't help sinking under the misery of a forlorn prisoner. I seemed to have already become a long-forgotten being among my peers. My friends didn't stop by anymore at my gate to call me out, even for appearance's sake. I, therefore, disconsolately picked up the blossoms beaten down by the rain under the old persimmon tree beside the twig fence during the hours of envy when all the world seemed to belong to my friends. Thus, I taught myself resignation early in my life. The opening of school was the only hope that I had to cling to. The school, which had closed down because of the war, was to reopen soon, and then Father's order of confinement would lose effect, and my nightmarish house imprisonment would eventually end.

Maternal Grandmother stretched her back, pausing for a moment from shelling peas. Thanks to Grandmother, who kept silently moving her fingers all day long without ever saying a word to anybody, the major portion of the harvested peas had been sorted. But the pods that were still in storage in a corner of the barn showed signs of germinating. The moisture-saturated pods thrust up pale yellow sprouts. The task of shelling the peas before they became inedible fell to Maternal Grandmother. For some reason, all the family seemed to take it for granted that pea shelling was solely and entirely Maternal Grandmother's charge. And she herself seemed to take it for granted as well; she spent all her waking hours shelling the clammy things. Well, it may be more accurate to say that, because she regarded pea shelling as her appointed task and jealously engaged in it, lest someone should take the work away from her, all the others abstained from helping. At any rate, once she sat down with a basket of pea-pods, Maternal Grandmother kept quietly moving her hands, seemingly oblivious to the passage of time. From time to time she poured her heavy sighs into the bamboo basket along with the green peas.

Even though her patience and perseverance were truly extraordinary, sitting thus immobile in one posture seemed to cause her occasional backaches. Thus, she now pushed the bamboo basket aside and shook her skirt. She rubbed her hands on her skirt and moved close to me. I smelt her peculiar odor in the lukewarm breath that descended on my forehead. I guessed what was forthcoming. Sure enough, a chilly hand that made my body shiver crept into my pants. I had never, even once, felt comfortable lying thus under Maternal Grandmother's gaunt hands.

"It's round as an apple, just like his maternal uncle's."

I knew, without looking, that Maternal Aunt was pulling her summer quilt up to her crown. Aunt had been lying almost continuously for quite some days now on the warmer part of the floor because something was evidently wrong with her respiratory system. Aunt always pulled up her quilt like that whenever Maternal Grandmother mentioned Maternal Uncle.

"Who do you like better, your maternal uncle, or your paternal uncle?"

This was the unreasonable question Maternal Grandmother

had got into the habit of posing to me. At first I was extremely dis-
concerted when she asked me that question. For one thing, it was a
question meant for extorting one answer. It was always Maternal
Uncle she mentioned first in the question. But my situation did
not allow me to pick out either one as my favorite. If I were to tell
the truth I would have had to say that I liked both of them. But
Maternal Grandmother was demanding that I pick one of the two.

"Do you like your maternal uncle, or your paternal uncle?"

But I knew that the important thing was neither the question
nor my answer. I had long ago figured out that the question, posed
without any emotion or stress, was simply an introductory remark
to her long, rambling discourse. So, it was only the first couple of
times that the question threw me into confusion. I therefore lay
there silently, pretending not to have heard the question. Then
Grandmother would put on an expression of regret.

"I know. The arm always bends inward."*

But it was only for a moment that the look of regret shaded her
face. Her face regained equanimity soon enough, and she began
her discourse.

"If you are to be really worthy of being Kwŏn Kiljun's nephew,
you must first of all know what kind of a person he was. Unless you
know what kind of a person your maternal uncle was, you're not fit
to claim kinship with him. No, you're not."

The maternal uncle that my maternal grandmother described
always wore a football player's uniform. And he dashed about like a
thoroughbred on the infinitely vast playground rapidly constructed
in my imagination. And he kicked the ball up sky-high, with a perfectly graceful motion. He excelled in studies too, to be sure, but
he was a genius in sports. And among sports, football was his specialty; he was the leader of his school football team from middle
school to college.

The first time Maternal Grandmother felt pride in her son as a
football player was at the very first football match she attended in
her life. At the time Maternal Uncle was a high school senior.
Maternal Grandmother, who had not wanted her only son to grow

---

*"The arm always bends inward" is an expression commonly used in Korea
to signify that people always favor their friends and close relatives over
strangers and distant kin. In this case, since the boy lives with his paternal
uncle and as he belongs with the uncle in the same patrilineal family,
which is the primary source of one's identity, he cannot but feel closer kinship to his paternal uncle than to his maternal uncle.—*Translator*

up to be a professional athlete, was dumbfounded after the game was over, when hordes of schoolgirls rushed over to her and addressed her as "mother," as if she had been their mother-in-law. Even more amazingly, the girls praised her son to the skies, as if he had been their husband.

She was not one to brook such forwardness in nubile girls, and she chased them away after giving them a smart lecture, but the incident was not altogether displeasing to her. From then on, it became an important task for her to scold away with a stern lecture the schoolgirl fans who besieged her and her son.

"You should've seen your uncle that time . . . that time when the goalkeeper of the opposite team fell backward, struck by the ball your uncle had kicked. That'd have made it easier for you to answer—that you like your maternal uncle better than your paternal one."

Maternal Grandmother was a woman of few words. But once she started talking about her son there was no stopping her. She was putting all her strength into her words, in an effort to implant deep into my heart the image of her splendid son. Sometimes she demanded that I describe my maternal uncle's features, as if afraid I might forget his face.

It is true that my maternal uncle was a splendid young man, worthy of any mother's pride. Even though there were some exaggerations and embellishments in Grandmother's memory, that he was an excellent football player and a much-admired figure are demonstrable truths.

He was a brilliant and handsome man. His face was white as porcelain, and the sharp nosebridge and dark eyebrows gave him a truly distinguished look. His smiles, which revealed two neat rows of clean teeth, and his well-proportioned body exuded refinement and good breeding. Several times we had had him and his friends as guests for a few days. One time he came with quite a number of them, all carrying rucksacks. The young men, who said they were on their way to Chiri-san Mountain, played harmonicas and guitars all night long in the guest room. That night, one of his friends said he'd give me instructions on how to kiss girls, and rubbed his coarse jaw on mine and made me scream and flee from the room. That was when I was five years old. There was a time also when a beautiful young woman was in the group. That was the year before the war broke out, and that time also he and his numerous friends carried on gleefully for five days, incurring the silent displeasure of my paternal grandmother, and putting Mother in an embarrassing position.

Uncle's friends seemed to be treating him and the young woman like a royal couple. The group also locked themselves up in the room for hours at a stretch and seemed to be earnestly discussing something. Mother explained later on that they were in flight at the time, after a clash with leftist students with whom they were in long-standing opposition. Except for the period of about a month after the outbreak of the war, when Maternal Uncle was hiding himself in the dug-out cave in the bamboo grove behind our house, these were about all the contacts I had had with him.

My feelings toward my uncle formed through such short encounters were closer to reverence than love as a kinsman. There were many things about him that could inspire my adoration. His comely features and cultured manners and speech had an almost feminine refinement; but his adroit movements and clear-cut decisiveness, which came from his almost limitless energy, bespoke manliness itself. The fact that he was the leader of an organization at such an early age proved him to be a man of extraordinary qualities, and made him seem even more distinguished in my eyes. To me, the wondrous combination of such diverse abilities in one human being was an eternal enigma.

My paternal uncle was three years older than my maternal uncle. In spite of his seniority, however, he was much more immature in his actions than my maternal uncle. His method of "rewarding" the labors of the special agents who had been hired to detect illegal home brewing and clandestine butchery made him famous in the vicinity for awhile. The agents had earned the resentment of the villagers for their unmerciful vigilance. In the middle of a large gathering of villagers in the village square, my uncle gave each of the agents a large bucket of plain water to drink. He termed this a way of rewarding their diligent labors in detecting clandestine brewing. Each of the agents had to gulp down the enormous amount of water, kneeling and with guns aimed at the napes of their necks. Then they were required to chant, marking time by striking their enormously swollen bellies, "I am the grandson of the yeast! I am the bairn of the cow! My father is an ox! A swine is my mother!" exactly one hundred times. Then they were asked to entertain the villagers with songs—any song. Their hoarse singing, which sounded more like the bellowing of calves, sounded so miserable that the villagers who had been writhing and giggling all along stopped laughing in the end.

All his actions were comic and preposterous in such a way. There is also the famous anecdote of his "marriage" with the daughter of a small landowner in the neighboring village. With a notorious hoodlum of the village officiating, he "married" the daughter of Mr. Ch'oe in a sham ceremony. The ceremony also took place in the village square, and it was a completely modern, Western-style ceremony, too. To it were invited, or summoned, Mr. Ch'oe and the bride's husband as guests. As soon as the ceremony was over, Uncle handed the bride over to the hoodlum who officiated and went directly up to Mr. Ch'oe. That day Mr. Ch'oe was beaten till he fainted away by the ruffian who kept calling him "father." That was in repayment for the atrocious thrashing he had received at the hands of Mr. Ch'oe's servants on the moonlit night he jumped over the wall of Mr. Ch'oe's house while drunk, after having yearned for his daughter for a long time.

My two uncles were thus antithetical. Whereas my paternal uncle's enlistment in the Red Army was a blind and impulsive involvement in the whirlwind of events, just like his leap over Mr. Ch'oe's wall in a drunken state, my maternal uncle's activity in the right-wing movement and his volunteering for officership in the Republic's army were decisions grounded firmly on principle and made after careful weighing and examining of the meaning and consequences. Although they had not met often, my two uncles seemed to like each other well enough. If they hadn't, it would have been impossible for my maternal uncle to remain safe in hiding for over a month under the communist rule. Saying that it was only ignorant and poor men like himself who would wear red armbands, my paternal uncle treated my maternal uncle with respectful courtesy. It may have been an expression of envy and admiration for one who had received a higher education than himself. At any rate, Paternal Uncle frequently bestowed kindly attention on his in-law relation who had to stay hidden in a cave. To Mother, he explained his kindly attentions by saying that it was in consideration of their mutual nephew, and the position of Father and Mother.

But my maternal uncle was different. Even though inwardly he felt warmly toward my paternal uncle who was so cheerful and frank, outwardly he always cast cold glances at his counterpart who went around acting like a playful urchin. His intuition proved right. My paternal uncle, who seemed to have so much affection for my maternal uncle, dispatched his men to the cave in the bamboo grove on that mad dawn of the communists' retreat. It was a few hours after Maternal Uncle, following a hearty supper, had silently disappeared without saying a word to anyone in the family.

I could hear Aunt coughing. Covered with the thin quilt up to her head, and lying still on her back on the warmer part of the

floor, she was racked by coughs that constricted her respiratory
organs. I could hear Maternal Grandmother murmuring. And I
could hear the noise of the thinning and thickening rain.

"He always disliked anything the least bit sloppy. I bet he died
as neatly as was his wont in everything. I'm sure only one bullet
struck him, in the heart or in the head, so that he died instantly,
without writhing or suffering pain."

It seems that Maternal Grandmother was severely shocked by
what the villager had recounted thoughtlessly a few days earlier. It
may be that the images of variously disfigured corpses went in and
out of the guest quarters of our house all night long and disturbed
the dreams of an unhappy old woman. It is certainly possible that
they did. Maternal Grandmother was praying that her only son had
met his death in battle in as neat and peaceful a posture as restful
slumber. She prayed ardently that Satan's bullet had struck him in
a vital spot, so that he crossed the boundary between this world
and the next instantly, not only without bodily pain but also without feeling sorrow at leaving his old, widowed mother without a
son in this sorry world. She murmured stubbornly that her son
died with all the parts of his body intact, and that he could never
have met the fate of those ghosts in ancient tales who had to linger
in this world wandering over hills and plains in search of their scattered body parts.

But the voice was weakening perceptibly. Aunt's coughs, on the
other hand, became more high-pitched. Grandmother's murmurs
were becoming more and more subdued under the continuously
intruding noise of the rain.

5

The day appointed by the blind fortune-teller was inexorably
approaching. The rain poured on, and everyone was tired. With
the exception of Paternal Grandmother, everyone was completely
exhausted. Worn out by waiting, and by the rain.

The steppingstones in the river that served as a bridge between
our village and the next had sunk long ago under the rising water.
After that, a thick rope had been tied across the stream, so that
grown-ups forded the river against the rapid current that came up
to the waist by holding onto the rope, and children were carried
across piggyback on the grown-ups' shoulders. But, as the water
was now deeper than a grown-up's height, it had become utterly
impossible to cross the river. Thus, traffic to town had as good as

closed down. There were people who averred they saw things like pigs, oxen, and uprooted pine trees being washed down the river from upstream, but Father brushed off such rumors as nonsense. According to Father, our village was located on the upstream shore of the Sŏmjin River, so that such things could not happen unless there was a great flood. But it was certain that this year's rainy spell was unusually long and heavy. As a consequence traffic to and from the village was tied up, which gave Paternal Grandmother grave worry.

"He's certain to be coming by the road from the town. How terrible it is that the river's so swollen!"

There was a toad that had taken up abode in the dirt veranda of our house for many days despite my manifold persecutions. It seemed to deem itself lucky to have found a shelter at all after having its cave wrecked by the long rain. Pitiable as it was, my mischievousness was aroused by the absurd sight it presented as it dragged its clumsy body around under the wooden floor or on the dirt veranda. On the third day, I turned it bellyside up and, inserting a barley straw in its anus, blew into the straw until its belly was puffed up like a rubber ball. After that it disappeared for an afternoon. But the next morning it was back on the dirt veranda, claiming its right of residence. Squatting on the stepping stone, it gazed vacantly with its protruding eyes at the water dripping from the eaves.

On one of those days, trouble was discovered in the barn. It was not the kind of trouble that broke out suddenly one morning, but rather a gradual development over many days. However, as no one had noticed it, we were all aghast at the discovery. A mist began rising from the bags of barley that had been stored in the barn as soon as they were reaped. As the peas had done some time ago, the grain was now sending up pale yellow sprouts. It was lucky that Father made the discovery when he went in to set mousetraps; otherwise, all the family would have simply had to starve until harvest in the autumn. Suddenly the entire family went around busily, as in the peak farming season. To store the barley bags so as to prevent further damage was a big problem. We installed a storage platform of wooden bars in the barn to provide ventilation space between the floor and the barley bags, and spread the steaming barley on all the level places in the house to let it dry. Wherever I went—bedrooms, kitchen, everywhere—there was barley. I detested barley, and not only because it felt rough in the mouth and gave me tummy aches. Whenever I saw the slit in the barley grain I recalled a legend Paternal Grandmother had told me.

Once upon a time there lived a boy whose father was ill with a fatal disease. The boy consulted a doctor, who prescribed a concoction made out of people's livers. The boy therefore killed three people he met on his way home—a scholar, a monk and a madman—and made a broth with their livers. Upon drinking it, the father's disease was completely cured. The boy buried the corpses in a sunny place. The next year a strange plant was seen growing on the tomb, and its grain was what we now call barley. The slit in the barley grain is thus the slit the boy made in the bodies of the men for the purpose of taking out their livers.

It was very uncomfortable inside the house with its floors all covered over with such an unpleasant grain. I felt cornered and bound. But Paternal Grandmother was a woman of truly amazing determination. Even in the midst of all the fuss, she simply went on with her plans. First, she ordered Mother to take out of the chest her treasured silk cloth and sew a Korean outfit for Uncle. In her opinion a Korean suit is the most dignified and comfortable garment for indoors. And she made Mother prepare Uncle's favorite dish—fried squash slices—in mountainous heaps, despite Mother's protest that it would get spoiled and become inedible in two days. She seasoned the fern fronds herself, and complained that plants didn't grow as they ought to because the times were hard. All the dishes that spoiled quickly were heavily salted or deep-fried to prevent spoilage. At last the preparations were almost complete. There was enough food to give an ordinary village-scale feast for country people like us. As she looked around the kitchen, Grandmother's face lit up with the pride of one who has accomplished an important task. Now she had only one more thing to worry about.

"He's sure to be coming by the road from town. How unfortunate it is that the river's so swollen!"

"What's there to worry about? Even if the river's a bit swollen, how could it hinder his coming, if he's destined to come? He knows traffic often gets tied up in the rainy season, so he'll take the stone bridge and come by the circular road."

Father brushed aside Grandmother's worry, to put her mind at ease, but Grandmother shook her head.

"Of course he'll take the circular road. But that's four miles longer. Four miles sounds pretty short, but think of walking four more miles in this rain. And his feet frostbitten, too!"

Paternal Aunt came the day before the appointed day. As soon as she arrived, she inspected the cupboards and shelves in the kitchen and complimented Mother and Paternal Grandmother for their thoroughness. She seemed quite satisfied with the preparations that had been made. Aunt had as complete a faith in the homecoming of my uncle as did Paternal Grandmother. It was she who had introduced Grandmother to the blind fortune-teller. As she was thus the one who induced my grandmother's complete faith in the fortune-teller, it was understandable that her belief in Uncle's homecoming was as firm as Grandmother's. But even her idea of a proper welcome for the returning uncle was so perfectly identical with Paternal Grandmother's that my mother, though she was chary of complaints against her in-laws, marvelled secretly to Maternal Grandmother and Maternal Aunt at the resemblance of taste between her mother- and sister-in-law. It was not as if Mother was not hoping for Uncle's return. Even Maternal Aunt, who hardly ever spoke in those days, and Maternal Grandmother, who had once invoked curses upon communist partisans, silently wished for the happy reunion of the relations as they watched the heated preparations. But wishing and believing are two different things. I also ardently wished for my uncle's return. But even in my childish judgment it did not seem very likely that an event like that could occur as easily as predicted. If Uncle were to come, in what status and by which road would he be coming?

I had chanced to overhear Father talking to Mother in the kitchen. Father said that such a thing was impossible. If one detached oneself even a little from Paternal Grandmother's touching faith—and it was a complete, unshakable faith—and examined the matter with any objectivity at all, the impossibility of the prediction being fulfilled was so clear that it made our hearts ache. As a last resort, Father even thought of the possibility of Uncle's having surrendered himself to the police somewhere. But he quickly dismissed the idea. Had that been the case, we would have had by now some notice of interrogation from the police. Father knew better than anybody else that our family was under surveillance. From time to time, a man could be seen sauntering up and down along our twig fence and casting suspicious glances into the house. Though outwardly we had freedom of movement, we were like fish securely cooped inside the net drawn by the man. I knew from long before that the man sometimes dropped in at our neighbor Chinku's to gather information about what was going on in my house, and once or twice he even called my father out to a tavern for a talk.

I shuddered most of all when the man came into view. His appearance had dreadful significance for me. It always awakened anew my guilty conscience, which I was trying to lull to sleep. The

sight of him made me recall Paternal Grandmother's words that I
was a butcher of men who had sold my uncle for a sweet. Father
should have struck me dead that night with the wooden pillow. It
gave me excruciating pain to behold Father's face as he returned
from a talk with that man.

The only way I had of escaping from my paternal grandmother's censure that kept reviving in my memory was to imagine myself
dying in the most pitiful fashion. That was the only way of evading,
even temporarily, the tormenting consciousness of guilt. I imagined the scene in which the whole family, especially my paternal
grandmother, shed tears without end in front of the dead youth.
The greater Paternal Grandmother's sorrow and regret, the more
consolation I felt. But, when I woke up from the daydream, I always
found myself as impudently alive as ever, and I could not but dread
meeting Paternal Uncle face to face. Because of this guilt, while I
ardently wished for my uncle's return, I also secretly harbored the
horrible wish that I might never have to face Uncle again—that
Uncle had died long ago in some steep, deserted valley, and his
body would never be found. The anticipated day, which was just
one day away now, really filled me with mortal dread. I was so terrified that I prayed today would never end.

But I think my terror and anxiety were nothing compared with
the pain my father endured. I had heard Father pleading in the
kitchen with Mother, who was complaining about Paternal
Grandmother's excessive vigilance.

"I feel the same as you do. It's a hundred to one that he won't
come. And even if he does by some extraordinary chance, it won't
be the kind of event Mother expects it to be. That I know better
than you do. But what can I say to Mother? It's best simply to do
everything she bids us. That's better than making her think we're
trying to thwart her joy and giving her a grievance. Don't you think
so?"

Father was appealing to Mother by telling her of his own agony
at having to follow his old mother's lead, even feigning assiduity in
doing so, while he knew the waited-for event would be an impossibility. Even though Paternal Grandmother's faith, nourished by
her boundless motherly love, moved our hearts at first and made
us pray for the fulfillment of her expectation, we were far from
having the same faith ourselves. We were only hoping and waiting
with her because we did not want on any account to disappoint the
old lady. Father had already foreseen the despair that would follow
if Grandmother's expectation was disappointed, and what would
result from that despair. But there was nothing any of us could do

except try our best not to cross the old lady. It was a pity that the blind fortune-teller, reputed to be divinely inspired, had not told Grandmother which road Uncle would be taking to return home.

It was already night. The rain, which thinned down from around dusk, was now a mere misty drizzle. Into the hazy halo of the lamp hung on the gatepost, the rain descended in sprinkles of powdery drops, as if it, too, was quite exhausted. Although there had been no express order, ever since the beginning of the war, the whole village was in the habit of extinguishing all lights after suppertime. However, we had hung out a lamp tonight, letting it keep vigil through the night like a lonely sentinel. It was, of course, at Paternal Grandmother's insistence. Who knows, she said, even though Uncle was slated to come between eight and ten o'clock in the morning, he might show up in the middle of the night due to some sudden change of plan. Grandmother did not want it to look as if the family was unprepared for his return.

"It was for an occasion like this that we have saved up the expensive kerosene."

She ordered one more lamp to be hung from the eaves and warned us not to let the lamps die out in any of the rooms. She explained very succinctly the reason we had to keep the house as bright as day.

"We have to keep the lamps burning bright so he can spot the house from far, far away and run all the way home, knowing his mother's waiting for him with wide-open eyes all through the night."

The night deepened. Even so, nobody seemed to be thinking of going to bed. No one in the family had the guts to spread out bedding when Paternal Grandmother was tensely surveying every corner of the house. The weather also seemed to be flattering my grandmother. The long, fierce rain had changed to a drizzle in the evening, and then by degrees withdrew out of sight and out of hearing, so that as the night deepened even the dripping from the eaves ceased. And the cool wind that carries away humidity began to blow. Well, the rainy spell had lasted long enough, and it was time for the rainy front to retreat. But Grandmother quickly related the change in the weather to the forthcoming happy event of the morrow, to her great satisfaction.

It must have been long past midnight. I had left the inner room to come to the guest room and lie down beside Maternal Grandmother. Neither my maternal aunt nor my maternal grandmother was asleep. I suppose they couldn't fall asleep, because of all the tense excitement in the inner quarters. Aunt was lying still

on her back, facing the ceiling, and Grandmother was seated leaning on the wall, facing the door. My eyes were tracing the flickering
shadow of the lamp's sooty flame on the ceiling. My ears were wide
open, and were listening to the songs of the night in the distant
grass beyond the darkness outside the door.

All around was quiet. The house couldn't be quieter, even had
everyone been asleep. It was so perfectly still that the stillness
rather hampered my listening to the sound of darkness. It was as if
my auditory organs were paralysed under the pressure of the stillness that weighed all around. So much so that I sometimes suspected that the sounds that came to my ears were not sounds that actually existed in the world but rather some illusion created by my
bewitched brain. But collecting myself and listening again, I
seemed to be hearing some wakeful being besides myself patiently
filing away with a sharp file in the darkness at the edge of the vast
stillness. For a long time I had been concentrating on distinguish-
ing the chirping of the crickets from that of the katydids amid the
whisper of the wind, and was relishing the sweet and sour notes of
those sounds. Suddenly, amidst the murmur of insects, an unfamiliar sound intruded, and its strangeness made me tense. But the
sound ceased as unexpectedly as it began. It fled, just as I was
about to grasp the tail end of it, and I felt again that I might have
been bewitched by something. But the sound came again after a
pause. It was very distinct this time. It was not loud, but it was distinctive among the many hushed sounds of the night. It was like
the sound children made when they blow into the mouth of an
empty bottle or like the siren of a ship on a distant sea. It was, at
any rate, a faint but pregnant sound. It was also a very obscure
sound, and I was completely at a loss as to the direction it was coming from. It seemed now to be coming from somewhere around
the river's shore outside the village, or from the kitchen garden of
our house, right outside the door. I lay bewitched by the strange,
secretive sound that stole through the stillness of the night. Like a
boy chasing fox fire in the graveyard, my consciousness, drawn by
the mysterious strain of the eerie sound, was already rushing to the
river's shore.

"It's the king snake calling up the snakes."

Grandmother's words coiled round my body like a huge snake
darting out its forked tongue, and I could hardly breathe. It was
my beloved maternal aunt who chased away the chilly feel of the
snake against my body. I had a protector. I was infinitely thankful
that I was not the only one to have heard the sound. Aunt was
already sitting up beside me and staring at the door. Grandmother

twitched her lips, preparatory to saying something more. Aunt put her hand on my shoulder and gave Grandmother a sideways stare.

"Don't."

But Grandmother kept twitching her lips. Had Aunt not subdued her once more, Grandmother would surely have said something.

"Please don't!"

Aunt pulled me under her quilt. Buried snugly under Aunt's armpit, I heard the sound again. The sound, like a ship's siren from a distant sea, once more scattered chill all over the room. This time, too, it was hard to tell whether the sound was coming from the river's shore or from the kitchen garden of our house. Then there was a long interval. The snake's call sounded for the third time, and then came no more. But the aftertaste of the sound lingered in the room for a long time and kept our mouths shut. Maternal Grandmother was still sitting in an awkward posture, stooping forward toward the door. Waves of emotion crossed her face. Sometimes she would look vacantly into space, like a person hit hard on the head, but the next moment she would gaze beyond the door with narrowed eyes, like someone trying to work out a very complicated problem. At last she turned towards me and Aunt.

"Tongman," she called. "Tongman, my dear."

But when my eyes met hers she averted her face. After some hesitation, she slowly opened her mouth again.

"Do you think so, too?" she asked, apropos of nothing, and again hesitated for a long while.

"Do you also think that what happened to your uncle happened because of me?"

I decided to answer the question. There was such urgency in the voice asking the question that I thought I had to say something in response. But I realized the next moment that no answer was needed. She was not looking at me, nor was she paying any attention to me. She was completely absorbed in her own thoughts. She would not have heard me even if I had said anything in response.

"No! What happened that night was none of my willing. I'd no thought of spying on anybody. I'd been to the outhouse and saw the light in the inner room and heard whispering voices, so I just went nearer to see what was going on. Who'd have known it'd bring about such consequences? A team of horses couldn't have dragged me there if I'd known such a thing was going to happen. I'm not saying I did well to be so curious. I know I shouldn't have done it, but it wasn't because of me that things ended that way.

Even if it hadn't been for me, your uncle would've returned to where he came from, as he was fated to do. That was his lot."

Aunt hugged me tightly. With my face buried snugly between Aunt's breasts, I heard Grandmother's murmurs in a dreamy coziness. Then, my whole body loosened up as after a heavy flogging and violent weeping, and drowsiness utterly overwhelmed me. Even in my dreamy exhaustion I vowed to myself that I would marry my aunt for sure when I grew up, and I stopped heeding Grandmother's muttering.

6

I was far from refreshed when I woke up from the sound of Paternal Grandmother's furious reproaches, uttered just inside the gate. Although the sky was brightening, it was still early dawn. Summer nights are short, and, as I had gone to sleep long past midnight, to wake up in early dawn meant I had as good as skipped sleeping that night. I felt a numbing pain inside my head, and my eyelids kept sliding down. But my condition was vigor itself compared with the rest of the family's. Because of many days of fatigue and tension, Father's face was swollen and yellow as if jaundiced, and Mother had become gaunt as a mummy. Maternal Grandmother and Maternal Aunt weren't doing any better. But Paternal Grandmother was energetically imperious, loudly scolding the weary family from early dawn. She was giving Mother and Father a horrendous reprimand.

The lamp hung on the gatepost had died out. The wind must have blown out the flame—the oil can was more than half full, and the glass shade was wet with drops of water. The extinguished lamp had infuriated Paternal Grandmother. She took it as a proof of Father and Mother's insufficient devotion. Grandmother's ire was not soothed even after she gave Father and Mother a severe reproof. She declared that this proved to her that Father and Mother were unfit to be trusted with Uncle's welfare, and announced her resolution to take charge of the keys to the barn and the safety cabinet until she saw signs of improvement.

"I won't say anything more this morning, because a woman shouldn't raise her voice on the morning of festivity. I'll leave the rest up to you. I won't move a finger, but just entertain myself watching what you do." Then she clicked her tongue in self-pity, as she turned around to head for the inner quarters. "Lucky woman I am, to have such a thoughtful older son!" She strode across the yard toward the inner room. "What sins am I expiating, to be blessed with a son and a daughter-in-law like them?" she grumbled to herself as she passed in front of the guest room, loud enough to be heard by neighbors.

Paternal Grandmother was as good as her word. She really did not move a finger. After she went into her room, slamming the door shut, she did not utter a single comment on what was going on outside. Instead, she kept a keen watch over what was happening in the yard through the glass pane of the small window, and a disapproving, discontented look did not leave her face. All of us in the family came out with brooms, rags, or dusters and, with a keen consciousness of supervisory eyes upon us, swept the yard, scrubbed the floor, cleaned cobwebs, and tidied the house. Both aunts also joined in, and the house regained the neat appearance it had had before the long rain. Maternal Aunt and Paternal Aunt went into the kitchen with Mother to prepare breakfast, and Father and I dug a deep ditch between the footpath leading from the gate to the yard and the kitchen garden, sweating profusely, to drain the water from the yard.

The sky was still cloudy. We had hoped to see the sun for the first time in a long while, but the sky did not look cheerfully disposed. Nevertheless, a patch of the western sky was clear, and there was a cool wind that drove away the clouds. There was no sign anywhere of a renewal of rain. Even that much beneficence was a blessing to us. Not only my family but everybody felt the same. Village people who dropped in on us from early morning began their greetings by talking of the weather, and the women went in and out of the kitchen. My house overflowed with village people, as on a feast day, and the members of the family were kept busy responding to questions from inquisitive neighbors. What the neighbors were most curious about was to what extent the members of our family believed in the prophecy. Of course they did not use words like "superstition." Although they marvelled at the fact that one word from a fortune-teller led to such large-scale preparations, they were polite enough not to treat it as mere foolishness, at least in our hearing. They tended rather to be sympathetic, and commented encouragingly that the devotion of the family, if nothing else, would bring Uncle back. Father simply smiled. Father saw, in the attitude of some of the people who spoke thus, that they were amusing themselves with what was going on in our house. Some of them were taking exactly the tone of the doctor who tells his dying patient he'll recover in a few days. As the appointed hour drew near,* more and more people gathered, so that our yard was teeming with people as on a village festival day. It looked as if everyone in the village who could walk had come. I could see the stranger smoking a cigarette, sitting on the porch of Chinku's house. My house was bustling like a marketplace, and the family had still not had breakfast. Grandmother had forbidden us to eat, as all of us were to eat with Uncle when he came. It wasn't as if we were starving, so I resolved to be patient, but my stomach howled pitifully.

At last it was eight o'clock, the beginning of the period appointed by the fortune-teller. Time sped by amid the tense excitement of everyone. Soon it was nine o'clock, and then it was approaching ten o'clock. But the long-awaited Uncle did not show up.

After the villagers had all dispersed, we sat down to a late, late breakfast. Only the village head and Chinku's family remained, try-ing to console us. Paternal Grandmother remained in the inner room, and the rest of the family sat around the table set in the side room. The spoons moved slowly although the table was luxuriously laden with colorful dishes. Paternal Grandmother refused to eat breakfast, even though she told the family to go ahead and eat. Her spirit was not weakened, even though the time appointed by the blind seer was quite past and gone. Well, she still *looked* spirit-ed, anyway. She said that from the first she had not thought the hour was all that important. What was important, according to her, was the day, not the hour. She said that there could be accidental errors even in events supervised by Heaven; and man cannot always move exactly according to schedule. She insisted one must make allowances for slight errors even in the prophecy of divine seers. For Grandmother, the day has only just begun. She said that, since Uncle would not fail to come that day, she would wait a little longer and have her first meal of the day with her son. She did not betray any tiredness.

Our dog Wŏlly, who had been peering in at the rooms, stand-ing with his forefeet on the edge of the living-room floor and

---

*The fortune-teller had predicted that the uncle would return in *Chinsi*, the hour of the dragon, which in this story appears to be between eight and ten o'clock in the morning, but which in fact is between nine and eleven o'clock in the morning. The author seems to have been slightly mixed up about the period divisions.—*Translator* smacking his lips, suddenly stepped down to the dirt veranda. Then he barked, turning to the gate. The shouting of children followed hard upon. Father's spoon stopped in midair, and all our movements instantly ceased. Children's exclamations were rapidly approaching our house. Flinging the spoon away, I ran outside. The noise instantly surrounded our gate. I was hit by the shouts of the children in the middle of the yard. The first thing that came into my view was a pack of children with gaping mouths. All of them had rocks or sticks of wood in their hands. The children hesitated a little before the gate, not daring to rush into the house, and raised their weapons threateningly. One of the boys threw his rock forcibly. Where the rock fell I beheld the thing.

There was a long object sliding into the house. It was a huge snake, longer than a man's height. My whole body constricted the moment I saw its horrible bulk slithering with its yellowish scales glittering dazzlingly, reviving in my memory the eerie whisper of the night before. But I was a boy, and a snake meant an adventure. Horror had a momentary grip on me, but the next moment I was as excited as any of the other boys who kept screaming and throwing rocks. I could not control the aggressive, destructive urge that male children instinctively feel towards all reptiles. I ran over to the barn and fetched the big wooden staff that Father used when carrying heavy things on an A-frame. I raised both hands high in the air, ready to strike the snake dead if it moved an inch closer to me, but a hand grabbed my arm roughly. I looked around to see that it was Maternal Grandmother. At the same moment, there arose a piercing scream from behind me.

"Aaaack!"

With that, Paternal Grandmother fell on the floor, as limply as a piece of worn-out clothing. Maternal Grandmother twisted the staff from my grasp. Her eyes glared at me in silent reprimand.

The unexpected appearance of the huge snake threw the whole house into utter confusion. The most urgent problem was Paternal Grandmother, who had fainted. The family gathered in the inner room to massage her limbs and spray cold water on her face in an effort to revive her. The village people, who had dispersed, gathered in the house once more, and talked and exclaimed so noisily that it was like sitting in the middle of a whirlwind. Only Maternal Grandmother did not lose her calm amidst the noise and confusion. As if she were simply carrying out a prearranged procedure, she put things in order one by one with a truly amazing composure. First of all, she drove away the people. With the help of the village head and Chinku's father, she drove out all the village people who came for the show and locked the gate fast. The children and grownups who had been driven out of the gates came round to the part of the twig fence next to a persimmon tree. Taking advantage of the heated confusion, the snake had slid down the kitchen garden through the brown mallows and lettuces and had already coiled itself around the upper branches of the persimmon tree. With its yellow body wound around the persimmon bough, it kept darting its wiry tongue in and out. It must have suffered a deadly blow, for its tail was more than half cut from the body and dangled precariously. The tireless children had followed it up to the persimmon tree and were still throwing rocks and sticks.

"Who's that throwing rocks?"

Maternal Grandmother's reprimand was as sharp as a sword.* All the throwing ceased. Then Grandmother began to slowly walk up to the persimmon tree. Nothing happened even when she stood just below the tree with the coiled snake, and sighs of relief escaped from the people who had been watching her with breathless suspense. She did not waver a bit, even though the snake's fiery dots of eyes gleamed in all directions and it raised and lowered its head threateningly. She slowly lifted both her hands and clasped them palm-to-palm on her bosom.

"My poor boy, have you come all this way to see how things are going in the house?" Grandmother whispered quietly, in the tone of one singing a lullaby to a fretful baby. Somebody giggled. Instantly, Grandmother's eyes grew sharply triangular.

"Which mongrel is sniggering there? Come up here at once! I'll wring your neck!"

Everybody became still as death at Grandmother's fiery rebuke. Grandmother turned to the snake again.

"As you can see, your mother's still in good health and everybody's doing all right. So put your mind at ease and make haste on your way."

The snake did not stir a muscle. It only darted its wiry tongue in and out and raised its head a couple of times.

"You mustn't linger here crouching like this anymore when you have such a long way to go. You shouldn't, you know, if you

---

*The giant, venomless snake was believed to have supernatural properties and powers. It was believed that spirits of the dead could enter it to visit people in this world. It behoved people, therefore, not to hurt it but to conciliate it by all means.—*Translator*

don't want to grieve your family overmuch. I know how you feel, but you must consider others' feelings, too. How would your mother feel if she knew you were lingering here like this?"

Maternal Grandmother was earnestly entreating, as if the snake had been a real live human being. But, however ardently she pleaded, the snake did not show any inclination to move away. A neighborhood woman then told Grandmother the method for expelling snakes. The woman, whose body was hidden from view and whose voice only could be heard, said that you could chase away snakes with the smell of burning hair. At Maternal Grandmother's bidding, I hurried into the inner room to get some of Paternal Grandmother's hair.

Paternal Grandmother was lying under a quilt, stiff as a corpse. Although she was breathing, she was still unconscious. I urgently demanded some of Paternal Grandmother's hair from the family members sitting around the unconscious form with ashen-grey faces, waiting for the arrival of the doctor. My demand must have sounded preposterous. It took quite a long time to explain for what purpose Grandmother's hair was needed. It took awhile longer for Paternal Aunt to collect a handful of hair from the unconscious old lady with a fine-toothed bamboo comb. The hair collected from repeated combing was given to me at last. When I came out to the yard, Maternal Grandmother had in the meanwhile prepared a small tray laden with a few dishes. On the round tray were Uncle's favorite dishes of fried squash slices and seasoned fern, and there was also a large bowl of cold water. After taking the knot of hair from me and putting it on the ground, Maternal Grandmother slowly raised her head and looked up at the persimmon tree.

"These are what your mother has prepared for many days for you. Even though you can't taste them, take a good look at them at least. They're all proofs of your mother's devotion. It's not that I'm trying to get rid of you. You must understand that. Please don't blame me too much for the bad smell. It's just to hurry you along on the long way you have to go. Put your worries at rest about your family and just take good care of yourself on the long way ahead of you."

As she finished talking, she turned up the live coal in the tinder bowl. When she placed the knot of hair on it, it burned with a sizzling sound. The smell of burning protein quickly spread all around. What happened next drew an exclamation of astonishment from everyone. The huge snake, which had till then been immobile as a rock despite all Grandmother's entreaties, slowly began to move. Its body, which had been coiled around the persimmon tree, smoothly unwound itself, and it slithered down to the ground. After hesitating a little, it slowly and waveringly crept towards Grandmother. Grandmother stepped aside to make way. She followed its tail as it slid away and kept chasing it, making a swishing sound with her lips. Like one chasing away sparrows from the fields, Grandmother swished and even clapped her hands. The snake crawled over the ground noiselessly, twitching its gleaming scales. All the members of the family also spilled out to the living-room floor and fearfully watched it sliding across the yard. Wŏlly, whose tail clung to his inner thighs, dutifully barked with a fear-strained voice from beneath the living-room floor. The snake slowly coursed its way through the empty space between the barn and kitchen, its half-detached tail shakily trailing behind.

"Swish! Swish!"

Spurred on from behind by Grandmother's hoarse voice, the snake had already slid past the well and crossed the backyard. Before it now was the densely overgrown bamboo grove.

"Thank you, dear. Just trust your brother to take care of all the household, and think only of keeping your body whole for your long, long journey. Don't worry at all about what you're leaving behind here, and take good care of yourself. That's a good boy. Thank you, dear."

Standing beside the well, Maternal Grandmother saw the snake off with earnest entreaties until it completely disappeared through the bamboo trees and the bamboo shoots that had sprouted thickly during the long rain.

Chinku's father arrived with a doctor from a neighboring village. Paternal Grandmother regained consciousness several hours after she had fainted. On waking up from her stupor of a few hours, she looked around the room like one who had been on a few months' trip to a faraway place.

"Is it gone?" were her first words after regaining consciousness. Paternal Aunt quickly understood and nodded. Paternal Grandmother lowered her eyelids, as if to say that was all that mattered. Paternal Aunt quickly recounted all that had happened after Paternal Grandmother had fainted away. She told how Maternal Grandmother chased away the neighbors, reasoned with the snake under the persimmon tree, made it come down from the tree by burning Paternal Grandmother's hair, and saw it off every step of the way until it disappeared through the bamboo grove. Mother occasionally added details to Paternal Aunt's account. Paternal Grandmother was weeping quietly. Tears gushed endlessly from her eyes, flowed down her sunken cheeks, and wetted the pillow-

case. After she had heard all, she told Father to go and ask
Maternal Grandmother to come to the inner room. Maternal
Grandmother, who had been resting in the guest room, followed
Father into the inner room. It was the first time Maternal
Grandmother had stepped into the inner room since the day of
the unhappy clash between the two in-laws.

"Thank you," Paternal Grandmother said huskily, raising her
sunken and lusterless eyes to Maternal Grandmother.

"You're welcome." Maternal Grandmother's voice was also tear-
fully husky.

"I heard it all from my daughter. You did for me what I
should've done. What a difficult and fearsome thing you have done
for me."

"It's all past now. Don't exert yourself anymore with talking,
but try to regain your strength."

"Thank you. Thank you so very much." Paternal Grandmother
held out her hand. Maternal Grandmother took it. The two grandmothers just held hands for awhile, unable to speak. Then Paternal
Grandmother expressed her remaining worry.

"I wonder if it went on its way all right."

"Don't worry. It must have found a comfortable place by now,
and is keeping a protective eye on this house."

Even that brief conversation drained Paternal Grandmother's
strength, and she fainted. Everyone sat around her until she fell
asleep with difficulty and then, leaving only Paternal Aunt to watch
over her, we all came out of the room to breathe a little.

Paternal Grandmother fainted again that night. She vomited
the few spoonfuls of broth and herb medicine we had spooned
into her mouth. From the next day, it was as if her consciousness
was playing hide-and-seek in and out of her body like a playful
urchin, and there was not a moment's rest for anyone in the house.

Grandmother struggled on for a week, though she had lost
control of her body. On the last night of the seventh day, the old
lady who always thought more of the son away from the house than
the son at home closed her eyes softly, like a spent candle flame
quietly going out. It may be that in Grandmother's long life the
happiest and proudest times were the few days she commanded
and scolded the family with amazing vigor, without sleeping and
eating, in rapturous expectation of her younger son's return—like
the last radiant soaring of the candle flame before going out. On
her deathbed, Grandmother held my hand and forgave me all my
misdeeds. I also in my heart forgave her everything.

It was a long, weary rainy spell indeed.

About the Book

These seven stories, dramatic and thought-provoking, provide a compelling picture of Korean life in the 1940s–1990s.

Family and community ties, respect for tradition, survival in the face of repeated national disasters and wrenching social upheaval—these are among the themes evoked in the collection. The narratives make palpable the lives and emotions of characters from differing backgrounds, all of whom must negotiate the same historical legacy and contradictory modern developments.

Suh Ji-moon is professor of English at Korea University. Her publications include *Faces in the Well*, and her translation of *The Rainy Spell and Other Korean Stories* received the Republic of Korea Literature Award.